PERSPECTIVES ON
CONTEMPORARY ISSUES

EIGHTH EDITION

PERSPECTIVES ON
CONTEMPORARY ISSUES

 **READING ACROSS THE DISCIPLINES**

KATHERINE ANNE ACKLEY
Professor Emeritus, University of Wisconsin at Stevens Point

CENGAGE
Learning·

Australia • Brazil • Mexico • Singapore • United Kingdom • United States

CENGAGE
Learning®

Perspectives on Contemporary Issues: Reading Across the Disciplines, Eighth Edition
Katherine Anne Ackley

Product Director: Monica Eckman

Product Manager: Vanessa Coloura

Senior Content Developer: Kathy Sands-Boehmer

Product Assistant: Claire Branman

Marketing Manager: Kina Lara

Senior Content Project Manager: Michael Lepera

Senior Art Director: Marissa Falco

Manufacturing Planner: Betsy Donaghey

IP Analyst: Ann Hoffman

Senior IP Project Manager: Kathryn Kucharek

Production Service/Compositor: Lumina Datamatics, Inc.

Text and Cover Designer: Lisa Kuhn Buchanan

Cover Image: Michael Mann/ Getty Images

Part Opener Images:
Part 1: Ecopic/Veer;
Part 2: Corbis Photography/Veer

For product information and technology assistance, contact us at **Cengage Learning Customer & Sales Support, 1-800-354-9706**

For permission to use material from this text or product, submit all requests online at **www.cengage.com/permissions**. Further permissions questions can be emailed to **permissionrequest@cengage.com**.

Library of Congress Control Number: 2016943328

Student Edition:

ISBN: 978-1-305-96937-7

Loose-leaf Edition:

ISBN: 978-1-337-09433-7

Cengage Learning
20 Channel Center Street
Boston, MA 02210
USA

Cengage Learning is a leading provider of customized learning solutions with employees residing in nearly 40 different countries and sales in more than 125 countries around the world. Find your local representative at **www.cengage.com**.

Cengage Learning products are represented in Canada by Nelson Education, Ltd.

To learn more about Cengage Learning Solutions, visit **www.cengage.com**.

Purchase any of our products at your local college store or at our preferred online store **www.cengagebrain.com**.

Printed in the United States of America
Print Number: 03   Print Year: 2017

For my family

CONTENTS

PREFACE

Perspectives on Contemporary Issues: Reading across the Disciplines, Eighth Edition, presents an approach to thinking, reading, and writing that views learning as the interconnectedness of ideas and disciplinary perspectives. Contemporary issues engage the students, while the readings provide rich material for class discussion and writing topics. The essays by authors from a variety of disciplines and professions focus on individual, national, and global issues. Regardless of their majors, students will enhance their skills through the writing assignments.

The goals of *Perspectives on Contemporary Issues: Reading across the Disciplines* are as follows:

- To sharpen students' thinking skills by presenting them with a variety of perspectives on current issues
- To give students practice in both oral and verbal expression by providing questions for discussion and writing after each selection
- To provide students with a variety of writing assignments representing the kinds of writing they will be asked to do in courses across the curriculum
- To encourage students to view issues and ideas in terms of connections with other people, other disciplines, or other contexts

The questions for discussion and writing encourage critical thinking by asking students to go well beyond simple recall of the readings and to use higher-order skills such as integration, synthesis, or analysis of what they have read. Most of the questions are suitable for work in small groups, as well as for class discussion.

NEW TO THIS EDITION

Learning Objectives. Each chapter in Part One is preceded by several learning objectives highlighting the concepts in the chapter.

MindTap. Each chapter in Part Two begins not only with an overview of the chapter but also with a question to prompt students to think about the subject of that chapter. At the end of each chapter, students are asked to reflect on the issues/ideas presented by the readings in that chapter. Eighteen articles are available online through the Questia website and include additional questions for discussion.

New Readings.   There are eighteen new readings in print in this edition, all of them published recently. Together with the Questia articles, thirty-six of the fifty titles in the book are new. These new readings cover topics of contemporary interest, and their writers sometimes take controversial positions on the issues under discussion.

Sleeker, Slimmer Text.   This book has fewer pages than previous editions, making it more manageable to cover in a one-semester class. Parts Two to Five in previous editions are now clustered together, with individual chapter titles noting the subject of each chapter.

MLA Updates.   This edition has been updated to reflect guidelines from the 2016 *MLA Handbook for Writers of Research Papers,* Eighth Edition.

READING SELECTIONS

The book has two parts, and the reading selections are organized by broad disciplinary areas:

- Chapters 8 and 9 cover the broad areas of popular culture, the arts, and media studies. Readings cover such subjects as music and video games, media violence, advertising, Hollywood films, television, and the visual arts.
- Chapters 10 to 14 address such matters as education, poverty and homelessness, gender and sex roles, race and ethnicity, and psychology and human behavior.
- Chapter 15 focuses on bioethical and environmental issues, with writers giving opinions on the sale of organs, environmental issues, and the crisis of rapid species extinction.
- Chapter 16 addresses marketing, the American consumer, and the workplace, with readings on the spread of commercialization, the difficulties employers face in finding workers, and the problems of a worker has when seeking a job.

The selections in each chapter encourage students to consider issues from different perspectives because their authors come from a wide range of disciplinary backgrounds and training. Sometimes the writers cross disciplinary lines in their essays. The individual perspectives of the writers may differ markedly from students' own perspectives, thus generating discussion and writing topics.

ACTIVITIES AND ASSIGNMENTS

After each selection,

- Students can make a personal response to some aspect of the reading.
- Each reading is also followed by several questions for class or small-group discussion. These questions invite students to consider rhetorical strategies

of the piece, think of larger implications, discuss related issues, or make connections between the readings and their own experiences. Many of these questions are appropriate for writing topics as well, and many others will prompt students to discover related topics on which to write.

Toward the end of each chapter, a section called "Perspectives on ..." provides writing topics based on ideas generated by the collected readings in that chapter. These writing assignments are arranged in two categories:

- Suggested writing topics are suitable for synthesis, argumentation, and other modes of writing such as the report, the letter, the personal essay, and the comparison and contrast essay.
- Research topics are suitable for development into research papers.

Finally, each chapter in Part Two concludes with a section called "Responding to Visuals," which features two photographs or other visual images. These images relate to the thematic focus of the chapter and are accompanied by questions on rhetorical strategies and other relevant matters.

A DEFINITION OF ISSUES

Given the title of this textbook, a definition of *issues* is in order. An issue is usually taken to mean a topic that is controversial, that prompts differences of opinion, or that can be seen from different perspectives. It often raises questions or requires taking a close look at a problem. Although this is not primarily an argument textbook, the inclusion of topics and essays guaranteed to spark controversy is deliberate. Many of the readings will prompt students to take opposing positions. Some of the readings are provocative; others may anger students. Such differences of opinion generate lively class discussions and result in writing opportunities that engage students.

ONLINE RESOURCES

MindTap® English for Ackley's *Perspectives on Contemporary Issues: Reading Across the Disciplines,* Eighth Edition, engages students to help them become better thinkers, communicators, and writers by blending course materials with content that supports every aspect of the writing process. Interactive activities on grammar and mechanics promote application in student writing, and an easy-to-use paper management system allows for electronic submission, grading, and peer review while tracking potential plagiarism. A vast database of scholarly sources with video tutorials and examples supports each step of the research process, and professional tutoring guides students from rough drafts to polished writing. Visual analytics track student progress and engagement with seamless integration into campus learning management system that keeps all course materials in one place.

ACKNOWLEDGMENTS

I would like to thank the following reviewers for their helpful suggestions on this new edition: Gretchen DiGeronimo, Becker College; David Green, Mass Bay Community College; Lilia Joy, Henderson Community College; Nancy Lee-Jones, Endicott College and Catherine Pavlich, Oregon Coast Community College. As always, I thank my husband, Rich, and my family: Heather, Brian, Elizabeth, and Lucas Schilling; Laurel, Gianni, Zack, and Celia Yahi; Jeremy, Jenni, and Che White; Robin Ackley-Fay and Terry Fay; and Jon Ackley.

A special thank you to Professor Beate C. Gilliar, Professor of English at Manchester University, North Manchester, Indiana, and the following students in her expository and critical writing course: Samantha Baker, Megan Batten, Shelby Covington, Stephanie Griffith, Brandon Hite, Catherine Lange, David Lloyd, Amy Luthanen, Holly Pawlak, Rebecca Pendergrass, Alison Scholtfeldt, Kristen Wolf, Maria Villafuerta, and Carol Yañez.

I am especially thankful for the gracious willingness of these students to share their written work for use in this textbook: Rita Fleming, Nate Hayes, Shawn Ryan, Elizabeth Schilling, Clorinda Tharp, Michael Vawter, and Laurel Yahi.

Finally, I give a special thank you to my editor, Kathy Sands-Boehmer, who has once again been a joy to work with.

PART 1

WRITING CRITICALLY AND CONDUCTING RESEARCH

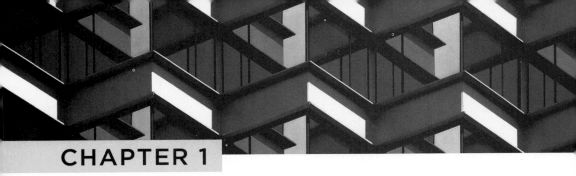

CHAPTER 1
READING CRITICALLY

MindTap® Start with a warm-up activity, and review the chapter Learning Objectives.

RHETORICAL ANALYSIS OF A WRITTEN WORK

Reading critically is the process of making a careful, thoughtful, and thorough consideration of a piece of writing by looking at its different parts, that is, making a **rhetorical analysis** of the work. **Rhetoric** is the study or examination of written or spoken language, particularly the way in which a writer communicates to an **audience**; **analysis** is the process of taking something that is whole and complex and breaking it into its individual components to better understand it. Thus, a rhetorical analysis is a close examination of not just what a work says but also how it says it. Although you will not be expected to do a formal rhetorical analysis of every piece you read, you will want to read critically, especially when considering the selections in this textbook. You will want to pay attention to various aspects of the piece as you read for two reasons: first, to understand the written work, and second, to assess it. You read for meaning first because, obviously, you must understand what you read before you can examine it. Once you develop a clear understanding of a piece of writing, you have a solid basis for moving beyond comprehension to evaluation.

The process of reading critically involves examining an author's ideas and the evidence the author has supplied in support of those ideas. It means that you try to recognize the difference between reasonable, logical assertions and those that are unreasonable or lack credibility. It requires you to distinguish between fact and opinion; to sort out the evidence an author cites; and to evaluate that evidence in terms of its relevance, accuracy, and importance. Thus, reading critically means that you actively engage in what you read, you analyze it, and you evaluate it. Learning to be a critical reader also helps make you a better writer. The best writers are often those who read widely. If you pay attention to not only what the authors you are reading have to say but also to the ways in which they use language, structure their essays, and develop their ideas, you will learn some valuable lessons for your own writing.

The following questions to ask about a written work are useful for getting the most from your reading. They provide guidelines for reading that will also be helpful for any kind of writing required in your college courses, especially the one for which you are using this textbook. If you read the assigned selections carefully, you will very likely be fully prepared to write on one of the topics that end each chapter. Certainly, reading critically is a necessity for any of the varieties of writing and strategies discussed in Part One: summary, critique, argument, synthesis, and the research paper.

MindTap® Read, highlight, and take notes online.

Questions to Ask about a Written Work

What Does the Title Tell You?   Before you read, consider the title. A title often not only reveals the subject of the piece, but it can also tell you something about the way in which the subject will be treated. It may indicate the position the author takes on the subject or reflect the tone of the piece. (**Tone** refers to the writer's attitude toward the subject and audience, which is conveyed largely through word choice and level of language usage, such as informal or formal, colloquial, or slang.) A number of essays in this textbook have revealing titles. For instance, the title "Why Legalizing Organ Sales Would Help to Save Lives, End Violence" in Chapter 15 clearly indicates the position of its author, Anthony Gregory, on the subject of legalizing the sale of human organs. You cannot tell from the title alone what his arguments are, but you can expect him to argue in favor of legalizing organ sales. Similarly, the title in Chapter 9 "Why I Just Asked My Students to Put Their Laptops Away" sets up the expectation that author Clay Shirkey will explain his decision to ban electronic devices in his classroom.

What Do You Know about the Author?   If information about the author is provided, read it. Knowing who the author is, what his or her profession is, and what his or her publications are, for example, gives you an idea of the authority from which the author writes. In magazines, journals, and collections of essays, such as those you will use in many of your college courses, the headnote often tells you about the author. The headnote is the information located between the title and the beginning of the essay, usually highlighted or set off from the body of the essay itself. The title of the Clay Shirkey article mentioned above becomes all the more intriguing when you learn in the headnote that he is a professor of media studies, which seems at odds with his decision to not allow students to use their laptops in class. Another example is the headnote for Karen Sternheimer's "Do Video Games Kill?" (Chapter 8):

> *Karen Sternheimer, whose work focuses on youth and popular culture, teaches in the sociology department at the University of Southern California, where she is also a distinguished fellow at the USC Center for Excellence in Teaching. She is author of* Pop Culture Panics: How Moral Crusaders Construct Meanings of Deviance and Delinquency *(2015);* Celebrity Culture and the American Dream: Stardom and Social Mobility *(2011);* It's Not the Media: The Truth about Pop Culture's Influence on Children *(2003);* Kids These Days: Facts and Fictions about Today's Youth *(2006); and* Connecting Popular Culture and Social Problems: Why the Media Is Not the Answer *(2009). Her commentary has been published in several newspapers, and she has appeared on numerous television and radio programs. This article appeared in* Contexts, *a quarterly publication of the American Sociological Association.*

The information about Sternheimer's professional interests as an instructor in the sociology department at the University of Southern California, the titles of her books, and the fact that she is invited to write and speak on her research interests all indicate that she is qualified to write on the subject of the relative harm of video games. The place of publication is also important in establishing Sternheimer's credentials as an authority on her subject: journals or periodic publications of professional associations are usually juried (indicating that not everyone who submits an article will be published), and such publications enhance their authors' scholarly reputations. Such qualifications do not guarantee that you will agree with the author's perspectives on a given subject or that you must adopt her position, but they do give clues as to how well informed about her subject the writer might be.

What Is the Purpose?   Good writers have clear purposes in mind as they plan and draft their work. Most nonfiction writing falls into the categories of **persuasive**, **expository**, and **expressive** writing. These forms of writing are used to achieve different goals, and they adopt different strategies for achieving those goals. In **persuasive writing**, the emphasis is on the reader: the writer's purpose is to convince the reader of the validity of his or her position on an issue and sometimes even to move the reader to action. In **expository writing**, the goal is to inform or present an objective explanation. The emphasis is on ideas, events, or objects themselves, not on how the writer feels about them. Much of the writing in college textbooks is expository, as are newspaper, magazine, and professional journal articles, and nonfiction books. Expository writing can take many forms, including cause–effect analysis, comparison–contrast, definition, and classification. **Expressive writing** emphasizes the writer's feelings and subjective view of the world. The writer's focus is on personal feelings about, or attitude toward, the subject. A journal or diary includes expressive writing. Persuasive, expository, and expressive writing often overlap, but usually a writer has one main purpose. From the opening paragraphs of a written work, you should be able to determine its general purpose or aim. A clearly implied or stated purpose helps the writer shape the writing, and it helps the reader understand and evaluate the work.

Who Is the Intended Audience?   Writers make assumptions about the people they are writing for, including whether their audience will be sympathetic or opposed to their positions, how informed their readers are about the subjects they are writing on, what their education level is, and similar considerations. These assumptions that writers make about their readers directly influence the tone they use; the evidence they select; the way in which they organize and develop their writing; and even their sentence structure, word choice, and diction level. Knowing whom the writer is addressing helps you understand the writer's point of view and explain the choices the writer has made in writing the piece. In writing for college courses, students usually assume a general audience of people like themselves who are reasonably intelligent and interested in what they have to say. However, professional writers or scholars often write for specific audiences, depending on the publications in which their writing appears. Knowing whether an audience is familiar with a subject or whether the audience is specialized or general also governs what kinds of evidence to offer and how much to include. Where the writing is published gives you a good idea of who the audience is. Take, for instance, Karen Sternheimer's "Do Video Games Kill?" (Chapter 8), mentioned earlier. Her piece appeared in a publication of the professional society associated with her area of expertise, sociology. However, *Contexts* is not a professional journal but rather, according to the website of the American Sociological Association (www.asanet.org), "a quarterly magazine that makes cutting-edge social research accessible to general readers. We're the public face of sociology." Knowing this, you can expect the article to be written in accessible language, addressed to an audience familiar with social issues who will need to be presented with convincing or persuasive evidence in support of her thesis.

What Is the Thesis or Main Idea?   The **thesis** states the main idea of the entire essay. Sometimes it is embodied in a single sentence—the thesis statement—and sometimes it is expressed in several sentences. If the main idea is not explicitly stated, it should be clearly implied. Whether the thesis is explicit or implicit, it is a necessary component of a clearly written work. A thesis helps the writer focus the writing and guides the organization and development of key ideas. It also helps to provide direction to the reader by making clear what the point of the essay is, thereby assisting the reader's understanding of the piece.

What Are the Key Ideas and Supporting Evidence or Details?   For this step in your critical reading, you should underline or highlight the major points of the essay. One important tool for an active, critical reader is a pen or pencil. As you read, underline, star, or in some way highlight major points of development. Look for topic sentences of paragraphs. Although the thesis statement answers the question, What is this essay about? the topic sentence answers the question, What is this paragraph about? If a topic sentence is not clearly stated, it should be clearly implied.

What Helpful Marginal Notes Can You Make as You Read?   In the margins, write your response to a passage or make note of words, phrases, or entire passages you think are important to the piece. Make notes about the evidence or details that support major points. If you have a question about something that the author says, write it in the margin for later consideration. If you are not sure of the meaning of a word, circle it and look it up in a dictionary after you have finished reading. Finally, if you are struck by the beauty, logic, or peculiarity of a passage, note marginal comments on that as well.

Can You Summarize What You Have Read in Your Own Words?   This is the point at which you test your understanding of what you have read. Go back now and look at your underlining and notations. Then try to state in your own words what the writing is about and the main points that the writer makes. If you can accurately summarize a piece of writing, then you probably have a good idea of its meaning. Summarizing also helps you recall the piece later, perhaps in class or in small-group discussions. Incidentally, summarizing is also a good strategy for your own study habits. After reading an assignment for any of your courses, try to write or tell someone a summary of your reading. If you cannot express in your own words the major ideas of what you have just read, you should reread. For a more detailed discussion of writing a summary, see Chapter 3.

How Would You Evaluate What You Have Read?   When you are sure that you understand what you have read and can summarize it objectively, you are ready to respond. You can evaluate something in many ways, depending on its purpose. First, consider whether the author achieves the stated or implied purpose and whether the thesis or main idea is thoroughly explained, developed, or argued. Has the writer supplied enough details, examples, or other evidence? If you are evaluating an argument or persuasion essay, is the evidence convincing to you? Does the piece make a logical and reasonable argument? Are you persuaded to the writer's position? What questions do you have about any of the writer's assertions? Do you wish to challenge him or her on any points? If the purpose of the essay is to describe, has the writer conveyed to you the essence of the subject with appropriately vivid language? For any piece of writing, you can assess how well written it is. Is it organized? Is the writing clear to you? Does the introduction give you enough information to get you easily into the essay, and does the conclusion leave you satisfied that the writer has accomplished the purpose for the essay? In Chapter 4, Writing a Critique, you will find a more detailed discussion of how to evaluate a passage or an entire essay.

GUIDELINES FOR READING CRITICALLY

☐ Consider what the title tells you about the essay.
☐ Try to learn something about the author.
☐ Determine the purpose of the writing.
☐ Determine the audience for whom the piece was written.
☐ Locate the thesis statement or main idea.
☐ Locate key ideas and supporting evidence or details.
☐ Make marginal notes as you read, including not only a summary of key ideas but also your questions about the content.
☐ Summarize what you have read.
☐ Evaluate what you have read.

EXERCISE

Read the following opinion piece critically and carefully, following the steps outlined in the guidelines by answering these questions:

- What does the title tell you about the article before you begin reading it?
- What does the information in the headnote indicate about the author's qualification to write on the subject of the article?
- What is the purpose of the article?
- Who seems to be the intended audience?
- What key ideas and supporting evidence does the author provide?
- How would you summarize the highlights of the article?
- How well do you think the author supported his main idea or thesis? Are you convinced by what he says?

Your instructor may want you to write out your rhetorical analysis or bring your notes to class for classroom discussion.

"CULTURE BUNDLING" AND OTHER OBSTACLES TO A REAL GUN CONTROL DEBATE

KEN WHITE

Ken White is an attorney in Los Angeles. His experience includes working as Assistant District Attorney in Los

*Angeles for six years, prosecuting federal fraud cases.
Since 2005, he has been co-owner of his own firm,
which specializes in all kinds of criminal defense,
including white collar crime. His particular expertise is
First Amendment litigation. This article was published
in the Op-Ed section of the* Los Angeles Times.

I enjoy unproductive talk. Bloviating, berating, snarking, and
swearing about politics are all pleasures, and not even particularly guilty ones. Most of the time, I remember that my
self-indulgence doesn't accomplish much. It pleases me, it
entertains like-minded people and it reaffirms whatever my
"team" already believes. But it doesn't persuade. It neither seeks
nor finds common ground.

Much of our modern American dialogue about gun rights
and gun control is like that. We yell, we signal to the like-
minded, we circle our wagons, we take shots at opponents.

Imagine that we wanted to have a productive conversation.
Imagine that we wanted to identify our irreducible
philosophical and practical differences, seek areas of agreement
and change some minds. What might we do?

4   First, we could stop culture-bundling. We culture-bundle
when we use one political issue as shorthand for a big group of
cultural and social values. Our unproductive talk about guns is
rife with this. Gun control advocates don't just attack support
for guns; they attack conservative, Republican, rural and
religious values. Second Amendment advocates don't just attack
gun control advocates; they attack liberal, Democratic, urban
and secular values. The gun control argument gets portrayed as
the struggle against Bible-thumping, gay-bashing, NASCAR-
watching hicks, and the gun rights argument gets portrayed as
a struggle against godless, elitist, kale-chewing socialists.

That's great for rallying the base, I guess, but that's about
all. When you culture-bundle guns, your opponents don't hear
"I'm concerned about this limitation on rights" or "I think
this restriction is constitutional and necessary." They hear
"I hate your flyover-country daddy who taught you to shoot
in the woods behind the house when you were 12" and "Your
gay friends' getting married would ruin America and must be
stopped." That's unlikely to create consensus.

Second, we could recognize that accurate firearms
terminology actually matters to the debate. Confused gun
control advocates may suggest a ban on "semiautomatic

weapons," believing that means automatic rifles, when it actually refers to nearly every modern weapon other than bolt-action rifles and shotguns. Such linguistic flimsiness drives the perception that mainstream gun control advocates want to take away all guns.

If you think precision doesn't matter, forget about guns for a second. Imagine I'm concerned about dangerous pit bulls, and I'm explaining my views to you, a dog trainer—but I have no grasp of dog terminology.

Me: I don't want to take away dog owners' rights, but we need to do something about pit bulls. We need restrictions on owning an attack dog.

8   **You:** Wait. What's an "attack dog"?

Me: You know what I mean. Like military dogs.

You: Huh? Pit bulls aren't military dogs. In fact "military dogs" isn't a thing. You mean like German Shepherds?

Me: Don't be ridiculous. Nobody's trying to take away your German Shepherds. But civilians shouldn't own fighting dogs.

12 **You:** I have no idea what dogs you're talking about now.

Me: You're being both picky and obtuse. You know I mean hounds.

You: Hounds? Seriously?

Me: OK, maybe not actually "hounds." Maybe I have the terminology wrong. I'm not obsessed with violent dogs the way you are. But we can identify breeds that civilians just don't need to own.

16 **You:** Apparently not.

Third, and perhaps most importantly, we can't debate gun rights when we're terrible at talking about rights in general. The 2nd Amendment debate is full of assertions like "My right not to be shot outweighs your right to own a gun" and "I have an absolute right to own any gun I want." How can we evaluate these assertions, except on a visceral level?

When it comes to rights, we've lost the plot, particularly since 9/11. We don't know where rights come from, we don't know or care from whom they protect us, we don't know how to analyze proposed restrictions on them, and brick by brick we've built a fear-based culture that scorns them in the face of both real and imagined risks. We've become a nation of civic illiterates, mystified by the relationship between individuals and the government.

It is therefore inevitable that talk about gun rights will be met with scorn or shrugs, and that discussions of what restrictions are permissible will be mushy and undisciplined. Unless we approach all rights in a principled manner—whether it's the right to free speech in the face of offense, or the right to due process in the face of the war on terrorism—we're not going to have a productive debate about any of them.

20   I know. Productive debates sound like hard work. Unproductive debates are more fun. But can we leave those to Facebook?

RHETORICAL ANALYSIS OF VISUALS

Rhetorical considerations apply to visual images as well as to written forms of communication. Whether you are critiquing an essay in a book or periodical, a visual art form, or an Internet website, questions of audience, tone, purpose, organization, content, and meaning apply. With visuals, as with written works, you must consider perspective or **point of view, context,** and **connotation.** Connotation—the emotional associations of a thing—is perhaps even more important when viewing visuals than in reading words. Just as words have associations that go beyond the literal term or add layers of meaning to what they denote ("the dictionary definition"), so images have powerful associations. Images often have the ability to express things—emotions, nuances, insights—in a way that words cannot. They can reveal what is difficult to put into words by conveying impressions or depicting in sharp detail what it would take a great many words to describe or explain, including subtleties of meaning that emerge only after thoughtful consideration and careful perusal of the image. Visuals also have the potential to argue a viewpoint or persuade an audience; their authors use strategies to present a viewpoint or make a statement that is similar to those used by authors of the written text.

We see images daily in a variety of forms—in photographs, drawings, paintings, pictures, brochures, advertisements, CD album covers, posters, and Internet web pages, and of course on television and in film. Most of these images go unexamined because we see so many images in our lives that we simply do not have time to analyze them all. But when we find it useful to consider an image closely, how do we analyze it? What can we say about it? How can we express in words what an image means or implies? The answer is that analyzing images critically requires skills that are quite similar to those for analyzing a piece of writing critically. Just as writers select details and organize essays to make specific points, so too do artists shooting a scene or painting a picture select details and arrange them in order to convey specific ideas or impressions. Writers and artists alike make judgments that in turn shape how readers or viewers perceive their work.

Analyzing a visual involves doing a close "reading" of the image and asking a series of questions about it. In looking critically at a visual image, you want to consider many aspects of it: what do you see when you first look at it? How do you respond initially? What details does the image highlight? What other details are included and what might have been excluded? How does the positioning of various elements of the image emphasize its meaning? The following list of questions will help you analyze the visual images that are located throughout the textbook in each of the chapters in Part Two. The answers you get when you ask these questions can give you a greater understanding of the images you are scrutinizing. Most of the visual images reproduced in this textbook are photographs or drawings, so the first set of questions is designed to help you in your analysis of them. However, the questions can easily be adapted to other kinds of images, such as advertisements, newspaper page layouts, and Internet web pages. Furthermore, television, film, music videos, and documentaries also convey messages through images that can be analyzed rhetorically in much the same way as the other forms of visual communication can be.

Questions to Ask about a Visual Image

- **What is your overall immediate impression of the image?** First impressions often linger even after rethinking one's initial response, so what strikes you immediately about an image is particularly important.

- **What detail first catches your attention?** After noting your immediate overall response, consider what detail or details first attract you. Is it the prominence, size, or positioning of the subject? Is it the colors or absence of them? Is it the size, the physical space it occupies? More than likely, the artist wanted you to notice that detail first, and very likely it is an integral part of the "message" or "statement" the image makes.

- **What details emerge after you have studied the image for a while?** Do you detect any pattern in the arrangement of details? If so, how does the arrangement of details function to convey the overall impression?

- **How does the arrangement of objects or people in the picture help draw your attention to the central image, the one you are initially drawn to?** Are some things placed prominently in the center or made larger than others? If so, what is the effect of that arrangement? How does the background function in relation to what is placed in the foreground?

- **If the image is in color, how does the artist use color?** Are the colors selected to represent certain emotions, moods, or other qualities? If it is in black and white, what use does the artist make of the absence of color? Does the artist use degrees of shading and brightness? If so, to what effect?

- **From what perspective does the artist view the subject?** Is it close to or far away from the subject? Is the subject viewed straight-on or from the side? Why do you think the artist selected this particular perspective? How might a shift in perspective alter the view of the subject, not just physically but on the level of meaning as well?

- **What emotions does the image evoke in you?** Why? Which details of the image convey the strongest emotion?

- **Has anything important been left out of the image?** What might have been included, and why do you think it was left out?

- **What is happening in the picture?** Does it tell a story or give a single impression?

- **What does the picture tell you about its subject?** How does it convey that message?

- **If there are people in the image, what can you tell about them?** What details tell you those things? Is it the way they are dressed? Their physical appearance? What are they doing?

- **Does the picture raise any questions?** What would you like to ask about the image, the activity, or the people in it? How would you find the answers to your questions?

EXERCISE

James Schnepf/Getty Images

FIGURE 1.1 *What is your initial reaction to this photograph?*

Ask the relevant questions for analyzing visuals listed earlier as you study the following photograph (Figure 1.1). Then, selecting the details you believe are important, write an analysis of the photograph in either full-length essay or one-paragraph format, depending on what your instructor asks you to do. If your assignment is to write an essay-length analysis, begin with an introductory paragraph that includes a thesis statement or a statement of the main idea of the photograph. This thesis should reflect your understanding of what the photograph means to you—its message, its story, what it suggests symbolically, or whatever ultimately you decide about the photograph. The rest of the paper should draw on details from your answers to the questions as you explain or support your thesis statement. If your assignment is to write a paragraph-length analysis, begin with a sentence that states your understanding of the main idea of the photograph. This is your topic sentence. The rest of the paragraph should supply supporting details from the image that explain or support your topic sentence.

Here are some questions specific to this photograph that you might want to think about as you work through the questions listed earlier:

- Besides showing the tattoo, what effect is achieved by looking upward from about chest high?

- Identify the main images in the tattoo. What do the choices that he made to have tattooed on his body suggest to you about the man?

- Do the earrings, nose ring, and stud add anything to your image of the man?

- What does the man's shaved or bald head add to the overall effect?

- Does the man's stance—the way he is standing, the shape of his shoulders, the position of his arms—tell you anything about what he is thinking or how he views himself? Is the man anticipating a challenge? Contemplating something? Feeling secure about himself?

- Comment on the layout of the image, especially the effect of the palm tree fronds behind the man's head.

Questions to Ask about an Advertisement

Advertising is a powerful and pervasive force in our world. Ads have the ability to affect how we think, act, and even feel about ourselves and others. Ads can shape, reflect, or distort both individual perceptions and social values, and they do so by employing some of the classic strategies of argument and persuasion: they have a proposition, they know their audience, they make appeals, they use comparisons and examples, and they particularly want to persuade us to action. In addition to the questions to ask about visual images, the following questions will help you analyze both print and nonprint advertisements:

- **What is the message of the advertisement?** What does it say to the potential buyers of the product? That is, what is its argument?

- **Who is the intended audience?** How can you tell?

- **What strategies does the ad use to convey its message?** What appeals—to logic, to emotion, to ethics, or to shared values—does it use? Does it rely primarily on only one appeal, or does it combine them? How do the specific details convey that message?

- **How does the text—the actual words used—convey the message of the advertisement?** How are words arranged or placed in the ad and why are they placed that way? If a nonprint ad, how are the voice-overs or dialogue used to convey the message?

- **How would you describe the style and tone of the advertisement?** How do they help convey the message or sell the product?

EXERCISE

- Select a print advertisement for analysis. Ask the questions noted in the previous section and write an analysis based on your notes, assessing the effectiveness of the ad in achieving its purpose. Attach a copy of the advertisement with your analysis when you hand it in to your instructor.

- Select two advertisements for the same kind of product (for instance, clothing, toothpaste, or laundry detergent). Apply the questions noted in the previous section and choose the one that you think is more effective at selling or promoting the product. Formulate a thesis sentence that states your preference, and use details from your scrutiny of both of them to support that statement. If the advertisements are print, attach copies of them if possible.

Questions to Ask about a Newspaper Page

Newspapers can shape reader response in the choices they make about the layout of text and photographs. Although we like to think that newspapers are unbiased in their reporting of news items, reading just two different newspapers on the same subject reveals that the choices a newspaper makes about a news item have a huge influence on the impressions it leaves on readers. Just the visual effect of a page layout alone tells us many things. What page an article or picture appears on and where on the page it is located represent a judgment on the part of the paper about the importance of the article or image and cannot help but shape how readers respond to it. Consider the following list about photographs and news articles when looking at a newspaper page:

- **Where in the paper is the article or photograph placed?** Front-page placement indicates that the newspaper considers it more important as a news item than placement on the inside pages.

- **How are photographs and news articles positioned on the page?** Items that are placed high on the page or in the center of the page are likely to draw the attention more readily than those placed low or off center.

- **How large are the photographs or the headlines?** Visually, larger photographs or headlines are likely to draw attention and interest more quickly than smaller ones.

- **Are photographs in color or black and white?** Choosing to run a picture in color indicates a value judgment that the paper has made about the interest or newsworthiness of the image.

EXERCISE

- Select a newspaper page for analysis. Front pages are particularly important in newspapers for attracting reader attention, so perhaps you will want to analyze the front page of the newspaper. Ask the questions listed earlier and write an analysis based on the answers to your questions. What article(s) does the newspaper think more important than others? How are photographs used on the page? Attach the page or a copy of it with your analysis when you hand it in to your instructor.

- Select two different newspapers covering the same news story and compare their treatment of the story. How do the two newspapers compare and contrast in their handling of the story? Is one more effective than the other in reporting it? Formulate a thesis that reflects your ultimate judgment of the two papers' treatment of the news story and support that thesis with details gathered from your comparison of the two. Attach the pages or copies of them with your analysis when you hand it in to your instructor.

RHETORICAL ANALYSIS OF WEBSITES

The Internet provides a seemingly endless variety of sites to visit for every taste and interest. Web pages can function rhetorically to influence visitors to the site in much the same way as other forms of discourse. The very way in which the web page is constructed can work to produce a desired effect, especially if the constructor of the site wishes to persuade an audience, sway opinion, or impose a particular point of view. A rhetorical analysis looks at the ways a site achieves its stated or implied purpose. Because websites vary considerably in their reliability and currency, you will find additional information about evaluating them in Chapter 7. Many of the same questions one asks when evaluating a website apply when doing a rhetorical analysis of it. What follows are some questions to ask as you analyze the rhetorical effectiveness of a website whose goal is to inform, educate, or entertain.

Questions to Ask about a Website

- **Who created the web page?** Is it an individual, an organization, a government agency, an educational institution, or a corporation? Does the text at the site give you information about the author? If not, why do you think that information is not provided? Does the site tell you how to contact the author?

- **What audience does the web page target?** How can you tell? Is the intended audience stated or implied? Does it make assumptions about values, beliefs, age, sex, race, national origin, education, or socioeconomic background of its target audience?

- **What is the purpose of the website?** Does the web page want to inform, entertain, sell, argue a position, or persuade people to change their minds or to take action? If it has more than one purpose, what combination of purposes does it have? Is the implied purpose the same as the stated purpose? Does the text state one purpose while word choice, graphics, and page layout suggest or imply another? For instance, a political candidate's website might state that it has no intention of bringing up an opponent's past wrongdoings, while the very fact of stating that there are past wrongdoings to bring up casts doubt on the character of the opponent.

- **What rhetorical appeals does the written text make?** Does the text of the website make an appeal to logic or reason? Does it appeal to emotions? If emotions, which ones does it appeal to—pity, fear, joy, anger, sympathy?

- **How would you evaluate the content?** Does the website cover the topic thoroughly? Does it use language that you understand? Does it offer links and, if so, how many links? Are the links still active? What is the quality of the links?

- **What use does the site make of color?** How does the background color choice affect the mood and tone of the page? Is it a vibrant color or a sober one? Does it intrude on the text or enhance it?

- **What do you observe of the page layout?** Is there space between items on the page or are things cramped together? How does the use of space on the page affect your overall impression of the page and your ability to read it?

- **What gets loaded first when you go to the web page?** Where is that material positioned? What is loaded later or positioned low on the page? Sometimes certain components of a web page are purposely programmed to load first in order to further emphasize the purpose of the site.

- **Are graphics on the web page static or active?** Is the print used for the text large, small, or a mix of both? If a mix, what does larger print emphasize that smaller print doesn't? What font is used? Are bold print, italics, or underlining used, and if so, to what effect? Is there a banner? What purpose does the banner serve?

- **If photographs or other images are used, what is their function?** Do they illustrate or help explain something, give information, or serve to decorate the page?

- **Does the web page make use of contrasts of light and dark?** If so, what is the effect of those contrasts?

EXERCISE

Locate two websites on the same topic and compare and contrast their rhetorical effectiveness by applying the relevant questions listed earlier. After deciding which one you think is more effective, write an analysis in which your thesis states which site you prefer. Use details from your perusal of both of them as proof or evidence to support your thesis statement.

Forums on the Web

In addition to websites that people go to for information, entertainment, or news, the Internet has available a number of forums for people to participate in, such as chat rooms, newsgroups, discussion lists (listservs), blogs, and social networking sites. Although most websites are fairly dynamic in that they are (or should be) regularly updated, forums typically change throughout the day. Popular forums such as **list-servs**, **blogs**, and **social networking sites** are capable of influencing people's views or the way they think about the topics being discussed at the sites; they even have the potential to actually bring about changes because of the high degree of involvement that they have generated among visitors to their sites. Another distinguishing characteristic of such sites is that people are invited to participate in an ongoing, ever-changing discussion. People who become members of these sites have an opportunity to be not just passive readers but also active writers.

Listservs.   Listservs are e-mail–based discussion groups linked to specific topics. Listservs function as forums for the exchange of ideas, where members can debate, discuss, post news items, seek or give advice, and share in a community of people who have in common their interest in the topic of the listserv. Although listservs have official websites where people can subscribe, read the rules for posting, and locate archived postings, among other things, the real activity takes place through e-mail. Members can elect to receive messages either individually as they are posted or in digests that are sent daily, or whenever a specific number of messages have posted. Members are usually required to follow certain standards, primarily those related to conduct and appropriate content, and often the listserv has a moderator who monitors the content of messages to make sure that posts do not violate those rules. Listservs typically archive messages by date, subject of message, and/or author, and these archives can be viewed by nonmembers as well as members. They vary widely in membership numbers, from just a few people to thousands. Because listservs attract people with at least the subject of the listserv in common, they can create a strong sense of community among subscribers. Although listservs are good for reading what many people have to say on various subjects related to the primary topic of the discussion group, postings are, in general, unedited and may not be completely reliable. On the other hand, a posting that seems wrongheaded or erroneous is likely to be corrected or at least commented on by other members of the group.

Blogs.   The term *blog* (web log) describes an activity that people had been doing long before the term was coined: maintaining a website where they record personal thoughts and provide links to other sites. Many of them are essentially personal pages that bloggers (owners of the sites) update daily. They provide a forum for the bloggers themselves to argue, explain, comment on, vent frustrations, air opinions, or just gossip, while visitors to the site can express their own opinions or make observations. Membership is not required; anyone can read and respond to anyone's blog. In addition to online journals, blogs can be news summaries, collections of bits and pieces from other websites, and valuable resources for instant access to the latest news. Thus blogs have been described as a cross between an online diary and a cybermagazine, but one of the key characteristics of the most successful or popular blogs is that they are constantly updated. Although just a few years ago there were only a small number of blogs, today there are millions of them. Many blogs are run by professionals like educators, reporters, researchers, scientists, and political candidates, with visits to the sites numbering in the thousands and in a few cases millions, but the vast majority are run by individuals who see them as chatty, stream-of-consciousness journals and whose readership is very limited.

A few blogs have attracted so many readers that they have achieved or exceeded the kind of readership that large newspapers enjoy. Because of the sheer number of readers and their ability to communicate instantly with other bloggers around the world, a few blogs have been responsible for bringing to light events or issues that mainstream media have ignored by focusing public attention on a current issue. Blogs with the most impact on public affairs appear to be those with large numbers of daily visitors, and they tend to have the most influence in politics. Blogs have certain common features, including making it convenient for people to post or respond to the blog owner, posting messages in reverse chronological order for others to read, and providing links to other blogs and websites. However, blogs differ greatly in the quality and reliability of the information at the site. Blogs by definition are logs or journals and as such are often unedited, not-very-well-thought-out musings on a variety of topics. Be very careful when choosing blogs to follow and even more careful in accepting as truth what you read on a blog. You can apply the same questions to blogs that you would use for analyzing other websites rhetorically, but keep in mind the special nature of blogs and how their unrestricted, constantly changing content is very likely slanted or biased to fit the viewpoint of the blogger.

Social Networking Websites.   There are many online services dedicated to establishing networks among people. Some are fairly limited to certain groups of people, such as those graduating from a particular high school or college or those belonging to certain ethnic, religious, or even family groups. Two worldwide, all-encompassing, and well-established services are Facebook and Twitter. Facebook users can register personal information, communicate with friends and colleagues, post pictures, and establish networks with people all over the world. Twitter is similar in purpose to Facebook but is a microblogging site that limits messages to 140 characters. Twitter emerged as a significant service when users began posting what was happening at moments of key social and political unrest or upheaval. As with all websites with countless users of all political, social, economic, and ethnic backgrounds, postings can be extremely biased and inaccurate.

EXERCISE

Select one of the following:

- Locate two listservs on topics that interest you and read a few days' worth of posts. How do they compare and contrast? What is your impression of the sense of community among the members? What sorts of posts do people send?

Do they stay on topic? Do the listservs have moderators? If you were going to join a listserv, which one would you prefer?

- Locate several blogs on a topic that interests you—baseball, water skiing, crime prevention, politics, a hobby, your major—and assess their rhetorical effectiveness, using the guidelines discussed.

- Follow a thread or two on a social networking service, and assess the sorts of postings people make. How would you characterize the sense of community among the posters? How would you rate the quality of the comments? What conclusions can you draw about the usefulness or purpose of the service?

MindTap Reflect, personalize, and apply what you've learned.

CHAPTER 2
THE WRITING PROCESS

LEARNING OBJECTIVES

Students will demonstrate an ability to do the following:

☐ Generate and develop their own ideas for a writing topic.

☐ Meet challenges that present themselves in the writing process by drafting, revising, and proofreading an essay.

☐ Produce an essay that shows awareness of audience, conveys an appropriate tone, is organized and focused, and demonstrates a command of spelling and grammar.

MindTap® Start with a warm-up activity, and review the chapter Learning Objectives.

THE PROCESS

Writing for any purpose involves a progression of stages that begins with determining your purpose, then finding what you want to say, developing a strategy for organizing your thoughts, writing a rough draft, revising, editing, and last, proofreading the final copy. All writers, not just college students, benefit from treating a written endeavor as a process. Even professional writers plan, draft, revise, and edit before turning in their work. This chapter discusses the challenges that writers face in the writing process, suggests ways to meet those challenges, and provides guidelines for revising and editing their paper. The guidelines presented here assume that you are writing for a college class and that your instructor has given you at least a general or broad subject area to write about with a specified purpose. Often instructors give students a number of choices, but they still outline their expectations for the assignment.

The writing process can be frustrating because it is made up of many components. The key to writing well is to take those components in turn, focusing on each stage rather than worrying about producing a perfect end product right from the beginning of the assignment. It takes time to discover how you are going to approach an assignment, what you have to say about your topic, and how you are going to organize your ideas into a clear, coherent whole. Good writers know that writing often involves false starts, wrong turns, and dead ends; but they also know that giving the writing assignment thought and taking time to prewrite, plan, draft, and revise will produce a sense of satisfaction when they hand in their finished paper to the instructor.

MindTap   Read, highlight, and take notes online.

CHALLENGES IN THE PREWRITING STAGE

Prewriting is the first stage of any writing project and includes everything you do before you write your first draft. At this stage, you want to think about the best approach to your subject. You want to determine your purpose, identify your audience, and explore ideas. Whether your instructor has given you a specific assignment or you are to select your own from a variety of possibilities, you need to spend time thinking about the assignment, identifying what you already know about it, discovering what you need to know, and narrowing your focus from a general subject to a specific topic. The practices used in prewriting usually spill over into other stages of the writing process as well. Through drafting, revising, editing, and producing the finished product, you are thinking about your topic, discovering new strategies or information, and determining how best to organize, develop, and polish your piece.

Challenge: Determining a Purpose.   A paper without a purpose wanders aimlessly, making the writing task difficult. As a result, the paper is vague and fails to engage reader interest.

Meeting the Challenge. Make sure that you understand the requirements of the assignment and spend time thinking about how best to satisfy those requirements. As mentioned in Chapter 1, most writing can be classified as one of several types: argumentative, expository, or expressive. These types take many forms and have differing purposes. Are you to argue a position, persuade an audience to take action, explain a phenomenon, analyze an event, conclude something, or describe or narrate an experience? Are you to write a summary or a critique? Perhaps you are to examine the ideas of several people on a specific topic, arrive at your own conclusions, and then incorporate the comments of those people into your own argument or explanation. It is crucial that you know what you hope to accomplish with the piece of writing at the beginning of each written assignment. Knowing your purpose puts you on the right track for the other stages of the process.

Challenge: Identifying Your Audience.   Even with a clear understanding of purpose, you may not achieve your goal if you do not know the audience you are to address in the assignment.

Meeting the Challenge. Often the nature of a writing assignment will help determine your audience. For college work, your audience may be your instructor alone, but more often it includes your writing group, your classmates, or an audience whom you identify specifically for the assignment. Ask yourself whether you are writing to a group of peers, to an older or younger audience, to those in authority, or to the general public. Each audience requires a different approach to your subject if you are to achieve your purpose. For instance, if you are to argue a position on a controversial topic, it makes a difference whether you write to people who agree with you or to those who disagree with you. Your argument is likely to be more effective if you write to an audience who needs to be convinced because such an audience requires strong proof or persuasive evidence. If your purpose is to explain, illustrate, or analyze, your audience is likely to be informed in general, but not have a deep understanding of your subject. Unless instructed otherwise, assume an intelligent audience of nonspecialists who are interested in learning more about the topic of your paper. Imagining this audience will keep you from having to define or explain every term or concept and will give you room for interesting, informative, and/or intriguing material about the topic. Whether your instructor tells you what audience to write for or leaves the selection of an audience up to you, knowing whom you are writing to or for will help you determine details you need to include in your paper.

Challenge: Generating Ideas and Discovering Your Topic.   Students sometimes are stumped right at the beginning of the writing process because they believe they have nothing to say. This early challenge requires an investment of time that will make the drafting process go much more smoothly later on.

Meeting the Challenge. After establishing your purpose and audience, turn your thoughts next to the task of coming up with ideas or details that you can use in your paper. A number of useful exercises will help you discover what you know about your subject, generate ideas for your paper, and open up ways for you to narrow your subject to a workable topic. Keep in mind the distinction between **subject** and **topic:** subject is the general area of investigation or thought, whereas topic is one narrow aspect of that subject. These exercises will help you come up with ideas for your topic:

- **Brainstorming or free writing.** This act involves simply writing without stopping for a set time, noting everything that occurs to you as you think about your subject. Time yourself for five or ten minutes while you write on a blank sheet of paper or your computer everything that occurs to you about your broad subject in an effort to narrow to a workable topic. When your time is up, read through everything that you have written. Look for ideas that you think are promising for your assignment, and if you need to explore them further, brainstorm or freewrite on those, or try one of the other exercises for generating ideas.

- **Asking questions.** A good way to find out more about your subject is to simply ask questions about it. The most obvious questions are those that journalists routinely use: Who? What? When? Where? Why? How? Depending on your initial broad subject area, any of the following may help you come up with ideas for your paper: Who is affected? Who is responsible? What does it mean? When did it happen or take place? How is it done? Why does it matter? How does it work? What are its components? What happened? Where did it happen? Why did it happen? As you can tell, not every question is relevant for a subject, but asking some of them about your subject when appropriate alerts you to areas that you may need to explore and helps anticipate the kinds of questions readers may have when reading your paper.

- **Making lists.** List everything you know or are curious about for the subject you are working on. Listing is similar to brainstorming but involves just making a simple list of ideas, thoughts, or information related to your subject. Sometimes seeing ideas, concepts, or key words in a list leads to further development of those things.

- **Clustering around a central idea.** Clustering involves placing a key word or central idea in the center of your page and writing related words, phrases, or ideas around this central idea. As you move out from the central point by creating related ideas, you may see patterns emerge or recognize ways to develop your topic.

- **Talking to others.** Discussing your subject with other people can be enormously helpful, whether it be friends, classmates, or your instructor. Often discussing a subject out loud with someone else helps you clarify thoughts or discover new ideas or approaches.

- **Researching.** Reading about or researching your subject will give you information, details, or arguments that you can use in your writing assignment. If you use the Internet to locate information, be cautious about which sources you accept. Keeping in mind the guidelines in Chapter 1 on evaluating Internet sources, choose your search engine from among the best known or most used; they are likely to be the most reliable.

If you use any of these techniques—brainstorming/freewriting, asking questions, listing, clustering, talking to others, researching your area of interest—you should be able to come up with narrow aspects of the general subject from which you can select what you want to write about. If one technique does not work, try another, and keep at it until you are satisfied with the topic you have generated.

Challenge: Adopting an Appropriate Tone.   Conveying the wrong tone, or attitude toward subject and audience, suggests to your readers that you are not comfortable with your purpose, topic, or nature of your audience or that you are unsure of yourself as a writer.

Meeting the Challenge. Adopt a suitable tone to your purpose and audience and that accurately conveys your attitude toward your subject. Tone is conveyed through word choice, diction, and even the way you structure sentences. It reflects your attitude toward your subject and your view of yourself as a writer. Thus, you want to use language that reflects your confidence as a writer and that successfully achieves your purpose. Again the questions of why you are writing, what you hope to achieve, and to whom you are writing are important. You want to be authoritative but not overly artificial and stilted, nor do you want to be too informal. Before writing your first draft, you should be aware of the tone you will take in your paper. Even if your audience is your peers, you would not write in an assignment the way you might talk to them if you were chatting informally outside the class. Likewise, if you attempt a very formal tone that seems unfamiliar to you, the result is likely to be stiff and unnatural. Because tone is linked to purpose and audience, when you have those clearly in mind, you will have a better idea of the tone you should adopt.

CHALLENGES IN THE DRAFTING STAGE

Having determined your purpose, audience, topic, and tone, you are ready to write. The first draft represents your unpolished initial effort to create the entire essay, to put all of your ideas about your topic into an organized, coherent whole. Your drafting process often begins with fashioning a working title that best reflects what you plan to do in the paper and writing a paragraph that introduces your topic by providing a context or background for it and that leads to a **thesis or central idea statement.** This is followed by the **body of your paper,** the paragraphs between your introductory and concluding paragraphs, where you will want to construct fully developed paragraphs, each of which is focused on one specific topic or main idea—often stated in a **topic sentence**—that is related to your thesis. Finally, you will bring your paper to an end by writing an appropriate **conclusion.**

Challenge: Drafting a Working Title.   The title is the first thing that your readers see, so a weak or misleading title does not make a good first impression.

Meeting the Challenge. In the draft stage, do your best to come up with a working title, one that best reflects what you think you are going to do in your paper. You will almost surely change your title as your paper goes through various drafts, and you may even want to wait until you have written a draft or two before you create your title. However, many writers find it helpful to have a title in mind as one more aid in focusing the direction of the paper. Titles serve a useful purpose. For example, if you knew nothing but the title of Jeff Madrick's "The Cost of Child Poverty" (Chapter 11), you would have a fairly good idea of what his article is about. On the other hand, a colorful title may serve to capture or reflect what the paper is about, but in an intriguing way. Thus, Will Wright's title "Dream Machines" (Chapter 3) does not tell readers what his topic is, but it is enticing. As it happens, Wright never uses the phrase "dream machines" in his article, but the content of his piece very clearly indicates what he means by his title.

Challenge: Writing an Introduction.   After reading your title, your audience reads the first paragraph of your paper, the introduction. If this introductory paragraph does not adequately set the stage for the rest of the paper, you might lose your readers right at the beginning.

Meeting the Challenge. Draft an introduction that presents your topic and prepares for the rest of the paper. Writing instructors often advise students to begin with a general statement that serves to intrigue readers or catch their attention. That general sentence leads to more specific sentences, which in turn lead to an even more specific one, the thesis statement. The first paragraph not only introduces readers to the specific focus of the paper but also sets the tone, prepares readers for what is to follow, and engages their interest. As with your title, you may not be satisfied with your introduction in the first draft or two. You may not know exactly how to introduce your paper until you have organized your thoughts and written at least one complete draft. Do not get frustrated if you cannot think of a good introduction as you begin the draft stage. Because of its importance, you will want a working introduction, but most likely your finished version of the introduction will come only after you are fully satisfied with the body of your paper. Professional writers often take more than one paragraph to introduce their topic, especially for longer pieces such as the readings in this textbook and other articles that you will read in your classes or leisure time. Note, though, that the opening paragraphs—whether one, two, or three—always state or imply the subject and in most cases the position of the writer on that subject.

An example of an effective introduction is the opening paragraph of Anne Trafton's "When Good People Do Bad Things" (Chapter 14):

> When people get together in groups, unusual things can happen—both good and bad. Groups create important social institutions that an individual could not achieve alone, but there can be a darker side to such alliances. Belonging to a group makes people more likely to harm others outside the group.

Trafton's paragraph is a model of how to introduce one's subject, entice readers, and set the stage for what the paper will do. Her opening sentence is a general statement, but it also tells readers the specific subject of her article, group behavior. Her next sentence is also general but still about group behavior, and it introduces another element: the darker side of group behavior. Then, her closing sentence explicitly states what that "dark side" is—harming those not in the group—and implicitly promises that she will explain what she means by that enticing statement.

Challenge: Avoiding Unclear or Weak Focus.   If your essay does not have a clearly recognizable central purpose that is strong or complex enough to warrant a full exploration in your paper, readers will be lost.

Meeting the Challenge. You can sharpen, clarify, or strengthen your focus with a relevant introduction and clear thesis or statement of purpose. Throughout the essay, keep your central purpose in mind and include only material that relates to that purpose. Not every kind of writing requires a thesis, but most do, especially the kinds of writing that you will do for your college courses. Not every thesis needs to be stated explicitly, either, but there must always be some clearly implied central point to your writing. For instance, the introduction and thesis in Diane Ravitch's "Critical Thinking? You Need Knowledge" (Chapter 10) quickly establishes the focus of her article and her position on it. Clarifying the focus early on works for both the writer in the process of drafting the essay and readers of the final version:

> The latest fad to sweep K–12 education is called "21st-Century Skills." States—including Massachusetts—are adding them to their learning standards, with the expectation that students will master skills such as cooperative learning and critical thinking and therefore be better able to compete for jobs in the global economy. Inevitably, putting a priority on skills pushes other subjects, including history, literature, and the arts, to the margins. But skill-centered, knowledge-free education has never worked.

Ravitch begins with a simple statement of fact about the "21st-Century Skills" initiative in primary and secondary education. Her next sentence expands on and defines essentially what that initiative does. In her third sentence, she narrows her focus by introducing the specific topic that she wants to address, the danger that she sees in a skill-based curriculum. Her fourth sentence indicates her viewpoint on that initiative and, as a result, sets up an expectation that she will tell readers why she thinks it will not work.

Challenge: Developing a Strategy for Organizing Your Paper.   In the same way that an essay without a clear purpose leaves readers confused, so does a paper that is not organized in a logical or sensible way.

Meeting the Challenge. The key questions of how you will organize your essay and what strategies you will use to develop and support your thesis assume primary importance as you begin to draft the body of your paper. Here again, a strong thesis statement will be invaluable in helping you plan your essay. After all, if it serves to direct readers of your paper, it must beforehand direct you as the writer of the paper. As noted earlier in the comments about both Anne Trafton's "When Good People Do Bad Things" (Chapter 14) and Diane Ravitch's "Critical Thinking? You Need Knowledge" (Chapter 10), both writers set up the subject of their articles and the direction it will go. Your goal as you think about organizing your paper is first to get a thesis or central idea firmly in place early on. Your thesis is essentially a guideline or a bare-bones sketch of what you will discuss in the rest of your paper.

Although your thesis is in a sense a directional statement for the paper's organization and development, more considerations come into play in planning the body of the paper. Using the thesis as your guide, write down the major points that you want to make in support or explanation of that thesis. For each major point, make a list of minor points or supporting examples or illustrations that you will use to make that point. Ask yourself if the major points are in a logical order or if they need to be shifted about to make them logical. Consider whether every major point does indeed support, illustrate, or in some way relate to your overarching purpose or thesis. If not, discard the irrelevant ones and look for more directly relevant points. Your chief concern when considering how to organize your paper is always directly connected to whether the points you make support or illustrate your position or in same way advance the development of your paper.

Writers use many different **rhetorical modes** or patterns to organize and develop their ideas, depending on their purposes, whether those are persuasive, expository, or expressive purposes. Whatever a writer's purpose, some fairly standard models can help to organize written work. These include **argumentation/persuasion, narration, description,** or expository modes such as **cause–effect analysis, classification-division, comparison/contrast,** and **definition.** These various ways of organizing and developing ideas are almost never used in isolation. Seldom will you find a piece of writing that does not combine two or more of these strategies, and they are all equally useful, depending on your purpose for writing, the audience you are writing to, and the context you are writing in. You will notice as you read the essays in this textbook that all of the writers employ a variety of strategies to achieve their purpose.

Challenge: Drafting the Body of Your Paper.   No matter how strong your title and introduction, the success of your writing efforts lies largely in how well you explain, defend, or develop your central point in the body of your paper.

Meeting the Challenge. The body of your paper should consist of a number of paragraphs that relate directly to your thesis. A successful writer ensures that each paragraph in the body contains key ideas, supporting evidence, detailed explanation, or other information that directly advances the purpose of the paper.

A **typical paragraph** in the body of the paper focuses on one topic related to the thesis of the paper; has a topic sentence that expresses that single topic; contains perhaps seven to ten supporting sentences; and has a concluding sentence that leads to the next paragraph:

- **Topic sentence.** Each of the paragraphs in the body of the paper should have a topic sentence or a clear statement of purpose. Remember that the thesis statement answers the question "What is this essay about?" In the same way, the topic sentence answers the question "What is this paragraph about?" As with a thesis, if your topic sentence is not clearly stated, it should be clearly implied.

- **Supporting sentences.** Sentences in the paragraph should have a logical organization, should support only the topic of that paragraph, and should lead clearly and smoothly from one to another. They are used to support the topic sentence, that is, to explain it, illustrate it, amplify or expand on it. Paragraphs contain details related to and supportive of the focus of the paragraph and include a mix of both general and specific or detailed statements.

- **Concluding sentence(s).** The final sentence or sentences summarize the connections between the sentences and bring the paragraph to closure. Sometimes, the final sentence points to the subject of the next paragraph.

Challenge: Providing Transition.   Transition is the linking or connecting of ideas or statements. If you do not use words that show the connection between ideas, clauses, sentences, and paragraphs, your writing will seem to be a series of disconnected statements.

Meeting the Challenge. Providing effective transition helps the reader follow what you are saying. Whether at the sentence, paragraph, or whole-essay level, you need to make connections clear to your readers. In any kind of writing, you want to try to be as coherent as possible; you will go a long way toward achieving that goal when you provide clear markers to help your readers follow the development of your paper and see connections between ideas and points. We have many tools with which to link or show the connection between thoughts and ideas.

Repeating key words and using pronouns to refer to nouns are two very common ways to provide transition. Here is a paragraph from Clay Shirkey's "Why I Just Asked My Students to Put Their Laptops Away" (Chapter 9):

> Despite these rationales, the practical effects of my decision to allow technology use in class grew worse over time. The level of distraction in my classes seemed to grow, even though it was the same professor and largely the same set of topics, taught to a group of students selected using roughly the same criteria every year. The change seemed to correlate more with the rising ubiquity and utility of the devices themselves, rather than any change in me, the students, or the rest of the classroom encounter.

In the first sentence, "these rationales" refers to what Shirkey wrote in the previous paragraph. Next, in expanding on "grew worse over time" in the first sentence, he states what that distraction was, followed by a transitional marker "even though" and the repetition of "same." In sentence three, "the change" repeats the word in the previous sentence, and "rather than" is a transitional phrase.

- **Another way to make sure that your sentences and paragraphs flow is to use transitional words or phrases to help** achieve clarity or coherence. The following are just a few examples of the many words and phrases that we use to make transitions clear:

  - **To show addition:** furthermore, in addition, also, again, too, as well as, another
  - **To show consequence:** therefore, as a result, because, consequently, thus, then, hence, so that, for this reason, because
  - **To show contrast:** on the other hand, however, in contrast, instead, conversely, on the contrary, but, yet, compared to
  - **To show similarity:** likewise, similarly, in the same way, moreover, analogous to
  - **To illustrate:** for example, such as, in particular, to illustrate, for instance, for one thing, to explain, namely, that is, in this case
  - **To show time relationship:** later, earlier, afterward, before, next, eventually, at length, before long, meanwhile, subsequently

- **To make a concession:** although, even though, still, of course, while it may be true, in spite of, at any rate
- **To emphasize:** importantly, unquestionably, without a doubt, of prime importance, certainly, undeniably
- **To summarize:** in brief, in summary, in essence, in other words, to conclude, generally, in any event, on the whole, as I have shown

Challenge: Distinguishing among Levels of Generality.   A paper that stays only at the general level usually lacks substance; not providing enough detail or specificity will likely weaken your overall effect.

Meeting the Challenge. One feature of a fully developed paper is the use of exemplification, details or illustrations. Whenever you make a general statement, make sure the following sentences provide specifics about that general statement. When you feel that you have not said enough to convincingly or fully develop or explain your central idea, ask yourself where you can add examples or illustrations. Examples and illustrations are crucial to writing, no matter what the primary purpose is. Without them, writing stays at the general or abstract level and leaves readers only vaguely understanding what the writer means. They make meaning clear and help make writing more interesting, livelier, and more engaging than an essay without details. Examples may be brief and numerous or extended and limited in number, and they may take the form of narratives. They do not have to begin with the words *for example* or *to illustrate* nor ostentatiously announce that an example is coming. Most of the readings in this textbook contain examples of one kind or another to both illustrate and argue their theses. It would be difficult to find an effective piece of writing that does not use examples of some sort.

An example of the use of details to illustrate meaning appears in this paragraph of Emily Alpert Reyes's "'Men Are Stuck' in Gender Roles, Data Suggest" (Chapter 12):

> Gender stereotypes do seem to have loosened: The Global Toy Experts survey found that most mothers would let their own sons play with dolls and dress-up sets, even if they shied from buying them for other boys. Parents in some parts of Los Angeles said their boys got barely any flak for choosing pink sneakers or toting dolls to school. And in a recent online survey by advertising agency DDB Worldwide, nearly three-quarters of Americans surveyed said stay-at-home dads were just as good at parenting as stay-at-home moms.

The opening clause is a generality, and the rest of the paragraph consists of specific examples to illustrate what that general statement means. How might the impact or effectiveness of the paragraph change if you alter the position of the sentences?

Challenge: Drafting Your Concluding Paragraph.   Without a concluding paragraph, readers are left with a feeling that you have not finished whatever points you have been making.

Meeting the Challenge. Write a final paragraph that brings the paper to a satisfying end. For a long paper, such as a research project, your conclusion may take more than one final paragraph, but no matter its length, a paper should have a conclusion. You may not be ready to write your conclusion when you write the first draft of your paper because the conclusion should come logically from all that has gone before. Sometimes you need to write several drafts before you can write your conclusion. When you are ready to write it, you have many approaches to choose from. Sometimes writers simply restate their introductions, but try to be more imaginative. You don't have to restate major points, as they should be clear in readers' minds, but referring to them or highlighting them lends emphasis to what you have written and stresses its significance. Try to leave your readers with something to think about: stress the importance of what you have written, suggest a course of action, or point to questions raised by your paper that need further study or exploration. You might refer back to your introduction by mentioning a detail or image from it, or end with an amusing anecdote or a humorous or striking comment. No matter what strategy you choose for concluding your paper, readers should feel that they have come to a satisfactory end. Will Wright, in "Dream Machines" (Chapter 3), concludes his essay about the importance of game playing in this way:

> Games are evolving to entertain, educate, and engage us individually. These personalized games will reflect who we are and what we enjoy, much as our choice of books and music does now. They will allow us to express ourselves, meet others, and create things we can only dimly imagine. They will enable us to share and combine these creations, to build vast playgrounds. And more than ever, games will be a visible, external amplification of the human imagination.

Wright's concluding paragraph makes reference to the points that he has made about games, summarizes his conclusions about their importance, and ends with a statement about their long-term influence on the imagination.

REVISING YOUR PAPER GLOBALLY

After you have written a draft of your paper, set it aside for a while—a few hours, overnight, a day or two if you have the time—and then return to it to closely reexamine and revise what you have written. Revision is a crucial step in the writing process, for it is here that you turn your draft into a polished piece of writing. The word *revision* means to look again or revisit, and that is what you do at this stage: examine the substance of your paper with a critical eye, looking for ways to improve what you have written. While you might have done some rewriting when drafting your paper, the really serious work comes during revision. This section suggests approaches to revising your paper. Your first concern when revising is to consider whole-essay or "global" matters, so reread your entire paper to begin the revision process. Don't worry at this time about whether you have made grammatical errors or whether every word is spelled correctly. These are matters that you will address after you have worked on larger issues. In the global revision stage, you may find yourself deleting or moving entire sections of what you wrote in the draft stage until you are satisfied with the focus, organization, and development of your essay.

Revision addresses the issues of purpose, audience, organization, and content, which include the development of ideas, and both the introduction and conclusion of your essay. Apply the same questions to your own writing that you ask when evaluating the writing of others, as detailed in Chapter 1 on critical reading. Writers use many techniques to make the revision process meaningful. You truly want to revise, not simply rewrite, your paper, so leave some time between drafts to give yourself a fresh perspective on what you have written. Obviously that means not starting any writing project at the last minute. You will find that it works to your advantage to begin writing as soon as possible after getting an assignment. The more time you have to draft and revise, the more satisfied you are likely to be with your final effort. When revising, try reading your paper out loud and listening to how it sounds, or read it to someone else to get feedback from an objective audience. Revise passages that sound awkward or seem to lead nowhere; move things around if the paper seems disorganized; and look for ways to improve the development of every point you make. Include entire paragraphs in the revision process. Make sure that every paragraph is itself fully explained and that each paragraph directly relates to your central purpose. Consider how well your introduction truly focuses on your paper and whether your concluding paragraph gives a sense of closure to the paper.

Of prime importance is the question of whether all components of your paper are directly related to your thesis. Remember that your thesis indicates the central idea of your paper, suggests the direction you will take with that idea, states your position on a topic, or asks a question that you will answer in the course of your paper. After you have read through your arguments or supporting examples or illustrations, ask yourself if you have left any important points out. Are there places where readers might argue with or take exception to what you have written and, if so, how would you respond? Consider addressing those matters in your paper, anticipating reader responses. For instance, if the purpose of the essay is to describe, have you conveyed the essence of the thing with appropriately vivid words? If your purpose is to argue or persuade, is your evidence convincing? Is the argument logical and reasonable? Have you avoided fallacies in the logic of your argument? Ask yourself if the essay has a clear plan or organizing principle and if your final paragraph brings your paper to a satisfactory conclusion.

GUIDELINES: A CHECKLIST FOR REVISING GLOBALLY

☐ Does your introduction focus on the main point or thesis of the paper? Does it state your purpose clearly? Does it create interest or otherwise pique reader curiosity?

☐ Is your audience clearly defined, and do you consistently write to that audience throughout the paper?

- [ ] Have you chosen an appropriate tone for your topic? Is that tone consistent throughout the paper?
- [ ] Is the essay organized logically?
- [ ] Do paragraphs have clearly stated or implied topic sentences? Are they developed in a coherent, logical way?
- [ ] Have you provided transition from thought to thought or point to point?
- [ ] Does your paper distinguish among levels of generality within paragraphs and within the essay as a whole?
- [ ] Do any passages need to be clarified?
- [ ] Does anything you have written need to be shifted to somewhere else in the paper or deleted entirely?
- [ ] Does your final paragraph bring your paper to a satisfactory end?

ILLUSTRATION: REVISING GLOBALLY

The following example illustrates how the revision process works. These are the opening paragraphs of a draft of Elizabeth's research paper "Then and Now in China: Comparing Revolutionary with Modern Ballet." The final version appears as the first two paragraphs of her paper, located in Chapter 7. Sources used in these paragraphs appear afterward in the correct MLA format.

DRAFT WITH
REVISIONS NOTED:

Elizabeth's second sentence states essentially the same thing, so she deleted the unnecessary words. This sentence is not relevant.

The sentence is wordy and redundant as written; deleting unnecessary words and changing "through the creation of" to "creating" tightens the sentence and reduces clutter.

China has a long history of ~~forcing women into subservient roles,~~ viewing **them** women as second-class citizens. Historically, the male dominated culture expected women to serve men, often as slaves or concubines. ~~The plight of a Chinese woman was once controlled first by her father and then by her husband, with whom her father had arranged the relationship.~~ Typically, artistic endeavors, including operas, ballets, writings, and art, perpetuated these traditional roles of women, ~~keeping them in their submissive places through the creation of~~ creating compliant female characters who rarely challenged their male counterparts. The ballet, still valued and cherished by Chinese citizens of all socio-economic levels, especially created a canvas for developing cultural expectations.;

and citizens of all socio-economic levels valued and continue even today to cherish Chinese ballet. Over time, interactions with Western culture have influenced the way Chinese society sees women, and modernization of women's roles has occurred. Yet, artists seem unhurried to incorporate these modern roles to the stage. This slowness, however, may be intentional, as artists work to influence their audiences. At the height of the spread of Communism, China entered an organized political period called the Cultural Revolution, a time when the government was heavy handed in influencing culture and focused on imposing Mao's ideals into the State. Since the 1960s, the West has had a variety of influences on Chinese culture, but not in all genres. Though interactions with Western culture since the 1960s have helped modernize the way that Chinese society views women and their roles, artists seem unhurried to incorporate these changes to the stage. Despite changes in Chinese society since the Cultural Revolution, modern Chinese ballet continues to reflect the traditional attributes of female characters and to rely on revolutionary plots.

After the Great Leap Forward in the 1950s, Mao Zedong's power and popularity began to dissipate because of his failure at modernizing the economic system of China. Because Mao feared that the new leaders would take the State in the wrong direction; as a result,, he instigated the Cultural Revolution exert that his power over the State and citizens still remained strong to maintain his influence over the State and its citizens (Trueman). As detailed in Patricia Ebrey's explains in *Sourcebook of Chinese Civilization*," The aim of the Cultural Revolution was to attack the Four Olds—old ideas, old culture, old customs, and old habits—in order to bring the areas of education, art and literature in line with Communist ideology" (Ebrey). To align society with his philosophy, Mao completely overhauled the Chinese culture. The Communist regime deemed non-supporters of Mao's views and the values of the State as an "enemy [enemies] of the party and people" (Ebrey). In order to avoid persecution or arrest, Chinese citizens complied with the government's mandates. Ultimately, the Cultural Revolution especially affected the arts so strongly

Elizabeth noticed that she could write a more effective sentence and provide variety by shifting words about.

Elizabeth removed irrelevant or unnecessary details, combined essential ideas, and narrowed her focus.

This is a general statement of her central idea. Her specific form of proof or support is stated at the end of the second paragraph.

Not relevant to her central point.

The original wording was clumsy.

The introduction to the quotation seemed awkward. This revision makes the transition into the quotation smoother. Elizabeth changed the singular word in the quotation to the plural, which she puts in brackets to indicate that it is her word. The plural noun now agrees with what it refers to, "non-supporters."

that ~~in fact,~~ for a period of time there was absolutely no music in China. Eventually, Mao's wife, Jiang Qing, fostered the production of eight "Model Operas" that applied the acceptable revolutionary themes; and were performed continuously with mandatory attendance (Ebrey). ~~Different than preceding eras, the Cultural Revolution has had a significant, long-lasting effect on the Chinese society, especially on the arts, and yet, e~~Even though *the regime's policies* ended long ago, modern Chinese ballets still rely on ~~the~~ strong elements ~~found in~~ of the "Model Eight" (Mittler 380). Nowhere is this more evident than in the ties between the late 1950s ballet *The White-Haired Girl* and the 1990s ballet *Raise the Red Lantern*.

Wordy and not directly relevant.

This sentence states explicitly how she will support her more general central idea at the end of the first paragraph.

Works Cited

Ebrey, Patricia. *A Visual Sourcebook of Chinese*

    Civilization: Cultural Revolution. 26 Nov. 2001,

    depts.washington.edu/chinaciv/tg/tfront.pdf.

Mittler, Barbara. "Eight Stage Works for 800 Million

    People: The Great Proletarian Cultural Revolution

    in Music—A View from Revolutionary Opera." *The*

    Opera Quarterly, vol. 26, nos. 2–3, 2010, pp. 377–401.

Trueman, Chris. "The Cultural Revolution." *History*

    Learning Site, 3 Mar. 2016, www.historylearningsite

    .co.uk/modern-world-history-1918-to-1980/

    china-1900-to-1976/the-cultural-revolution/.

Elizabeth's revisions eliminate wordiness and unnecessary information and combine components of some sentences for better effect. Her first two paragraphs comprise her introduction, and her thesis comes at the end of her second paragraph

REVISING FOR STYLE AND CLARITY

Besides being focused, organized, and developed well, your paper will be more successful if it is written in an engaging style. **Style** in writing refers to your overall written effect and is characterized by such things as word choice, tone, and sentence structure or **syntax** (the arrangement of words or phrases to create sentences). **Throughout the revision process, whether globally or at the individual sentence level, look for clumsy, wordy, ineffective, or unclear passages.** If you find that you have written several very short simple sentences in a row, for instance, try combining them. Look for ways to vary sentence structure and length to avoid monotony or choppiness, and select words and details for greatest effect and interest. Use language that is appropriate for your topic and idiomatic, avoiding slang and clichés. Structure sentences to their best advantage, as Elizabeth has done in the revision example earlier. Consider ways to reword what you have written so that it more accurately reflects what you mean. Watch out for some fairly common pitfalls in sentence construction, such as wordiness, misplaced modifiers, **passive voice for active voice,** and faulty parallelism.

ILLUSTRATION: REVISING FOR STYLE AND CLARITY

In her expository writing class, Professor Gilliar assigned students to write a cover letter for a job application. She then selected passages from the students' work and asked them to edit the passages and explain how the reworked versions are more effective than the original. Here are examples of the process that the students went through in doing this exercise.

1. ORIGINAL SENTENCE: Not only through my passion but also through my experience conducting research and interviews, I plan to make a difference in the outreach of a news organization.

    Revised Version 1:
    With my strong passion for improving the lives of others and my savvy approach to conducting research and interviews, I will thoroughly inform my readers and move them to action.

    Rationale for rewrite:
    The first sentence is too vague with phrases like "my experience" and "make a difference." In addition, the first sentence doesn't explain what "my passion" really is or what the "outreach of a news organization" aims to do. So, the revised sentence states what the passion is for and better explains the experience of conducting research and interviews. Rather than stating "the outreach of a news organization," I stated my aims of writing for a newspaper: inform readers and move them to action. Moreover, I said "I will" rather than "I plan" because it's more decisive and shows that this is something I'm going to do no matter what.

2. ORIGINAL PASSAGE: I have had a lot of fine experiences while at school that prepared me for the challenges at your competitive company. There are many ways that allow me to apply the multiple skills and expertise I have to offer.

    Revised Version 1:
    As a college student, I have conducted rigorous research and conveyed my findings in understandable, concise reports. My savvy approach to research,

coupled with my excellent interpersonal skills, makes me an excellent candidate for your company.

Rationale for rewrite:
This revised version is much more specific and clearly indicates the experience I have learned at school. It touches upon the skills rather than simply saying "I have skills."

Revised Version 2:
As a college student, I researched the difference in symptoms of patients with latent tuberculosis compared to the symptoms of patients with active tuberculosis in the laboratory, collected all of my data in a research report that was published in a local science journal, and presented my findings at a Science Seminar that was attended by a large number of fellow science students, faculty, and staff members. Through this experience, I gained several skills including collecting and recording data in the laboratory, organizing the data in a professional format that led to acceptance by a local journal, and professional communication skills through my presentation of my findings. All of these skills make me a top candidate for the position you are offering.

Rationale for rewrite:
This rewrite explains specifically what my experience at college was and what skills were gained from these experiences that would make me a better candidate.

3. ORIGINAL SENTENCE: My natural ability and passion for writing can only be rivaled by my desire to write.

    Revised Version 1:
    I possess a natural ability to write, evidenced by my winning an English Department award for the best essay in my writing class, which is complemented by my desire to write.

    Rationale for rewrite:
    Ability and passion are fine qualities, but evidence to support such claims gives the sentence weight. A "desire" for writing is also important, so I chose to keep that word and stated that the "natural ability" is complemented by the "desire" to write, thus making me highly marketable by showing both stamina and ability.

    Revised Version 2:
    Writing is a natural ability, a passion, and a desire of mine. I constantly jot down notes, write in my journal, or make lists of ideas and prompts.

    Rationale for rewrite:
    The rivalry between "natural ability and passion" and the "desire to write" is not one of compelling logic. It is more powerful to put these factors together to work as a team of a love for writing.

    Revised Version 3:
    My natural ability and passion for writing allow me to produce effective, professional work of the kind that your prestigious company values.

Rationale for rewrite:
This version shows how my writing would help the organization. It is written more gracefully than the previous version, and it is easier to understand what I mean.

GUIDELINES: A CHECKLIST FOR REVISING FOR STYLE AND CLARITY

☐ Have you used colorful, engaging, and/or lively language?
☐ Have you constructed sentences that are varied in structure and length?
☐ Have you avoided slang and clichés?
☐ Have you avoided wordiness?
☐ Are verbs active rather than passive?
☐ Have you avoided shifts in verb tense?
☐ Are equal sentence parts parallel and modifiers correctly placed?
☐ Can you combine short sentences into longer, more complex ones to avoid a choppy effect?
☐ Have you written with clarity and grace, to the best of your ability?

EXERCISE

Imagine that you are applying for your dream job and want to explain in your cover letter why you would be a good choice. Compose a paragraph for this hypothetical job application. Select one or two sentences that you think would make you stand out from the other applicants and revise the sentence(s). For each revised version, write an analysis of why the revision is an improvement over the previous draft. Do this until you are satisfied that your final version is the best that you can write. Spend time reflecting on how your selection evolved from being acceptable to being outstanding. Be prepared to share your work with your classmates or hand it in to your instructor.

ILLUSTRATION: REVISING AT THE SENTENCE LEVEL

As noted earlier, revision at the sentence level focuses on style, clarity, or effectiveness. The following examples illustrate just a few of the writing problems that you might discover in a careful rereading of your draft. They represent some of the most typical sentence-level challenges.

1. **Revising to avoid wordiness and passive construction:** My first day on campus was one of learning my way around.
   Revised: I spent my first day on campus learning my way around.
   Rationale: The revised sentence avoids the passive construction and reduces the wordiness that of "my first day . . . was one of" causes.

2. **Revising to avoid dangling modifiers:**
   a. Standing straight and breathing hard, my mother's face appeared in the aisle.

   Revised: My mother, standing straight and breathing hard, appeared in the aisle.

   Rationale: The revision shifts the modifying phrase "standing straight and breathing hard" to apply to "mother," not just to her face.

   b. Entering the classroom late, a pop quiz had already been collected.

   Revised: Entering the classroom late, I learned that a pop quiz had already been collected.

   Rationale: In the original, the "dangling" modifier does not clearly modify anything in the sentence, whereas the revision clarifies who entered the classroom.

3. **Revising to avoid awkward construction:** That really hit home to me, the fact that other people were having the same experiences of shyness as me when it came to meeting people for the first time.

   Revised: I realized that others were just as shy as I when meeting new people.

   Rationale: The revision removes unnecessary words and makes the meaning straightforward rather than getting lost among the excess words.

4. **Revising to make equal sentence parts parallel:**
   a. He is polite, gracious, considerate, and has high standards.

   Revised: He is not only polite, gracious, and considerate, but he also has high standards.

   b. Classes are limited and not a big variety.

   Revised: Classes are limited and lack variety.

   c. We worked on his reading skills, interaction with others, or I simply read to him.

   Revised: We worked on his reading skills and interaction with others; sometimes, I simply read to him.

   Rationale: In each of the original sentences, different parts of speech are linked. The revisions avoid that error by linking nouns with nouns and verbs with verbs.

EDITING YOUR PAPER

While sentence-level revision aims to increase the clarity and effectiveness of your work, sentence-level editing focuses on grammar, mechanics, and punctuation. **Grammar** refers to such things as avoiding sentence fragments and run-on or fused sentences; subject-verb and pronoun-antecedent agreement; correct use of case for nouns and pronouns; and using adjectives and adverbs correctly. **Mechanics** refers to spelling words correctly, including correct hyphenation; correct use of italics; and use of capital letters, numbers, and abbreviations. **Punctuation** involves using correctly such things as commas, colons, semicolons, apostrophes, and quotation marks. Although the most important aspect of your writing is your content—what you say, how well you say it, and how well you present it—you also want to pay attention to these matters, especially if you know that you have problems in certain areas. If you have trouble with writing sentence fragments or run-ons, get confused about apostrophe or comma use, or misspell the same words all the time, make a conscious effort to look for those trouble spots. Errors at this level distract your reader from what you are saying, and too many such errors weaken your effectiveness as a writer.

GUIDELINES: A CHECKLIST FOR EDITING YOUR PAPER

- ☐ Are your words spelled correctly?
- ☐ Are sentences complete?
- ☐ Have you avoided fragments and run-on sentences?
- ☐ Are sentences punctuated according to standard conventions; that is, are commas, colons, semicolons, and apostrophes used correctly?
- ☐ Do pronouns and antecedents agree?
- ☐ Do subjects and verbs agree?
- ☐ Have you used pronouns in the correct case, that is, subjective pronouns like "I," "he," "we," and "they" used in subject positions and "me," "him/her," "us," and "them" used in object positions?

ILLUSTRATION: EDITING FOR ERRORS IN GRAMMAR AND PUNCTUATION

Misspelling: There opening hours show that **their** willing to devote **alot** of time to **acomodating** customer needs.

Edited: Their opening hours show that **they're** willing to devote **a lot** of time to **accommodating** customer needs.

Fragment: In college, it's nothing to have a class of 150 to 200 **students. Whereas** in high school, my classes never had more than 30 students.

Edited: In college, it's nothing to have a class of 150 to 200 **students, whereas** in high school, my classes never had more than 30 students.

Comma splice: When making drives, one group of hunters stays in one **area, another** group walks through a nearby area and tries to make the deer move toward the group that is standing.

Edited: When making drives, one group of hunters stays in one **area; another** group walks through a nearby area and tries to make the deer move toward the group that is standing.

Run-on or fused sentence: There were no cars zooming or people **talking the only** sound came from the forest creatures.

Edited: There were no cars zooming or people **talking. The only** sound came from the forest creatures.

Misuse of semicolon: Basic communication has only two people **involved; the** sender and the receiver.

Edited: Basic communication has only two people **involved: the** sender and the receiver.

Pronoun-antecedent disagreement: A student who wants to improve **their grade** can ask for a tutor at the writing lab.

Edited: A student who wants to improve **his or her grade** can ask for a tutor at the writing lab. OR, **Students who want** to improve **their grade** can ask for a tutor at the writing lab.

Subject-verb disagreement: The **number** of violent crimes in my old neighborhood **have gone** done dramatically in the last decade.

Edited: The **number** of violent crimes in my old neighborhood **has gone** done dramatically in the last decade.

Incorrect pronoun case: Both **Steve and myself** loved hunting.

Edited: Both **Steve and I** loved hunting.

Incorrect apostrophe use: My **parent's** have been married for 30 years.

Edited: My **parents** have been married for 30 years.

PROOFREADING

Leave time to proofread your final version and make any last-minute corrections, preferably on the word processor, but if necessary, written neatly in ink. At this final stage, you are looking for careless or previously undiscovered errors that you can fix easily. You might discover a misspelled word or a comma in the wrong place, or you might notice that you have left a word out. If you have given yourself time to write several drafts, edit, and revise, the proofreading stage should just be a final check of work well done.

MindTap   Reflect, personalize, and apply what you've learned.

CHAPTER 3
WRITING A SUMMARY

MindTap°   Start with a warm-up activity, and review the chapter Learning Objectives.

WRITING A SUMMARY

Students often must write both informal exercises and formal papers based on readings in their textbooks. In writing assignments for the course using this textbook, for instance, you will find frequent use for information or ideas discussed in the readings. For formal writing assignments, you may be instructed to choose among the writing topics that end each chapter in Part Two, or you may be asked to suggest your own topic for a paper on a reading or readings. You may choose to argue in favor of or against a position another author takes; you may use information from one or more of the readings to write an essay suggested by a particular chapter; you may decide to compare and contrast two or more essays in a chapter or explain various perspectives on an issue. At some point, you may want to use some of the readings from this or another textbook in combination with other print and Internet resources in a research paper. This chapter and the next three introduce several specific types of assignments that you may be asked to write. This chapter focuses on the summary.

Summarizing produces an objective restatement of a written passage in your own words, in a much shorter version than the original. The purpose of a

summary, sometimes called a **précis,** is to highlight both the central idea or ideas and the major points of a work. A summary does not attempt to restate the entire reading. You might summarize an entire book in the space of a paragraph or perhaps even a sentence, although you will not do full justice to a lengthy work that way.

Many writing assignments call for summarizing. Your instructor may ask you to write a summary of an essay, or a passage from one, to gauge your understanding. Such an assignment may be informal, something that you write in class as a quiz or an ungraded journal entry, or you may be assigned a formal summary, a longer piece that you write out of class in detail and with care. Many kinds of writing include summaries as part of the development of their main ideas. For instance, if you are asked to report on an individual or group research project for a science class, you will probably summarize your purpose, methodology, data, and conclusions. If you write an argumentative paper, you may need to summarize either opposing viewpoints or your own supporting evidence. A research paper often includes summaries of information from source materials, and the research process itself necessitates summarizing portions of what you read. Reviews of books or articles almost always include summaries of the works under discussion, and essay questions on an examination often require summaries of information or data. Across the curriculum, no matter what course you are taking, you will probably be asked to summarize.

Summaries serve useful purposes. Professors summarize as they lecture in order to convey information in a condensed way when a detailed review would take far too much time. Textbook chapters often present summaries of chapter contents as part of chapter introductions (as in Part Two of this textbook). In this textbook, some of the questions for small-group and class discussion following the readings ask you to summarize major points or portions of readings in order to facilitate your understanding of the text. That process, in turn, enhances the quality of your classroom experience and develops your abilities to follow the discussion intelligently and to make useful contributions to the discussion yourself. Your instructor may ask you to write a summary of a piece you have read as a formal assignment. Summarizing is also an excellent strategy to enhance your own study habits. After reading an assignment for any of your courses, try to write a summary of the reading. If you cannot put into your own words the major ideas of what you have just read, you may need to go back and reread the material.

Outside the classroom and the academic environment, summaries routinely give brief introductions, overviews, and conclusions of subjects at hand. In business, industry, law, medicine, scientific research, government, or any other field, both managers and workers often need quick summaries to familiarize themselves with the high points or essence of information. Knowing how to summarize accurately is a useful skill in both your academic writing and your profession or job.

A Summary Is Not a Substitute for Analysis.   Do not mistakenly assume that putting another person's words into your own words is an analysis. Instead, **a summary is a brief, concise, objective restatement of the important elements of a piece of writing of any length,** from a paragraph to an entire book. A summary may be brief, as in a one-paragraph abstract that precedes a report or long paper and gives a very short overview of it, or it may be several paragraphs or even pages in length, depending on the length of the writing or writings being summarized. You may summarize as an informal exercise for your own purposes or as a formal assignment that you hand in to your instructor for evaluation.

Abstract.   An abstract, like all summaries, is a condensed, objective restatement of the essential points of a text. Its distinguishing characteristic is its brevity. Abstracts are usually quite short, perhaps 100 to 200 words, whereas summaries may be much longer, depending on the length of what is being summarized. As with all summaries, an abstract helps readers determine quickly whether an article or a book will be of interest or use. It can also serve as a brief guide to the key points before reading an article or as an aid in recalling the contents of the piece after reading it. You will almost always find an abstract before the beginning of a research paper or an article in the sciences. Following this is the abstract that precedes a research paper by Laurel Yahi titled "Effects of His Mother's Death on Joseph's Social and Emotional Development." This abstract provides a broad overview of her paper, including her major points and conclusions. In her paper, she discusses or develops each of these components at length, providing examples and supporting evidence where necessary. In 161 words, the abstract condenses a paper of more than 2,000 words to its most essential points. You can see how an abstract, like summaries of other lengths, is useful for getting a quick overview of a report or an essay.

MindTap®   Read, highlight, and take notes online.

Effects of His Mother's Death on Joseph's Social and Emotional Development

LAUREL YAHI

Abstract

Four-year-old Joseph suddenly lost his mother two years ago. I have observed Joseph in my home daycare for 50 hours a week since his mother's death. With ample opportunity to observe him in this natural setting, I set about determining whether his mother's death might have long-term effects on Joseph's social and emotional development. At play, when working alone, at lunch time, and nap time, Joseph's cognitive abilities, vocabulary skills, willingness to listen to and obey adults, and social interaction skills appear normal for his age. He is well liked by the other children in the daycare. His progress, determination to learn, and intellectual growth all reflect a natural resiliency that lets him grow and mature without serious developmental problems. With a strong support system and a loving family, he should be able to grow into a healthy adult with no lasting negative effects on his ability to form relationships and participate fully in social settings, and enjoy good emotional health.

Formal and Informal Summaries.   Informal summaries are primarily for personal use and are usually not handed in for evaluation by an instructor. Formal summaries are those that others will read and are sometimes graded assignments. In either case, the process for writing a summary is virtually the same. Although the process is the same for both an assignment that you will hand in to your instructor and a summary for your own use, a formal summary requires the kind of care that you give to longer writing assignments. The following directions will help you prepare and draft your formal summary:

Prewriting

1. Begin by carefully reading the work. Make a mental note of its thesis or main idea, but do not write anything in the margins yet. If you try to highlight for a summary on your first reading, you might end up underlining or noting too many things. Wait until you have read the entire selection through once before writing anything.

2. After your first reading, write in your own words the thesis or central idea as you understand it. Then go back to the article, locate the thesis or main idea, underline it, and compare it with the sentence you wrote. If your sentence differs from the sentence(s) you underlined, rephrase your own sentence.

3. Next, read the article again, this time looking for major points of development or illustration of the thesis. As you reread, make marginal notes and underline, circle, or in some way mark the key supporting points or major ideas in the development of the thesis.

4. After you have finished reading, look at your notes and state in one sentence, in your own words, the thesis and each major point. Do not include details or minor supporting evidence unless leaving them out would misrepresent or unfairly represent what you are summarizing. If the writing you are summarizing comes to any important conclusions, note them as well in one sentence in your own words.

5. If you are still unclear about which are major and which are minor points, give the piece another reading. The more you read it, the better you understand its purpose, method of development, and major points.

Writing Your Summary

1. In your opening sentence, state the author's full name, the title of the work, and the thesis or main idea. Write in complete sentences, whether your summary is 100 words or 500 words long.

2. Use the author's last name when referring to what he or she says in the article or when quoting the author directly.

3. Use attributive tags throughout; that is, use words and phrases that attribute or point to your source. Such tags serve the purpose of reminding your readers who you are quoting or summarizing. They may take the form of the author's last name or pronouns referring to the author, credentials of the author, published source of the material, or other information that identifies the author (for example, "Wright, in his *Wired* Magazine article, argues that").

4. Do not use the exact words of the author unless you use quotation marks around those words. The summary must use your own wording. Use direct quotations sparingly, and only for a significant word, phrase, or sentence. Make sure that anything you put in quotation marks uses the exact wording of the article.

5. Use present tense to describe or explain what the author has written ("Wright explains" or "Wright concludes").

6. Provide clear transitions from point to point, just as you would in a longer assignment, and write in clear, coherent language.

7. Edit what you have written before turning it in to your instructor.

The key to summarizing accurately is knowing what is important and therefore must be included, and what is secondary and therefore should be omitted. Here you see the usefulness of the guidelines for critical reading. When you read critically, you identify the main idea or thesis of the selection, and you highlight or in some way mark major points. A summary must include the main idea of what you are summarizing, and it should include major points, and only major points. Thus, if you learn to read critically, you can write a summary.

GUIDELINES FOR WRITING A SUMMARY

- ☐ On your first reading, mentally note the thesis or central idea of the work or passage you are summarizing without writing anything down.
- ☐ After your first reading, write down your understanding of the thesis, locate the thesis in the work, underline it, check what you have written against it, and adjust your own sentence if necessary.
- ☐ Now reread the work, noting key points, either in the margin, by highlighting, or on a separate piece of paper.
- ☐ When you have finished your second reading, once again write in your own words a one-sentence summary of the thesis or central idea. Use the author's name and title of the reading in that sentence.
- ☐ Write in your own words a one-sentence summary of each major point the author has used to develop, illustrate, or support the thesis or central idea. State only essential details related to each major point.
- ☐ Do not include minor points unless you believe their omission would give an unfair representation of what you are summarizing.
- ☐ Where appropriate, write in your own words a one-sentence summary of any conclusion from the piece.
- ☐ Use attributive tags throughout your summary.
- ☐ Keep your summary short, succinct, and focused on the central idea and major points of the piece you are summarizing.
- ☐ Edit for grammar, punctuation, and spelling before handing in your assignment.

EXERCISE

Read "Dream Machines" by Will Wright, take notes, and write a summary of it. The personal response and questions for class or small-group discussion that follow the article may help you write your summary. Your instructor may want you to hand in your work or use it as part of a class or small-group discussion of the article.

DREAM MACHINES

WILL WRIGHT

Will Wright has created more than a dozen games, beginning with SimCity *in 1989, but he is perhaps best known for* The Sims *(2000). Wright was awarded a lifetime achievement award by Game Developers Choice in 2001. His latest software game series,* Spore, *is based on the model of evolution and scientific advancement. This article first appeared in* Wired.

The human imagination is an amazing thing. As children, we spend much of our time in imaginary worlds, substituting toys and make-believe for the real surroundings that we are just beginning to explore and understand. As we play, we learn. And as we grow, our play gets more complicated. We add rules and goals. The result is something we call games.

Now an entire generation has grown up with a different set of games than any before it and it plays these games in different ways. Just watch kids with a new videogame. The last thing they do is read the manual. Instead, they pick up the controller and start mashing buttons to see what happens. This isn't a random process; it's the essence of the scientific method. Through trial and error, players build a model of the underlying game based on empirical evidence collected through play. As the players refine this model, they begin to master the game world. It's a rapid cycle of hypothesis, experiment, and analysis. And it's a fundamentally different take on problem-solving than the linear, read-the-manual-first approach of their parents.

In an era of structured education and standardized testing, this generational difference might not yet be evident. But the gamers' mindset—the fact that they are learning in a totally new way—means they'll treat the world as a place for creation, not consumption. This is the true impact videogames will have on our culture.

Society, however, notices only the negative. Most people on the far side of the generational divide—elders—look at games and see a list of ills (they're violent, addictive, childish, worthless). Some of these labels may be deserved. But the positive aspects of gaming—creativity, community, self-esteem, problem-solving—are somehow less visible to nongamers.

I think part of this stems from the fact that watching someone play a game is a different experience than actually holding the controller and playing it yourself. Vastly different. Imagine that all you knew about movies was gleaned through observing the audience in a theater—but that you had never watched a film. You would conclude that movies induce lethargy and junk-food binges. That may be true, but you're missing the big picture.

So it's time to reconsider games, to recognize what's different about them and how they benefit—not denigrate—culture. Consider, for instance, their "possibility space": Games usually start at a well-defined state (the setup in chess, for instance) and end when a specific state is reached (the king is checkmated). Players navigate this possibility space by their choices and actions; every player's path is unique.

Games cultivate—and exploit—possibility space better than any other medium. In linear storytelling, we can only imagine the possibility space that surrounds the narrative: What if Luke had joined the Dark Side? What if Neo isn't the One? In interactive media, we can explore it.

Like the toys of our youth, modern videogames rely on the player's active involvement. We're invited to create and interact with elaborately simulated worlds, characters, and story lines. Games aren't just fantasy worlds to explore; they actually amplify our powers of imagination.

Think of it this way: Most technologies can be seen as an enhancement of some part of our bodies (car/legs, house/skin, TV/senses). From the start, computers have been understood as an extension of the human brain; the first computers were referred to as mechanical brains and analytical engines. We saw their primary value as automated number crunchers that far exceeded our own meager abilities.

But the Internet has morphed what we used to think of as a fancy calculator into a fancy telephone with email, chat groups, IM, and blogs. It turns out that we don't use computers to enhance our math skills—we use them to expand our people skills.

The same transformation is happening in games. Early computer games were little toy worlds with primitive graphics and simple problems. It was up to the player's imagination to turn the tiny blobs on the screen into, say, people or tanks. As computer graphics advanced, game designers showed some Hollywood envy: They added elaborate cutscenes, epic plots, and, of course, increasingly detailed graphics. They bought into the idea that world building and storytelling are best left to professionals, and they pushed out the player. But in their rapture over computer processing, games designers forgot that there's a second processor at work: the player's imagination.

12 Now, rather than go Hollywood, some game designers are deploying that second processor to break down the wall between producers and consumers. By moving away from the idea that media is something developed by the few (movie and TV studios, book publishers, game companies) and consumed in a one-size-fits-all form, we open up a world of possibilities. Instead of leaving player creativity at the door, we are inviting it back to help build, design, and populate our digital worlds.

More games now include features that let players invent some aspect of their virtual world, from characters to cars. And more games entice players to become creative partners in world building, letting them mod its overall look and feel. The online communities that form around these imaginative activities are some of the most vibrant on the Web. For these players, games are not just entertainment but a vehicle for self-expression.

Games have the potential to subsume almost all other forms of entertainment media. They can tell us stories, offer us music, give us challenges, allow us to communicate and interact with others, encourage us to make things, connect us to new communities, and let us play. Unlike most other forms of media, games are inherently malleable. Player mods are just the first step down this path.

Soon games will start to build simple models of us, the players. They will learn what we like to do, what we're good at, what interests and challenges us. They will observe us. They will record the decisions we make, consider how we solve problems, and evaluate how skilled we are in various circumstances. Over time, these games will become able

16

to modify themselves to better "fit" each individual. They will adjust their difficulty on the fly, bring in new content, and create story lines. Much of this original material will be created by other players, and the system will move it to those it determines will enjoy it most.

Games are evolving to entertain, educate, and engage us individually. These personalized games will reflect who we are and what we enjoy, much as our choice of books and music does now. They will allow us to express ourselves, meet others, and create things that we can only dimly imagine. They will enable us to share and combine these creations, to build vast playgrounds. And more than ever, games will be a visible, external amplification of the human imagination.

PERSONAL RESPONSE

Comment on your own experience with game-playing. If you are a player, explain its appeal; if you are not a player, explain why you think it does not appeal to you.

Questions for Class or Small-Group Discussion

1. Wright comments that society, especially "elders," sees only the negative effects of videogames (paragraph 4). What are those negative effects? Can you account for this view that videogames have a negative effect on the culture? In your experience, is Wright correct that "elders" view videogames negatively?

2. State in your own words what you understand Wright to mean when he says that "it's time to reconsider games, to recognize . . . how they benefit—not denigrate—culture" (paragraph 6).

3. Explain what you understand Wright to mean by the phrase "possibility space" (paragraph 7).

4. How effective do you find Wright's argument? What evidence or supporting proof does he supply? Do you think that his argument would convince those who have only negative opinions about videogames?

MindTap®   Reflect, personalize, and apply what you've learned.

CHAPTER 4

WRITING A CRITIQUE

LEARNING OBJECTIVES

Students will be able to do the following:

Produce a written critique that has these components:

- ☐ An introduction stating the name of the essay being evaluated
- ☐ A brief, objective summary of the essay
- ☐ An analysis of how well the essay achieves its stated purpose
- ☐ A personal response to the essay
- ☐ A conclusion

MindTap® Start with a warm-up activity, and review the chapter Learning Objectives.

THE CONNECTION BETWEEN READING CRITICALLY AND WRITING A CRITIQUE

Recall the guidelines for reading critically outlined in Chapter 1. The final step is to evaluate what you have read. **A critique is the written form of an evaluation of a passage or an entire work.** Reading critically is the biggest aid to writing a critique; applying the guidelines for reading critically is a crucial part of preparing to write a critique. You will need to understand not only the purpose of the piece and its central idea but also the writer's main points. Reading critically enriches your understanding of a work and its components, enabling you to focus your critique. So the first step in writing a critique is to read critically and, in the process, to determine your opinion of the piece.

Apply the guidelines detailed in Chapter 1, but especially look for the following: thesis and purpose of the writing, who the likely intended audience is, key ideas or supporting evidence for the thesis, the author's use of language, how well the piece is organized, and how successfully the piece has achieved its stated or implied goal. You may need to read the piece several times before you are clear on your own viewpoint and therefore prepared to write.

MindTap   Read, highlight, and take notes online.

WRITING A CRITIQUE

When you write a critique, your goal is to make a formal analysis of and response to a piece of writing, whether a selected passage or an entire essay. Your purpose encompasses both explaining and evaluating a piece of writing. **A critique differs from a summary, which is an objective restatement in your own words of the original material. When you summarize, you leave out your personal or subjective viewpoint. In a critique, you begin objectively but then add your own subjective response to the work.** The components of your critique paper are as follows: introduction, summary, analysis, personal response, and conclusion. Before you begin to draft your critique, you will need to think about each of these components. Prewriting exercises are excellent preparation for the draft stage.

Prewriting

Determine Your Position.   To convince an audience that your analysis and response are reasonable or valid, you must convey your views confidently. Thus, before you even begin writing your critique, you must have a clear idea of your own viewpoint on the work. A firm conviction of your own position will help persuade an audience that your critique is sensible and fair.

How do you arrive at your position? You do so by carefully reading and rereading the piece that you are to critique, by thinking seriously about what the piece says and how it says it, and by assessing how persuaded you are as a reader by what the author has said. This stage in the writing process is crucial for helping you formulate and make concrete the points you want to make in the formal assignment.

As with other kinds of writing, any number of tools for generating writing ideas can be used to help you arrive at your position when writing a critique. The following suggestions are variations on those mentioned in Chapter 2, but here they are worded specifically to help you discover your response to a piece of writing that you are to critique.

- **Freewriting.** As soon as you have read the work, write for five to ten minutes on any impressions of any aspect of the piece that occur to you. Write down everything that comes to mind, no matter how jumbled. When your time is up, select a phrase or word that seems important to your purpose, no matter how vague it is, and write a sentence with the phrase or word in it. Put that sentence at the top of another blank piece of paper, and repeat the process of writing for another five or ten minutes without thinking very deeply or long about what you are writing. If you do this several times, you should end up with a fairly good idea of the position you want to take in the analysis/assessment part of your paper. If you find that you cannot write very much, go back and reread the piece. It may be that you missed some important points on your first read-through and that a second or even a third reading will greatly clarify your position or view on the work.

- **Summarizing.** A summary of the piece is the first main part of your critique, but the act of summarizing can be a key part of your prewriting efforts. If you get stuck on generating ideas by brainstorming, perhaps you do not completely understand the work. This may be the writer's fault, and that criticism may become a part of your critique, but assuming that the piece itself is clearly written, it may be helpful for you to put in your own words what the author says. Doing that may help you discover the position you will take in your critique of the piece.

- **Listing.** Another way to discover your viewpoint is to simply list terms or phrases describing your response to the piece you are critiquing. Then, study your list and group related ideas together. Do you see a pattern? Does one dominant viewpoint emerge from these groupings? If so, write a statement reflecting that pattern or viewpoint. That should give you a sense of your position when it comes to writing your assessment of and response to the work.

- **Asking questions.** Asking questions is a very useful tool for generating ideas, perhaps most useful when thinking about and drafting your response to a piece of writing. The discussion on analysis that follows suggests a number of useful points to consider when assessing the success of a writer's argument, language, evidence, and logic. Turning them into questions in the prewriting stage can help you arrive at your overall response to the work and to discover your own position in relation to that of the writer whose work you are critiquing. Because the response section of a critique expresses your personal, subjective reaction to the work, you will want to ask yourself these questions:

  - Do you agree with the writer's position on the subject? Why or why not?
  - What reasons can you give for supporting or disagreeing with the writer?
  - Are you convinced by the writer's logic, evidence, and language? Why or why not?
  - If you are not convinced, can you give other evidence to counter the arguments or evidence of the writer?

You need not go into great detail in the response section of your paper, but you do need to explain your reasons for your response. **Give careful thought, then, not only to *what* you think of the piece of writing but also to *why* you think that way.** What specific elements of the work influence your reaction to the work? As with freewriting, summarizing, and listing, write out your questions and answers, either on paper or on your computer. Review what you have written and consider whether you have left anything unasked or unanswered.

WRITING A CRITIQUE: PREPARATION AND PREWRITING

☐ First read the text carefully, applying the guidelines for reading critically (Chapter 1).
☐ Brainstorm, summarize, list, and/or ask questions.
☐ Determine the main points, the chief purpose, and the intended audience.
☐ Identify arguments that support or develop the main point.
☐ Locate evidence used to support the arguments.
☐ Determine any underlying biases or unexamined assumptions.

Drafting Your Critique

When you are satisfied with your prewriting activities and feel that you have generated enough ideas to write your critique confidently, you are ready to write your first draft. As with all writing assignments, you will likely write several drafts of a paper before you reach the final version.

COMPONENTS OF A CRITIQUE

The following section lists the components of a formal critique and gives directions for writing each of those components. In general, a written critique includes these components: (1) an introduction; (2) an objective, concise summary of the work or passage; (3) an objective analysis of the author's presentation; (4) a subjective response detailing your opinion of the author's views; and (5) a conclusion.

1. Introduction.   The first paragraph of your critique should name the author and title of the work that you are critiquing. Do not neglect this information, as it immediately tells readers the subject of your critique. Then, give a very brief overview of the piece in two to four sentences. Your intent in the introduction is not to summarize the piece but to tell readers its purpose. Generally, stating the thesis or central idea of the piece along with a highlight or two and/or its major conclusion(s) will be enough to convey its essence and provide background for the rest of your paper. Finally, your introduction should state your own thesis. In one sentence, indicate your assessment of the passage or work that you examined. Your thesis statement should be worded to reveal your position to readers before they begin reading the body of your paper.

2. Summary.   The first section in the body of your critique should offer an objective summary of the piece. This summary states the original author's purpose and includes key ideas and major points. Where appropriate, include direct quotations that are particularly important to the development of the piece, but quote sparingly: the summary should be largely in your own words. Use direct quotations only when your own words would not do justice to the original. Do not write anything evaluative or subjective at this point. Your purpose here is to give a fair and accurate summary of the intent and main points of the work you are analyzing.

3. Analysis.   Once you have summarized the work by stating its purpose and key points, begin to analyze the work. Your goal is to examine how well the author has achieved the purpose and to consider the validity or significance of the author's information. Do not try to look at every point the author makes; rather, limit your focus to several important aspects of the piece. Remain as objective as possible in this section, saving your personal opinion of the author's position for the response section of your critique. Different purposes for writing—persuasive, expository, and expressive—require application of different criteria to judge a writer's success in achieving the intended purpose. In general, however, certain considerations help in the assessment of any piece of writing. **Questions about validity, accuracy, significance, and fairness help you evaluate any author's success or failure.**

Assess Persuasive Writing. Recall that in Chapter 2 argumentative writing is defined as a mode of persuasion in which the goal is either to convince readers of the validity of the writer's position (argument) or move readers to accept the author's view and perhaps even act on it (persuasion). This means that the writer must supply evidence or proof to support his or her position in such a way as to convince readers that the position is valid, whether they agree with the position. If the purpose is to persuade, the supporting evidence or proof must be so convincing that readers adopt the position themselves. Chapter 5 is devoted to a fuller discussion of writing an argument, so you may want to look at that chapter. In any event, when assessing the success of another writer's argument, you should gauge how well that writer has used the standard strategies for argumentation. Furthermore, pay attention to the writer's use of language. Finally, assess the validity of the argument by examining the evidence the writer presents to support his or her position and the logic of his or her conclusions.

Look Closely at a Writer's Language. In particular, make sure that the writer defines any words or terms that may be unclear, abstract, or ambiguous. Ask yourself whether the writer's language seems intended to intimidate or confuse readers or whether the writer attempts to manipulate readers by relying on emotionally loaded words. Does the writer make sarcastic remarks or personal attacks? Ultimately, examine a writer's evidence to evaluate credibility and fairness. Good writers do not rely on manipulative language, unclear terms, or loaded or sarcastic words to achieve their purposes.

Examine a Writer's Use of Appeals. Appeals are persuasive strategies that support claims or assertion or that respond to opposing arguments. They call upon logic, ethical considerations, or emotion to convince. An appeal to reason or logic uses statistics, facts, credible authority, expert testimony, or verifiable evidence to support claims in a reasoned, unemotional way. Karen Sternheimer in "Do Video Games Kill?" (Chapter 8) relies on statistics to counter the claim that there is a causal relation between video games and the impulse to commit murder. Ethical appeals call upon shared values or beliefs to sway readers or motivate them to act. Jeff Corwin in "The Sixth Extinction" (Chapter 15) calls upon shared beliefs and the common good to urge individuals to become socially responsible for ultimately ensuring the future of mankind by taking care of all living creatures on Earth, not just humans. Emotional appeals use heavily charged language to evoke feelings of pity, awe, sympathy, or shock, for instance, rather than intellectual responses not tied to the feelings. Mike Rose uses emotional appeal in the brief excerpt from his book *Why School?* (Chapter 10) with his example of the man with a disability who has struggled to learn to read and write in order to create a better world for himself and his family. A balance of these three kinds of appeals makes the best arguments. As you examine a writing for the appeals used, determine how balanced they are. If a writer relies heavily on one kind of appeal to the exclusion of the others, especially if the main appeal is to emotion, the argument is probably weak.

Evaluate a Writer's Evidence. A writer should support any generalizations or claims with ample, relevant evidence. As a critical reader, consider the kinds of evidence used and the value or significance of that evidence. Evidence may take many forms, including hard fact, personal observation, surveys, experiments, and even personal experience. In evaluating evidence, ask how well the writer provides a context or explanation for the evidence used. Consider whether the writer establishes the significance of the evidence and how it is relevant to the thesis or central point. For instance, factual evidence may be supplied in the form of statistics, facts, examples, or appeals to authorities. Statistics can be manipulated to conform to the needs of the person using them, so make sure that they are based on a large and representative sample; the method of gathering the statistics yields accurate results; and the statistics come from reliable sources. Look closely at statements of facts as well; they should give accurate, complete, and trustworthy information. Examples are specific instances or illustrations that reveal a whole type, and they should give believable, relevant, reliable, and representative support for an author's thesis. Finally, authorities are people who have the training or experience needed to make trustworthy and reliable observations on matters relating to their areas of expertise. In completing a critique, make sure, as far as possible, that the piece under study appeals to believable and credible authorities.

Judge a Writer's Logic. Argumentative or persuasive writing must portray a logical, reasonable, and accurate reasoning process supplemented by relevant, sensible supporting proofs. You will be in a good position to evaluate a writer's reasoning process if you are mindful of any pitfalls that undermine the success of the argument. Evaluating the writer's logic is part of the process of critiquing a work. *For a discussion and examples of common flaws or fallacies, see the section on assessing evidence in Chapter 5.*

WRITING A CRITIQUE: QUESTIONS FOR ANALYSIS AND EVALUATION

- ☐ Has the author clearly stated or implied a thesis, main idea, or position?
- ☐ Has the author written to a clearly identifiable audience?
- ☐ What rhetorical strategies in the development and organization of the essay does the writer use? Is the development appropriate to the purpose?
- ☐ Is the essay logically and clearly organized?
- ☐ If the writing is an argument, does the author use verifiable facts or convincing evidence?

□ If the essay seeks to explain, define, describe, or accomplish some other purpose, has the writer supplied enough details to clearly achieve the stated or implied purpose?

□ Are language and word choice accurate, imaginative, correct, and/or appropriate?

□ Does the text leave any unanswered questions?

4. Response.   In this part of your critique, express your own position relative to that of the writer of the piece and give reasons why you believe as you do. You may find yourself in total agreement or absolutely opposed to the author's position, or you may place yourself somewhere in between. You may agree with some points the author makes but disagree with others. No matter what position you take, you must state your viewpoint clearly and provide reasons for your position. These reasons may be closely linked to your assessment of key elements of the paper, as laid out in your assessment section, or they may spring from ideas that you generated in your prewriting activities.

5. Conclusion.   The final paragraph of your critique should reiterate in several sentences your overall assessment of the piece, the conclusions you have drawn from your analysis, and your personal response to the work. This section is not the place to introduce new material; rather, it is an opportunity to provide an overall summary of your paper. You want your readers to feel that you have given them a thorough and thoughtful analysis of the work under consideration and that you have brought your comments to a satisfying close.

GUIDELINES FOR WRITING A CRITIQUE

□ **Begin with an introduction.** The introduction familiarizes readers with the work under discussion, provides a context for the piece, and states your thesis. State the author's name and the title of the piece.

□ **Summarize main points.** The summary tells readers what major points the writer makes to support his or her position.

□ **Analyze how well the writer has achieved the purpose of the piece.** The analysis tells readers what aspects of the work you have examined. In general, assess the overall presentation of evidence, judging its validity, accuracy, significance, and fairness.

□ **Explain your response to the piece.** The response section tells readers your personal viewpoint by explaining the extent to which you agree or disagree with the author and why.

□ **Conclude with your observations of the overall effectiveness** of the piece and your personal views on the subject. The conclusion summarizes for readers the results of your analysis and your overall judgment of the piece.

HANDLING SOURCE MATERIAL

Verb Tenses, Quoting, Paraphrasing, and Citing Sources. As you draft your critique, keep in mind the following notes about verb tense and handling source material:

- **Verb tense.** Whenever you write about or refer to another person's work, use the present tense: "Lane Wallace *argues* ..." or "Wallace *asserts* that. ..." Use the past tense only to refer to something that happened before the time span of the essay: "**Wallace** offers a 'cautionary tale' by relating the experiment that Bell Telephone made in 1952 to expand their managers' education ..." (par. 7).

- **Handling quotations and paraphrases.** When writing a critique, you will often want to quote a passage directly or paraphrase it. In either case, you must cite the source where the original appears and use **attributive tags (words that identify the source)** to give credit to the source. At the first mention of the author's name, use full name; thereafter, use just the last name (or a pronoun when the antecedent is clear).

- Full details about handling source material appear in Chapter 6, with further examples in Chapter 7, but here are examples of quotations from Lane Wallace's "Liberal Arts and the Bottom Line," reprinted later in this chapter.

Quoting part of a sentence:

Wallace refers to Friedman's philosophy of the bottom line as "the almighty measure of success" (par. 2).

The quoted material is attributed to Wallace, with quotation marks around words taken directly from the source. The paragraph number in parentheses locates where the material appears in the article.

Paraphrasing (putting in your own words) some of Wallace's main points:

Wallace offers a "cautionary tale" by relating the experiment that Bell Telephone made in 1952 to expand their managers' education and thereby better equip them to make sound business decisions (par. 7).

The words *cautionary tale* are Wallace's, so you must use quotation marks around them. The rest of the sentence paraphrases what Wallace says in her article.

Quoting a passage that is in quotation marks in the article:

Wallace begins her essay with a reference to economist Milton Friedman's often quoted observation that "'the business of business is business'" (par. 1).

The single mark within the double indicates that the material is in quotation marks in the original. Do not insert a space between the single and double quotation marks.

Quoting material but leaving a word out to make the sentence grammatically correct:

In contrast, she says, the liberal arts student learns to be "a good global citizen, ... balancing the numbers with more intangible metrics of success" (par. 14).

The **three spaced periods (ellipsis points)** indicate where the word appears in the original.

Adding an explanatory phrase, using brackets to indicate that the addition is yours:

> Wallace writes of the current interest in solving "the growing number of 'wicked' problems confronting [business executives]" (par. 4).

The words *business executives* do not occur in this passage from paragraph 4, so the word *them* is replaced with the bracketed information. Note also that "wicked" is in quotation marks in the original, hence the single quotation marks around it.

One of your primary obligations in any writing that incorporates the words or ideas of other authors is fairness to those you borrow from. Along with that is the obligation to be as clear and accurate as possible for your readers. Quoting and paraphrasing your sources and using attributive tags help you realize those obligations.

Citing Source Material

You have several options for citing source material, depending on the assignment. If the assignment is for everyone in the class to critique the same reading in your textbook and that reading is your only source, your instructor may tell you that it is not necessary to give a page number or to construct a separate "Work Cited" entry at the end of your paper. You must always name the author and title of the work you are critiquing in your opening paragraph, so that information is clearly stated from the beginning. It is quite useful for you to identify which paragraph your paraphrase or quotation is taken from, however, especially if the assignment is to critique a reading in this textbook, as paragraphs are numbered.

Even if everyone is critiquing the same reading, your instructor may want you to cite the source anyhow, just to get in the habit of citing sources. You will certainly want to cite your source if the assignment is to choose any reading in this textbook to critique and students are all doing different readings. In the case of the Lane Wallace reading that follows, and if your paper uses only that source, this is how you would cite it:

Work Cited

Wallace, Lane. "Liberal Arts and the Bottom Line."

Perspectives on Contemporary Issues: Reading across the

Curriculum. 8th ed., edited by Katherine Anne Ackley,

Cengage, 2018, pp. 59–63.

The heading "Work Cited" is singular because there is only one source named. This format identifies the specific reading, beginning with the author, last name first, followed by the title of the reading. Next comes the name of the book in which the article appears. The edition number follows the name of the book, and that is followed by the name of the editor, preceded by the words *edited by.* A shortened title of publisher and the date of publication follow. The inclusive page numbers identify specifically which pages in the book the article is on. Note the punctuation between each component of the citation.

If you supplement your critique with readings from other sources, then you will need to create a Works Cited list, with the word *Works* made plural because more than one source is listed. The list is alphabetical. Here is a hypothetical Works Cited list that includes the Wallace reading and additional sources:

Works Cited

Davis, Wes. "The 'Learning Knights' of Bell Telephone."

Nytimes.com, 16 June 2010, www.nytimes

.com/2010/06/16/opinion/16davis.html?_r=0.

Neem, Johann. "The Liberal Arts, Economic Value, and

Leisure." *Insidehighered.com*, 23 Oct. 2012, works

.bepress.com/johann_neem/16/.

Wallace, Lane. "Liberal Arts and the Bottom Line."

Perspectives on Contemporary Issues: Reading across the

Curriculum. 8th ed., edited by Katherine Anne Ackley,

Cengage, 2018, pp. 59–63.

GUIDELINES: HANDLING SOURCE MATERIAL IN A CRITIQUE

- ☐ Use present tense when referring to what the writer says in the work.
- ☐ Use past tense only to refer to events that happened before the article was written.
- ☐ When quoting directly, use exact words and cite the source of material.
- ☐ Use attributive tags, such as *the author says, comments, points out, observes, argues*, or similar words and phrases.
- ☐ When quoting directly, use brackets to enclose anything that you have added and ellipses to indicate where you have omitted words.
- ☐ When paraphrasing, use your own words and cite the source of material.
- ☐ The first time you mention the author, use his or her full name. Thereafter, use last name only. Never use first name only to refer to an author.
- ☐ If you use more than one source in your critique, alphabetize the sources in a separate list labeled "Works Cited" at the end of your paper.
- ☐ If you use one source, list it as a "Work Cited" or, if everyone is critiquing the same reading and your instructor agrees, omit that page.

Read Lane Wallace's "Liberal Arts and the Bottom Line" and prepare for class discussion by considering how you would critique the piece. Your instructor may ask you to write your critique and hand it in or use it in a small group discussion of the article.

LIBERAL ARTS AND THE
BOTTOM LINE

LANE WALLACE

Lane Wallace, columnist for The Atlantic *and editor for* Flying Magazine, *has written six books for NASA on flight and space exploration. She has also worked as a writer and producer on a number of television and video projects. Her book* Unforgettable *(2009) is a collection of some of her best adventure tales; her latest book,* Surviving Uncertainty: Taking a Hero's Journey *(2012), explores positive ways to handle life's unexpected adventures. She is an honorary member of the United States Air Force Society of Wild Weasels and won a 2006 Telly Award for her work on a documentary of the experimental aircraft X-3 crash,* Breaking the Chain. *This piece was published in* The Atlantic.

The popularity of the late economist Milton Friedman's philosophy among business people has never surprised me much. After all, telling business people that "the business of business is business" is rather like telling people that eating dessert is actually good for you. It tells your audience what they want to believe, and relieves their guilt feelings about doing what they want to do anyway. No need to worry about pesky issues like employee welfare, environmental impact (unless required), or improving the social fabric of the community. No need to weigh the intangible costs to others of moving a business overseas, closing a factory for a quick profit, or paving roads through the Amazon to extract and export the oil.

By concentrating on the bottom line as the almighty measure of success, Friedman's philosophy also tends to focus employees on numbers as a measure of their own success. That focus, of course, encourages employees to work harder to increase those numbers. Which, in turn—surprise, surprise!—improves the company's bottom line even more. It's an incredibly convenient system that offers the appeal of neat and clean boundaries, and maximum profit for the company. Really . . . what's not to like?

What's not to like, of course, is an uneasy feeling that sets in, periodically, that perhaps the world isn't as neat as Friedman's economic model suggests. That by focusing exclusively on their own bottom lines, businesses can do extraordinary harm. (See: recent economic meltdown and the BP oil disaster in the Gulf of Mexico.)

4   As a result of some of those recent disasters, as well as increasingly complex global markets and a growing belief that today's business executives need what investment icon Charlie Munger calls a "latticework of frameworks" to solve the growing number of "wicked" problems confronting them, a movement has begun to change what business students learn. At undergraduate and graduate business schools across the country—including Wharton, Harvard, Stanford, Yale and a host of other big names—curricula are being changed to include a greater focus on multi-disciplinary approaches, ethics, critical and integrative thinking, and even, in some cases, history and literature.

Roger Martin, the dean of the Rotman School of Management at the University of Toronto, has said openly that he's trying to create the first "liberal arts MBA." And when I asked David Garvin, a professor at the Harvard Business School and co-author of the recently published *Re-thinking the MBA: Business Education at a Crossroads* what he thought about that, he answered, "Is business education becoming more like the liberal arts? If the question is, 'are we trying to teach more about how to be a well-rounded human being who happens to be practicing business,' the answer is absolutely, 'yes.' "

On one level, these changes are an effort to assuage society's concerns about bloodthirsty and uncaring business executives bringing down economies or risking the destruction of an entire coastline in the name of profit. But on another level, they reflect a growing belief that the kind of complex, critical thinking and ability to look at problems in larger contexts and from multiple points of view that a liberal arts education instills (at least in theory) actually leads to better decision-making skills in business executives.

It's a viewpoint I actually endorse. Quite enthusiastically, as a matter of fact. But I recently came across a bit of history (in a New York Times article) [Davis, Wes. "The 'Learning Knights' of Bell Telephone." New York Times 16 June 2010: A31.] that offered a bit of a cautionary tale on this front—at least in terms of businesses buying into the goal of making managers more well-rounded human beings.

8   In 1952, the president of Bell Telephone of Pennsylvania apparently became concerned that his managers, most of whom had purely technical backgrounds, did not have the broader knowledge they required to make superior business decisions. "A well-trained man knows how to answer questions," the Bell executives were reported as reasoning. "But a well-educated man knows what questions are worth asking."

Bell paired up with the University of Pennsylvania to offer a 10-month immersion course in the Humanities and Liberal Arts for up-and-coming Bell managers. The managers studied history and architecture. They read classics like James Joyce's *Ulysses* and poetry by Ezra Pound. They toured art museums and attended orchestral concerts. They argued philosophy from multiple points of view.

At the end of the 10 months, the managers were reading far more than they had before—if, in fact (as the article's author pointed out), they'd even *read* before. They were far more curious about the world around them. And in the polarized world of the early 1950s, at the height of McCarthyism, the Bell managers now "tended to see more than one side to any given argument." As hoped, they were far more equipped to make better and more thoughtful decisions, and to figure out what questions were worth asking.

By all appearances, the program was a rousing success, as well as a ringing endorsement of the benefits of a liberal arts education. There was, however, an unexpected twist in the program's impact on the Bell managers. After learning about how much more there was in life than business, one of the questions they apparently decided was worth asking was, "why am I working so darn hard?" As the article put it, "while executives came out of the program more confident and more intellectually engaged, they were also less interested in putting the company's bottom line ahead of their commitments to their families and communities."

12   Within a few years, Bell had discontinued the program.

It's an interesting and—when you think about it—completely reasonable outcome. Aside from developing the ability to think critically and approach subjects from multiple perspectives and disciplines, the idea of a liberal arts education is to develop—as Professor Gavin said—a more well-rounded person. And being a workaholic is antithetical to a well-rounded person's psyche.

The current movement to make business students "more well-rounded human beings who happen to practice business" will almost assuredly create managers who think more about long-term consequences, impact on external audiences, being a good global citizen, and balancing the numbers with more intangible metrics of success. They may also be far more agile and creative thinkers who find successful middle ground between entrenched or polarized camps, generate more innovative solutions to sticky problems, and devise ingenious ways to responsibly benefit both their companies and the communities they serve.

But these more well-rounded managers may also go home earlier, or choose options—for themselves or for their companies—that put some other value above maximizing profit for the company or its shareholders. [As] Adam and Eve discovered, a little knowledge can be a very dangerous thing.

16   The question will be, somewhere down the line, what businesses or shareholders think of all that. For all the lip service we pay to wanting more well-rounded managers and responsible corporations, are we prepared to back that when it's our own income, stock or profit that's affected by those more balanced and responsible decisions? Or will we gravitate once more to Friedman's far less conflicted philosophy that—whatever else can be said about it—conveniently aligns the numbers-oriented thinking and motivation of managers with the best interests of their employers?

MindTap®   Reflect, personalize, and apply what you've learned.

CHAPTER 5
WRITING AN ARGUMENT

LEARNING OBJECTIVES

Students will demonstrate an ability to do the following:

- ☐ Write an argumentative essay on a controversial subject with a narrowed focus, an awareness of audience, and appropriate use of tone.

- ☐ Write an argumentative essay that analyzes the main arguments opposed to their own position.

- ☐ Write an argumentative essay with logical and persuasive use of facts, evidence, or other means of convincing readers of the validity of their position.

MindTap Start with a warm-up activity, and review the chapter Learning Objectives.

ARGUMENTATION

Much of the writing that you do for your college classes is argumentation. It may not be called that formally, but any writing exercise that asks you to state a position and defend it with evidence that is true or reasonable is a form of argument. Whenever you state your opinion or make an assertion and back it with proof, you are making an argument. As you can see, just about any writing that has a thesis or implicit central idea that requires evidence or proof is a form of argument. Whether you provide evidence to explain, illustrate what you know, inform, prove a point, or persuade, if you take a position on a subject and support or develop it with evidence to demonstrate that it is valid or sound, you are making an argument.

Oftentimes, students are specifically assigned the rhetorical mode of argumentation, a reasoning process that seeks to provide evidence or proof that a proposition is valid or true. **An argument sets forth a claim in the form of a thesis statement, refutes the arguments of the opposition—sometimes giving in or conceding to certain points—and presents a coherent, organized set of reasons why the claim is reasonable. To demonstrate that your position is logical or right, you must offer reasons why you believe that way in order to convince your audience.** An argument may have several goals or purposes, either singly or in combination, such as to show relationships between things (**causal argument**), to explain or define something (**definition argument**), to evaluate something or support a position on it (**evaluative argument**), to inform (**informative argument**), or to sway an audience to change a position or take action on something (**persuasive argument**). Argumentation is a useful tool for developing critical thinking because doing it well requires close analysis of your own ideas as well as those of others. Writing an argument involves the same general procedure as that detailed in Chapter 2 on the writing process: prewriting or planning, drafting, revising, and editing.

MindTap   Read, highlight, and take notes online.

NARROWING YOUR FOCUS AND DISCOVERING YOUR POSITION

All arguments begin with a position, claim, or proposition that is debatable and that has opposing viewpoints. Statements of fact are not debatable; abstract generalizations are too vague. If your position is not debatable, there is no argument. Furthermore, in an argument, your goal is to convince those opposed to your position or who are skeptical of it that yours is valid or true. You might even want to persuade your audience to abandon their position and adopt yours or go beyond that and perform some action. Your first step, then, is to select a controversial subject or issue in which you have a strong interest. That begins the process that will ultimately lead you to the position that you want to argue.

A good starting point for discovering a topic to argue is to make a list of controversial issues currently in the news or being discussed and debated publicly or among your friends or family. *Remember that this is only a starting point.* These general topics are far too broad for a short paper, but they give you a beginning from which to start narrowing your focus. From your list, select the subjects that interest you most or that you feel strongly about and develop a series of questions that you might ask about them. This process of considering a variety of views when contemplating a topic you would like to argue helps you solidify your position. For instance, you might ask the following: Should bilingual education be offered in public schools? Should the Electoral College be abolished? Is affirmative action a fair policy? Should schools be required to provide bully awareness programs? Although such questions seldom have absolutely right or wrong answers, it is useful to frame your position by saying (or implying), "Yes, bilingual education should be offered in public schools," or, "No, affirmative action is not a fair policy." But making up your mind about how you feel about an issue is only the beginning. You must also convince others that your position is logical, reasonable, or valid. You do that by providing strong evidence or reasons to support your position and by anticipating and addressing the arguments of those who do not agree with you.

The following list of potentially controversial subjects may give you an idea of the kinds of general topics that can be narrowed for an argumentative paper. To this list, add others that appeal to you as potential topics for an argument. Then, select those subjects that you have the strongest interest in or hold opinions about and, taking each in turn, spend some time writing down questions that come to mind about that subject, issues related to it that you are aware of, and/or what your preliminary position on the subject is: What is the controversy? Who is affected by it? Why is it controversial? What is the context or situation? What is your position on

POSSIBLE SUBJECTS FOR ARGUMENTATION

Adolescents tried as adults	English-only movement	National security
Advertising images	The environment	Nuclear energy
Affirmative action	Free agency in sports	Nuclear proliferation
Airline security	Gender issues	Nuclear waste
Animal rights	Gender roles	Off-shore oil drilling
Bilingual education	Genetic engineering	Ozone layer depletion
Bullying	Global warming	Patriot Act
Censorship	Gun control/gun rights	Pay inequity
Civil rights	Home schooling	Regulating toxic emissions
College—is it for everyone?	Human cloning	Space exploration
Compensation for organ donors	Illegal aliens	Special interest groups
Controversial speaker on campus	Immigration	Sports violence
Cyber bullying	Intellectual freedom	Steroids and athletes
Cyber stalking	Intellectual property rights	Stereotypes in mass media
Drunken driving or DUI punishment	Internet: government control	Strip mining
Electoral College	Land minds	Sweatshops
Eliminating the grading system	Landfills	Terrorism in America
Embryo or stem cell research	Media violence	Water pollution

that controversy? Why do you believe as you do? What evidence or proof do you have to support your position? What do those opposed to your position argue?

At this stage, you are simply **brainstorming or freewriting** to see what you know about certain self-selected subjects that you would be comfortable with developing into an argument paper. When you have finished, examine the results of your brainstorming session and narrow your list to the one or two that you have the most to say about or feel most strongly about. Brainstorm further on those issues by framing questions about the subject or trying to identify the problem associated with it. Keep in mind that you not only want to find an issue or issues that you have a strong interest in, but you must also consider the implications of the position you take on that issue. How will you convince your audience that your position is reasonable or logical? How can you best defend your position? How can you best meet the arguments of those opposed to you?

You are looking for a topic that poses a question or problem you believe that you know the answer or solution to. This is your position. Once you know your position, you are ready to commit time to thinking about and researching the best evidence or proof to support your position.

Examples of Narrowing a Focus

1. Consider the suggestion that the grading system at the college level be abolished. You might wonder: Should the grading system be abolished? Who would benefit from abolishing the grading system? Why should the grading system be abolished? Why should the grading system not be abolished? What would replace the grading system were it abolished? How would abolishing the grading system affect students and instructors? Would it change the dynamics of the learning process?

2. Imagine that the office in charge of programming at your campus wants to bring a controversial person for its speaker series. Suppose you are a student at a private faith-based liberal arts college and the speaker is an avowed atheist, or suppose you are a state-funded liberal arts university and the speaker is a religious-right fundamentalist. Who would support bringing this speaker to campus? Who would oppose it? What reasons might both those in favor of and against bringing the speaker to campus give to support their positions? Are there contexts or situations where it might be appropriate and others where it would not? Which side would you support in such a controversy?

3. Erin was intrigued by an essay that she read on advertising images of women, so she began the process of discovering her position on that topic by thinking about the very general subject "advertising images." Here are the questions she asked and the thoughts that she jotted down:
   - Do advertising images affect behavior?
   - Isn't it the purpose of an ad to influence behavior?
   - So what if advertisements do affect behavior? What's the harm?
   - Such power might influence behavior the wrong way.

- What is the wrong way? Affects self-esteem. Makes people feel inadequate. Reduces women to objects.
- What about men? Ads affect them too.
- Some ads set up unrealistic, even impossible-to-attain, images of men and women. Young or old, male or female.
- Ads present false images of relationships between men and women. Ads focus a lot on sex and on attacking people's vulnerabilities.
- Who bears responsibility? Advertisers. They need to consider the effects of their ads.
- What should they do? Modify images that attack and weaken self-esteem.
- Topic: advertisers' responsibility for their ads.

Her questions, answers, and ideas may look rambling, but they ultimately led her to her topic, which she refined by focusing specifically on ads featuring women that have the potential to affect self-esteem and body image.

4. Rita became interested in the current controversy over whether women had truly achieved pay equity with men in the workforce. Therefore, when her English instructor assigned an argumentative essay using source materials, Rita chose that subject for her paper. Her question was, "Have women really achieved equality in the workplace?" Her reading in this area led her to the conclusion that, no, despite everything that has been done to make women equal to men in employment, they have not yet achieved that goal. Although she found that there are differences not only in earnings but also in rates of promotion and representation at higher, managerial ranks, she decided to focus her paper on just the issue of the wage gap. The proposition that she formulated for her paper is the following: Despite decades of struggling for women's pay equity in the workplace, the wage gap between men and women remains unacceptably wide. You will find Rita's paper later in this chapter.

GUIDELINES FOR NARROWING YOUR FOCUS AND DISCOVERING YOUR POSITION

- ☐ Jot down a controversial or arguable subject that you have a strong interest in or about which you have an opinion.
- ☐ Ask questions about that subject from as many angles as you can think of.
- ☐ Write down ideas that occur to you as you ask questions.
- ☐ Repeat the brainstorming process by asking more questions and writing more thoughts as they occur. At this stage, you are working toward a defensible position on a fairly narrow topic.
- ☐ Consider how you might defend your position, how you would counter the arguments against it, and what evidence you might need.
- ☐ Begin the process of thinking about, researching, and writing your paper on that narrow topic.

STRUCTURING AN ARGUMENT

Structuring an argument is similar to structuring most other kinds of writing. Recall that in Chapter 2, the typical essay has certain components: a title, an opening paragraph that introduces the topic by providing a context or background for it and that leads to a thesis statement or clearly stated central idea; fully developed paragraphs in the body of the paper that advance, support, illustrate, or otherwise relate to the thesis; and a conclusion. Effective arguments follow that pattern, with some additions or variations. In formal argumentation, these parts of your essay might be labeled differently, but they are essentially the same. For instance, a thesis might be called a proposition or position statement, but it is still the central idea of the paper. Development might be referred to as offering supporting proof by refuting the opposition, making concessions where necessary, and offering evidence in a logical, well-reasoned way.

What follows are various components of a well-organized and well-developed argument. The discussion in general assumes a traditional, formal Aristotelian mode of argument, with the goal of proving one's proposition or thesis while countering or refuting the opposition, but there are other approaches that use different lines of reasoning. Two of the most prominent are the Toulmin and Rogers. The Toulmin approach, like the Aristotelian, views argument as oppositional, with a goal to proving one's position; the Rogerian, on the other hand, uses conflict-resolution based on compromise, a goal that searches for common ground or mutual agreement rather than refuting the opposition. These three approaches are discussed in more detail in the section labeled "Strategies for Arguing Effectively," under the heading "Follow a Logical Line of Reasoning."

Introduction.   The opening of your argument lays the groundwork for the rest of the paper by establishing the tone that you will take, providing any clarification or preliminary information necessary and/or giving a statement of your own qualifications for asserting a position on the topic. Here is an opportunity to provide a context for your argument, establish your initial credibility, and connect with your audience. Credibility is the level of trustworthiness your audience perceives in you. If you can convey an impression that you are credible early in your paper, your audience may be more willing to think of you as reliable or trustworthy and therefore be more receptive to your argument. Otherwise, they may dismiss your evidence, question your motive, or simply refuse to accept what you are saying.

Context.   When explaining background or situation, you establish a context within which your audience is to consider your argument. Establishing tone is part of the context. You might provide a striking quotation, cite statistics, or define the problem or controversy in terms that everyone agrees on. Diane Ravitch in "Critical Thinking? You Need Knowledge" (Chapter 10) provides a context for her argument that "skill-centered, knowledge-free education has never worked." Ravitch needs to establish this context immediately in order to explain both her title and the reason for the essay. When an issue is particularly controversial, writers may not be able to establish sympathy with readers. Nevertheless, some sort of context or reason for writing needs to be established early in the essay. We see this in Anthony Gregory's "Why Legalizing Organ Sales Would Help Save Lives, End Violence" (Chapter 15). Gregory takes a usually unpopular position on the issue of legalizing live organ donations by countering some of the moral and ethical objections to doing so. The issue of voluntary, compensated organ sales, particularly of kidneys, has been debated for years, rather heatedly at times. Gregory has to couch his argument in non-offensive and conciliatory tones in order to avoid offending readers from the start.

Credibility.   Any number of strategies help to establish credibility in an argument. Beginning with your introduction and continuing throughout your argument, demonstrating to your readers that you are fully informed, reasonable, and fair establishes credibility and makes your audience more receptive to your position. Using trustworthy outside sources to support, explain, defend, or back general statements demonstrates that your position is based on more than just your personal opinion. To show that others, perhaps professionals with more experience than you, have done research or hold similar views reflects well on your own credibility. Furthermore, citing sources or statistics shows that you have done your homework, that you are familiar with or knowledgeable about your subject, and that you know what others have to say about it. These things go toward establishing your credibility as a writer. Using hard data such as facts or statistics also helps, as does acknowledging and countering viewpoints opposed to yours.

Statement of the Case.   As clearly as possible in your opening paragraph(s), provide a rationale or need for what you are arguing. Provide a context for the argument, give relevant background material, or explain why you believe as you do. Establishing need helps to convey your credibility by showing that you are knowledgeable about your subject. It is also a good strategy for connecting with your audience. In stating the case for the argument, you might explain that it is worth upholding or endorsing because it has some bearing on the lives of readers or the common good of a community or society. You may also want to indicate the degree to which a particular issue or policy is controversial. Take, for instance, Jeff Corwin's opening in "The Sixth Extinction" (Chapter 15): "There is a holocaust happening. Right now. And it's not confined to one nation or even one region. It is a global crisis. Species are going extinct en masse." Corwin's compelling first few sentences strongly suggest a need to look at the issue of species extinction.

Proposition.   The proposition is an assertion or claim about the issue. It is effectively the same as a thesis or position statement and should be stated clearly near the beginning of the essay. In "The Collective Conscience of Reality Television" (Chapter 9), Serena Elavia opens with an example of a dramatic emotional scene captured on camera for the viewing audience of a popular reality television show. This opening leads to her assertion: "Networks are willing to show almost everything, regardless of the impact on its cast members, until their viewers get upset, lash out on social media, or threaten to stop watching entirely. What viewers will or won't watch matters immensely to networks; in fact, they seem function as the networks' sole 'conscience.'" In most arguments, as Elavia does in hers, you must make your position clear very early and then devote the rest of your paper to providing supporting evidence, details, or facts to "prove" that your position is a logical or reasonable one. The strength of your argument will come from your skill at refuting or challenging opposing claims or viewpoints; giving in or conceding on some points; and then presenting your own claims, evidence, or other details that support your position.

Refutation of Opposing Arguments.   It is not enough to find evidence or facts that argue your own position and therefore prove its validity; you must also realize that those opposed to your position will have their own evidence or facts. You must try to project what you think others may say or even try to put yourself into their position. An excellent strategy for argumentation, therefore, is to first look at the claims of others and challenge or dispute them. One of the chief strengths of a good argument is its ability to counter evidence produced by the opposing side. In fact, you must imagine more than one opposing side. Rarely is an issue represented by just two equal and opposing arguments. Often it is represented by multiple viewpoints. Obviously you cannot present every aspect and every position of an issue, but you must demonstrate that you are aware of the major viewpoints on your subject and that the position you have taken is a reasonable one. The preparatory step of anticipating or imagining the opposing position(s) will be a huge help in developing your own argument. Ask yourself what you think will be the strategy of those opposed to your position and how you can best address that opposition and counter it with your own logical reasoning. Ignoring an opposing opinion is a major fault in argumentation because it suggests that you have not explored enough aspects of the topic to warrant the position you are taking. For more on refutation, see the section on anticipating the opposition in the section on strategies for effective argumentation later.

Concessions to Opposing Arguments.   Often, some of what those opposed to your position argue is valid or irrefutable. A very effective, necessary, and wise strategy is to make concessions to the opposition. It helps establish your reliability as a fair-minded person. The act of acknowledging limitations or exceptions to your own argument and accepting them actually strengthens your argument. It indicates your commitment to your position despite its flaws, or suggests that, even flawed, your position is stronger than the positions of those opposed to it. It is best to make these concessions or acknowledgments early in your paper rather than later. For more on making concessions, see the section on conceding to the opposition in the section on strategies for effective argumentation.

Development of Your Argument.   In this stage of the process, you present evidence or proof to persuade your audience of the validity of your position. Your argument will be most effective if it is organized with the least convincing or least important point first, building to its strongest point. This pattern lends emphasis to the most important points and engages readers in the unfolding process of the argument as you move through increasingly compelling proofs. A successful argument also gives evidence of some sort for every important point. Evidence may include statistics, observations or testimony of experts, personal narratives, or other supporting proof. You need to convince readers by taking them from some initial position on an issue to your position, which readers will share if the argument succeeds. The only way to do this is to provide evidence that convinces readers that your position is a right or valid one.

Conclusion.   In the closing paragraph(s) of your paper, you have a final opportunity to convince your audience that the evidence you have presented in the body of your paper successfully demonstrates why your proposition is valid. You may want to summarize your strongest arguments or restate your position. You may want to suggest action, solutions, or resolutions to the conflict. This final part of your paper must leave your audience with a feeling that you have presented them with all the essential information they need to know to make an intelligent assessment of your success at defending your position and possibly persuading them to believe as you do.

GUIDELINES: BASIC STRUCTURE OF AN ARGUMENT

- ☐ **Introduction**—Familiarizes audience with subject, provides background or context, conveys credibility, and establishes tone.
- ☐ **Statement of the case**—Provides rationale or need for the argument.
- ☐ **Proposition**—Asserts a position or claim that will be supported, demonstrated, or proved in the course of the paper.
- ☐ **Refutation of opposing arguments**—Mentions and counters potential evidence or objections of opposing arguments.
- ☐ **Concession**—Acknowledges validity of some opposing arguments or evidence.
- ☐ **Development of the argument**—Offers convincing, creditable evidence in support of proposition.
- ☐ **Conclusion**—Brings paper to a satisfactory end.

STRATEGIES FOR ARGUING EFFECTIVELY

Whereas the previous section outlines the essential structure of an argument, the following comments will also help you write an effective argument.

Know Your Audience.   A consideration of who your audience is will help you anticipate the arguments of those opposed to you. Many instructors tell students to imagine an audience who disagrees with them. After all, there really is no argument if you address an audience of people who believe exactly as you do. Knowing your audience will help you figure out what strategies you must use to make your position convincing. Imagine that you are addressing an audience who is either indifferent to or opposed to your position. This will help direct the shape of your argument because such an audience will require solid evidence or persuasive illustrations to sway its opinion.

Establish an Appropriate Tone. Tone refers to the writer's attitude toward his or her subject. As a writer of argument, you want your audience to take you seriously, weigh what you have to say in defense of your position, and, ideally, not only agree that your reasoning is sound but also agree with your position. Therefore, try to keep your tone sincere, engaging, and balanced. You do not want to take a hostile, sarcastic, or antagonistic tone because then you risk alienating your audience. If you are too light, flippant, or humorous, your audience might believe you to be insincere or not truly interested in your topic.

Anticipate the Arguments of the Opposition. As mentioned earlier, one key aspect of argumentation is refuting arguments of those who hold opposing opinions. How do you anticipate what those opposed to your position believe? Perhaps you are already familiar with opposing positions from your own observations or discussions with others, but a good step in your preparation is to look for articles or books that express an opinion or a position that you do not share. Read the arguments, determine the authors' positions, and note the evidence they produce to support their positions. How can you refute them? What evidence of your own contradicts them and supports your own position? Sometimes students find themselves being convinced by the arguments of others and switch their positions. Do not worry if that happens to you. In fact, it will probably aid you in your own argument because you are already familiar with the reasoning of that position and can use the new evidence that persuaded you to find fault with your old position.

Keep in mind that this strategy of refuting an opposing argument does not always require disproving the point. You may also question its credibility, challenge the point, identify faulty logic, or otherwise cast doubt on it. Take care when challenging the opposition that you are on solid ground and can back up your own claims with proof. Attacking a point by simply declaring it wrongheaded or insubstantial without having your own solid evidence considerably weakens your argument. So look for any of the following ways to challenge the opposition:

- **Question the validity of data or evidence: Are statistics accurate?** What is the source of data? Can it be trusted to be accurate? Does the opposition skew or slant data to fit its own needs?

- **Question authority: What are the credentials of authorities cited in arguments?** Do their credentials qualify them to have informed opinions on the topic? Do they have questionable motives?

- **Challenge the logic of the opposition: What fallacies do you find?** What flaws in the reasoning process are there?

Make Concessions.   Sometimes it is necessary to concede a point to the opposition—that is, to acknowledge that the opposition has made a reasonable assertion. Making a concession or two is inevitable in arguments of complex issues. Conceding to the opposition is actually a good strategy as long as you follow such a concession with even stronger evidence that your position is the reasonable one. You agree that the opposition makes a good point, but you follow that agreement with an even more persuasive point.

Follow a Logical Line of Reasoning

Aristotelian Logic. Formal, classic argumentation typically follows one of two common lines of reasoning, **deductive** and **inductive** reasoning. In deductive reasoning, you move from a general principle, or shared premise, to a conclusion about a specific instance. Premises are assumptions that people share, and the conclusion will be implied in the premises or assumptions. The traditional form of deductive reasoning is the **syllogism,** which has two premises and a conclusion. A **premise** is defined as an assumption or a proposition on which an argument is based or from which a conclusion is drawn. The premises are often referred to as major and minor, with the major premise being the general truth and the minor premise a specific instance. The classic syllogism, offered by Aristotle (384–322 BCE), a Greek mathematician and logician, is the following:

> **Major premise:** All men are mortal.
> **Minor premise:** Socrates is a man.
> **Conclusion:** Socrates is mortal.

This simple example of syllogism indicates the basic formula: A is B. C is B. Therefore A is C. Arguments are described as valid when the premises lead logically to the conclusion. If they do not, the argument is invalid. Similarly, an argument is said to be sound if the argument is valid and leads to the conclusion; it is unsound if the argument is valid but does not lead to the conclusion or if the conclusion is valid but the argument is not. Here is another example:

> **Major premise:** Driving while drunk is illegal.
> **Minor premise:** Joe was drunk when he drove home from the party.
> **Conclusion:** Joe committed a crime.

In contrast, inductive reasoning moves from a number of specific instances to a general principle. Rather than begin with a shared assumption or generalization, you must provide sufficient data or evidence that the generalization is warranted. Your intent is to show the general pattern by presenting relevant specific instances as evidence. To avoid being accused of overgeneralizing or making a hasty generalization, you must provide enough data, examples, or specific instances to ensure that your audience is satisfied with your conclusion. In contrast to deductive reasoning, which rests on certainties (shared or commonly acknowledged truths), inductive reasoning relies on probability (the likelihood that something is true).

Example.

Observation one: Students entering the classroom have wet hair and damp clothes.

Observation two: Students typically come from outside the building to class.

Conclusion: It must be raining outside.

With induction, you must be very careful that your data do indeed warrant your conclusion. For instance, consider the following example of **hasty generalization:**

Observation one: The daily high temperatures for the last several days have been unusually high.

Observation two: I don't remember it ever being this hot during the summer.

Conclusion: We must be experiencing global warming.

Obviously there is not enough evidence in either of the observations to establish that global warming accounts for the recent high temperatures.

Although formal argumentation is useful when arguing in abstract or ideal disciplines, such as mathematics, it is less effective in complex, real-world situations—that is, the kinds of arguments in which you are likely to be engaged. Aristotle himself realized that syllogistic reasoning, which deals in absolutes, is not suited to all arguments and that many arguments depend on an informal logic of probabilities or uncertainties. His study of this system of reasoning was known as **rhetoric,** which he defined as "the faculty of discovering in any particular case all of the available means of persuasion." Formal syllogistic logic typically leads to one correct and incontrovertible conclusion, while informal or rhetorical logic allows for probable or possible conclusions. As in syllogistic logic, the reasoning process must be rational and practical.

The Toulmin Model of Reasoning. A model of informal argumentation, or practical reasoning, is that described by Stephen Toulmin, a twentieth-century philosopher, mathematician, and physicist. This method is not as constrictive as formal syllogistic reasoning because it allows for probable causes and reasonable evidence. With this method, an argument is broken down into its individual parts and examined: each stage of the argument leads to the next. Toulmin defined argumentation as a process or logical progression from **data** or **grounds** (evidence or reasons that support a claim) to the **claim** (the proposition, a debatable or controversial assertion, drawn from the data or grounds) based on the **warrant** (the underlying assumption). The *claim* is the point your paper is making, your thesis or arguable position statement. *Data* or *grounds* constitute your proof and demonstrate how you know the claim is true or the basis of your claim. *Warrants* are the underlying assumptions or inferences that are taken for granted and that connect the claim to the data. They are typically unstated or implied and can be based on any of several types of appeals: logic, ethics, emotion, and/or shared values.

This view of argumentation as a logical progression has similarities to formal argumentation but does not rely on inductive or deductive reasoning that leads inevitably to one true conclusion. Rather, it relies on establishing the relationship between data and the claim by offering evidence that supports the warrant and leads to the best possible, the most probable, or the most likely conclusion. In such reasoning, the argument often attempts to defuse opposing arguments with the use of **qualifiers** such as *some, many, most, usually, probably, possibly, might,* or *could.* Qualifiers indicate awareness that the claim is not absolute but reasonable in the specific instance. This step reveals how sure you are of your claim.

The argument should also recognize any **conditions of rebuttal**—that is, exceptions to the rule. Rebuttals address potential opposing arguments, usually by showing flaws in logic or weakness of supporting evidence. An argument will also, if necessary, make **concessions** or acknowledgments that certain opposing arguments cannot be refuted. Often **backing**—additional justification or support for the warrant—is supplied as a secondary argument to justify the warrant. To succeed, an argument following the Toulmin model depends heavily on the strength of its warrants or assumptions, which in turn means having a full awareness of any exceptions, qualifications, or possible reservations.

Rogerian Argument. Based on the work of the American psychologist Carl R. Rogers, this approach adopts the stance of listening to arguments opposed to your own with an open mind, making concessions, and attempting to find a common ground. Thus, it attempts to compromise rather than assume confrontational or adversarial opposition. The Rogerian approach is well suited to subjects that are particularly explosive or controversial, when the writer knows that the audience will be hostile or hold opinions and beliefs different from her own. This approach to argumentation differs from both the Aristotelian and Toulmin methods by focusing on conflict resolution, with both sides finding aspects of the issue that they can agree on. An argumentative essay using the Rogerian method will usually begin with a statement of common beliefs or goals and then proceed in the body of the paper to give as reasonable an explanation of the writer's position as possible without being overtly defensive or aggressive. The conclusion will present a position that encompasses the concessions the writer has made.

Use Appeals Effectively.   An appeal is a rhetorical strategy whose object is to persuade. Appeals go beyond fact or logic to engage the audience's sympathy, sense of authority or higher power, or reason. Aristotle maintained that effective persuasion is achieved by a balanced use of three appeals to an audience: *logos* (**logic**), *ethos* (**ethics**), and *pathos* (**emotion**) related to the words *pathetic, sympathy,* and *empathy.* Other appeals may be used, such as shared values. In the Toulmin method, appeals support warrants. The appeal to ethos is a strong characteristic of Rogerian argumentation, with its emphasis on finding a common ground and its genuine attempts to understand opposing arguments and resolve conflicts. But a good argument does not rest solely on any one appeal. Thus, a good argument will use sound reasoning or apply inductive or deductive reasoning (**logic**), it will call upon recognized authority or establish the credibility of its sources (**ethics**), and it will reach audience members on an affecting, disturbing, touching, or other poignant level (**emotion**). An argument may also make appeals to the audience on the basis of shared values, such as human dignity, free speech, and fairness.

Logical appeals offer clear, reasonable, well-substantiated proofs, including such things as data, statistics, case studies, or authoritative testimony or evidence, and they acknowledge and refute the claims of the opposition. We see such a logical appeal in Greg Kaufman's "Ignoring Homeless Families" (Chapter 11) when he cites statistics to support his point about the dramatic increase in the number of homeless families.

Ethical appeals are often made in the introduction and conclusion because they are not based on statistics or hard data. Rather, they take advantage of the beliefs or values held by the audience and often help establish context. In "The Sixth Extinction," an essay about the potential for half of the Earth's species to disappear by the end of the century (Chapter 15), Jeff Corwin cites the work of scientists around the world who are helping to reverse the trend, and then he concludes with an ethical appeal: "These committed scientists bring great generosity and devotion to their respective efforts to stop the sixth extinction. But if we don't all rise to the cause and join them in action, they cannot succeed. The hour is near, but it's not too late." Corwin calls on the shared interests and values of his audience to take action to help prevent global disaster.

Emotional appeals can be quite effective but must not be overdone, certainly not to the exclusion of logical appeals. Many writers use it to some degree, but sparingly. Thus, Jeff Madrick in "The Cost of Child Poverty" (Chapter 11) makes an emotional appeal in his conclusion when he refers to "the reduction in the suffering of innocents," but he has not based his entire argument on that one point.

Use Analogy.   An analogy is a comparison of two things in order to show their similarities. Often the comparison is of a difficult or unfamiliar concept to a simpler or more familiar one, an excellent way to advance your argument. As a strategy in argumentation, you want to make the point that if the situation in the example is true or valid, it will be true or valid in the situation you are arguing. When Maria Konnikova in "The Real Lesson of the Stanford Prison Experiment" (Chapter 14) refers to the Stanford prison experiment as *"Lord of the Flies* in the psych lab," she is confident that her readers will be familiar with *Lord of the Flies* and thus instantly get the point that she is making about the prison experiment. You must choose your comparisons wisely and avoid making false comparisons: if the argument is weak for your example, it will be weak for the argument you are making.

Assess the Evidence.   Reading critically is important in argumentation. You can build your own argument by trying to keep an open mind when analyzing the arguments of those opposed to your position as you read in search of evidence to support your position. What questions should you ask when analyzing the positions of those opposed to you? Consider the following: What is the writer's purpose? How well does he or she achieve that purpose? What evidence does the writer give in support of that purpose? How does the writer know the evidence is true? What is the argument based on? Has the writer omitted or ignored important evidence? Does the writer's argument lead to a logical conclusion? Sometimes something that seems to be logical or reasonable turns out to be false. Are you convinced that the writer's sources are trustworthy? What sort of language does the writer use? Is it clear and fair? Does the writer use words that are heavily charged or "loaded" and therefore likely to play on emotions rather than appeal to reason? Does the writer make any of the common fallacies (errors of reasoning) associated with attempts to be logical and fair?

Avoid Common Rhetorical Fallacies.   Part of your strategy in writing a good argument is to evaluate your own reasoning process as well as that of other writers, especially those whose works you may use in support of your own argument. A fallacy is a flaw or an error in reasoning that makes an argument invalid or, at best, weak. Look for these **common flaws** or **fallacies** in your own writing or in that of any writing you analyze:

- *Ad hominem* **arguments.** This Latin term means "against the man" or "toward the person" and applies to arguments that attack the character of the arguer rather than the argument itself. *Ad hominem* arguments often occur in politics, for instance, when opponents of a candidate refer to personal characteristics or aspects of the candidate's private life as evidence of his or her unsuitability to hold office. **Examples:** Arguing that because someone has been in prison, you shouldn't believe anything she says is an *ad hominem* attack. Arguing that a candidate would not make a good senator because he is a single parent or that a candidate would not be effective as mayor because she is homosexual ignores the more important questions of qualifications for the office, the candidate's stand on issues relevant to the position, the candidate's experience in political office, and similar substantive considerations.

- **Circular reasoning or begging the question.** This error makes a claim that simply rephrases another claim in other words. It assumes as proof the very claim it is meant to support. **Examples:** This sort of logic occurs in statements such as "We do it because that's the way we've always done it," which assumes the validity of a particular way of doing things without questioning or examining its importance or relevance. Other examples are stating that your candidate is the best person for an office because she is better than the other candidates, or a parent replying "because I said so" when a child asks why he or she must do something.

- **Either–or reasoning.** If a writer admits only two sides to an issue and asserts that his or her is the only possible correct one, the writer has probably not given full thought to the subject or is unaware of the complexity of the issue. Most arguable topics are probably complex, and few are limited to either one or another right viewpoint. Be wary of a writer who argues that there is only one valid position to take on an issue. **Example:** Arguing that if a fellow citizen does not support your country's involvement in war as you do, he or she is not patriotic. The implication is that "either you are for your country or you are against it, and the right way is my way."

- **Emotionally charged language.** Writers may rely on language guaranteed to appeal to their audiences on an emotional level rather than an intellectual level. This appeal can be effective when used sparingly, but it becomes a fault in logic when the argument is based entirely on such language. Arguments on ethical or moral issues such as abortion or capital punishment lend themselves to emotional appeals, but arguments on just about any subject may be charged with emotion. This fallacy can appeal to any number of emotions, such as fear, pity, hatred, sympathy, or compassion. Emotionally charged language also includes **loaded words,** those whose meanings or emotional associations vary from person to person or group to group, and **slanted words,** those whose connotations (suggestive meaning as opposed to actual meaning) are selected for their emotional association. **Examples:** Evoking images of dirty homeless children in rags living on dangerous streets and eating scraps of garbage when arguing for increased funds for child services is an appeal to the emotions. Abstract words, such as *democracy, freedom, justice,* or *loyalty,* are usually loaded. Words may be slanted to convey a good association, such as those used in advertisements—cool, refreshing, or smooth—or to convey a bad association—sweltering, noisy, or stuffy. **In argumentative writing, loaded or slanted language becomes problematic when it is used to deceive or manipulate.**

- **False analogy.** A writer may falsely claim that, because something resembles something else in one way, it resembles it in all ways. This warning does not deny that analogy has a place in argument. It can be an extremely useful technique by emphasizing a comparison that furthers an argument, especially for a difficult point. Explaining a difficult concept in terms of a simpler, more familiar one can give helpful support to readers. However, make sure that the analogy is true and holds up under close scrutiny. **Example:** A controversial analogy that is sometimes used is the comparison of America's internment of American citizens of Japanese descent during World War II to Hitler's concentration camps. On some levels, the comparison is justified: people in the U.S. internment camps were held against their will in confined areas guarded by armed soldiers, they often lost all of their property, and some were even killed in the camps. On the other hand, they were not starved to death, exterminated, or used as subjects of medical experiments. The analogy is useful for making a point about the unfair treatment of American citizens during wartime, but many would argue that the analogy breaks down on some very important points.

- **Faulty appeal to authority.** Stating that a claim is true because an authority says it is true may be faulty if the authority is not an expert in the area being discussed, the subject is especially controversial with much disagreement over it, or the expert is biased. Such false appeals often appear in advertising, as when an actor who portrays a lawyer on a television series appears in an advertisement for a real-life law firm. Similarly, actors who portray doctors on medical television shows are often used in advertising health and beauty products to present an appearance of authority. The underlying assumption seems to be that audience members will equate the fictional lawyer's or doctor's words with those of an actual lawyer or physician.

- **Hasty generalization.** A writer makes a hasty generalization if he or she draws a broad conclusion on the basis of very little evidence. Such a writer probably has not explored enough evidence and has jumped too quickly to conclusions. **Examples:** Assuming that all politicians are corrupt because of the bad behavior of one is an example of making a hasty generalization. Assuming that all rock musicians use hard drugs before performances because of the highly publicized behavior of one or two musicians is an example of faulty generalization.

- **Oversimplification.** In oversimplification, the arguer offers a solution that is too simple for the problem or issue being argued. This fault in logic overlooks the complexity of an issue. **Examples:** Arguing that the problem of homelessness could be solved by giving jobs to homeless people overlooks the complexity of the issue. Such a suggestion does not take into account matters such as drug or alcohol dependency that sometimes accompanies life on the streets or a range of other problems faced by people who have lost their homes and learned to live outdoors. Arguing that the crime rate will go down if we just outlaw handguns overlooks such important considerations as crimes committed with weapons other than handguns and the likely probability that the criminal underworld would continue to have access to guns, illegal or not.

- *Non sequitur.* This Latin term, meaning "does not follow," refers to inferences or conclusions that do not follow logically from the available evidence. *Non sequiturs* also occur when a person making an argument suddenly shifts course and brings up an entirely new point. **Examples:** The following demonstrates a *non sequitur:* "My friend Joan broke her arm during a gymnastics team practice after school. After-school activities are dangerous and should be banned." Reminding a child who will not eat his or her food of all the starving children in the world is a line of reasoning that does not follow. If the child eats his or her food, will that lessen the starvation of other children? If the child does not eat the food, can the food itself somehow aid those starving children?

- *Post hoc, ergo propter hoc* **reasoning.** This Latin term means "after this, therefore because of this." It applies to reasoning that assumes that Y happened to X simply because it came after X. **Example:** Accusing a rock group of causing the suicide of a fan because the fan listened to the group's music just before committing suicide is an example of such reasoning. Although the music might be a small factor, other factors are more likely to account for the suicide, such as a failed love relationship, feelings of low self-worth, or personal despair for a variety of reasons.

- **Red herring.** A red herring diverts the audience's attention from the main issue at hand to an irrelevant issue. The fallacy is to discuss an issue or a topic as if it were the real issue when it is not. Writers of mystery fiction often use red herrings to distract readers from identifying the stories' criminals. That is part of the fun of reading a mystery. But an argumentative writer who tries to use red herrings probably does not have enough relevant supporting evidence or does not recognize the irrelevance of the evidence. **Examples:** Arguing against the death penalty on the grounds that innocent people have been executed avoids the issue of why the death penalty is wrong. Citing the execution of innocent people is a red herring. Similarly, calling attention to the suffering of a victim's family when arguing for the death penalty shifts focus away from the relevant reasons for capital punishment.

- **Stereotyping.** Another form of generalization is stereotyping, that is, falsely applying the traits of a few individuals to their entire group or falsely drawing a conclusion about a group on the basis of the behavior or actions of a few in that group. Stereotyping is also oversimplification because it ignores the complexity of humans by reducing them to a few narrow characteristics. Stereotyping produces a false image or impression of a large number of people who have a certain thing in common—most frequently race, ethnicity, gender, or sexual preference—but also such widely differing things as occupation, hair color, speech habits, or educational level.

- **Examples:** Any assertion about an entire group of people on the basis of a few in that group is stereotyping. Arguing that women are not suited for combat because women are weaker than men is a stereotype based on the fact that the average woman is weaker than the average man. Not all women are weaker than men.

GUIDELINES: STRATEGIES FOR CONSTRUCTING A CONVINCING ARGUMENT

- ☐ **Know your audience.** Whether identified by your instructor or left up to you, imagine an audience opposed to your position. This helps you understand what evidence you need to make your argument convincing.

- ☐ **Establish appropriate tone.** Your attitude toward your subject is important in making your argument convincing. Using the appropriate tone strengthens your argument.

- ☐ **Anticipate the arguments of those opposed to you.** Anticipating and countering others' arguments strengthens your own position.

- ☐ **Make concessions where necessary.** Acknowledging truths in the arguments of others reveals that you are aware of those truths but are still committed to your own position. Follow such concessions with your own even stronger evidence, proof, or support.

- ☐ **Follow a logical line of reasoning.** Whether formal or informal, inductive or deductive, or some other method recommended by your instructor, your argument must be reasonable and sound.

☐ **Use appeals effectively.** Appeals to logic, ethics, emotions, or shared values all help develop your argument. Be cautious when appealing to emotions; such appeals are all right in small measure, but your main appeals should be to logic and/or ethics.

☐ **Assess the evidence.** Examine carefully the evidence you use for your argument. Weak or flawed evidence weakens your own argument.

☐ **Look for flaws in your own and others' reasoning process.** Avoid fallacies or errors in reasoning in your own writing and examine the arguments of others for such flaws.

SAMPLE ARGUMENT

On the following pages you will find Rita Fleming's argumentative paper annotated with marginal comments on her strategies. In addition to noting Rita's argumentative strategies, pay attention to the ways in which she uses sources to bolster her argument. **Note that she follows MLA style guidelines for handling source material as outlined in Chapters 6 and 7.**

Fleming 1

Rita Fleming

English 102–2

Professor White

6 Nov. 2017

Women in the Workforce: Still Not Equal

According to the Department of Labor's Women

Bureau, nearly seventy-two million American women,

over half of those over the age of 16, are in the civilian

Rita's opening paragraph gives background information.

labor force, and over half of those women work full

time, year round. Many people have the perception that

women's large presence in the workforce in combination

with federal laws that prohibit job discrimination means

Fleming 2

She asserts the importance of the issue by appealing to the common good.

that women enjoy equality, especially pay equity, with men in the workplace. However, recent class-action sex-discrimination suits brought by women workers against large corporations suggest that millions of women feel discriminated against in the workplace. Furthermore, a look at labor statistics compiled by the federal government reveals that women on average are still paid significantly less than men. Despite decades of struggling for women's equality in the workplace, the wage gap between men and women remains unacceptably wide.

Her proposition states her position.

Some argue that workplace inequity has disappeared as a result of federal legislation that makes discrimination in employment illegal. It is true that efforts to correct disparities between men's and women's wages have a long history. Executive Orders have been legislated to fight discrimination in employment, beginning in 1961 with President John F. Kennedy's Executive Order 10925 creating a President's Committee on Equal Employment Opportunity prohibiting discrimination on the basis of sex, race, religious belief, or national origin. The Equal Pay Act of 1963 prohibits paying women less than men working in the same establishment and performing the same jobs, and Title VII of the 1964 Civil Rights Act prohibits job discrimination on the basis of not only race, color, religion, and national origin but also sex. It is also true that when the Equal Pay Act was signed, women working full-time, year round made only 59 cents on average for every dollar a man made, whereas that the figure had increased to

Rita acknowledges the opposition and makes concessions.

Fleming 3

78 cents on average in 2013 and has hovered around that figure since. Yes, women have made gains over the past decades, but is 78 cents for every dollar a man makes acceptable? If women are truly equal to men in this society, why are their average earnings not equal?

Having made concessions, she reaffirms her position.

Some people refuse to believe that women's pay is not equal to men and argue that the 78 cents statistic simply does not take into account such variables as the kinds of jobs women and men work as well as, education, experience how long workers have been on the job, and the number of hours worked. A commentator for *CNN Money* calls the 78 cents argument "spurious" and "bogus," noting that "the statistic lumps together women and men who work different hours" (Furchgott). However, Sara Ashley O'Brien, in her report for *CNN Business*, says that "even after you drill down into specific occupations, the wage gap persists." She notes, for instance, that elementary and middle school female teachers "hold more than 70% of the jobs" but earn only "87 cents to the man's job" for the same work. Depending on the profession, the gap can be "even more pronounced," as in retail sales, where "women earn 70 cents to the dollar" (O'Brien). Statistics such as these are supported by data from various government agencies such as the Bureau of Labor Statistics and the Census Bureau as well as independent research agencies like the Pew Research Center. All point to the fact that women of all races and colors, of all educational levels, and of all ages, consistently make

Rita mentions a frequent argument against her position and gives an example of the sort of language used by opponents of her position.

She counters the opposition with data of her own that support her position.

She names her sources and establishes their credentials while reaffirming her position.

Fleming 4

less on average than their male counterparts (U.S. Dept. of Labor, *Current Population Survey*). As the American Association of University Women [AAUW] reports in *The Simple Truth about the Gender Pay Gap*: "Among the many occupations for which the Bureau of Labor Statistics collects data that allow for valid comparison, women's earnings are higher than men's in only a handful" (16). While this exact ratio varies state by state, the gap between women's and men's earnings exists in every state.

Rita cites a number of reasons why there is a gender wage gap.

There are many reasons for this inequity. One reason is that most women work in service and clerical jobs, including such occupations as secretaries, teachers, cashiers, and nurses. For instance, the Women's Bureau report *Women in the Labor Force 2014*, notes that in 2011, 91.1% of registered nurses and 81.8% of elementary and middle school teachers were women (U.S. Dept. of Labor). The Bureau of Labor Statistics reports similarly that in 2014 97.0% of preschool and kindergarten teachers, 95.1% of dental hygienists, and 97.9% of secretaries were women (*Women in the Labor Force 2014*). These statistics have not changed much in the years since then. Women also tend to work at jobs that pay less than the jobs that men typically work at. Eitzen and Zinn point out that, as the economy shifted in recent times from being manufacturing-based to being more service oriented, a dual labor market emerged. Characterized by two main types of jobs, primary and secondary. They define primary jobs as usually stable, full-time jobs with high wages, good

Fleming 5

benefits, and the opportunity to move up the promotion ladder, whereas secondary jobs are unstable, normally part time, with few benefits and little opportunity for advancement (218). Unfortunately, large corporations have been eliminating many primary jobs and creating new, secondary jobs to take their places, and it is mostly women who are hired to fill these secondary positions.

The term "occupational segregation" is used to describe the phenomenon of women workers being clustered in secondary or low-paying jobs (Andersen and Collins 238). Women are simply not crossing over into traditionally male-dominated occupations at a very high rate. This does not mean that women do not have opportunities or are not educated. In fact, surprisingly, the wage gap is greater than one might expect at the professional level: female professionals (doctors, lawyers, dentists) make substantially less than what male professionals make. Female physicians and surgeons aged 35–54, for instance, earned 69% of what male physicians and surgeons made (International Labor Organization). Furthermore, advancement to higher-paid positions is slower for women than it is for men; and advancement to positions with "chief" in the title, such as chief operating officer, is perhaps slowest of all ("Status of Women"). Statistics such as these reveal that many workplaces are still plagued by old, outdated stereotypes about gender-based occupations.

Another explanation for the wage gap is that women earn less because of the differences in years of experience on

Rita continues to explain, backing assertions with supporting proof.

Fleming 6

the job. Collectively, women earn less because they haven't worked as many years as men have in certain professions (Robinson 183–84). Women often drop out of the job market to have their families, for instance, while men stay at their jobs when they have families. Yet another reason for the wage gap, according to the AAUW is that "the gender pay gap also grows with age, and differences among older workers are considerably larger than gaps among younger workers" (12). In contrast, the rates for young women coming of age in the 1990s reflect women's social and legal advances. The report notes that "in 2013, for full-time workers ages 20–24, women were paid 90 percent of what men were paid on a weekly basis. Among workers 55–64 years old, women were paid only 77 percent of what their male peers were paid" (12). This is great news for young women but a dismal reality for the significantly large number of working women who fall into the older age group.

Reasons to account for the persistence of a wage gap are many, but sometimes there is no explanation at all. Analysts have tried to determine why, as the U.S. Census Bureau figures reveal, men of every race or ethnicity earn more than women at every educational level (Julian and Kominski). The reality is, as a Bureau of Labor Statistics report notes, that "there is a substantial gap in median earnings between men and women that is unexplained, even after controlling for work experience . . . education, and occupation" (US Dept of Labor, *Women in the Labor Force: A Databook*). We see

Fleming 7

this in the results of surveys such as those conducted in late 2015 by McKinsey & Company and LeanIn. org, a nonprofit organization focused on women's advancement. Emily Peck, Executive Business and Technology editor at *HuffingtonPost*, suggests that "the big, ugly, hard-to-fix issue . . . is gender bias." She believes that "sexism has (mostly) moved . . . into something we now call unconscious bias – the things a lot of us believe about women without even realizing it, . . . [such as] that women are less competent than men" (Peck). Other commentators make similar statements to explain the wage gap. Given this explanation, one has to ask if the reason that women are paid less than men for the same or equal work is simply discrimination, what can be done to correct the wage differential between men's and women's earnings?

Rita suggests an explanation for the seemingly inexplicable.

Laws have failed to produce ideal results, but they have done much to further women's chances in the workplace and they give women legal recourse when they feel that discrimination has taken place. Therefore, better vigilance and stricter enforcement of existing laws should help in the battle for equal wages. Heidi Hartmann suggests that businesses themselves "must also mitigate occupational segregation" by hiring more women for non-traditional jobs, raise women's wages, and ensure that more women sit on committees and boards that determine corporate policies (Hartmann). Young women should be encouraged to train for primary jobs, while

Rita ends by suggesting actions to address the problem that she has substantiated in her paper.

Fleming 8

those who work in secondary jobs should lobby their legislators or form support groups to work for better wages and benefits. Working women can join or support the efforts of such organizations as 9to5, the National Association of Working Women. Women's position in the workforce has gradually improved over time, but given the statistics revealing gross differences between their wages and those of men, much remains to be done.

Works Cited

American Association of University Women. *The Simple Truth about the Gender Pay Gap.* Spring 2016, www. aauw.org/files/2016/02/SimpleTruth_Spring2016.pdf.

Andersen, Margaret L., and Patricia Hill Collins, editors. *Race, Class and Gender: An Anthology.* 8th ed., Cengage, 2010.

Eitzen, Stanley D., and Maxine Baca Zinn. *Social Problems.* 12th ed., Prentice Hall, 2010.

Furchgott-Roth, Diana. "The Gender Wage Gap is a Myth." *MarketWatch*, 26 July 2012, www.marketwatch.com/ story/the-gender-wage-gap-is-a-myth-2012-07-26.

Hartmann, Heidi. "America's Gender Pay Gap is a Record Low, But Hold the Celebration." *Fortune*, 22 Sept. 2015, fortune.com/2015/09/22/americas-gender-pay-gap-is-at-a-record-low-but-hold-the-celebration/.

Julian, Tiffany, and Robert Kominski. *Education and Synthetic Work-Life Earnings Estimates.* United States Census Bureau, September 2011, www.census.gov/ prod/2011pubs/acs-14.pdf.

International Labor Organization. *Gender Inequality and Women in the US Labor Force.* 2016, www.ilo.org/ washington/areas/gender-equality-in-the-workplace/ WCMS_159496/lang--en/index.htm.

O'Brien, Sara Ashley. "78 Cents on the Dollar: The Facts about the Gender Wage Gap." *CNN Money*, 14 Apr. 2015, money.cnn.com/2015/04/13/news/economy/ equal-pay-day-2015/.

Peck, Emily. "At This Rate, It'll Take 100 Years to Get Pay Equity at Work." *HuffingtonPost*, 30 Sept. 2015, www. huffingtonpost.com/entry/gender-equality-at-work_ us_560b00a4e4b0af3706de64c4.

Robinson, Derek. "Differences in Occupational Earnings by Sex." *Women, Gender, and Work,* edited by Martha Fetherolf Loutfi, International Labor Office, 2001.

"Status of Women in the States." Institute for Women's Policy Research, 2015, www.iwpr.org/initiatives/states/ the-status-of-women-in-the-states.

United States. Department of Labor. Bureau of Labor Statistics. *Women in the Labor Force: A Databook.* Dec. 2014, www.bls.gov/opub/reports/cps/women-in-the-labor-force-a-databook-2014.pdf.

United States. Department of Labor. Bureau of Labor Statistics. *Current Population Survey Annual Average Data Tables.* Table 39, 2015, www.bls.gov/cps/ cpsaat39.htm.

EXERCISE

Read the following essay and analyze its effectiveness as an argument by considering the strategies that the author uses. Write out your analysis to hand in to your instructor, or take notes in preparation for class discussion. Here are some points to consider:

1. On the basis of information about the author provided in the headnote, how well suited do you think she is to write on the subject of this essay?
2. Describe the tone adopted by the author. What audience is she writing to?
3. Where does the author state her thesis or proposition?
4. What appeals does the author rely on? How credible or convincing do you consider those appeals? Explain your answer.
5. What evidence does the author supply to support her argument? Do you find the evidence persuasive?
6. How well does the author anticipate opposing opinions? Does she make any concessions to opposing opinions?
7. Is the author guilty of any flaws in her reasoning?
8. Are you convinced by the author's argument? Why or why not?

THE GENDER WAGE GAP—
A MYTH THAT JUST WON'T DIE

ABIGAIL HALL

Abigail Hall is an assistant professor in economics at the University of Tampa. While working on her Ph.D., she was a research fellow with the Independent Institute, and the JIN Fellow in Economics at the Mercatus Center at George Mason University. The Independent Institute is a nonprofit, nonpartisan, scholarly research and educational organization that sponsors in-depth studies of critical social and economic issues.

This past year I was on the academic job market, applying for faculty positions at a variety of colleges and universities. As a woman making a critical career move, I've been up to my eyeballs in cover letters, resumes, statistics about cost of living, state income taxes, health insurance, and, of course, salary information.

Chances are you've heard the statistic on numerous occasions, "women earn 77 cents for every dollar a man earns—for exactly the same work." I certainly heard this several times throughout my job search in various contexts. This issue of the supposed "gender wage gap" came up again recently during the 2015 Oscars when actress Patricia Arquette used the platform to call for wage equality stating,

> To every woman who gave birth, to every taxpayer and citizen of this nation, we have fought for everybody else's equal rights. It's time to have wage equality once and for all. And equal rights for women in the United States of America.

Social media exploded. Bloggers, politicians, and others applauded Arquette for her statements. The familiar and rallying cry of "equal pay for equal work" was everywhere. While few would disagree with the sentiment that men and women should receive the same compensation for the same services, the position espoused by Arquette and others that women are systematically underpaid is just plain *wrong*. Of the many economic-related fallacies to be cited as gospel on a regular basis, this one drives me positively insane.

4   Let's take a look a closer look at this statistic.

The first thing to notice is that the "77 cents on the dollar" metric isn't comparing apples to apples. It is a comparison of *gross* income. That is, it compares the income of *all* women to that of *all* men. It fails to take into account important factors—like education, experience, or even just comparing people in the same career. You wouldn't compare the incomes of elementary school teachers with Bachelor's degrees to those of individuals with PhDs in physics and complain that there is a "teacher-physicist wage gap"—but this is precisely what this statistic does.

When you take these characteristics into account, the purported "gap" all but disappears.

One important variable to consider is the type of careers men and women select. Simply put, men and women tend to choose different jobs. Looking at data from 2010 on undergraduate majors in the U.S., one sees certain fields are heavily dominated by men and vice versa.

8   Consumer and human science majors, for example, are about 88 percent female. Eighty-seven percent of library science majors are women. Women also heavily dominate healthcare majors and educational fields, with females representing 80 percent or more of these majors.

By contrast, other disciplines are largely populated by men. Males comprise some 96 percent of military and applied science majors. Eighty-three percent of engineering students are men. Eighty-two percent of computer science majors are male, as are 70 percent of economics majors.

In addition to selecting different jobs, women and men also differ in the number of hours they choose to work. Men are much more likely to work full-time hours or more a week (40+ hours). Women are much more likely to work part-time (less than 35 hours per week). Not surprisingly, people who work part-time jobs tend to earn less than people who work full-time jobs.

(Note: women actually tend to earn *more* than men with the same part-time jobs.)

12   When women do find themselves in male-dominant fields, they actually tend to do *better* than their male counterparts in terms of finding a job. Take, for example, academic jobs. One study from 2010 looked specifically at applications for tenure-track jobs in electrical engineering and physics. They found that while women comprised only 11 percent of engineering applicants and 12 percent of physics applicants, they were *much* more likely to receive job offers. In fact, the study found that 32 and 20 percent of job offers went to female candidates in engineering and physics, respectively.

The gender wage gap falls completely apart if one thinks of it from the perspective of an employer. Suppose you own an accounting firm. Further suppose that the gender wage gap is real—women and men do the exact same work, but you can pay the women in your firm 77 cents for every $1 you pay your male employees.

You need to hire five new accountants. What are your options?

A. You can hire male CPAs at a price of $50,000 each, per year ($250,000 per year for all five),

16   Or

B. You can hire female CPAs at a price of $38,500 each (77% of the male wage), per year ($192,500 per year for all five). What would you do? Hire the women, of course! In fact, you'd be foolish to hire any men at all! You'd get the same work from either group of employees, but by hiring women you'd save $57,500 every year.

The same goes for other businesses. If men and women were truly providing "equal work," but women were systematically paid less than their male counterparts, entrepreneurial business leaders could make a killing hiring women. The fact that we don't observe this is yet another indication that the statistic is seriously flawed.

Now, some will point to the statistics on the careers men and women tend to choose and say that women aren't really "free" to choose their careers. This is not only incredibly patronizing, but it ignores the fact that women in the U.S. are not only well-educated, but also well-informed when it comes to selecting careers. It's not as if women are unaware that social workers and schoolteachers tend to earn less than engineers. We choose careers just as men do. We consider what we think is most important when selecting a career, look at our options, and make the best choices we can.

20   When it comes to issues of gender equality, there are a variety of issues to discuss. When having these discussions, however, it's important for women and men to discuss the facts and present correct information. Otherwise, we not only perpetuate incorrect information, but we ultimately fail to advance these issues in any meaningful way.

MindTap   Reflect, personalize, and apply what you've learned.

CHAPTER 6

WRITING A SYNTHESIS AND DOCUMENTING SOURCES

LEARNING OBJECTIVES

Given an assignment to write an essay that incorporates two or more articles, students will produce a written work that does the following:

- ☐ Adopts a position on the same topic as the articles.
- ☐ Demonstrates understanding of the articles by avoiding simple summaries and drawing connections between them and their own ideas.
- ☐ Incorporates material from the articles as support or illustration.
- ☐ Integrates and documents source material using the assigned documentation style.

MindTap® Start with a warm-up activity, and review the chapter Learning Objectives.

SYNTHESIS

A synthesis draws conclusions from, makes observations on, or shows connections between two or more sources. In writing a synthesis, you attempt to make sense of the ideas of those sources by extracting information relevant to your purpose. The ability to synthesize is an important skill, for people are continuously bombarded with a dizzying variety of information and opinions that need sorting out and assessment. To understand your own thinking on a subject, it is always useful to know what others have to say about it. You can see the importance of reading and thinking critically when synthesizing the ideas of others. The sources for a synthesis may be essays, books, editorials, lectures, movies, group discussions, or any of the myriad forms of communication that inform academic and personal lives. At minimum, in a synthesis you will be required to reflect on the ideas of two writers, assess them, make connections between them, and arrive at your own conclusions based on your analysis. Often you will work with more than two sources; certainly you will do so in a research paper.

Your purpose for writing a synthesis will be determined by the nature of your assignment, although syntheses are most commonly used to either explain or argue. Perhaps you want to explain how something works or show the causes or effects of a particular event. You may argue a particular point, using the arguments of others as supporting evidence or as subjects for disagreement in your own argument. You may want to compare or contrast the positions of other writers for stating your own opinion on the subject. When you write a research paper, you must certainly synthesize the ideas and words of others. Whether your synthesis paper is a report or an argument, you must sort through and make sense of what your sources say. Sometimes you will want to read many sources to find out what a number of people have to say about a particular subject in order to discover your own position on it.

Synthesis, then, involves not only understanding what others have to say on a given subject but also making connections between them, analyzing their arguments or examples, and/or drawing conclusions from them. You routinely employ these processes in both your everyday life and in your courses whenever you consider the words, ideas, or opinions of two or more people or writers on a topic. Each chapter in Part Two ends with a list of suggestions for writing. Many of the topics require that you synthesize material in the readings of that chapter. These topics often ask you to argue, to compare and contrast, to explore reasons, to explain something, to describe, or to report on something, using at least two of the essays in the chapter.

In all cases, no matter what your purpose for writing the synthesis, you will need to state your own central idea or thesis early in your paper. In preparation for writing your essay, you will complete a very helpful step if you locate the central idea or thesis of each of the works under analysis and summarize their main points. The summary is itself a kind of synthesis, in that you locate the key ideas in an essay, state them in your own words, and then put them back together again in a shortened form. This process helps you understand what the authors believe and why they believe it. Furthermore, your own readers benefit from a summary of the central idea or chief points of the articles you are assessing. As you write your essay, you will not only be explaining your own view, opinion, or position, but you will also be using the ideas or words of the authors whose works you are synthesizing. These will have to be documented, using the appropriate formatting for documenting sources illustrated in this chapter. See the box "Guidelines for Writing a Synthesis" for step-by-step directions on writing your synthesis.

MindTap® Read, highlight, and take notes online.

GUIDELINES FOR WRITING A SYNTHESIS

☐ **Determine your purpose for writing by asking yourself what you want to do in your essay.** Without a clear purpose, your synthesis will be a loosely organized jumble of words. Although your purpose is often governed by the way in which the assignment is worded, make sure you understand exactly what you intend to do.

☐ **Consider how best to accomplish your purpose.** Will you argue, explain, compare and contrast, illustrate, show causes and effects, describe, or narrate? How will you use your sources to accomplish your purpose?

☐ **Read each source carefully and understand its central purpose and major points.** If you are unclear about the meaning of an essay, reread it carefully, noting passages that give you trouble. Discuss these passages with a classmate or with your instructor if you still lack a clear understanding.

☐ **Write a one-sentence statement of the central idea or thesis and a brief summary of each source you will use in your paper.** This process will help clarify your understanding of your sources and assist you in formulating your own central idea. These statements or summaries can then be incorporated appropriately into your synthesis.

☐ **Write a one-sentence statement of your own thesis or central purpose for writing the synthesis.** This statement should be a complete sentence, usually in the first paragraph of your essay. The thesis statement helps you focus your thoughts as you plan your essay by limiting the nature and scope of what you intend to accomplish. It is also a crucial aid to your readers, because it is essentially a succinct summary of what you intend to do.

☐ **Develop or illustrate your thesis by incorporating the ideas of your sources into the body of your paper, either by paraphrasing or by directly quoting.** Part of your purpose in writing a synthesis is to demonstrate familiarity with your sources and to draw on them in your own essay. This goal requires that you make reference to key ideas of the sources.

☐ **Document your sources.** Keep in mind the guidelines for documenting all borrowed material.

CITING AND DOCUMENTING SOURCES USING MLA STYLE

Although Chapter 7 on writing a research paper addresses in detail the matter of citing and documenting a variety of sources, you will need some guidelines for handling sources when writing a synthesis paper. No matter what your purpose or pattern of development, if you draw on the writing of someone else, you must be fair to the author of the material you borrow. Whether paraphrasing an author's words or quoting them exactly as they appear in the original text, whenever you use the ideas or words of another, you must give credit to your source. In academic writing, credit is given by naming the author of the borrowed material, its title, the title of the container (such as a book that holds a number of essays or other work, a periodical, or a website) the date of publication or location where it appears, and the page number or numbers where the information is located, if the work is paginated.

The rest of this chapter introduces some basic skills needed to incorporate the words and ideas of others into your own written work. **Because the chapter focuses on how to draw material on two or more sources in a collection such as this or a similar text book, the examples will largely be from print sources that are paginated. For other kinds of sources, see Chapter 7.** The discussion begins with guidelines for documenting sources, goes on to provide examples of paraphrasing and quoting, illustrates some useful tools for handling and integrating source materials, and ends with directions for documenting sources from collections of essays, such as this textbook. The guidelines used in this chapter follow Modern Language Association (MLA) documentation style. (*Note:* If your instructor prefers that you use American Psychological Association [APA] style or gives you a choice of styles, refer to guidelines for APA documentation style that appear in Chapter 7.) MLA style is used primarily in the humanities disciplines, such as English and philosophy, whereas other disciplines have their own guidelines. If you learn the skills necessary for paraphrasing, quoting, and documenting the material located in this textbook or in any collection of readings, you will be prepared to incorporate library and Internet resources, as well as other materials, into long, complex research papers. For more discussion of MLA style, with sample works-cited entries for a broad range of both print and nonprint sources, including the Internet, see Chapter 7.

IN-TEXT CITATIONS AND LIST OF WORKS CITED

The MLA style of documentation requires that you give a brief reference to the source of any borrowed material in a parenthetical note that follows the material. This parenthetical note contains only the last name of the authority and the page number or numbers on which the material appears, or only the page number or numbers if you mention the author's name in the text. This in-text citation refers to specific information or ideas from a source for which you give complete bibliographic information at the end of the paper in the works-cited list. With the name of the author (or title, if no author's name) given in the paper itself, your readers can quickly locate full details of your source by looking at the alphabetical list of all the works that you drew upon in your paper.

The parenthetical citation is placed within the sentence, after the quotation or paraphrase, and before the period. If punctuation appears at the end of the words you are quoting, ignore a comma, period, or semicolon but include a question mark or exclamation mark. In all cases, the period for your sentence follows the parenthetical citation.

The name or title that appears in the parenthetical citation in your text corresponds to an entry in the works-cited list at the end of your paper. This list is labeled "Works Cited." Individual entries in this list contain complete bibliographic information about the location of the works you reference, including the full name of the author (if known), the complete title, the place of publication, and the date of publication (if known).

Treat World Wide Web and other electronic sources as you do printed works. This means name the author, if known, or the title if no author is named. If you use a source with no page numbers, such as a website or a film, you cannot give a page number in the parenthetical citation.

Illustration: In-Text Citations and Works-Cited Entries. The following examples show formats for citing sources in the text of your paper. The works-cited formats for many of the references are included here. You can find more examples in Chapter 7.

- **Book or article with one author.** Name of the author followed by the page number:

  (Crichton 441)

  Source as it appears on the list of works cited:
  Crichton, Michael. "Patenting Life." *Perspectives on Contemporary Issues: Reading across the Disciplines.* 7th ed., edited by Katherine Anne Ackley, Cengage, 2015, pp. 441-445.

- **Book or article with two or three authors.** Last names of authors followed by the page number:

  (Pojman and Pojman 110), (Newton et al. 24)

  Sources as they appear on the list of works cited:
  Pojman, Paul, and Louis P. Pojman. *Environmental Ethics.* Wadsworth, 2011.
  Newton, Lisa H., et al. *Watersheds 4: Ten Cases in Environmental Ethics.* Wadsworth, 2005.

- **Book or article with more than two authors.** Name just the first author followed by "et al." (Latin for "and others") and then the page number:

  (Mitchell et al. 29)

  Source as it appears on the list of works cited:
  Mitchell, James, et al. *Herbal Supplements: Benefits and Dangers.* Global Health Press, 2017.

> **COMMENT**
>
> *When there are two or more authors, reproduce the names in the order in which they appear on the title page. If they are not listed alphabetically, do not change their order.*

- **Article or other publication with no author named.** Give a short title followed by the **p**age number, if available:

  ("New Year's Resolutions" 11), ("Banned Books Week")

Sources as they appear on the list of works cited:

"New Year's Resolutions." *Columbia City Post and Mail* [Indiana], 2 Jan. 2017, p. 11.

"Banned Books Week: Celebrating the Freedom to Read." American Library Association, 2016, www.ala.org/bbooks/bannedbooksweek.

- **If you cite two anonymous articles beginning with the same word,** use the full title of each to distinguish one from the other:

  ("Classrooms without Walls" 45), ("Classrooms in the 21st Century" 96)

  Sources as they appear in the list of works cited:

  "Classrooms without Walls." *21ˢᵗ Century Teacher*, Oct. 2017, pp: 44–49.

  "Classrooms in the 21st Century." *Journal of Teacher Education*, Sept./Oct. 2017, pp. 94–98.

- **Two works by the same author.** Give the author's name followed by a comma, a short title and the page number:

  (Rose, *Back to School* 57), (Rose, *Why School?* 78)

  Sources as they appear in the list of works cited:

  Rose, Mike. *Back to School: Why Everyone Deserves a Second Chance at Education.* The New Press, 2012.

  ———. *Why School? Reclaiming Education for All of Us.* The New Press, 2009.

COMMENT *Three hyphens followed by a period indicate that the author's name is identical to that in the preceding entry. The entries themselves are alphabetized by the first letter of the titles of the works.*

- **An Internet work.** Use author's last name or short title:

  (Tublin)

  Source as it appears on the list of works cited:

  Tublin, Patty Ann. "What Everyone Ought to Know about Millennials." *HuffingtonPost.com*, 22 Nov. 2015, www.huffingtonpost.com /dr-patty-ann-tublin/what-everybody-ought-to-know-about-millenni-als_b_7999816.html.

- **An article from an electronic database.** Use author's last name and page number:

  (Strauss 5)

  Source as it appears on the list of works cited:

  Strauss, Valerie. "Why We Are Looking at the 'Value' of College All Wrong." *The Washington Post*, 1 Nov. 2014, p. 5. *Academic Search Premier*, www .ebscohost.com/academic/academic-search-premier.

GUIDELINES FOR DOCUMENTING SOURCES

☐ Provide a context for your paraphrase or quotation by naming the author or the title of the work, or by using attributive tags, such as *observes, comments, points out,* or *argues.*

☐ Provide a citation every time you paraphrase or quote directly from a source.

☐ Give the citation in parentheses following the quotation or paraphrase.

☐ In the parentheses, give the author's last name and the page number or numbers from which you took the words or ideas, if available. Do not put any punctuation between the author's last name and the page number.

☐ If you name the author as you introduce the words or ideas, the parentheses will include only the page number or numbers. If your source is from the Internet, has no page numbers, and you name the author in your text, no parentheses are needed, though some instructors ask that you repeat the author's name after the borrowed material.

☐ At the end of your paper, provide an alphabetical list of the authors you quoted or paraphrased and give complete bibliographic information, including not only author and title but also where you found the material. This element is the Works-Cited page.

PARAPHRASING

Paraphrasing is similar to summarizing in that you restate in your own words something someone else has written, but a paraphrase restates everything in the passage rather than highlighting just the key points. Summaries give useful presentations of the major points or ideas of long passages or entire works, whereas paraphrases are most useful in clarifying or emphasizing the main points of short passages.

To paraphrase, express the ideas of the author in your own words, being careful not to use exact phrases or key words of the original. Read your source carefully, more than once if necessary, and then write down what you understand the source to say. It will help if you put the source aside or do not look at it when restating the material in your own words. Then you won't be tempted to use the exact words of the original. Another approach is to jot down a few notes while you are reading and then, without looking at the original source, use your notes to write what you recall of the passage. After you have finished paraphrasing a section, compare what you have written to make sure it is fair to the original and does not use exact words. Paraphrases are sometimes as long as the original passages, but usually they are shorter. The purpose of paraphrasing is to convey the essence of a sentence or passage in an accurate, fair manner and without the distraction of quotation marks. If your paraphrase repeats the exact words of the original, then you are quoting, and you must put quotation marks around those words. A paper will be more interesting and more readable if you paraphrase more often than you quote. Think of your own response when you read something that contains quotations. Perhaps, like many readers, you will read with interest a paraphrase or short quotation, but you may skip over or skim quickly long passages set off by quotation marks. Readers generally are more interested in the ideas of the author than in his or her skill at quoting other authors.

GUIDELINES FOR PARAPHRASING

- ☐ Read the passage carefully, perhaps taking a few notes, and then try to recall without looking at it what the essential ideas are.
- ☐ Restate in your own words the important ideas or essence of a passage.
- ☐ Do not look at your source when paraphrasing. This will help you avoid using the exact words. Do not repeat more than two or three exact words of any part of the original, unless you enclose them in quotation marks. If you must repeat a phrase, clause, or sentence exactly as it appears in the original, put quotation marks around those words. Give the source of the paraphrased information either in your text or in parentheses immediately after the paraphrase.
- ☐ Check that you have paraphrased fairly and accurately by comparing your paraphrase to the original words.
- ☐ In your paper, use attributive tags or the author's name when paraphrasing.
- ☐ Try to paraphrase rather than quote as often as possible, saving direct quotations for truly remarkable language, startling or unusual information, or otherwise original or crucial wording.

Illustration: Paraphrasing.   This section provides examples of paraphrases using selected passages from the sources indicated.

1.   **Source:** Isaacson, Walter. *Einstein: His Life and Universe.* Simon, 2007.

> **Original** (page 54): Among the many surprising things about the life of Albert Einstein was the trouble he had getting an academic job. Indeed, it would be an astonishing nine years after his graduation from the Zurich Polytechnic in 1900—and four years after the miracle year in which he not only upended physics but also finally got a doctoral dissertation accepted—before he would be offered a job as a junior professor.

> **Paraphrase:** In his biography of Albert Einstein, Walter Isaacson notes the rather surprising fact that Einstein not only had trouble finding a teaching job after college graduation, but that it took nine years to do so (54).

COMMENT

Even when you put the material into your own words, you must cite the source and give a page number where the paraphrased material is located. Use attributive words or tags ("In his biography of Albert Einstein, Walter Isaacson notes . . .").

2. **Source:** Kluger, Jeffrey. "The War on Delicious." *Time*, 9 Nov. 2015, pp. 30-36.

Original (page 32): The modern American diet is a huge, sprawling, bib-under-the-chin affair of generous portions served up on demand. Most primarily, that has meant a diet heavy in red meat and processed meat.... Now this is being called into question by doctors, by public health advocates and by the World Health Organization (WHO), which has not just America's well-being in mind but also that of the entire globe.... In a sweeping review released on Oct. 26, the WHO officially identified processed meat as a Group 1 carcinogen, meaning the quality of the evidence firmly links it to cancer.

Paraphrase: In a cover story for *Time* magazine, Jeffrey Kluger reports on the results of a recent study by the World Health Organization on the dangers of red and processed meats. The report identifies processed meat as "a Group 1 carcinogen," which "firmly links it to cancer" (32).

COMMENT

When it is clear that you are paraphrasing from the same source in two or more consecutive sentences and you have named the author or source in the first sentence, you need give only one parenthetical citation at the end of the series of sentences. Note also that key terms from the original are placed in quotation marks to indicate that they are not the student's own words.

3. **Source:** "Beyond Distrust: How Americans View Their Government." *PewSocialTrends.org*, 23 Nov. 2015, www.people-press.org/2015/11/23 /beyond-distrust-how-americans-view-their-government/.

Original: [T]he American public is deeply cynical about government, politics and the nation's elected leaders in a way that has become quite familiar. ... Majorities want the federal government to have a major role in addressing issues ranging from terrorism and disaster response to education and the environment. And most Americans *like* the way the federal government handles many of these same issues, though they are broadly critical of its handling of others – especially poverty and immigration.

Paraphrase: According to a 2015 study by the Pew Research Center on the attitudes of Americans toward the United States Government, Americans have a "deeply cynical" opinion of the government, admiring its handling of some issues but remaining critical of its involvement in other areas ("Beyond Distrust").

COMMENT

For Internet or other electronic sources without pagination, many instructors recommend that you repeat the author's name in parentheses after all paraphrases and direct quotations, even if the name is already included in the text.

QUOTING

When you want to include the words of another writer, but it is not appropriate to either paraphrase or summarize, you will want to quote. Quoting requires that you repeat the exact words of another, placing quotation marks before and after the material being quoted. **A crucial guideline requires that you copy the words exactly as they appear in the original text.** To omit words or approximate the original within quotation marks is sloppy or careless handling of your source material.

Be selective in the material you choose to quote directly, however. You should usually paraphrase the words of another, restating them in your own language, rather than relying on exactly copying the words. How do you know when to quote rather than paraphrase? You should quote only words, phrases, or sentences that are particularly striking or that must be reproduced exactly because you cannot convey them in your own words without weakening their effect or changing their intent. Quote passages or parts of passages that are original, dramatically worded, or in some way essential to your paper. Otherwise, rely on paraphrasing to refer to the ideas of others. In either case, document your source by identifying the original source and the location of your information within that source.

GUIDELINES FOR QUOTING

☐ Be selective: Quote directly only words, phrases, or sentences that are particularly striking or original, or whose meaning would be lost in a paraphrase.

☐ Quote directly passages that are so succinct that paraphrasing them would be more complicated or take more words than a direct quotation would require.

☐ Enclose the exact words you are quoting between quotation marks.

☐ Do not change any word of the original unless you indicate with brackets, ellipses, or other conventions that you have done so.

☐ Provide the source of your quoted material either in your text or in parentheses following the material.

Illustration: Quoting.   This section provides examples of quotations using selected passages from an article called "Mad for Dickens" by Joshua Hammer. The source for all examples in this section is the following:

Hammer, Joshua. "Mad for Dickens." *Smithsonian,* February 2012, pp. 70-78.

1. **Original** (page 72): Dickens burst onto the London literary scene at age 23, and as the world celebrates his 200th birthday on February 7, "The Inimitable," as he called himself, is still going strong.

   Quotation: In an article about writer Charles Dickens' 200th birthday, Joshua Hammer observes that Dickens was only 23 when he "burst onto the London literary scene" (72).

- *Place double quotation marks before and after words taken directly from the original.*
- *When the quoted material is an integral part of your sentence, do not capitalize the first letter of the first word.*
- *Where possible, name the author whose ideas or words you are quoting or paraphrasing.*
- *Giving information on the source material helps provide a context for the quoted and paraphrased material.*
- *In parentheses after the quotation, state the page number in the source where the quotation is located (hence the phrase "parenthetical citation"). This example contains only the page number because the author's name is mentioned in the text. If the text had not given the author's name, it would be included in the parenthetical citation.*

2. **Original** (page 74): The Dickens family was forced to move frequently to avoid debt collectors and, in 1824, was engulfed by the catastrophe that has entered Dickens lore: John was arrested for nonpayment of debts and jailed at Marshalsea in London.

   Quotation: Hammer comments that "the Dickens family was forced to move frequently to avoid debt collectors and, in 1824, . . . [Dickens' father] John was arrested for nonpayment of debts" (75).

- *When a quotation preceded by* that *forms an integral part of your sentence, do not capitalize the first word in the quotation, even when it is capitalized in the original.*
- *Use the ellipsis (three spaced periods) to indicate the omission of text from the original.*
- *Use brackets to enclose explanatory material not given in the quotation itself.*

3. **Original** (page 72): The word "Dickensian" permeates our lexicon, used to evoke everything from urban squalor to bureaucratic heartlessness and rags-to-riches reversals.

   Quotation: In discussing the influence of Dickens two centuries after his birth, Hammer notes: "The word 'Dickensian' permeates our lexicon from urban squalor to bureaucratic heartlessness . . ." (73).

COMMENTS

- *If your direct quotation is preceded by introductory text and a colon or comma, capitalize the first letter of the first word of the quotation.*
- *If you quote something that appears in quotation marks in the original source, use single marks within the double quotes.*
- *If your quotation appears to be a complete sentence but the actual sentence continues in the original, you must use the ellipsis at the end of your quotation to indicate that.*
- *If an ellipsis comes at the end of a quotation, the closing quotation mark follows the third period, with no space between the period and quotation mark. The parenthetical citation follows as usual.*

Combination of Paraphrase and Direct Quotation.   The following example illustrates how one can combine paraphrasing and quoting for a balanced handling of source material.

4. **Original** (page 75): With his father incarcerated, Charles, a bright and industrious student, was forced to leave school at around age 11 and take a job gluing labels on bottles at a London bootblacking factory. "It was a terrible, terrible humiliation," Tomalin told me, a trauma that would haunt Dickens for the rest of his life.

   Paraphrase and Quotation: The young Charles had to leave school and work in a factory when his father was sent to jail, an experience that Hammer describes as "a trauma that would haunt Dickens for the rest of his life" (75).

INTEGRATING SOURCE MATERIALS INTO YOUR PAPER

When quoting or paraphrasing material, pay special attention to your treatment of source materials. Authors have developed many ways of skillfully integrating the words and ideas of other people with their own words. Your paper should not read as if you simply cut out the words of someone else and pasted them in your paper. You can achieve smooth integration of source materials into your text if you keep the following suggestions in mind:

- **Mention the cited author's name in the text of your paper to signal the beginning of a paraphrase or quotation:**

  Hammer notes that Dickens' meteoric rise to fame came at quite a young age for a writer, describing him as "newly famous [and] upwardly mobile" (75).

- **Mention the source if no author is named.** This practice gives credit to the source while providing an introduction to the borrowed material:

  A *U.S. News & World Report* article notes that, although no genes determine what occupation one will go into, groups of genes produce certain tendencies—risk-taking, for instance—that might predispose one to select a particular kind of work ("How Genes Shape Personality" 64).

> **CAUTION**
>
> ▶ **AVOID DROPPED QUOTATIONS**
> Never incorporate a quotation without in some way introducing or commenting on it. A quotation that is not introduced or followed by some concluding comment, referred to as a "dropped" quotation, detracts from the smooth flow of your paper.

- **Give citations for all borrowed material.** State the authority's name, use quotation marks as appropriate, give the source and page number in a parenthetical citation, give some sort of general information, and/or use a pronoun to refer to the authority mentioned in the previous sentence. **Do not rely on one parenthetical citation at the end of several sentences or an entire paragraph:**

  > **Regna Lee Wood** has also researched the use of phonics in teaching children to read. **She** believes that the horrible failure of our schools began years ago. Wood notes that "it all began in 1929 and 1930 when hundreds of primary teachers, guided by college reading professors, stopped teaching beginners to read by "matching sounds with letters that spell sounds" (52). **She** adds that since 1950, when most reading teachers switched to teaching children to sight words rather than sound them by syllable, "fifty million children with poor sight memories have reached the fourth grade still unable to read" (52).

- **Vary introductory phrases and clauses.** Avoid excessive reliance on such standard introductory clauses as "Smith says," or "Jones writes." For instance, vary your verbs and/or provide explanatory information about sources, as in the following examples:

  > Michael Liu notes the following:
  > Professor Xavier argues this point convincingly:
  > According to Dr. Carroll, chief of staff at a major health center:
  > As Marcia Smith points out,

- **The first mention of an authority in your text (as opposed to the parenthetical citation) should include the author's first name as well as last name.** The second and subsequent references should give the last name only (never the first name alone).

  > **First use of author's name in your paper: Susan Jaspers** correctly observes that . . .
  > **Second and subsequent mentions of that author: Jaspers** contends elsewhere that . . .

- **Combine quotations and paraphrases.** A combination provides a smoother style than quoting directly all of the time:

  > W. H. Hanson's 2014 survey of college students reveals that today's generation of young people differs from those he surveyed in 2003. Hanson discovered that today's college students "are living through a period of profound demographic, economic, global, and technological change." Since these students of

the first decade of the 21st century see themselves living in a "deeply troubled nation," they have only guarded optimism about the future (32–33).

- **For long quotations (more than four typed lines), set the quoted material off from the text (referred to as a block quotation).** Write your introduction to the quotation, generally followed by a colon. Then begin a new line indented half an inch from the left margin, and type the quotation, double spaced as usual.

- **Do not add quotation marks for block quotations indented and set off from the text. If quotation marks appear in the original, use double quotation marks, not single.** If you quote a single paragraph or part of one, do not indent the first line any more than the rest of the quotation.

- **For block quotations, place the parenthetical citation after the final punctuation of the quotation.** See the following example of a block quotation:

> In her article exploring the kind of workforce required by a high-tech economy, Joanne Jacobs suggests that many of today's high school graduates lack crucial skills necessary for jobs in the rapidly growing technical and computer industries. For instance, a number of corporations agreed on the following prerequisites for telecommunications jobs:
>
> - Technical reading skills (familiarity with circuit diagrams, online documentation, and specialized reference materials).
> - Advanced mathematical skills (understanding of binary, octal, and hexadecimal number systems as well as mathematical logic systems).
> - Design knowledge (ability to use computer-aided design to produce drawings). (39–40)

USING ELLIPSIS POINTS, SQUARE BRACKETS, SINGLE QUOTATION MARKS, AND "QTD. IN"

This section offers some additional guidelines on the mechanics of handling source materials and incorporating them into your paper.

Ellipsis Points

- **If you want to omit original words, phrases, or sentences from your quotation of source material, use ellipsis points to indicate the omission.** Ellipsis points consist of three spaced periods, with spaces before, between, and after the periods. In quotations, ellipses are most frequently used within sentences, almost never at the beginning, but sometimes at the end. In every case, the quoted material must form a grammatically complete sentence, either by itself or in combination with your own words.

  Original: The momentous occurrences of an era—from war and economics to politics and inventions—give meaning to lives of the individuals who live through them.

Quotation with an ellipsis in the middle: Arthur Levine argues, "The momentous occurrences of an era . . . give meaning to lives of the individuals who live through them" (26).

- **Use ellipsis marks at the end of a quotation only if you have not used some words from the end of the final sentence quoted.** In that case, include four periods. When the ellipsis coincides with the end of your own sentence, use four periods with no space either before the first or after the last.

  Quotation with an ellipsis at the end: You know the old saying, "Eat, drink, and be merry. . . ."

- **If a parenthetical reference follows the ellipsis at the end of your sentence, use a space before each period and place the sentence period after the final parenthesis:**

  According to recent studies, "Statistics show that Chinese women's status has improved . . ." (*Chinese Women* 46).

- **Ellipsis points are not necessary** if you are quoting a fragment of a sentence, that is, a few words or a subordinate clause, because context will clearly indicate the omission of some of the original sentence.

  Sociobiologists add that social and nurturing experiences can "intensify, diminish, or modify" personality traits (Wood and Wood 272).

Square Brackets.   Sometimes you will need to change slightly the punctuation or verb tense of a quotation to make your own sentence grammatically correct, or you might need to add clarification or identification to a quoted passage. On these occasions, you will use square brackets. Although you should look for ways to integrate source material into your text that avoid overuse of square brackets, the following guidelines apply when changing source material is unavoidable.

- **If you want to change a word or phrase to conform to your own sentence or add words to make your sentence grammatically correct, use square brackets to indicate the change.** The square brackets enclose only the changed portion of the original.

  Original: They were additional casualties of our time of plague, demoralized reminders that although this country holds only two percent of the world's population, it consumes 65 percent of the world's supply of hard drugs.

  Quotation: According to Pete Hamill in his essay "Crack and the Box," America "holds only two percent of the world's population, [yet] it consumes 65 percent of the world's supply of hard drugs" (267).

  Original: In a miasma of Walt Disney images, Bambi burning, and Snow White asleep, the most memorable is "Cinderella."

  Quotation: Louise Bernikow recalls spending Saturday afternoons at the theatre when she was growing up "in a miasma of Walt Disney images, . . . the most memorable [of which] is 'Cinderella'" (17).

COMMENT

> *This example illustrates the use not only of square brackets but also of ellipsis points and single and double quotation marks.*

- **Use square brackets if you add some explanatory information or editorial comment.**

    Original: Then, magically, the fairy godmother appears. She comes from nowhere, summoned, we suppose, by Cinderella's wishes.

    Quotation: Louise Bernikow points out that "she [the fairy godmother] comes from nowhere, summoned . . . by Cinderella's wishes" (19).

- **If the passage you quote already contains an ellipsis, place square brackets around your own ellipsis.** The brackets tell readers that the ellipsis without brackets is in the original and that the ellipsis in brackets is your addition. MLA notes that, alternatively, you can add an explanatory note in parentheses after the quotation, if you prefer.

    Original: She seemed normal, herself again. She wasn't trembling. And if this sudden belief was going to keep her happy he couldn't possibly begrudge it. But . . . but . . . he wished, all the same, it hadn't happened. There was something uncanny about thought-reading, about telepathy.

    Quotation with an added ellipsis: The husband in "Don't Look Now" is disturbed after an encounter that his wife has just described: "He couldn't possibly begrudge it. But . . . but . . . he wished, all the same, it hadn't happened. There was something uncanny about [. . .] telepathy" (Du Maurier 10).

    Alternative handling of added ellipsis: The husband in "Don't Look Now" is disturbed after an encounter that his wife has just described: "He couldn't possibly begrudge it. But . . . but . . . he wished, all the same, it hadn't happened. There was something uncanny about . . . telepathy" (Du Maurier 10; 1st ellipsis in original).

- **The word "sic" (meaning "thus" or "so") in parentheses indicates that an error occurs in the original source of a passage you are quoting.** Because you are not at liberty to change words when quoting word for word, reproduce the error but use (sic) to indicate that the error is not yours.

    Original: Thrills have less to do with speed then changes in speed.

    Quotation: Dahl makes this observation: "Thrills have less to do with speed then (sic) changes in speed" (18).

Single Quotation Marks

- **If you quote text that itself appears in quotation marks in the original, use single marks within the double that enclose your own quotation.**

Original: This set me pondering the obvious question: "How can it be so hard for kids to find something to do when there's never been such a range of stimulating entertainment available to them?"

Quotation: Dahl is led to ask this question: "'How can it be so hard for kids to find something to do when there's never been such a range of stimulating entertainment available to them?'" (18–19).

Qtd. In.

- **If you quote or paraphrase material that is quoted in an indirect source, use the abbreviation "qtd." with the word "in."** An indirect source is a second-hand one that quotes or paraphrases another's words, unlike a primary source, which is the writer's own work. In college research papers, you want to use primary sources as often as possible, but you are likely to have occasion to use secondary sources as well. Use "qtd. in" whenever you quote or paraphrase the published account of someone else's words or ideas. The works-cited list will include not the original source of the material you quoted or paraphrased but rather the indirect source, the one where you found the material. You will likely be using the single quotation marks within the double because you are quoting what someone else has quoted.

  Original: Printed in bold letters at the entrance of the show is a startling claim by Degas' fellow painter Auguste Renoir: "If Degas had died at 50, he would have been remembered as an excellent painter, no more; it is after his 50th year that his work broadened out and that he really becomes Degas."

  Quotation: Impressionist painter Auguste Renoir observed of Degas: "'If Degas had died at 50, he would have been remembered as an excellent painter, no more; it is after his 50th year that his work broadened out and that he really becomes Degas'" (qtd. in Benfey).

GUIDELINES FOR INTEGRATING SOURCE MATERIALS INTO YOUR PAPER

- ☐ Avoid "dropped" quotations by introducing all direct quotations.
- ☐ Use the author's name, where appropriate, to signal the beginning of a paraphrase or quotation.
- ☐ Use attributive tags, short identifying words, phrases, or clauses that identify source and introduce borrowed material.
- ☐ Cite sources for all borrowed material, either as attributive tags or parenthetically after the quotation or paraphrase.
- ☐ Name a source title if the source does not list an author's name.
- ☐ Vary the way you introduce source material.
- ☐ Try combining direct quotations and paraphrases in the same sentence.
- ☐ Become familiar with appropriate uses of ellipsis points, brackets, single quotation marks, and "qtd. in."

DOCUMENTING SOURCES IN A COLLECTION OF ESSAYS

You have been reading about and looking at examples of one important component of source documentation: in-text citations. The other component is the alphabetical list, appearing on a separate page at the end of your paper, of all the works that you quoted from or paraphrased. This is the list of works cited. Each entry in the list begins with the author's name—last name first—followed by the title of the article, book, or other source and information about its place and date of publication. The author's name (or title of the work, if it is published anonymously) in the text's parenthetical citation refers to one item in this list at the end of the paper.

You will find more discussion of documenting sources in Chapter 7, but the brief treatment here gives useful guidelines for short papers using materials reprinted in a collection of essays, such as this textbook. Although the examples in this section illustrate how to document materials reprinted in this textbook, the guidelines apply to any collection of essays. Because much of *Perspectives on Contemporary Issues* is a collection of other people's works, not the editor's, you will probably not have occasion to use the words or ideas of Ackley herself. However, because you are not reading the essays in their original source, you must indicate that you have read them in her book.

Citing One Source in a Collection.   Suppose your paper quotes or paraphrases a statement from a reading in the seventh edition of *Perspectives on Contemporary Issues,* Donna Beegle's "All Kids Should Take 'Poverty 101.' " After you write either the exact words of Beegle or paraphrase her words, open a parenthesis, write the author's last name and the page number where you read the words with no punctuation between them, and then close the parenthesis (Beegle 345-347). Do not write the word *page* or *pages* nor insert a comma between the author's name and the number of the page. If Beegle's piece is the only one you use in your paper, write "Work Cited" (note the singular form of "Work") at the end of your paper and enter complete bibliographic information for the article:

Work Cited

Beegle, Donna. "All Kids Should Take 'Poverty 101.' "

Perspectives on Contemporary Issues: Readings across

the Disciplines. 7th ed., edited by Katherine Anne

Ackley, Wadsworth Cengage, 2015, pp. 345–347.

Citing Two or More Sources in a Collection.   If you draw material from two or more works in a collection, MLA style recommends that you create an entry for the collection and then cross-reference each work to that collection. That is, you need not repeat the full information for the collection with the citation for each essay.

Instead, list the collection by the editor's name, giving full bibliographic information. Then list separately each article you use by author and title, but after each essay title, give only the collection editor's name and the inclusive page numbers of the essay.

For example, suppose you write a paper on the power of words and images to affect behavior. In your essay, you use information from several essays in the seventh edition of this textbook. Here is how your Works Cited page might look:

Works Cited

Ackley, Katherine Anne, editor. *Perspectives on Contemporary Issues: Readings across the Disciplines.* 7th ed., Wadsworth Cengage, 2015.

Beegle, Donna. "All Kids Should Take 'Poverty 101.'" Ackley, pp. 345–347.

Friedman, Thomas. "Pass the Books. Hold the Oil." Ackley, pp. 325–328.

Ravitch, Diane. "Critical Thinking? You Need Knowledge." Ackley, pp. 321–323.

STUDENT PAPER DEMONSTRATING SYNTHESIS WITH IN-TEXT CITATIONS USING MLA STYLE

Following is a student paper that synthesizes material from several works in one collection and follows MLA guidelines for paraphrasing and quoting. Michael Vawter, in "More than Just a Place," uses sources from a collection of essays, stories, and poems on the subject of the environment. His assignment in a literature and environment course was to explain a key theme or main point that several of the writers had in common. His paper may be used as a model for papers that you are asked to write using readings from this or any other textbook, or from a similar collection of works, such as the one that Michael uses. The marginal comments call attention to various strategies for writing an effective synthesis.

COMMENTS

- *While instructors may stipulate their own formatting guidelines for papers, typically you place your last name in the running head before the page number.*
- *Write your name, class, instructor's name, and date on the left-hand side above the title of the paper.*

- MLA style recommends using the day/month/year format for the date. Double-space between all lines of your paper, including between the date and your title and between your title and the first line of your paper.
- A works-cited list appears on a separate page at the end. The works-cited list gives full bibliographic information for the collection and cross-references the individual works to the collection.
- Works are listed alphabetically and each citation conforms in punctuation and spacing to the MLA style of documentation
- ·For more on using MLA style in writing that uses sources, including guidelines for formatting the works-cited list, see Chapter 7.

Michael Vawter

Prof. Weaver

FYS 101

13 Feb 2017

More than Just a Place

The opening paragraph introduces readers to the subject of the paper.

Science tells us that we are the product of two fundamental forces, our genetic code and our environment. These two factors have not only propelled our evolution as a species, but they have also given us our sense of personality, culture, and identity. While our genetic code is fixed, our cultural and physical environments can be fluid and ever changing. Feeling rooted or closely connected to the environment can be extremely beneficial for the development of personal and cultural wellness. To have this sort of connection with

Michael's thesis sets the direction of the paper.

one's environment, one must develop a strong sense of place and an identity that is grounded in location. We see the importance of place and its transcendence beyond just a physical location in the works of four writers as they reflect on their environments.

Scott Russell Sanders writes in *Staying Put* that one needs an adequate measuring stick to experience the world at large. He argues that a person can never fully appreciate any environment—or any aspect of nature for that matter—without having an environment of his or her own to compare it to: "How can you value other places if you do not have one of your own? If you are not yourself placed, then you wander the world like a sightseer, a collector of sensations, with no gauge for measuring what you see" (114). How can a person adequately understand the significance of any place he or she happens to spend time in without a reference point in the form of a home environment with which to identify?

Elsewhere, in his essay "Buckeye," Sanders argues that each of us has a responsibility to adopt our local environment and to care for it. He refers to the words of another writer, Simone Weil, who wrote: "'Let us love the country of here below. . . . It is this country that God has given us to love. He has willed that it should be difficult yet possible to love it'" (293). Sanders suggests here that the important thing is not caring for the environment at large, but rather caring for the specific chunk of it within which one lives. He argues that we are intrinsically tied to the environment that we inhabit, and that just as we cannot effectively enjoy nature by disassociating from our homes and haphazardly attempting to take all of it in at once, we cannot effectively protect nature by aiming to

When quoting more than three lines of vere, set them off in a block text. Indent half an inch from the left margin and put each new line of the poem on a new line. Put a period at the end and the inclusive line numbers in parentheses.

protect all of it instead of just concerning ourselves with our own areas. One's home, for Sanders, is more than just a place.

Sanders is not alone in his belief that nature—our environment—has a profoundly direct impact on our personal identities. Wendell Berry, in his poem "Stay Home," claims nature itself as his most beloved home and reveals the impact that nature has had on the shaping of his identity. He feels grounded and rooted whenever he is in the wild and derives pleasure from that profound sense of rootedness:

> I will be standing in the woods
>
> where the old trees
>
> move only with the wind
>
> and then with gravity.
>
> In the stillness of the trees
>
> I am at home. (8–13)

He seems to derive pleasure and fulfillment from being out in the woods, but this is not his focus. His emphasis is on his feeling at home—on the fact that these pleasurable experiences he derives from being in the woods are not just exciting, but are also grounding and definitive.

Michael provides transition as he moves from paragraph to paragraph. When quoting three lines or fewer of poetry, integrate them into the text and use a slash with spaces before and after to indicate line separation.

At the same time, Berry recognizes that other people have different homes and that they derive different sorts of identities based on those different homes. He seems to suggest that this is okay. As long as he can remain rooted to his own conception of "home," others can feel free to root themselves differently: "I am at home. Don't come with me. / You stay home too" (6–7; 13–14). The repetition of these lines at the conclusion of each stanza reinforces this view. Berry does not argue that everyone should find "home" by seeking to experience nature the way that he does. He seems to suggest that the important thing is to find your unique environment and unique source of grounding and to maintain them.

Writer bell hooks does not capitalize her name, so references to her name should be lowercased.

The impact of environment on rootedness is observable not only in the context of personal identity, but also in the context of cultural identity. In her essay "Touching the Earth," bell hooks argues that the African American people developed a unique cultural identity while enslaved in the South, and that this identity was tied at a fundamental level to their plantation environment and to the Southern land itself. When slavery in the U.S. was finally abolished and African Americans began migrating northward in search of new opportunities, many of them lost a certain element of their identity. Observing that many African Americans realized this and began travelling back to their homelands in the South, hooks writes: "Generations of black folks who migrated north . . . returned down home in search of a spiritual nourishment, a healing, that was fundamentally connected to reaffirming one's connection to nature" (172). The process of northward migration uprooted the African American people from their environment, which had a negative effect on their general wellness. Unfortunately, it also seems to have had a far-reaching effect on their general confidence as a race, as hooks

Michael now shifts to a discussion of the author Langston Hughes.

writes: "Learning contempt for blackness, [African American] southerners transplanted in the north suffered both culture shock and soul loss" (172). With their cultural confidence in shambles, the African American people who were scattered across the North began to be affected by the racist attitudes present in their surrounding environment. They began internalizing the lies perpetuated by those Northerners who didn't believe that African Americans were a competent race, and this in turn had a profoundly negative effect on American society as a whole. Uprooting oneself from a "home" environment and moving into a more hostile one is clearly a very dangerous pursuit.

The past environments of one's ancestors may even be a factor in rootedness and in cultural identity. In his poem "The Negro Speaks of Rivers," Langston Hughes suggests that his identity has been shaped not only by his own environment but also by the environments that played a role in his ethnic heritage. He defines himself not only in the context of his own environment, but also in the context of the environments of his African ancestors: "I bathed in the Euphrates when dawns were young. / I built my hut near the Congo and it lulled me to sleep. / I looked upon the Nile and raised the pyramids above it" (4–6). Hughes himself never slept in huts by the Congo or built pyramids by the Nile, but he considers himself to be a product of that environment nonetheless. His message here seems to be that a "rooted" person should be cognizant not only of his or her current environment but also of the environments that rooted their ancestors.

Hughes is far more than just cognizant of these extended roots, however. He insists that the Congo and the Nile have had a deep impact on him, though he has perhaps never seen them. He writes, "I've known rivers: / Ancient, dusky rivers. / My soul has grown deep like the rivers" (8–10). He recognizes that his ancestors were, in many ways, the direct product of interaction with these formidable rivers, and that this environmental impact has been passed down to him through stories, traditions, and possibly even genetic traits. His way of life as well as his way of thinking may have been directly influenced by his ancestors' relationship with rivers.

Home is more than a place. Home is not simply a building that one regularly inhabits, a town that one was born in, or a park that one enjoys walking through. Those buildings, towns and parks do directly influence us, however, and can even become a part of us; in fact, they *should* become a part of us. While at times it may be necessary to uproot oneself and move to a new environment—such as in the example of the northward migration of African Americans after their liberation—this uprooting can be a difficult and even painful process. In the fast pace of modern society, it can be easy for one to lose connection with the immediate environment and with one's true *home*. This type of disconnect should not be taken lightly. In order to firmly root oneself and obtain

Michael's conclusion brings his paper to a close by summarizing what he has gained from reading selected works of four writers on the importance of feeling connected to a place.

Michael's list of works cited includes four selections from an anthology as well as two works by the same author.

a profound and lasting sense of personal and cultural identity, one must have a home.

Works Cited

Anderson, Lorraine, et al., editors. *Literature and the Environment: A Reader on Nature and Culture.* Longman, 1999.

Berry, Wendell. "Stay Home." Anderson et al., pp. 222–23.

hooks, bell. "Touching the Earth." Anderson et al., pp. 169–73.

Hughes, Langston. "The Negro Speaks of Rivers." Anderson et al., pp. 168–69.

Sanders, Scott Russell. "Buckeye." Anderson et al., pp. 290–95.

---. *Staying Put: Making a Home in a Restless World.* Beacon, 1991.

The three hyphens indicate that the name is identical to that in the preceding entry; the entries themselves are listed alphabetically by the first letter of the title. Do not change the three hyphens to a long dash

MindTap   Reflect, personalize, and apply what you've learned.

WRITING A RESEARCH PAPER

MindTap® Start with a warm-up activity, and review the chapter Learning Objectives.

THE RESEARCH PROCESS

This chapter presents a brief overview of the key steps in locating a topic you want to spend time with, researching it, and writing a paper incorporating the sources you have used. Keep in mind the discussion in Chapter 6 on paraphrasing, quoting, and documenting sources. A research paper is likely to be much longer than a writing assignment generated from readings in this book, but otherwise little difference separates the processes of using materials from this textbook and using materials from other sources in terms of accuracy and fairness to your sources. Furthermore, the process of writing a research paper is not much different from that of writing any other paper, as explained in Chapter 2. To do your best work, you will go through the prewriting, drafting, revising, editing, and proofreading stages.

MindTap°   Read, highlight, and take notes online.

DEFINING YOUR PURPOSE

Your instructor will tell you whether your purpose in the research paper is to argue, explain, analyze, or come to some conclusion about something. Many instructors prefer that students write argumentative papers. In that case, you will make a judgment about your topic based on what you find in your research. Recall the discussion in Chapter 5 on writing an argument. The same guidelines apply whether you are writing a researched argument or one without sources. You will begin your research with an idea of what your position is, then research your subject extensively, arrive at an informed opinion, and finally defend that position by presenting evidence that seems valid (that is, logical and convincing) to you. If you want to go a step further and convince your audience to adopt your position or to act on suggestions you propose, then your purpose is persuasion.

On the other hand, some instructors direct students to explain or analyze something in their research papers. An informative paper does not necessarily address a controversial subject. If you are to write an explanatory paper, you will gather information about your topic and present it in such a way that your reader fully understands it. You will explain, describe, illustrate, or narrate something in full detail, such as what a black hole is, how photosynthesis works, the circumstances surrounding a historical event, and significant events in the life of a famous person.

Audience.   Having a clear sense of your audience will direct your research and help you write your paper. If you are writing an argument, the most useful audience to address is one that is opposed to your position or, at best, uncertain about where they stand on the issue. A good argument seeks to persuade or convince an audience, so anticipating readers who are not already convinced will help sharpen your argument. If your purpose is to explain, illustrate, or analyze, your audience is likely to be informed in general about the particular subject of your paper, but not in great depth. Unless instructed otherwise, assume an intelligent audience of nonspecialists who are interested in learning more about the topic of your paper. Imagining this audience will keep you from having to define or explain every term or concept and give you room for interesting, informative, and/or intriguing material about the topic.

FINDING A TOPIC

Once you know your purpose and audience, the next step in writing a research paper is to find a subject that you will be comfortable working with for many weeks and then narrow it to a specific topic. Some instructors assign topics, but most leave the choice to students. The freedom to choose your own research paper topic can be intimidating because so much depends on selecting the right topic. You want a topic that not only holds your interest but also offers you an opportunity to investigate it in depth.

The process of discovering or locating what you will write about involves first determining the broad subject you are particularly interested in pursuing. Once you have settled on the subject, you will need to narrow it to one specific aspect of that subject. For many research paper assignments, that topic will have to be arguable, one that requires you to investigate from several angles and arrive at and defend your own position. This position will be worded in the form of a hypothesis or thesis, stated most often as a declarative statement but sometimes as a question. Settling on your final topic takes time, so do some serious thinking about this important step as soon as the paper is assigned. You will be reshaping, narrowing, and refining your topic for much of the research process, so you do not want to switch subjects halfway through.

Any or all of the suggestions for generating ideas in the prewriting stage that are discussed in Chapter 2 would be useful when trying to discover a topic for your research paper. Brainstorming, making lists, clustering, even researching in a preliminary way and talking with others can be of use. Asking questions, thinking about your personal interests or personal opinion, and thinking about controversial topics can also be quite helpful in the process of narrowing down to a research topic that you are interested in pursuing.

Asking Questions.   One of the best ways to approach the research project is to ask questions about a subject that interests you and that seems worth investigating. As you read through the suggestions for locating a topic that follow, think in terms of questions that you might ask about the initial subjects you come up with. As you narrow your field of potential topics, look for those about which you can ask questions whose answers are neither too broad nor too narrow. You want the topic that you ultimately select to be challenging enough that your paper will be interesting to you as well as to your audience. Avoid topics about which questions are unanswerable or highly speculative. Your goal in the research process will be to arrive at an answer, insofar as that is possible, to your question.

Any of the topics listed as possible subjects of argumentation in Chapter 5 are appropriate for researched writing. Here are examples of questions that one might ask about various argumentative subjects when trying to generate ideas for a research paper:

- Under what conditions, if any, is censorship justifiable?
- Do advertising images of women set up impossible standards of femininity?
- What is the appropriate punishment for steroid use in athletes?
- Which plays a more prominent role in determining behavior, genes or environment?
- How dangerous is secondhand smoke?
- Should sex education be taught by parents or by schools?

- Are restrictions on freedom of speech necessary in time of war?
- How far should Homeland Security go to protect Americans from terrorists?
- Is there still a "glass ceiling" for women in the workforce?
- Does watching too much television have a harmful effect on preschool children?
- Should the Electoral College be abolished?
- Do women do better academically in all-female schools?
- Should there be a formal apology from the government for slavery?
- Should grades be abolished?
- What should be done about illegal immigrants in the United States?
- Should the federal government increase funding for the space program?
- Should college athletes be paid?

Generating Topics from Personal Interest.   One way to find a topic for your research paper is to begin with subjects you already know well, are interested in, or think you would like to improve your knowledge of. Consider topics that attracted your interest in high school or in previous college classes; any reading you have already done on subjects that appeal to you; or the kinds of things that capture your attention when you watch television news, read news magazines or newspapers, or select nonfiction books for leisure-time reading.

Generating Topics from Personal Opinions.   Virtually any topic can be turned into an argument, but opinions are always subject to debate. Therefore, one way to generate a research paper topic is to begin with your own strongly held opinions. Avoid a topic that is based entirely on opinion. Evaluative statements are especially good for argumentative papers because they are likely to have differing opinions. Once you say that something is the best, the most significant, the most important, or the greatest, for instance, you have put yourself in the position of defending that statement. You will have to establish your criteria for making your judgment and defend your choice against what others might think. Here are some ideas for this particular approach:

- The most influential person in the twenty-first century (or in America; in the world; in a particular field such as education, government, politics, arts, entertainment, or the like)
- The greatest basketball (or football, tennis, soccer, baseball) player (either now playing or of all time)
- The greatest or worst president
- The business or industry with the greatest impact on American life in the last decade (or last twenty years, last fifty years, or last century)

Because your conclusion on any of these or similar topics is your opinion, you need to establish criteria for your conclusion, describe the process you used to make it, and explain the logical basis for that process.

Generating Topics from Controversy.   Yet another way to discover a topic you find intriguing enough to commit many hours of time to is to think of controversial issues that always generate heated debate. These topics may be frequently discussed in newspapers, news magazines, and on television news programs and talk shows. They may be issues on which candidates for public office, from local county board members to state and federal officials, are pressed to take stands. Here are some examples of controversial statements:

- Media coverage of celebrity trials should be banned.
- Children whose parents are on welfare should be placed in state-run orphanages.
- Women should be barred from participating in combat duty.
- The federal government should stop funding projects in the arts and the humanities.
- The federal government should provide unlimited funds to support research to find a cure for AIDS.
- Children who commit murder should be tried as adults no matter what their age.
- America is obligated to provide military intervention to countries around the world.

Narrowing Your Subject to a Specific Topic.   Most research paper assignments are short enough that you simply must narrow your focus to avoid a too shallow or too hopelessly general treatment of your topic. Keep in mind the distinction between **subject** and **topic**: subject is the general area under investigation, whereas topic is the narrow aspect of that subject that you are investigating.

One way to get a sense of how a general topic can be narrowed is to look at the table of contents of a book on a subject that interests you. Notice the chapter headings, which are themselves subtopics of the broad subject. Chapters themselves are often further subdivided. You want to find a topic that is narrow enough that you can fully explore it without leaving unanswered questions, yet broad enough that you can say enough about it in a reasonably long paper.

To narrow your subject to a topic, take a general subject and go through the brainstorming process again, this time listing everything that comes to your mind about that particular subject. What subtopics does your subject have? What questions can you ask about your general subject? How might you narrow your focus on that subject? Ultimately, you want to generate an idea that gives focus to your preliminary library search.

FORMING A PRELIMINARY THESIS AND A WORKING BIBLIOGRAPHY

When you believe that you have narrowed your topic sufficiently, you are ready to form your preliminary thesis. This is the position that you believe you want to take on your topic, based on your early thinking about and narrowing down of a subject. Your preliminary or working thesis can be in the form of either a question or a statement. In much the same way as your final thesis gives direction and focus to your paper, your preliminary thesis gives you direction and focus in the research process. As you review potential sources and read about your topic, you may find yourself changing your preliminary thesis for any number of reasons. Perhaps your topic is too narrow or too new and you simply cannot find enough sources with which to write a fair and balanced research paper. Or you may discover that your topic is too broad to cover in a research paper and that you need to narrow your focus even more.

A common reason for changing a preliminary thesis is that, once you actually start reading sources, you discover that you want to change your initial position. You may discover that you were wrong in your assumption or opinion about your topic and that you are persuaded to change your position. Part of the pleasure in researching a topic is discovering new ideas or information, so it makes sense that your early views on your topic may shift as you learn more about it. More than likely, your final thesis will differ in some way from your preliminary thesis.

With your preliminary thesis in mind, you are ready to start the actual research process. First, you need to locate potential sources. A working bibliography is a list of sources you *might* use in your research paper, those that look particularly promising during a preliminary search. At this point, you will not have had time to read or even carefully skim all potential sources, let alone imagine how they fit together to support your working thesis. Your goal is to find the sources that are most relevant to topic and select from them the most useful ones to read carefully, taking notes as you read. One obvious place to start looking for sources is the library; another source is the Internet.

FINDING SOURCES

The Library.   Your library has a good number of valuable resources to help you in your search for materials on your research topic. Libraries house books, periodicals, and other materials that you can hold, leaf through, check out, and read. Furthermore, many libraries have special collections on specific subjects and offer access to online databases that they subscribe to. They also have CDs or DVDs that you can use, and your library may have print copies of sources that you cannot find on the Internet.

Online Catalog. Begin your library search for sources on your general subject or topic (if you have sufficiently narrowed your focus) by reviewing the online catalog for titles of potential sources. In this searching stage, you probably will not know titles of works or authors, so you will begin by looking under subject headings for titles that seem relevant to your research subject. Examining the table of contents and index of a source, reading the author's credentials, and scanning some of the text will help you narrow your focus if you haven't already done so.

The Internet.   To find Internet materials, you can use any of a number of equally good search engines available on the Web. Search engines collect many sites in their databanks; they return sites that match the keywords you type to begin your search. Be very careful when searching for sources on the Internet: keep in mind the guidelines in Chapter 1 on evaluating Internet sources. Begin by choosing your search engine from among the best known or most used; they are likely to be the most reliable. Commercially backed search engines are usually well maintained and frequently upgraded, thus ensuring reliable results.

Other Sources.   Do not overlook other excellent sources of information, such as personal interviews, surveys, lectures, taped television programs, films, documentaries, and government publications.

The Difference between Primary and Secondary Sources   *Primary* refers to original sources, actual data, or firsthand witnesses, such as interviews, surveys, speeches, diaries, letters, unpublished manuscripts, photographs, memoirs or autobiographies, published material written at the time of the event such as newspaper articles, and similar items. They are actual recorded accounts or documentary evidence of events. *Secondary* refers to sources like books and articles that discuss, explain, or interpret events or that are seen secondhand. They are written or recorded after the fact and represent processed information: interpretations of or commentary on events.

Reporting the Results of a Survey Using Tables and Graphs.   Surveys are another good primary source. For instance, in a group-written paper, four students were interested in the question of the influence of gender on academic success on their college campus. They prepared a survey that they distributed to classmates. Their paper reports the results of their findings based on 103 surveys and includes four charts and graphs that represent these findings. One of these is reproduced in the guidelines for putting all of the parts of a paper together later in this chapter.

GUIDELINES FOR DEVELOPING A WORKING BIBLIOGRAPHY

☐ List sources that sound promising for your research, recording titles and locations as you discover them.

☐ If the source is a library book, record the title, author, and call number.

☐ If the source is an article from the library, write the title of the piece, the name of its author, the title of the magazine or journal where it appears, the date of the issue, and the inclusive pages numbers. You will need all this information to find the article.

☐ For other sources in the library, such as videotapes, audiotapes, government documents, or pamphlets, write down as much information as you can find to help locate them. Write the location of any source, such as a special collection, government document, stack, and periodical.

☐ For a website, record the title; the author, if known; the date, if available; and the Uniform Resource Locator (URL) or, preferably, the DOI (digital object identifier), if available. The DOI remains the same, even if the URL changes. You may want to retrieve the full text files of websites that seem promising, as you discover them, to ensure their availability when you are ready to begin reading and taking notes.

CREATING A PRELIMINARY BIBLIOGRAPHY

Once you complete a list of sources to investigate, you need to evaluate them as potential references for your research paper. If you discover that you cannot use a source, cross it off your list or delete it from your bookmarked sites. When you find a source that definitely looks promising for your research topic, make sure that you have recorded all pertinent bibliographic information in the form in which it will appear on your list of works cited. Following the formatting guidelines for the works-cited page is essential because, although the list appears at the end of your paper, you will need to know how to make parenthetical citations in the text. You will recall that references within the text of your paper must correspond to sources in the list of works cited. This means using the last name of the author or editors, the title of the work if no author is named, or a shortened title if the work has no author or editor and a long title. The section in this chapter entitled "Documenting Sources" lists appropriate formats for various kinds of sources. Note the following sample work-cited formats for some common types of sources:

Book with One Author.

> Pollock, Jocelyn M. *Ethical Dilemmas and Decisions in Criminal Justice.* Wadsworth, 2013.

Journal Article with One Author.

> Wintroub, Michael. "Words, Things, Going Native, and Staying True." *American Historical Review*, vol. 120, no. 4, Oct. 2015, pp. 1185–1217.

Journal Article with Two Authors.

> Ender, Evelyne, and Deirdre Shauna Lynch. "On 'Learning
>
> to Read.'" *PMLA,* vol. 130, no. 3, May 2015, pp. 539–45.

Journal Article with No Author Named.

> "Class Action Suits in the Workplace Are on the Rise." *HR*
>
> *Focus*, April 2012, pp. 84–85.

Newspaper Article with Author Named.

> Stockman, Farah. "The Outcast Effect." *Boston Globe,* 13
>
> Nov. 2015, p. 4.

Magazine Article with Author Named.

> Hammer, Joshua. "Mad for Dickens." *Smithsonian*, February
>
> 2012, pp. 70–78.

Magazine Article with Author Named, Online.

> Sweet, Elizabeth. "Toys are More Divided by Gender Now
>
> than They Were 50 Years Ago." *The Atlantic,* 9 Dec. 2014,
>
> http://www.theatlantic.com/business/archive/2014/12/
>
> toys-are-more-divided-by-gender-now-than-they-were-
>
> 50-years-ago/383556/.

Magazine Article with No Author Named.

> "Mercury Rising." *National Geographic*, Dec. 2012, p. 35.

Chapter from a Collection of Essays.

> Smiley, Jane. "You Can Never Have Too Many." *The Barbie Chronicles: A Living Doll Turns Forty,* edited by Yona Zeldis McDonough, Touchstone/Simon, 1999, pp. 189–92.

Government Document.

> United States, Congress, House, Committee on Education and the Workforce. *Education Reforms: Hearing before the Early Childhood, Elementary and Secondary Education Subcommittee,* 21 Sept. 2011, https://www.gpo.gov/fdsys/pkg/CHRG-112 www.gpo.gov/fdsys/pkg/CHRG-112 hhrg68367/html/CHRG-112hhrg 68367.htm. 112th Cong., 1st sess.

As you record information in the proper format, alphabetize your list, placing new items in the appropriate alphabetical position. Then, when you need to assemble your list of works cited, just move the list to the file where you store your paper (or keep the list in the same file). As you evaluate sources to determine whether they are appropriate for your paper, delete those that you decide not to pursue further. Here is how a list of some of the works on the previous sample bibliography entries would look in a computer file:

> **Work Cited**
>
> "Class Action Suits in the Workplace Are on the Rise." *HR Focus,* April 2012, pp. 84–85.
>
> Ender, Evelyne, and Deirdre Shauna Lynch. "On 'Learning to Read.'" *PMLA,* vol. 130, no. 3, May 2015, pp. 539–45.
>
> "Mercury Rising." *National Geographic,* Dec. 2012, p. 35.
>
> Pollock, Jocelyn M. *Ethical Dilemmas and Decisions in Criminal Justice.* Wadsworth, 2013.

Smiley, Jane. "You Can Never Have Too Many." *The Barbie Chronicles: A Living Doll Turns Forty*, edited by Yona Zeldis McDonough, Touchstone/Simon, 1999, pp. 189–92.

Stockman, Farah. "The Outcast Effect." *Boston Globe*, 13 Nov. 2015, p. 4.

Sweet, Elizabeth. "Toys are More Divided by Gender Now than They Were 50 Years Ago." *The Atlantic*, 9 Dec. 2014, http://www.theatlantic.com/business/archive/2014/12/toys-are-more-divided-by-gender-now-than-they-were-50-years-ago/383556/.

United States, Congress, House, Committee on Education and the Workforce. *Education Reforms: Hearing before the Early Childhood, Elementary and Secondary Education Subcommittee*, 21 Sept. 2011, www.gpo.gov/fdsys/pkg/CHRG-112hhrg68367/html/CHRG-112hhrg68367.htm. *112th* Cong., 1st sess.

Wintroub, Michael. "Words, Things, Going Native, and Staying True." *American Historical Review*, vol. 120, no. 4, Oct. 2015, pp. 1185–1217.

EVALUATING PRINT SOURCES

Before you begin taking notes from any source, carefully assess its reliability. Ideally, your research should rely on unbiased, current, well-documented sources written by people with the authority to discuss the subject. However, you are likely to find a great number of sources that are written from particular perspectives that are out of date or incomplete, that are written by people with no authority whatsoever, or that do not document their own sources. Part of your job as a researcher is to try to discover these aspects of your sources, to reject those that are completely unreliable, and to use caution with sources when you lack complete confidence in them. Although you may never know for sure how much to trust a particular source, you can check certain things to help in your assessment.

Check for Bias.   Try to find out whether the author, publication, organization, or person being interviewed is known to give fair coverage. You need not reject sources outright if you know they take particular positions on subjects, especially controversial issues. However, your own paper should be as unbiased as possible, which requires acknowledgment of the known biases of your sources.

Check the Date of Publication.   For many subjects, current information is crucial to accurate analysis. If you are researching issues such as global warming, or controversial treatments for AIDS victims, for instance, you need the most recent available information. However, if you are examining a historical matter, such as the question of Richard III's guilt in his two young cousins' deaths, you can rely in part on older materials. You still want to look for the latest theories, information, or opinions on any subject you research, though.

Check the Author's Credentials.   Find out whether the author has sufficient education, experience, or expertise to write or speak about your subject. You can do this in a number of ways. Any book usually gives information about an author, from a sentence or two to several paragraphs, either on the dust jacket or at the beginning or end of the book. This information reveals the author's professional status, other books he or she has published, and similar information that helps to establish his or her authority. You can also look up an author in sources like *Contemporary Authors, Current Biography,* and *Who's Who.*

Check the Reliability of Your Source.   In evaluating a book, determine whether the publishing house is a respectable or familiar one. For a magazine, find out whether it is published by a particular interest group. Evaluation of a book could include reading some representative reviews to see how it was received when first published. Both the *Book Review Digest* and *Book Review Index* will help you locate reviews.

Check the Thoroughness of Research and Documentation of Sources.   If your source purports to be scholarly, well informed, or otherwise reliable, check to see how the evidence was gathered. Determine whether the source reports original research or other people's work and what facts or data support its conclusions. Look for references either at the end of chapters or in a separate section at the end of a book. Almost all journal articles and scholarly books document sources, whereas few magazine articles and personal accounts do. Also, consider how statistics and other data are used. Statistics are notoriously easy to manipulate, so check how the author uses them and confirm his or her fair interpretation.

EVALUATING INTERNET SOURCES

As with print sources, you must take care to evaluate any material you locate on the Internet before you use it in your paper. The Internet may pose more difficulty because its resources may offer fewer clues than a book or journal article might give. However, searching the Internet will turn up many useful sources, such as scholarly projects, reference databases, text files of books, articles in periodicals, and professional sites. You must apply the same sort of skills that you bring to critical reading when looking at an Internet website, particularly when searching for materials for a class assignment. You must ask a number of questions about the site before accepting and using materials that you locate on the Internet. Here is a list of questions that will help you evaluate Internet websites:

- **What do you know about the author of the site?** Is the author qualified to give information on the subject? Are the author's credentials, such as academic affiliation, professional association, or publications, easily verified? **Is the material on the website presented objectively, or does it reveal biases or prejudices?** The language used may be a clue, but probably the best way to discover a particular bias is to look at a great many sites (and other sources) on the same topic. When you understand the complexity of your topic and the variety of viewpoints on it, you should be able to determine whether a site is objective or subjective.

- **Is the information reliable?** Can you verify it? How does it compare with information you have learned from other sources? Does the site offer unique information, or does it repeat information that you can find at other sites?

- **How thoroughly does the website cover its topic?** Does it provide links to other sites for additional information? Does the site have links to related topics, and do those links work?

- **How accurate is the information?** This may be difficult to assess when you first begin your research, but the more you read about your topic and examine a variety of sources, the better able you will be to evaluate information accuracy.

- **When was the site last updated?** Is the information at the site current?

- **What is your impression of the visual effect of the site?** Are the graphics helpful or distracting, clear or confusing? Are words spelled correctly? Is the page organized well?

GUIDELINES: QUESTIONS TO ASK WHEN EVALUATING SOURCES

- ☐ Is the publication or site known to be fair, or does it have a bias or slant?
- ☐ Does the source seem one-sided, or does it try to cover all perspectives on an issue?
- ☐ Is the information current or outdated?
- ☐ Does the authority have respectable credentials?
- ☐ How reliable is the source?
- ☐ How thoroughly does the source cover its subject?
- ☐ Does the source offer adequate documentation for its information?
- ☐ If the source relies on research data, how was evidence gathered? Are statistics used fairly, or are they misrepresented?

TAKING NOTES

When you find an article, book, pamphlet, website, or other source you believe will be important or informative in your research, take notes from that source. There are several kinds of notes that you will take:

Summary.   A summary produces an objective restatement of a written passage in your own words. A summary is much shorter than the original work. Because its purpose is to highlight the central idea or ideas and major points of a work, make summary notes to record general ideas or main points of a large piece of writing—perhaps several pages, a chapter, or an entire article.

Paraphrase.   A paraphrase is a restatement of the words of someone else in your own words. Use paraphrasing when you want to use another writer's ideas but not the exact words, or to explain difficult material more clearly. Your own version of someone else's words must be almost entirely your own words. When incorporating paraphrased material into your research paper, you must be clear about when the paraphrased material begins and ends.

Direct Quotation.   A direct quotation is a record of the exact words of someone else. You will want to quote directly when the words are unique, colorful, or so well stated that you cannot fairly or accurately paraphrase them. Use direct quotations when you do not want to misrepresent what an author says or when the author makes a statement that you wish to stress or comment on. Use direct quotations sparingly and integrate them smoothly into your paper. Too many direct quotations in your paper will interrupt the flow of your own words.

Recording Source and Page Numbers.   Note taking is crucial to the success of your paper. You must take accurate and careful notes, reproducing an author's words exactly as they appear if you quote, completely restating the author's words if you paraphrase, and accurately capturing the essence of the material if you summarize. In any case, you will give a citation in your paper, so **you must record the source and page number for any notes.**

> **CAUTION**
>
> When taking notes, some students are tempted to write every detail as it appears in the original, thinking that they will paraphrase the material at some later time. They must then spend valuable time later rephrasing material when they should be concentrating on writing their papers, or else they take the easier route and use the direct quotations. The result may be a paper that is too full of direct quotations and lacking in effective paraphrases. Remember that you should quote directly only language that is particularly well expressed or material that you do not feel you can adequately restate in your own words. Your final paper should have far more paraphrases than direct quotations.

Where you record your notes does not matter, as long as you develop an efficient system. The important consideration is the accuracy and fairness of your notes. Traditionally, researchers used 4 × 6 inch cards because they are large enough to record ideas, summaries, quotations, or major points. When the note-taking part of the research ends, the researcher can shuffle the cards about, arranging them in the order that makes sense for the research paper. Some people like the note card system and work well with it, but most now prefer to use a computer as a more convenient way to record and store notes.

A computer can be very helpful for organizing and sorting notes. Most programs allow you to arrange your notes in numerical order. However, make sure to develop a filing system for your notes. If your program lets you create folders, you can keep your notes from different sources under specific headings, each with its own subheadings.

Place the subject heading at the beginning of your notes, and put the page number at the end. **Make sure that your notes clearly identify sources for all information.**

GUIDELINES FOR TAKING NOTES

- ☐ **Write the author's last name or title, if no author is named, and the page number from which the information is taken, if the source is paginated.** That is all the information you need, as long as you have a bibliography card or file for the source that lists complete bibliographic information.
- ☐ **Use subject headings as you take notes.** This labeling system will help you sort and arrange your notes when you write your paper.
- ☐ **Record only one idea or several small, related ones in each note.** This practice will help you organize your notes when you begin writing.
- ☐ **Place quotation marks before and after the material taken directly from a source.**
- ☐ **Don't rely on memory to determine whether words are identical to the original or paraphrased.**
- ☐ **Use notes to summarize.** A note may refer to an entire passage, an article, or a book, without giving specific details. Make a note to remind you that the information is a summary.
- ☐ **Use notes to record original ideas that occur to you while you are reading.** Make sure you identify your own ideas.

HANDLING SOURCE MATERIAL

Handling source material fairly, accurately, and smoothly is one of your main tasks in writing a successful research paper. More than likely, your instructor will evaluate your research project not only on how successfully you argue, explain, examine, or illustrate your topic but also on how skillfully you handle source materials. This means that you must take great care not only when you take notes but also when you transfer those notes into your paper. Always keep in mind that you must acknowledge the source for all borrowed material. Any information that you take from a source must be properly attributed to its author or, if no author, to its title. At the same time, you must not simply drop material into your text but be mindful of providing smooth integration of your source material into your own text.

After all, the text is your work: the thesis of the paper, the overall organization and development, transitions from point to point, general observations, and the conclusions are all yours. Your source materials serve to support, illustrate, develop, or exemplify your own words. Source materials must not interrupt the flow of your words or call attention to themselves. They are an important and integral part of your own paper.

Chapter 6 has detailed directions and summary guidelines for both paraphrasing source material and quoting directly. Chapter 6 also discusses some common tools for handling source material: ellipsis points, brackets, single quotation marks, and "qtd. in." The sample research paper located later in this chapter also gives examples of the correct handling of source material. The following guidelines highlight important points of the discussion of summarizing, paraphrasing, and quoting discussed in Chapter 6.

GUIDELINES FOR HANDLING SOURCE MATERIAL

☐ **Introduce or provide a context for quoted material.** "Dropped" quotations occur when you fail to integrate quotations smoothly into your text. The abrupt dropping of a quotation disrupts the flow of your text.

☐ **Name your authority or, when no author is named, use the title of the source.** Provide this information either in the text itself or in the parenthetical citation. Rely on standard phrases such as "one writer claims," "according to one expert," and the like to introduce quotations or paraphrases.

☐ **Use both first and last names of author at the first mention in your text.** After that, use just the last name. Always use last name only in parenthetical citations (unless you have sources by two authors with the same last name).

☐ **Acknowledge source material when you first begin paraphrasing.** Make sure you give some kind of signal to your reader when you begin paraphrasing borrowed material. This is particularly important if you paraphrase more than one sentence from a source. Otherwise, your reader will not know how far back the citation applies.

☐ **Quote sparingly.** Quote directly only those passages that are vividly or memorably phrased, so that you could not do justice to them by rewording them; those that require exact wording for accuracy; or those that need the authority of your source to lend credibility to what you are saying.

☐ **Intermingle source material with our own words.** Avoid a "cut-and-paste" approach to the research process. Remember that source materials serve primarily to support your generalizations. Never run two quotations together without some comment or transitional remark from you.

☐ **Make sure that direct quotations are exact.** Do not change words unless you use brackets or ellipses to indicate changes. Otherwise, be exact. For instance, if your source says "$2 million," do not write "two million dollars."

☐ **Make sure that paraphrases are truly your own words.** Do not inadvertently commit plagiarism by failing to paraphrase fairly.

AVOIDING PLAGIARISM

Giving proper credit to your sources is a crucial component of the research process. It is also one of the trickiest aspects of the process because it requires absolute accuracy in note taking. Many students have been disheartened by low grades on papers that took weeks to prepare, because they were careless or inaccurate in handling and documenting source materials.

Simply defined, **plagiarism** is borrowing another person's words without giving proper credit. The worst form of plagiarism is deliberately using the words or important ideas of someone else without giving any credit to that source. Handing in a paper someone else has written or copying someone else's paper and pretending it is yours are the most blatant and inexcusable forms of plagiarism, crimes that on some campuses carry penalties like automatic failure in the course or even immediate expulsion from school. Most student plagiarism is not deliberate, but rather results from carelessness either in the research process, when notes are taken, or in the writing process, when notes are incorporated into the student's own text. Even this unintentional plagiarism can result in a failing grade, however, especially if it appears repeatedly in a paper.

Keep the following standards in mind when you take notes on your source materials and when you write your research paper:

- **You commit plagiarism if you use the exact words or ideas of another writer without putting quotation marks around the words or citing a source.** The reader of your paper assumes that words without quotation marks or a source citation are your own words. To use the words of another without proper documentation suggests that you are trying to pass the words off as your own without giving credit to the writer.

- **You commit plagiarism if you use the exact words of another writer without putting quotation marks around those words, even if the paper cites the source of the material.** Readers assume that words followed by a parenthetical citation are paraphrased from the original—that is, that they are your own words and that the general idea was expressed by the author of the source material. Be especially carefully when you copy and paste from an Internet site: always use quotation marks around such material to remind yourself that they are the exact words.

- **You commit plagiarism if you paraphrase by changing only a few words of the original or by using the identical sentence structure of the original, with or without a source.** Again, readers assume that words without quotation marks followed by a parenthetical citation are your own words, not those of someone else. In a paraphrase, the *idea* is that of another; the *words* are your own.

- **You inaccurately handle source material when you use quotation marks around words that are not exactly as they appear in the original.** Readers assume that all words within quotation marks are identical to the original.

Obviously, accuracy and fairness in note taking are essential standards. Exercise care when you read your source materials and again when you transfer your notes to your final paper.

ILLUSTRATION: PLAGIARISM, INACCURATE DOCUMENTATION, AND CORRECT HANDLING OF SOURCE MATERIAL

The passage that follows is an excerpt from a reading in Chapter 10 of this book. Complete bibliographic information follows, as it would appear on your bibliography list and on the works-cited page of a research paper:

> Schilling, Heather. "The Anti-College Movement: Finding the Song in the Clamor." *Perspectives on Contemporary Issues: Reading across the Disciplines*. 8th ed., edited by Katherine Anne Ackley, Cengage, 2018, pp. 234–240.

Here is the passage:

One of the most compelling intangible benefits is something that critics of higher education have failed to consider and what colleges need to promote more: the transferrable skills that college students develop when they are deeply engaged in their education. These skills include collaboration, communication, time management, and structured independence, skills that carry into adulthood and manifest themselves in many ways. . . . Businesses want employees who possess collaborative skills and the ability to work through differences. While higher education does not necessarily measure graduates' abilities to collaborate or employ conflict resolution tactics, these transferrable skills are extremely important. . . . In the end, it is these transferable skills that separate college graduates from non-college graduates even further than the financial differences in income, and these immeasurable characteristics enable college graduates to enter the adult world prepared to interact successfully with colleagues and understand the importance of discovering work-life balance.

Now look at each of these sentences from a hypothetical research paper using information from the article. The commentary that follows identifies plagiarism, inaccurate handling of the source material, or correct handling of source material:

1. One of the most compelling intangible benefits of college is something that critics have failed to consider and what colleges need to promote more: the transferrable skills that college students develop when they are deeply engaged in their education.

[This is *plagiarism:* Put quotation marks around words taken directly from the original and name the source. Indicate omitted words with an ellipsis.

Correct: "One of the most compelling intangible benefits of college," notes Heather Schilling, "is something that critics . . . have failed to consider and what colleges need to promote more: the transferrable skills that college students develop when they are deeply engaged in their education" (238).]

2. According to Schilling, skills that students learn in college are collaboration, communication, time management, and structured independence (238).

[This is *plagiarism:* Put quotation marks around words taken directly from the original even when the source is named.

Correct: According to Schilling, college students learn "collaboration, communication, time management, and structured independence" (238).]

3. Business owners want to hire employees who know how to work collaboratively and are able to work through their differences (Schilling 238).

[This is *plagiarism:* Even though the source is cited, original words are changed only slightly and the original sentence structure is retained.

Correct: Businesses owners want employees with "collaborative skills and the ability to work through differences" (Schilling 238).]

4. Schilling points out that the skills students learned in college are what "separate them from those who didn't graduate even further than the financial differences in income" (238).

[This is *inaccurate documentation:* Words between quotation marks must be identical to the original. Use brackets to indicate a word or words added for clarification or to make the sentence read smoothly.

Correct: Schilling points out that skills students learned in college are what "separate [them] from non-college graduates even further than the financial differences in income" (238).]

5. In her article on the benefits of going to college, Schilling argues that it is the "intangible benefits" that help college graduates succeed by teaching them "to interact successfully with colleagues and understand the importance of discovering work-life balance" (238).

[This is **correct:** The text acknowledges the source and adequately paraphrases the general idea of the passage. Quotation marks enclose material taken directly from the original.]

Students are sometimes frustrated by these guidelines governing note taking and plagiarism, arguing that virtually everything in the final paper will be in quotation marks or followed by citations. But keep in mind that your final paper is a synthesis of information you have discovered in your research with your own thoughts on your topic, thoughts that naturally undergo modification, expansion, and/or revision as you read and think about your topic.

Probably half of the paper will be your own words. These words will usually include all of the introductory and concluding paragraphs, all topic sentences and transitional sentences within and between paragraphs, and all introductions to direct quotations. Furthermore, you need give no citation for statements of general or common knowledge, such as facts about well-known historical or current events. If you keep running across the same information in all of your sources, you can assume it is general knowledge.

GUIDELINES FOR AVOIDING PLAGIARISM

☐ **For direct quotations, write the words exactly as they appear in the original.** Put quotation marks before and after the words. Do not change anything.

☐ **For paraphrased material, restate the original thought in your own words, using your own writing style.** Do not use the exact sentence pattern of the original, and do not simply rearrange words. You have to retain the central idea of the paraphrased material, but do so in your own words.

☐ **When using borrowed material in your paper, whether direct quotations or paraphrases, acknowledge the source by naming the author or work as you introduce the material.** Doing so not only tells your reader that you are using borrowed material but also often provides a clear transition from your own words and ideas to the borrowed material that illustrates or expands on your ideas.

☐ Provide a parenthetical, in-text citation for any borrowed material. Give the author's last name if it is not mentioned in the text of the paper, followed by page number(s). If the source material is anonymous, use a shortened version of the title in place of a name.

☐ **Assemble all sources cited in your paper in an alphabetical list at the end of the paper.** This is your list of works cited, containing only those works actually used in the paper.

DOCUMENTING SOURCES

Follow the Appropriate Style Guidelines.   The examples of documentation and sample research papers that appear in this chapter all follow Modern Language Association (MLA) documentation style. That style governs because this textbook is often used in English courses, and English is located within the discipline of the humanities. However, your instructor may permit you to choose the style appropriate to the major field you intend to study. A section later in this chapter provides guidelines for writing a research paper using American Psychological Association (APA) style. That style is probably as commonly used as MLA in undergraduate course papers. In addition to MLA and APA, other frequently used documentation styles are the Council of Science Editors (CSE) and the Chicago Manual of Style (CMS). Following this summary of the chief differences among those four styles, the chapter lists stylebooks that give additional guidelines.

Style Guides.   To find full details on a particular documentation style, consult the following style guides:

MLA

Modern Language Association of America. *MLA Handbook for Writers of Research Papers.* 8th ed., MLA, 2016.

APA

American Psychological Association. *Publication Manual of the American Psychological Association.* 6th ed., APA, 2010.

CSE

Council of Science Editors. *Scientific Style and Format.* 8th ed., U of Chicago P, 2014.

CMS

University of Chicago Press Staff. *The Chicago Manual of Style.* 16th ed., U of Chicago P, 2010.

Turabian Kate L. *A Manual for Writers of Research Papers, Theses, and Dissertations.* 8th ed. Revised by Wayne C. Booth et al., U of Chicago P, 2013

SUMMARY OF DIFFERENCES AMONG DOCUMENTATION STYLES

☐ **MLA:** Used by writers in the many areas of the humanities (English, foreign languages, history, and philosophy); requires parenthetical in-text citations of author and page number that refer to an alphabetical list of works cited at the end of the paper.

☐ **APA:** Used by writers in the behavioral and social sciences (education, psychology, and sociology); requires parenthetical in-text citations of author and date of publication that refer to an alphabetical list of references at the end of the paper.

☐ **CSE:** Used by writers in technical fields and the sciences (engineering, biology, physics, geography, chemistry, computer science, and mathematics); requires either a name–year format or a citation–sequence format. The name–year format places the author's last name and the year of publication in parentheses, referring to an alphabetical list of references at the end of the paper.

☐ **CMS:** Used by some areas of the humanities, notably history, art, music, and theatre; requires a superscript number (for example,[1]) for each citation, all of which are numbered sequentially throughout the paper; no number is repeated. Numbers correspond either to footnotes at the bottoms of pages or a list of notes at the end of the paper. The first note gives complete information about the source, with shortened information for each subsequent reference to that source. A bibliography follows the notes, giving the same information, except for the page number, as in the first citation of each source. The information is also punctuated and arranged differently from the note copy. The Turabian book uses the same formatting style but is written specifically for college students.

Internet Citation Guides.   Many research resources, including guides for citing such sources, are available on the Internet. Your university librarian may have created a website where you will find the names of sites that give directions for citing electronic sources. Because Internet sites constantly change, URLs are not provided in the following list. You can locate the website by searching for the name. The ease of changing and updating Internet sites often means that they may have more current information than print guides offer. If you doubt the reliability and currency of a website, consult with your instructor about the advisability of using the site. Here are a few reliable sites that provide guidelines and models for finding and documenting sources. Many university libraries offer such services online:

- *Citing Primary Sources,* Library of Congress. Explains how to cite primary sources available online, such as films, music, maps, photographs, and texts. Covers MLA and Chicago styles.
- *Help with Citing Sources*, Indiana University. Covers MLA, APA, and Chicago.
- *MLA Style*, Modern Language Association of America. Includes list of frequently asked questions about MLA style.
- *Purdue Online Writing Lab, OWL,* covers both MLA and APA styles.

PARENTHETICAL DOCUMENTATION—CITING SOURCES IN THE TEXT

Recall from the discussion in Chapter 6 on documenting sources with in-text citations and the discussion in this chapter on taking notes that a crucial task of the researcher is to identify accurately sources for all borrowed material. This section expands the discussion from Chapter 6 with illustrations of treatments for several types of sources. It also includes guidelines for creating a list of works cited that incorporates a variety of sources, including electronic sources. These examples follow MLA guidelines as they appear in the *MLA Handbook,* eighth edition.

Parenthetical, In-Text Citations

Remember that you must name your source for any borrowed material. The parenthetical citation must give enough information to identify the source by directing your reader to the alphabetized list of works cited at the end of your paper. The citation should also give the page number or numbers, if available, on which the material appears.

Author–Page Format

MLA guidelines call for the author–page format when acknowledging borrowed material in the text of your paper. You must name the author (or source, if no author is named) and give a page number or numbers where the borrowed material appears in the source. The author's name or title that you give in your text directs readers to the correct entry in the works-cited list, so the reference must correspond to its entry on that list. Here are some examples:

Book or Article with One Author.   Author's last name and page number, without punctuation.
    (Smith 67)

Book or Article with Two Authors.   Both authors' last names followed by the page number.
    (Barrett and Rowe 78)

Note: Reproduce the names in the order in which they appear on the title page. If they are not listed alphabetically, do not change their order.

Book or Article with More Than Two Authors.   First author's last name followed by "et al." and page number.
    (Leitch et al. 29)

Article or Other Publication with No Author Named.   Short title followed by page number.
    ("Teaching" 10)

Note: When citing any source in a parenthetical reference in your text that appears on your works-cited list, use the full title if short or a shortened version. When using a shortened version, begin with the word by which the source is alphabetized.

Two Anonymous Articles Beginning with the Same Word.   Use the full title of each to distinguish one from the other.
    ("Classrooms without Walls" 45)   ("Classrooms in the 21st Century" 96)

Two Works by the Same Author.   Author's name followed by a comma, a short title, and the page number.
    (Heilbrun, *Hamlet's Mother* 123)   (Heilbrun, *Writing a Woman's Life* 35)

Works by People with the Same Last Name.   First and last names of author and page number.
    (Che White 16)

    Sources as they appear on the list of works cited:

    White, Che. "The Groundbreaking Musical *Rent.*" *Review of Contemporary Theatre,*
        vol.1, no.1, 2016, pp. 12–16.

    White, Jeremy. *Card Games You Never Knew Existed.* Leisure Games, 2016.

Exceptions to Author–Page Format Such as a Lecture or Television Program.   Many papers must accommodate some exceptions to the basic author–page parenthetical citation. For instance, for nonprint sources such as an Internet website, a lecture, a telephone conversation, a television documentary, or a recording, name the source in parentheses after the material without giving a page number:

("U.S. Technology in Iran")

Source as it appears on the list of works cited:

"U.S. Technology in Iran." Narrated by Lesley Stahl. *Sixty Minutes*, CBS, 21 Feb. 2016.

Citing an Entire Work.   You may want to refer to an entire work rather than just part of it. In that case, name the work and the author in the text of your paper, without a parenthetical citation:

Sir Arthur Conan Doyle's *Hound of the Baskervilles* features Watson to a much greater degree than do the earlier Holmes stories.

MLA suggests that this approach might be appropriate for Web publications with no pagination, television broadcast, movies, and similar works.

Citing a Work by a Corporate Author or Government Agency.   Cite the author's or agency's name, followed by a page reference, just as you would for a book or periodical article. However, if the title of the corporate author is long, put it in the body of the text to avoid an extensive parenthetical reference:

Testifying before a subcommittee of the U.S. House Committee on Public Works and Transportation, a representative of the Environmental Protection Agency argued that pollution from second-hand smoke within buildings is a widespread and dangerous threat (173–74).

Citing Internet Sources.   Works on the Web are cited just like printed works when citing sources in your text, that is, with author's name or short title if there is no author listed. A special consideration with Web documents is that they generally do not have fixed page numbers or any kind of section numbering. If your source lacks numbering, your parenthetical citation will give the author's last name if known, for example, (Plonsky), or the title if the original gives no author's name, for example, ("Psychology with Style"). If an author incorporates page numbers, section numbers, or paragraph numbers, you may cite the relevant numbers. Give the appropriate abbreviation before the numbers: (Plonsky, pars. 5–6). (*Pars.* is the abbreviation for *paragraphs.*) For a document on the Web, the page numbers of a printout should normally not be cited, because the pagination may vary in different printouts.

Remember that the purpose of the parenthetical citation is to indicate the location of the quotation or paraphrase in the referenced work and to point to the referenced work in the list of works cited. The entry that begins the reference in the works-cited list (that is, author's last name or title of work) is the same entry that should also appear in the parenthetical reference or in the body of the text.

GUIDELINES FOR PARENTHETICAL DOCUMENTATION

- ☐ **Name the source for all borrowed material,** including both direct quotations and paraphrases, either in your text or in parentheses following the borrowed material.

- ☐ **Give the citation in parentheses at the end of the sentence** containing the quotation or paraphrase.

- ☐ **In the parentheses, state the author's last name and the page number** or numbers from which you took the words or ideas, with no punctuation between the name and the page number.

- ☐ **When citing Internet or other sources such as television broadcasts, movies, or lectures that have no page numbers, use the author's last name in parentheses.** If you mention the author's name in your text, it is helpful to repeat it in the parenthetical citation as well, to indicate where the borrowed material ends, though MLA style does not require it.

- ☐ **For smooth transition to borrowed material, name the author or source as you introduce the words or ideas.** In that case, the parentheses will include only the page number or numbers.

- ☐ **At the first mention of an author in your text, use the author's full name.** Thereafter, use the last name only.

- ☐ **Create a page titled "Works Cited" at the end of your paper** that lists all sources quoted or paraphrased in the paper. Do not include any works that you consulted but did not directly use in your paper.

CREATING A WORKS-CITED PAGE USING MLA STYLE

The works-cited page of a research report lists in alphabetical order all the sources you cite in your paper. It comes at the end of your paper, beginning on a separate page.

Include an entry for every work quoted from, paraphrased, summarized, or otherwise alluded to in your paper. **Do not include on your list of works cited any sources you read but did not use in the paper.** You may want to include a list of works that informed your understanding of the topic but that you did not quote or paraphrase from in your final paper; to do so, create a separate page entitled "Works Consulted."

MLA guidelines emphasize flexibility and consistency in documentation in projects of any kind that require giving credit to borrowed material. Given the wide range of potential sources beyond traditional print and Web materials, such as television programs, videos, film, music, comic books, and other means of conveying information, the most helpful way of citing and documenting sources is to think of documentation as a series of core elements common across all kinds of sources. MLA guidelines provide a few principles that students can follow to document any borrowed material accurately and fairly. The goal is to make your documentation useful to readers, so the information you provide about your sources will include essential information that they can use to locate the sources themselves. The nine core elements for documenting all sources are the following. As MLA includes punctuation after each of the elements in its guide to illustrate which punctuation mark follows each element, those marks are included here. When documenting sources, begin with the first bulleted item and record any of the elements pertinent to your source in the order they are listed here:

- **Author(s) of the source,**
- **Title of the source,**
- **Container of the source,**
- **Other contributors,**
- **Version,**
- **Number,**
- **Publisher,**
- **Publication date,**
- **Location.**

Each of these elements is discussed below, with examples of how sources would look on a works-cited page. Most sources are unlikely to have all 9 elements, but you will record all of the elements that are relevant for each one.

See the examples in the previous section on documenting sources and those following as guides for documentation. For ease in locating the following examples, the numbers on this list correspond to the numbered illustrations which follow:

1. Source with one author
2. Source with two authors
3. Two works by the same author
4. Edited collection
5. Edited collection with two editors
6. Edited collection with more than two editors
7. Work with no author named
8. Book with subtitle
9. Story in a collection
10. Article in a journal
11. Article in a magazine
12. Television series or film
13. Episode in a television series
14. Article in a periodical

15. Article in a newspaper

16. Online article

17. Article contained in an online database

18. Movie contained in an online network

19. Introduction to a source

20. A translation

21. Edition of a book

22. Multivolume work

23. Quarterly journal article

24. Film or television series

25. Newspaper article, online

26. An entire website

27. Blog posting

28. Online source with DOI

29. Work by a corporate author

30. Congressional publication

31. Lecture

32. Letter

33. PDF file

34. Pamphlet

35. Sound recording

CORE ELEMENTS FOR DOCUMENTING SOURCES
Author of the Source

All sources whose authors are named begin with the author's last name, followed by a comma, and then the first name, followed by a period:

1. **Source with one author**

   Kolbert, Elizabeth. *The Sixth Extinction: An Unnatural History.* Henry Holt, 2015.

2. **Source with two authors**
   For a source with two authors, invert the first author's name, followed by the other author's name in normal order. List the names of the authors in the same order as they are listed on the title page, even if they are not in alphabetical order.

   Vaughn, Brian K., and Fiona Staples. *Saga.* Image Comics, 2012.

3. **Two works by the same author**
   For two works by the same author, list them in alphabetical order by title. For the second and subsequent books by the same author, type three hyphens followed by a period in place of the name.

   > Chabon, Michael. *Summerland.* Hyperion, 2011.
   > ———. *Telegraph Avenue: A Novel.* Harper, 2012.

4. **Edited collection with one author**
   Sometimes the person responsible for the work is not an author but rather an editor or some other person or persons who have produced the work. In that case, identify the role of the person, such as an editor.

   > Taylor, Helen, editor. *The Daphne du Maurier Companion.* Virago, 2007.

5. **Edited collection with two editors**
   For two editors, list the first editor's name in inverted order, followed by a comma, the word "and" and the second editor's name in normal order, followed by the word "editors."

   > Boyle, T.C., and Heidi Pitlar, editors. *The Best American Short Stories 2015.* Houghton Mifflin Harcourt, 2015.

6. **Edited collection with more than two editors**
   If more than two editors, list the first name in inverted order, a comma, the term "et al." ("and others"), followed by the word "editors."

   > Brandon, Lee, et al., editors. *Sentences, Paragraphs, and Beyond: With Integrated Readings.* Wadsworth, 2013.

7. **Work with no author named**
   If a work has no author named, begin your works-cited entry with the title of the work.

   > "Findings." *Harper's,* June 2016, p. 80.

Title of the Source

After the author's name, list the title of the source. If the source is self-contained, such as a book, a collection of essays, a play, or a film, italicize it. Include the subtitle after the main title.

8. **Book with subtitle**

   > Cummings, Claire Hope. *Uncertain Peril: Genetic Engineering and the Future of Seeds.* Beacon, 2008.

9. **Story in a collection**
   If the source is part of a larger container, such as a poem in a collection of poems or an essay in a collection of essays, place quotation marks around the title.

   > Erdrich, Louise. "The Big Cat." *The Best American Short Stories,* edited by T.C. Boyle and Heidi Pitlar, Houghton Mifflin Harcourt, 2015, pp. 72–81.

10. **Article in a journal**

The title of a periodical like a journal or magazine is italicized, while the title of the article is placed In quotation marks.

Nevens, Kate. "The Youth Are Revolting." *Harvard International Review,* vol. 34, no. 2, Fall 2015, pp. 32–35.

11. **Article in a magazine**

Alter, Charlotte. "Why America Needs More Female Cops." *Time,* 16 Nov. 2015, p. 25.

12. **Television series or film**

As with books and periodicals, television series and movie titles are italicized.

ER. Created by Michael Crichton, NBC, 1994–2009.
The Wizard of Oz. Directed by King Vidor et al., Warner Bros. Pictures, 1939.

Container of the Source

When the source being documented is part of a larger whole, think of the larger whole as the container. The title of the container is usually italicized, while the source itself is usually in quotation marks. In the previous section, the story in a collection and articles in a journal or magazine are all titles and in quotation marks, while their containers are italicized. Here are more examples:

13. **Episode in a television series**

"Haunted." *ER,* created by Michael Crichton, performance by Parminder Negra, season 15, episode 5, 30 Oct. 2008.

14. **Article in a periodical**

Nye, Joseph S. Jr. "The Decline of America's Soft Power." *Foreign Affairs,* May–June 2004, pp. 16+.

15. **Article in a newspaper**

Kingsolver, Barbara. "A Pure, High Note of Anguish." *Los Angeles Times,* 23 Sept. 2001, p. M1.

16. **Online article**

Benfey, Christopher. "The Alibi of Ambiguity." *The New Republic,* 7 June 2012, /newrepublic.com/article/103918/barbara-will-gertrude-stein-christopher-benfey.

17. **Article contained in an online database**

Sometimes the container of your source will be in a second container, for instance, a movie that you viewed on Netflix, an article collected in a reference database, or an online service offering full-text articles, such as *Questia.* In that case, add the relevant elements 3 through 9 after you provide information for your source.

Saey, Tina Hesman. "Editing Human Germline Cells Debated: New Techniques for Modifying Genes Raise Ethical Questions." *Science News,* 30 May 2015, pp. 16+. *Questia,* www.questia.com/read/1G1-416301739/editing-human-germline-cells-debated-new-techniques.

18. Movie contained in an online network

"Chapter 42." *House of Cards*. Season 4, episode 3, 4 Mar. 2016. *Netflix*, www.netflix.com/watch/80049214?trackId=13752289&tctx-=0%2C2%2C5b0f30b1-811a-40c6-8eae-cab155c4c935-11284855.

Other Contributors

Besides the author of a source, other people might have contributed to it, such as an editor, a translator, or someone who wrote an introduction for the source.

19. Introduction to a source

Green, Richard Lancelyn. Introduction. *The Adventures of Sherlock Holmes*, by Arthur Conan Doyle, edited by Richard Lancelyn Green, Oxford UP, 1994, pp. xi–xxxv.

20. A translation

Witten, Johann. "Letters to Christoph Witten, 3 December 1914, 5 December 1915, 9 September 1919, 18 September 1920." *News from the Land of Freedom: German Immigrants Write Home*. Translated by Susan Vogel, edited by Walter Kamphoefner, et al., Cornell UP, 1991, pp. 278–83.

Version

Some sources note that they have been issued in other forms or previous editions. If that is the case, indicate which version you are using.

21. Edition of a book

Symons, Julian. *Bloody Murder: From the Detective Story to the Crime Novel: A History*. 3rd edition, Pan Macmillan, 1992.

If a different publisher produced earlier editions, you have the option of naming the publisher and date for the other editions.

Symons, Julian. *Bloody Murder: From the Detective Story to the Crime Novel: A History*. Faber, 1972. Viking, 1985. Pan Macmillan, 1992.

Number

If your source is part of a numbered series, such as a multivolume work, indicate which volume you consulted. If it is a journal article with volume and issue number, include that information.

22. Multivolume Work

If you draw material from two or more volumes of a work, cite the total number of volumes in the entire work. When you refer to the work in the text of your paper, your parenthetical reference gives the volume number and page number.

Johnson, Edgar. *Charles Dickens: His Tragedy and Triumph*. Simon, 1952. 2 vols.

If you refer to only one volume of a multivolume work, state the number of that volume in the works-cited entry. Your parenthetical in-text citation supplies page number only, not volume and page.

> Johnson, Edgar. *Charles Dickens: His Tragedy and Triumph.* Vol. 2, Simon, 1952.

23. Quarterly journal article

> Sánchez-Moreno, Maria McFarland. "Winding Down the War on Drugs: Reevaluating Global Drug Policy." *Harvard International Review*, vol. 36, no. 4, Summer 2015, pp. 12–18.

Publisher

The publisher is often an organization or a business responsible for producing the source or making it available to the public.

> For books, look at the title page or the copyright page to locate the name of the publisher: Weir, Andy. *The Martian.* Crown, 2014.

24. Film or television show

For a film or television show, the publisher is generally the entity responsible for producing it.

> Scott, Ridley, director. *The Martian.* Twentieth Century Fox, 2015.

Publication Date

If your source was published at different times in different mediums, such as an online newspaper or magazine article that appeared in print earlier or later than the date on the website, list the date that is most relevant to your work. If you read the article online, list the date given there. If you read it in print, use that date.

25. Newspaper article, online

> Wilford, John Noble. "Malaria Is a Likely Killer in King Tut's Post Mortem." *New York Times*, 16 Feb. 2010, www.nytimes.com/2010/02/17/science/17tut.html?_r=0.

26. An entire website

If your source is a website as a whole, include the range of dates if it was developed over time.

> *The Purdue Online Writing Lab, (OWL).* 1995–2016, owl.english.purdue.edu/.

27. Blog posting

Blog postings, comments, and similar sources also record the time, so include that in your entry.

> Reynolds, Gretchen. "Exercise Makes Our Muscles Work Better With Age." *New York Times*, 30 Mar 2016, 5:45 a.m., well.blogs.nytimes.com/2016/03/30/exercise-makes-our-muscles-work-better-with-age/.

Location

Location of a source differs according to the type of source. In the examples of print sources noted in other elements, a page number or inclusive page numbers specify the location of the source. For online sources, the URL (with http:// deleted) or, if available, the DOI (digital object identifier), a series of digits, possibly with letters, that you precede with "doi:" in your works cited entry.

28. Online source with DOI

> Bourne, Matthew N. et al. "Eccentric Knee Flexor Strength and Risk of Hamstring Injuries in Rugby Union: A Prospective Study." *American Journal of Sports Medicine*, vol. 43, no. 11, Nov. 2015. Doi: 10.1177/0363546515599633.

Keeping in mind the nine elements that identify a source for readers, you can apply the principles of documenting sources for any number of different kinds of sources. The keyword is consistency. What follows are some miscellaneous sources that follow MLA guidelines for documentation.

29. Work by a corporate author

If the work is by a corporate author, such as a government document, or an agency report, begin with the corporate name. If it is a government agency, begin with the name of the government and then the name of the agency. If the corporate author and the publisher are different, begin with the corporate author's name, followed by the publisher's name. If the corporate author and the agency name are the same, begin with the title of the source, listing the name of the agency or organization as publisher. If two or more entries begin with the same government, use 3 hyphens for any of the names repeated in the previous entry.

> United States, Department of Justice. *A Guide to Disability Rights.* Department of Justice, Aug. 2014.

> ——, Department of Labor, Bureau of Labor Statistics. *Occupational Outlook Handbook, 2014–2015.* Government Printing Office, 12 Oct. 2016.

30. Congressional publications

For congressional publications, you may want to include the optional elements of the number and session of Congress, the chamber, and the type and number of the publication, if available.

> United States, Congress, Senate. *Limiting Certain Uses of the Filibuster in the Senate to Improve the Legislative Process.* Government Printing Office, 2015. 114th Congress, 1st session, Senate Resolution 20.

> ___, ___, House, Committee on Energy and Commerce. *Expressing he Sense of the House of Representatives that Gun Violence is a Public Health Issue.* Government Printing Office, 2015. 114th Congress, 1st session, House Resolution 289.

31. Lecture

> Chase, Carol. "The Role of First Responders in Medical Emergencies." Careers Club, Manchester High School, North Manchester (IN), 22 Dec. 2016.

32. **Letter**

> Webber, Jill. Letter to the author. 1 Oct. 2016. MS.

Note that *MS* represents a work prepared by hand. For machine-generated work, use *TS*, for typescript.

33. **PDF file**

> Ebrey, Patricia. *A Visual Sourcebook of Chinese Civilization: Cultural Revolution.* 26 Nov. 2001, depts.washington.edu/chinaciv/tg/tfront.pdf.

34. **Pamphlet**

> Tweddle, Dominic. *The Coppergate Helmet.* Cultural Resource Management, 1984.

35. **Sound recording**

List first the aspect of the recording you want to emphasize: composer, conductor, or performer. Give that name first, then the title of the recording or selection, the manufacturer, the year of issue (write *n.d.* if no date appears on the package or disc), and the medium (compact disc, audiotape, audiocassette). Do not enclose the name of the medium in italics or quotation marks.

> Uchida, Mitsuko, pianist. *Piano Sonatas in D,* KV. 284, *Sonata in B flat,* KV. 570, and *Rondo in D,* KV. 485. By Wolfgang Amadeus Mozart, Philips, 1986. CD.

GENERAL GUIDELINES FOR FORMATTING A LIST OF WORKS CITED

☐ Begin your list of cited works on a new page after the conclusion of your paper.

☐ Center the title "Works Cited" one inch from the top of the page.

☐ Continue the page numbers of the text, with a separate number for each of the Works-Cited pages.

☐ Alphabetize the list of sources.

☐ Begin the first line of each entry flush with the left margin. Indent the second and subsequent lines within each entry five spaces.

☐ Begin with the author's last name, followed by a comma and then the first name. For a source with two or more authors, invert only the first name. List the other name or names in normal order.

☐ Italicize the titles of books, journals, magazines, newspapers, and websites.

☐ Double-space within and between all entries.

☐ Place a period at the end of each entire entry.

Sample Works-Cited Pages.   Here is an alphabetized list of sources drawn from the examples on the previous pages, using a hypothetical student's last name.

White 15

Works Cited

Benfey, Christopher. "The Alibi of Ambiguity." *The New Republic*, 7 June 2012, newrepublic.com/article/103918 /barbara-will-gertrude-stein-christopher-benfey.

Bourne, Matthew N. et al. "Eccentric Knee Flexor Strength and Risk of Hamstring Injuries in Rugby Union: A Prospective Study." *American Journal of Sports Medicine*, vol. 43, no. 11, Nov. 2015. Doi: 10.1177/0363546515599633.

Erdrich, Louise. "The Big Cat." *The Best American Short Stories*, edited by T.C. Boyle and Heidi Pitlar, Houghton Mifflin Harcourt, 2015, pp. 72–81.

"Findings." *Harper's*, June 2016, p. 80.

Kingsolver, Barbara. "A Pure, High Note of Anguish." *Los Angeles Times,* 23 Sept. 2001, p. M1.

Kolbert, Elizabeth. *The Sixth Extinction: An Unnatural History*. Henry Holt, 2015.

Nye, Joseph S. Jr. "The Decline of America's Soft Power." *Foreign Affairs*, May–June 2004, pp. 16+.

Sánchez-Moreno, Maria McFarland. "Winding Down the War on Drugs: Reevaluating Global Drug Policy." *Harvard International Review*, vol. 36, no. 4, Summer 2015, pp. 12–18.

Symons, Julian. *Bloody Murder: From the Detective Story to the Crime Novel: A History*. 3rd edition, Pan Macmillan, 1992.

"U.S. Technology in Iran." Narrated by Lesley Stahl. *Sixty Minutes*, CBS, 21 Feb. 2016.

ASSEMBLING THE PARTS OF A RESEARCH PAPER

In general, putting a research paper together is not so different from writing any other kind of paper. Following the guidelines explained in Chapter 2 on the writing process, you will have the same components in a longer paper with sources as you do in a shorter one. You will have an introduction, though it is likely to be longer than in other writing assignments. You must have a thesis statement or clearly evident central idea. Your paper as a whole and individual paragraphs within it must be organized and fully developed. Sentences must be crafted grammatically and imaginatively, and your language should be idiomatic, colorful, and clear. You must provide transitions between points within paragraphs and from paragraph to paragraph throughout the paper, and you must have a conclusion that brings the paper to a satisfactory finish. Of course, a major difference between the research paper and other papers you will write for your college classes is that research papers incorporate the works of others. Thus, you will have in-text citations for all references to your sources and a work-cited list of all sources referenced in your paper. Your instructor may also ask you to include an outline of your paper.

The following sections will take you through the process of putting together your final paper. They address the following components:

- First page of paper without a separate title page
- Title page
- First page of a paper with a separate title page
- Pagination and spacing
- Tables, figures, and illustrations
- Outline page
- Introductory paragraph
- Body of the paper
- Conclusion
- Works Cited page
- The complete research paper

First Page of a Research Paper without a Separate Title Page.   If your instructor tells you that your research paper does not need a separate title page, follow these guidelines:

- Type your last name and the number 1 in the upper right-hand corner, one-half inch from the top of the page, flush with the right margin.
- Place your name, your instructor's name, the course title and section, and the date in the upper left-hand corner, one inch from the top of the paper and flush with the left margin.

- Double-space between each line.
- Double-space below the date and center your title.
- Do not italicize your title, enclose it in quotation marks, capitalize every letter, or place a period after it.
- Capitalize the first letter of every important word in the title.
- Double-space again and begin the body of your paper.

Nate Hayes

Professor White

English 102–8

15 April 2017

A Positive Alternative to Cloning

Since Dr. Ian Wilmut's successful cloning of a sheep in 1996, the debate over how far medical science should be allowed to go has grown increasingly heated. Some people are completely opposed to any kind of experimentation that involves genetic manipulation or the development of procedures that some consider should be reserved only for God.

Title Page.   Many instructors ask for a separate title page, especially if your research project is lengthy. If your instructor requires a title page, follow these guidelines:

- Center your title about one-third to halfway down the page.
- Do not italicize your title, enclose it in quotation marks, capitalize every letter, or place a period after it.
- Capitalize the first letter of every important word in the title.
- Underneath the title, about halfway down the page, write your name, centered on the line.
- Drop farther down the page and center on separate lines, double spaced, your instructor's name; the course name, number, and section; and the date.

Arthur of Camelot: The Once and Future King

by

Shawn Ryan

Professor Zackary

English 102–21

22 Apr. 2017

First Page of a Research Paper with a Separate Title Page.   If your instructor requires a separate title page, follow these guidelines for the first text page of your paper:

- Type your last name and the number 1 in the upper right-hand corner, one-half inch from the top of the page, flush with the right margin.
- Drop down two inches from the top of the page and center your title, exactly as it appears on your title page.
- Do not italicize your title, enclose it in quotation marks, capitalize every letter, or place a period after it.
- Capitalize the first letter of every important word in the title.
- Double-space and begin the body of your paper.

Ryan 1

Arthur of Camelot: The Once and Future King

North and west the wind blew beneath the morning

sun, over endless miles of rolling grass and far scattered

thickets . . . [and] Dragonmount, where the dragon had

died, and with him, some said, the Age of Legend—where

prophecy said he would be born again. (Jordan 13)

GRAPH I *Males vs. Females: Free Time Activities*

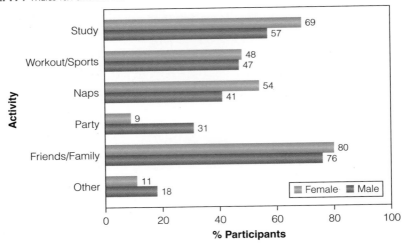

Source: Survey conducted by Margo Borgen, Morris Boyd, Maicha Chang, and Kelly Kassien, University of Wisconsin–Stevens Point, May 2016.

Pagination and Spacing.   The entire paper should be double-spaced, with each page numbered in the upper right-hand corner, one-half inch from the top and flush with the right margin. Begin with page 1 and include your last name before the page number.

Graphs, Figures, and Illustrations.   Place graphs, tables, figures, and illustrations close to the parts of the paper that they relate to.

Graph.   A graph is labeled *Graph*, given an Arabic number, and captioned. This information is capitalized as you would a title. **Place the label and caption above the graph on separate lines.** Place the label first, above the caption, flush with the left margin. Under it, place the caption flush with the left margin. Directly below the graph, place the name of the source and any additional comments, as illustrated here:

Figures and Illustrations.   Visual images such as photographs, charts, maps, and line drawings are labeled *Figure* (usually abbreviated *Fig.*), assigned an Arabic number, and given a title or caption. A label and title or caption are positioned **below the illustration and have the same margins as the text.** The following illustrates correct handling of a visual image:

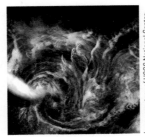

FIG. I *Whirlpool in the Air: a spinning formation of ice, clouds, and low-lying fog off the eastern coast of Greenland.*

Image courtesy of USGS National Center for EROS and NASA Landsat Project Science Office

Outline Page.   If your instructor requires a formal outline, place it immediately after the title page. Your instructor will tell you how detailed your outline should be, but follow these basic directions in most cases:

- Begin your outline with the thesis statement of your paper.
- Double-space between all lines of the outline.
- If your instructor requires a topic outline, use only short phrases or key words. If your instructor requires a sentence outline, write complete sentences.
- Use uppercase roman numerals (I, II, III) for each major division of your outline and capital letters (A, B, C) for each subdivision under each major division.
- If you find it necessary to further subdivide, use Arabic numerals (1, 2, 3) under capital letters and lowercase letters (a, b, c) under Arabic numerals.
- Number the outline page(s) with lowercase roman numerals (i, ii, iii, iv) placed in the upper right-hand corner, one-half inch from the top of the page and flush with the right margin. Include your last name.
- End with a statement summarizing your conclusion.

Here is a sample topic outline page from a student paper.

Ryan i

Outline

Thesis: An examination of some of the research on Arthurian legend suggests that the evidence supports the theory that a man like Arthur did exist.

  I. The birth of Arthur

      A.   The legend

      B.   Evidence of Tintagel

  II. The places and people most important to Arthur

      A.   Camelot

      B.   Glastonbury Abbey

      C.   Lancelot and Perceval

III. Arthur's impact on society

    A.   His image

    B.   The difference between the man and the legend

Conclusion: Arthur's existence as a man is indeterminable, but Arthur's presence in the minds and hearts of people everywhere gives credence to his existence as a leader of nations.

Introductory Paragraphs.   As for any other kind of writing assignment, begin with an introduction that provides background information that presents the topic of your paper or the direction your argument will take, or that in some way sets the stage for what follows. State your thesis or central idea early in the paper. If your topic is controversial, explain the nature of the controversy.

Body of the Paper.   Once you have introduced your topic sufficiently, begin developing your position or central idea, following the guidelines for developing your central idea detailed in Chapter 2. The body of your research paper will contain not only your argument, findings, or views but also supporting evidence from primary or secondary sources. Follow the guidelines for paraphrasing and quoting described earlier in this chapter and in Chapter 6.

Conclusion.   Recall from Chapter 2 that the conclusion brings the paper to a satisfying end, no matter what its length. Whether the assignment is a 500-word essay or a 5,000-word research paper, readers should not be left with unanswered questions and should have a sense that the writer has fully explained, argued, developed, or illustrated the central idea or thesis. A good conclusion forcefully reiterates the introduction, reinforces the writer's connection with the audience, looks to the future, reemphasizes the central argument, or suggests a course of action.

Works-Cited Page.   This is the last page of your research paper. Begin the list on a new page, continuing the pagination from the text of your paper. Place the page number in the upper right-hand corner, half an inch from the top, flush with the right margin just as you do for the rest of the paper. Follow the guidelines discussed in the section "General Guidelines for Creating a List of Works Cited."

STUDENT RESEARCH PAPER USING MLA STYLE

The following student research paper implements MLA style guidelines for incorporating and documenting source material as explained in Chapters 6 and 7. Marginal notes point out various components of the research paper.

Schilling 1

Elizabeth Schilling

Music and Politics in China

Dr. Cheng

17 November 2017

Then and Now:

Comparing Revolutionary and Modern Ballet

China has a long history of viewing women as second-class citizens. Historically, the male dominated culture expected women to serve men, often as slaves or concubines. Typically, artistic endeavors, including opera, ballet, creative writing, and art, perpetuated these traditional roles of women, creating compliant female characters who rarely challenged their male counterparts. The ballet, still valued and cherished by Chinese citizens of all socio-economic levels, especially created a canvas for developing cultural expectations. Though interactions with Western culture since the 1960s have helped modernize the way that Chinese society views women and their roles, artists seem unhurried to incorporate these changes to the stage. Despite changes within Chinese society since the Cultural Revolution, modern Chinese ballet continues to reflect the traditional attributes of female characters and to rely on revolutionary plots.

After the Great Leap Forward in the 1950s, Mao Zedong's power and popularity began to dissipate

Elizabeth's opening paragraph gives background information as a context for her central idea, stated in the last sentence.

Schilling 2

because of his failure to modernize the economic system of China. Because Mao feared that the new leaders would take the State in the wrong direction, he instigated the Cultural Revolution to maintain his influence over the State and its citizens (Trueman). As Patricia Ebrey explains in *Sourcebook of Chinese Civilization*, "The aim of the Cultural Revolution was to attack the Four Olds—old ideas, old culture, old customs, and old habits—in order to bring the areas of education, art and literature in line with Communist ideology" (Ebrey). To align society with his philosophy, Mao completely overhauled the Chinese culture. The Communist regime deemed non-supporters of Mao's views and the values of the State as "[enemies] of the party and people" (Ebrey). In order to avoid persecution or arrest, Chinese citizens complied with the government's mandates. Ultimately, the Cultural Revolution affected the arts so strongly that for a period of time there was absolutely no music in China. Eventually, Mao's wife, Jiang Qing, fostered the production of eight "Model Operas" that applied the acceptable revolutionary themes and were performed continuously with mandatory attendance (Ebrey). Even though Mao's policies ended long ago, modern Chinese ballets still rely on strong elements of the "Model Eight" (Mittler 380). Nowhere is this more evident than in the ties between the late 1950s ballet *The White-Haired Girl* and the 1990s ballet *Raise the Red Lantern*.

Although the source is named in her text, Elizabeth repeats the author's name in the parenthetical citation. There are no page numbers for her Web source

Elizabeth's second paragraph continues to give background information but narrows the focus.

Schilling 3

The sentence beginning "Nowhere is this more evident" specifies how she will support her more general statement at the end of paragraph one.

A basic similarity between *The White-Haired Girl* and *Raise the Red Lantern* can be seen in the progression of the protagonist in each ballet. J. Norman Wilkinson explains this common thread by noting that *The White-Haired Girl* revolves around the story of a young girl, His-erh, who is forced to work for a landlord who treats her brutally and eventually sells her into prostitution. Though the audience believes that she has died, they later discover that she has actually escaped to the wilderness. Because she has no food and little sunlight, her hair turns white, so other characters think that she is haunting the area. Eventually, some army men find her, one of whom is her former lover. Together they bring justice to the landlord, and she fights so that others can earn the rights that she has attained (169-72).

The author Wilkinson is named at the beginning of a series of sentences paraphrasing the source, ending with a direct quotation.

Raise the Red Lantern, adapted from the movie in 1991, is also about a young girl, Songlian. The ballet version begins with her moving into her master's home. As a concubine she has difficulties adjusting, struggling the first time that she is called to the dominating man's bedroom and feeling jealous of the other "top" mistresses. During her time there, she has a secret affair with her former lover. An envious fellow concubine sees them and tells their master; as a result, all three people are executed. Before they die, though, the two concubines forgive each other (*Raise the Red Lantern*).

The source is a film version of the ballet that Elizabeth summarizes.

Schilling 4

While they take place during different time periods, the two ballets share a similar theme. Each portrays the story of a woman owned by a man, one as a servant, the other as a mistress. To better the status of their families, both are placed in miserable and emotionally devastating positions. As strong women, both rebel against conforming to what is expected of them; they fight oppression from beginning to end. Although Songlian's master kills her and His-erh defeats her master, both women are eager for a true, free love with the man they have selected, not an arranged relationship. The real difference between the two female characters lies in the fact that Songlian does not get the chance to escape with her lover before she is caught and sentenced to death, while His-erh escapes and eventually lives to find her "true love" again and bring revenge upon her master.

All of this paragraph is in Elizabeth's own words, so no source is cited.

Even though decades have passed since the first of the "Model Eight" operas was performed, modern ballets reflect similar themes, explicitly demonstrating the lasting impact of the Cultural Revolution on the arts. *The White-Haired Girl*, one of the most respected pieces of the revolutionary era, played continuously for decades in a variety of formats. First performed as a ballet in 1958, composers modified the piece many times into appropriate revolutionary versions, removing a pregnancy as a result of rape and adding militant features (Wilkinson 171).

Schilling 5

In a similar manner, *Raise the Red Lantern* has undergone modification: Songlian is killed by her master in an ending that would never have appeared during the Cultural Revolution because it is not ideal for the "hero."

A main revolutionary aspect in *The White-Haired Girl* is its direct military features, fully embodying all the pomp and circumstance of a militant regime. "It is on this high and militant note that the ballet ends," Wilkinson notes (172). During the Cultural Revolution this ending would have had a strong effect on the Chinese citizens. According to Elizabeth Urban in her undergraduate thesis, *The White-Haired Girl* is considered one of the eight-model works because of its strong revolutionary themes (18). These themes encompass ideas from Mao's Yen'an Forum speech:

> There is absolutely no such thing in the world as love or hatred without reason or cause. As for the so-called love of humanity, there has been no such all- inclusive love since humanity was divided into classes. . . . There will be genuine love of humanity—after classes are eliminated all over the world. Classes have split society into many antagonistic groupings; there will be love of all humanity when classes are eliminated, but not now. We cannot love enemies, we cannot love social evils; our aim is to destroy them. (Wang)

One sees the application of Mao's words in *The White-Haired Girl*: His-erh and her landlord come from

Schilling 6

opposite ends of the societal spectrum and she is his property. Placed in this subservient and demeaning role, she can neither love him nor respect him, and yet it is her duty to serve him, sacrificing her own feelings. This theme also applies to the more recent ballet *Raise the Red Lantern* in which the protagonist, Songlian, finds herself in a similar submissive role as a mistress. The presence of revolutionary themes in both of these ballets demonstrates that, despite their differences, modern audiences desire and approve of revolutionary themes, perhaps because of the sense of security that tradition provides.

Each of the female characters strongly represents the masses, as well. In *The White-Haired Girl,* His-erh embodies the peasants as she rebels against the ruling social class. Similarly, as Paul Coughlin explains, Songlian of *Raise the Red Lantern* represents the inhibited masses, as a woman owned by a man; when she continually tries to rebel, she is further repressed and eventually killed (129). This contemporary ballet portrays revolutionary themes, fully representing the oppressed. The revolutionary theme runs deep in both of these popular ballets, illustrating the strong relationship between the two.

One can see that there are many similarities between the roles of the female characters in the two

Here, Elizabeth names her source, paraphrases information from it, and includes the page number after the paraphrase.

Schilling 7

ballets. The protagonists are both young women who make sacrifices for their families and must leave what they know to live with a man who treats them badly. According to Richard King, "The story [*The White-Haired Girl*] is not structured around her (His-erh), but around the ownership of her" (194). This statement could easily apply to the main character of *Raise the Red Lantern*. The strongest tie between the two heroines is their representation of the masses and the ways in which they demonstrate bravery. Even though the two ballets are from different time periods, their female central characters continue to serve as role models for Chinese women.

Elizabeth supplies explanatory information in brackets.

While the Cultural Revolution ended decades ago, it certainly had a lasting effect on the themes, plots and traits of the female characters of modern Chinese compositions no matter what their genre. Two prominent ballets, from time periods thirty years apart, fully demonstrate this heavy-handed influence. By recognizing the similarities and differences in character traits and noticing trends in revolutionary themes, one can see that *The White-Haired Girl* and *Raise the Red Lantern* are quite similar. With strong female characters, the ballets present Chinese audiences with the very models of the perfect Chinese woman that they desired.

Elizabeth's conclusion summarizes the main points of her paper.

Works Cited

Ebrey, Patricia. *A Visual Sourcebook of Chinese Civilization: Cultural Revolution*. 26 Nov. 2001, depts.washington. edu/chinaciv/tg/tfront.pdf.

Coughlin, Paul. "Iron Fists and Broken Spirits: Raise the Red Lantern as Allegory." *Screen Education*, vol. 36, Spring 2004, pp. 125–31.

King, Richard, editor. *Art in Turmoil: the Chinese Cultural Revolution, 1966–76*. UBC Press, 2010.

Mittler, Barbara. "Eight Stage Works for 800 Million People: The Great Proletarian Cultural Revolution in Music—A View from Revolutionary Opera." *The Opera Quarterly*, vol. 26, nos. 2–3, 2010, pp. 377–401.

Raise the Red Lantern (Ballet drama). Directed by Zhang Yimou, National Project for the Distillation of the Stage Arts, 2005. DVD.

Trueman, Chris. "The Cultural Revolution." *History Learning Site,* 3 Mar. 2016, www.historylearningsite. co.uk/modern-world-history-1918-to-1980/ china-1900-to-1976/the-cultural-revolution/.

Urban, Elizabeth C. "The Evolution of Revolution: The Dilemma of Censorship and Fifth Generation Filmmakers." Honors College thesis 88, Pace University, 2010. *Digital Commons, digitalcommons.pace.edu/ honorscollege_theses/88/*

Schilling 9

Wang, Rujie. "Lecture Notes: 'The White Haired Girl.'

"Chinese 220, Fall 2011. The College of Wooster,

Wooster, OH.

Wilkinson, J. Norman. "'The White-Haired Girl': From

'Yangko' to Revolutionary Modern Ballet." *Educational*

Theatre Journal, vol. 26, 1974, pp. 164–74.

WRITING A RESEARCH PAPER USING APA STYLE

The documentation style of the APA, also referred to as the *author–date system,* is used widely in the behavioral and social sciences. Its style differs from that of the MLA, used primarily in the humanities, in some significant ways. APA style cites sources in parenthetical notes in the sentences to which they refer, as does MLA style, but the contents of the notes differ. In the APA system, the year of publication is given in the parenthetical note, and page numbers are given only for quotations, not for paraphrases. Finally, sources are listed at the end of the paper on a page called *References* rather than *Works Cited,* and formatting for that page is quite different from formatting in MLA style. This section gives general guidelines for both parenthetical citations and composing a references page using APA style. The guidelines are accompanied by sample pages from a student research paper using APA documentation style. For complete guidelines on APA Style, consult the following book:

> American Psychological Association. *Publication Manual of the American Psychological Association.* 6th ed. Washington: APA, 2010.

For the latest updates on APA Style, go to the official website of the American Psychological Association, located at www.apastyle.org.

PARENTHETICAL CITATIONS USING APA STYLE

Quotations.

- Include the author's last name, a comma, the year the work was published, another comma, and the page number, preceded by the abbreviation *"p."* or *"pp.":*

    Many experts agree that "it is much easier and more comfortable to teach as one learned" (Chall, 2014, p. 21).

- If the source has two authors, name them both, and separate their names with an ampersand (&):

  > President Truman and his advisors were aware that the use of the bomb was no longer required to prevent an invasion of Japan by the Soviets (Alperovitz & Messer, 2012).

- Omit from the parenthetical citation any information given in the text:

  > Samuel E. Wood and Ellen R. Green Wood (2014a) note that sociobiologists believe that social and nurturing experiences can "intensify, diminish, or modify" personality traits (p. 272).

- If the author's name is given in the text, follow it with the year of publication in parentheses:

  > Nancy Paulu (2013) believes that children who are taught phonics "get off to a better start" than those who are not taught phonics (p. 51).

- For works with three to five authors, name all of the authors the first time you refer to the work, but give only the last name of the first author followed by "et al." in subsequent citations. For a work with six or more authors, give only the first author's last name, followed by "et al." for all citations, including the first.

- If the author's name is repeated in the same paragraph, it is not necessary to repeat the year. However, if the author is cited in another paragraph, give the year of the work again.

- For summaries and paraphrases, give author and year, but not the page number where the information appears:

  > Minnesota scientists have concluded that this data shows that genes are more influential than nurture on most personality traits (Bazell, 2007).

- If the source names no author, cite a short form of the title:

The twins were both born with musical abilities, but their unique experiences determined whether they acted on this ability ("How Genes Shape Personality," 2007).

Note: The first letter of each word in the short title is capitalized, but in the references list, only the first letter of the first word is capitalized.

- If you use two or more sources by the same author and they were published in the same year, add lowercase letters to refer to their order on the references page:

  > Wood and Wood (2014a) observe that . . .
  > Other authorities (Wood & Wood, 2015b) agree, pointing out that . . .

- If one of your sources quotes or refers to another, and you want to use the second source in your paper, use the words "cited in," followed by the source you read and the year the source was published. If you quote directly, give the page number of the source you read on which the quotation appeared:

  > Gerald McClearn, a psychologist and twin researcher at Pennsylvania State University, explained personality development realistically when he said:
  > " 'A gene can produce a nudge in one direction or another, but it does not

directly control behavior. It doesn't take away a person's free will' " (cited in "How Genes Shape Personality," 2007, p. 62).

- To cite electronic material, indicate the page, chapter, figure, table, or equation at the appropriate point in the text. Give page number(s) for quotations, if available. If the source does not provide page numbers, use paragraph number if available, preceded by the paragraph symbol or the abbreviation para. If neither page number or paragraph number is visible, cite the heading and the number of the paragraph so that the reader can locate the material at the website:

> (Merriwether2016, p. 27)
> (Johnson2015, para. 3)
> (Shaw, 2016, conclusion section, para. 1)

Abstract.   Papers written in APA style often have an abstract, which succinctly summarizes its important points, instead of an outline. Here is the abstract of the paper by a group of students who surveyed classmates on various study and leisure-time patterns to discover whether biological sex has an influence on academic achievement:

Effect of Biological Sex on Grades

Abstract

Can differences in academic achievement be explained on the basis of biological sex? We hypothesized that sex is not the dominating factor influencing the success of University of Wisconsin–Stevens Point (UWSP) students. We conducted a survey of 108 college students, investigating their pastimes, study habits, work schedules and housing status in addition to their grade point averages (GPA). The data showed a small difference in GPAs with respect to sex, but not large enough for sex alone to be the deciding factor. Our hypothesis that sex alone does not account for academic success was proved. We found that other factors, such as length of time spent studying, the number of hours of work per week, and time spent partying, all play significant roles as well.

APA-STYLE REFERENCES LIST

- Bibliographic entries for all works cited in a paper are listed in alphabetical order on a page entitled *References*.

- After the first line of each entry, use a hanging indentation of five spaces.

- Give the last names and only the initials of the first and middle names of authors.

- The year of publication, in parentheses, follows the author's name. If the source is a periodical, include month after the year.

- For a book, capitalize only proper nouns and the first word of the title and subtitle; italicize the title. Indicate location and publisher. For location, include both city and state, using the two-letter postal abbreviation for the state. If the publisher is foreign, name city and country.

- If a book is edited, place the abbreviation "Ed." or "Eds." in parentheses after the name(s) of the editor(s).

- If a citation names two or more authors, each name is reversed and an ampersand (&), not the word *and*, is placed before the last name.

- For an article, book chapter title, or title of an essay in a collection, capitalize as for a book title (see above) and do not use quotation marks or italicize.

- Capitalize the first letters of all important words in the name of the periodical and italicize it.

- Use the abbreviations "p." and "pp." for inclusive page numbers of articles in newspapers, but not in magazines and journals. If volume number is given for a periodical, place it after the name of the periodical and italicize it. If an issue number is also given, place it in parentheses after the volume number, but do not italicize it.

- If two or more works by the same author appear on the references list, put them in chronological order. Repeat the author's name each time, followed by the date in parentheses.

- If you cite two works of one author published in the same year, alphabetize them by title, and give each entry a lowercase letter: (2016a), (2016b).

- Words like "university" and "press" are spelled out, not abbreviated.

Below is a sample reference list:

References

Harnois, C. E. (2015). Race, ethnicity, sexuality, and women's political consciousness of gender. *Social Psychology Quarterly, 78* (4), 365–386.

Hopper, G. (2015). *Art, education, and gender: The shaping of female ambition.* New York, NY: Palgrave Macmillan.

Huang, C. (2014). Gender differences in academic self-efficacy: A meta-analysis. *European Journal of Psychology of Education, 28* (1), 1–35.

Immordino-Yang, M. H. (2016). *Emotions, learning, and the brain: Exploring the educational implication of affective neuroscience.* New York, NY: Norton.

Nye, J. R. (2015). Is the American century over? *Political Science Quarterly, 130* (3), 393–400.

Weis, M., Heikamp, T, & Tromsdorff, G. (2013). Gender differences in school achievement: The role of self-regulation. *Frontiers in Psychology,* 4, 442–52. Retrieved from http://www.ncbi.nlm.nih.gov/pmc/articles/PMC3713251/

SAMPLE PAGES FROM A STUDENT RESEARCH PAPER USING APA STYLE, WITH TITLE PAGE, ABSTRACT, BODY OF PAPER, AND REFERENCES

Here are sample pages, with marginal comments, of a student research paper illustrating in-text citations using APA style. The first several pages of the paper are given, along with the concluding paragraph and list of references.

Indicate what your running head is by writing the words "Running head" followed by a colon and title of article.

All pages are numbered, beginning with the first or cover page.

Running Head: USING READERS' THEATER TO DEVELOP FLUENCY IN STUDENTS WITH LEARNING DISABILITIES   1

Using Readers' Theater to Develop Fluency in Students with Learning Disabilities

Clorinda Tharp

Manchester University

Abstract

Successful readers must master reading fluency, which includes accuracy, automaticity, and prosody. The

Drop halfway down the page, center the information, and write your title on one line, name on the next, and academic affiliation on the third line.

Following the cover page, write your abstract. Include running head and page number.

Keywords highlight essential components of the paper and give readers important clues about the content of the paper.

repeated reading strategy, sometimes used to help develop fluency in young children, lacks motivation for students to reread a text several times. Readers' theater, however, combines the repeated reading strategy with an authentic performance, which research suggests is an excellent strategy for developing fluency for all types of learners, including those with disabilities. Research shows that performing motivates students to read more and promotes success. All ages and levels of readers can benefit from the use of readers' theater because teachers and students can alter the scripts to meet the needs of each student. Motivation, however, has ultimately made readers' theater the most successful at improving students' fluency.

Keywords: readers' theater, fluency, repeated reading, motivation, disabilities

Running head, in caps, appears on all pages. Repeat title, upper and lower cased, at the beginning of your paper, even though the running head is on the page.

USING READERS' THEATER TO DEVELOP FLUENCY IN STUDENTS WITH LEARNING DISABILITIES   2

Using Readers' Theater to Develop Fluency in Students with Learning Disabilities

Characterized by the ability to read quickly and accurately, good readers must master reading fluency. When good readers pick up books, their fluency allows them to read with accuracy, automaticity, and prosody, ultimately leading to better comprehension of the

USING READERS' THEATER TO DEVELOP FLUENCY IN
STUDENTS WITH LEARNING DISABILITIES   3

Clorinda's opening paragraphs provide background information to give a context for her research.

text. For quite awhile, teachers have recognized the importance of fluency, characterized by reading quickly and accurately, but unfortunately, they often ignore the importance of prosody. Prosody refers to the expression and phrasing one uses while reading orally or silently. A student with a disability may assume that good readers merely read quickly; thus, he or she may compete with others in the class to finish reading a book first. However, this strategy lacks the other key component of fluency, prosody. If a student lacks the ability to incorporate expression in his or her reading, then he or she may not fully comprehend the text. Additionally, a student with a disability may not even try to improve his or her fluency and reading skills due to a lack of motivation and repeated failure. Fortunately, readers'

Clorinda's thesis

theater provides an excellent strategy for developing fluency for all types of learners, including those with disabilities, because it incorporates repeated reading and motivates students.

The structure of the repeated reading strategy helps develop reading fluency because students read the same text several times to improve word recognition, speed, comprehension, and accuracy, but students lack the motivation to repeatedly read the same text (Corcoran, 2005, p. 106). In their article "Using Readers Theatre to Foster Fluency in Struggling Readers: A Twist on the

USING READERS' THEATER TO DEVELOP FLUENCY IN

STUDENTS WITH LEARNING DISABILITIES   4

Repeated Reading Strategy," Tyler and Chard (2000)

also suggest that repeated reading increases fluency

and comprehension when reading new text (p. 165).

Essentially, repeated reading equals practice which just

like in other disciplines helps develop skills. Samuels,

the originator of the repeated reading method in 1979,

suggests that musicians that repeatedly practice a piece

of music obtain more skills; therefore students, who

repeatedly read a passage become more fluent at reading

that passage and those skills transfer to new passages

as well (Graves, Juel, Graves, & Dewitz, 2011, p. 227).

Obviously, research suggests that the repeated reading

strategy increased fluency but lacks the motivation

component that students need to fully utilize the strategy.

Unfortunately, not all students are motivated to read the

same text over and over again. Some students get bored

or do not understand the purpose of repeated reading

and therefore do not benefit fully from the strategy.

Research suggests that "some [students] find the notion of

reading the same text over and over absurd, regardless

of the teacher's explanations" (Tyler & Chard, 2000,

p. 165). Motivation, therefore, would make the strategy

more successful at increasing fluency. However, reading

programs need strategies such as repeated reading to

promote fluency due to fluency's importance in reading;

With 3, 4, or 5 authors, give all surnames the first time the reference is cited. Thereafter, give only the first author's surname followed by et al.

USING READERS' THEATER TO DEVELOP FLUENCY IN
STUDENTS WITH LEARNING DISABILITIES   5

the key lies in finding the element of motivation in
repeated readings.

* * * * *

*Clorinda's
conclusion
summarizes the
results of her
research.*

In order to develop the fluency of all types of learners,
including those with disabilities, teachers must use a
combination of the repeated reading strategy along
with an authentic performance. Research shows that
performing a script motivates students to read more
and promotes success. When students are successful,
they perform the act of reading more readily and
consequently improve their skills. Reading fluency
increases readers' success which also helps develop
other essential skills such as comprehension. Primary to
upper elementary can benefit from the use of readers'
theater because the scripts can be altered to meet the
needs of each student. Differentiating the script helps
meet the needs of all types and levels of learners. The
motivation component of readers' theater has allowed it
to successfully improve students' fluency. Research has
shown that readers' theater has effectively motivated
struggling readers which have lead them to be more
successful readers. Consequently, students can continue
to improve their literacy skills in a positive and successful
manner.

USING READERS' THEATER TO DEVELOP FLUENCY IN

STUDENTS WITH LEARNING DISABILITIES   6

Running head and page number appear on the references page.

References

Clark, R., Morrison, T. G., & Wilcox, B. (2009). Readers' theater: A process of developing fourth-graders' reading fluency. *Reading Psychology, 30*(4), 359–385.

Corcoran, C. A. (2005). A study of the effects of readers' theater on second and third grade special education students' fluency growth. *Reading Improvement, 42*(2), 105–111.

Garrett, T. D., & O'Connor, D. (2010). Readers' theater: "Hold on, let's read it again." *Teaching Exceptional Children, 43*(1), 6–13.

Graves, M. F., Juel, C., Graves, B. B., & Dewitz, P. (2011). *Teaching reading in the 21st century: Motivating all learners.* Boston, MA: Pearson.

Tyler, B., & Chard, D. J. (2000). Using readers theatre to foster fluency in struggling readers: A twist on the repeated reading strategy. *Reading & Writing Quarterly, 16*(2), 163.

Young, C., & Rasinski, T. (2009). Implementing readers theatre as an approach to classroom fluency instruction. *Reading Teacher, 63*(1), 4–13.

MindTap   Reflect, personalize, and apply what you've learned.

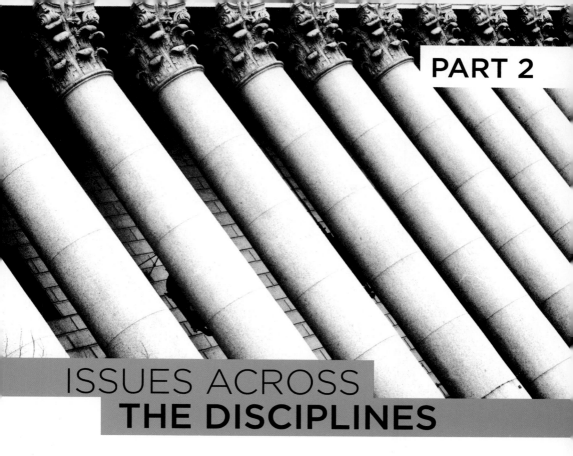

PART 2

ISSUES ACROSS
THE DISCIPLINES

POPULAR CULTURE AND THE ARTS

LEARNING OBJECTIVES

Students will demonstrate an ability to do the following:

- ☐ Critique the lyrics of selected rock, hip-hop, or gangsta rap music on the basis of their potential to demean or disrespect certain groups of people.

- ☐ Assess the arguments for and against the proposition that violent video games produce violent behavior in those who play them.

- ☐ Formulate arguments in favor of or against requiring that art be taught in public schools.

MindTap®   Understand the goals of the chapter and complete a warm-up activity.

CHAPTER OVERVIEW

The field of popular culture studies encompasses a wide range of subjects, most of which are designed to entertain. These include music, novels, videogames, and movies. Sports, politics, fashions, and fads are also aspects of popular culture. The focus of popular culture studies is on the choices that people make when searching for entertainment and how various components of popular culture affect behavior and influence attitudes and beliefs. Those who study popular culture are interested in why a particular game, movie, book, television, show, or song becomes wildly popular and how such popularity changes or influences people.

A strong and pervasive component of popular culture is video games, whether played on handheld electronic devices, on phones, in arcades, or on television. Critics of video games question whether they have any "redeeming social value," a question that applies particularly to games involving high-body-count killings by assault weapons and other powerful guns. With vivid graphics and sound effects, such games seem to their critics to condone violence and condition their players to be unfeeling or insensitive to real violence. The first reading in this chapter presents an intriguing commentary on the effects of playing violent video games on young people, Karen Sternheimer's "Do Video Games Kill?" Sternheimer cites newspaper articles and studies done following some high-profile school shootings in the late 1990s to support her argument. Although her article was published over a decade ago, you will find that her comments are remarkably relevant today. Unfortunately, there are many more recent school shootings that could be substituted for the examples that she uses.

While video games are a very recent development in popular culture, evidence suggests that music has been an integral part of humans' lives from their earliest existence. Song and instrumental music have spoken to, soothed, excited, and otherwise influenced humans of virtually all cultures and time periods in a seemingly endless variety of styles, subject matter, and methods of delivery. Each new musician, composer, or singer hopes to create a style uniquely his or her own, often acknowledging the influence of a previous form or artist. Sometimes a wholly new form of musical expression is created, from which generations of musicians and music lovers in turn take their inspiration.

Among the most controversial forms of contemporary music are certain types of rock, hip-hop, and gangsta rap. Their lyrics generate heated debate, with defenders of the music just as convinced of their legitimacy as their detractors are that such lyrics are abusive, misogynistic, and even dangerous. Like violent video games, sexually explicit and violently graphic music lyrics come under frequent and vocal attack from those who believe they have devastating effects on certain groups of people. In response to the defenders of such lyrics, Jennifer McLune asserts in "Hip-Hop's Betrayal of Black Women" that "women too are raised in this environment of poverty and violence but have yet to produce the same negative and hateful representation of black men that male rappers are capable of making against women." As you read her essay, think about your own reaction to and understanding of hip-hop and gangsta rap music.

Another area of popular culture is the creative arts, which includes not only music but also such things as painting, sculpture, photography, videos, filmmaking, and literature. Humans have always used a variety of creative ways in which to express themselves imaginatively. Researchers have discovered paintings in prehistoric caves that provide evidence of the earliest humans' compulsion to tell stories or depict significant aspects of their lives through pictures. Literature, too, has long been regarded as a significant art form. Indeed, some would claim that imaginative writing, whether a short story, a novel, a play, a poem, or some other form of creative expression, is just as crucial to the nurturing of the human soul as are visual arts and music. In the third reading in this chapter, Sarah Lewis makes a case for the "critical importance of the arts" in "Scientists Aren't the Only Innovators: We Really Need Artists." Consider your own view on the arts as you read her essay. Do you agree with her about the importance of arts and the power of the imaginative mind?

The subject of popular culture and the arts is so vast that these few readings serve only to indicate the breadth and depth of possible related topics and issues. Despite the persistence of art throughout time, the role of the artist in society and the relative value of art are frequently debated topics. Tastes change and differ from generation to generation and individual to individual, as do values and beliefs about what is important to sustain and nurture a society and the standards by which people judge the merits of works of art, or for that matter, many components of popular culture. Determining what makes an artwork, a song, a film, a play, a book, or a videogame "good" or "bad" is often a subjective response rather than a conscious application of objective standards. As you consider the points made by the writers in this section, also think about the kinds of creative art and entertainment that appeal to you. Think about the role that all of these forms of expression play in humans' lives: How might their absence affect humanity?

DO VIDEO GAMES KILL?

KAREN STERNHEIMER

Karen Sternheimer, whose work focuses on youth and popular culture, teaches in the sociology department at the University of Southern California, where she is also a distinguished fellow at the USC Center for Excellence in Teaching. She is the author of Pop Culture Panics: How Moral Crusaders Construct Meanings of Deviance and Delinquency *(2015),* Celebrity Culture and the American Dream: Stardom and Social Mobility *(2011),* Connecting Popular Culture and Social Problems: Why the Media Is Not the Answer *(2009),* Kids These Days: Facts and Fictions about Today's Youth *(2006), and* It's Not the Media: The Truth about Pop Culture's Influence on Children *(2003). This article appeared in* Contexts, *a quarterly publication of the American Sociological Association.*

As soon as it was released in 1993, a video game called *Doom* became a target for critics. Not the first, but certainly one of the most popular first-person shooter games, *Doom* galvanized fears that such games would teach kids to kill. In the years after its release, *Doom* helped video gaming grow into a multibillion-dollar industry, surpassing Hollywood box-office revenues and further fanning public anxieties.

Then came the school shootings in Paducah, Kentucky; Springfield, Oregon; and Littleton, Colorado. In all three cases, press accounts emphasized that the shooters loved *Doom*, making it appear that the critics' predictions about video games were coming true.

But in the ten years following *Doom*'s release, homicide arrest rates fell by 77 percent among juveniles. School shootings remain extremely rare; even during the 1990s, when fears of school violence were high, students had less than a 7 in 10 million chance of being killed at school.

During that time, video games became a major part of many young people's lives, few of whom will ever become violent, let alone kill. So why is the video game explanation so popular?

Contemporary Folk Devils

In 2000 the FBI issued a report on school rampage shootings, finding that their rarity prohibits the construction of a useful profile of a "typical" shooter. In the absence of a simple explanation, the public symbolically linked these rare and complex events to the shooters' alleged interest in video games, finding in them a catchall explanation for what seemed unexplainable—the white, middle-class school shooter. However, the concern about video games is out of proportion to their actual threat.

Politicians and other moral crusaders frequently create "folk devils," individuals or groups defined as evil and immoral. Folk devils allow us to channel our blame and fear, offering a clear course of action to remedy what many believe to be a growing problem. Video games, those who play them, and those who create them have become contemporary folk devils because they seem to pose a threat to children.

Such games have come to represent a variety of social anxieties: about youth violence, new computer technology, and the apparent decline in the ability of adults to control what young people do and know. Panics about youth and popular culture have emerged with the appearance of many new technologies. Over the past century, politicians have complained that cars, radio, movies, rock music, and even comic books caused youth immorality and crime, calling for control and sometimes censorship.

Acting on concerns like these, politicians often engage in battles characterized as between good and evil. The unlikely team of Senators Joseph Lieberman, Sam Brownback, Hillary Rodham Clinton, and Rick Santorum introduced a bill in March 2005 that called for $90 million to fund studies on media effects. Lieberman commented, "America is a media-rich society, but despite the flood of information, we still lack perhaps the most important piece of information—what effect are media having on our children?" Regardless of whether any legislation passes, the senators position themselves as protecting children and benefit from the moral panic they help to create.

Constructing Culpability

Politicians are not the only ones who blame video games. Since 1997, 199 newspaper articles have focused on video games as a central explanation for the Paducah, Springfield, and Littleton shootings. This helped to create a groundswell of fear that schools were no longer safe and that rampage shootings could happen wherever there were video games. The shootings legitimated existing concerns about the new medium and about young people in general. Headlines such as "Virtual Realities Spur School Massacres" (*Denver Post*, July 27, 1999), "Days of Doom" (*Pittsburgh Post-Gazette*, May 14, 1999), "Bloodlust Video Games Put Kids in the Crosshairs" (*Denver Post*, May 30, 1999), and "All Those Who Deny Any Linkage between Violence in Entertainment and Violence in Real Life, Think Again" (*New York Times*, April 26, 1999) insist that video games are the culprit.

These headlines all appeared immediately after the Littleton shooting, which had the highest death toll and inspired most (176) of the news stories alleging a video game connection.

Across the country, the press attributed much of the blame to video games specifically, and to Hollywood more generally. The *Pittsburgh Post-Gazette* article "Days of Doom" noted that "eighteen people have now died at the hands of avid *Doom* players." The *New York Times* article noted above began, "By producing increasingly violent media, the entertainment industry has for decades engaged in a lucrative dance with the devil," evoking imagery of a fight against evil. It went on to construct video games as a central link: "The two boys apparently responsible for the massacre in Littleton, Colo., last week were, among many other things, accomplished players of the ultraviolent video game *Doom*. And Michael Carneal, the 14-year-old boy who opened fire on a prayer group in a Paducah, Ky., school foyer in 1997, was also known to be a video-game expert."

12   Just as many stories insisted that video games deserved at least partial blame, editorial pages around the country made the connection as well:

> President Bill Clinton is right. He said this shooting was no isolated incident, that Kinkel and other teens accused of killing teachers and fellow students reflect a changing culture of violence on television and in movies and video games. (*Cleveland Plain Dealer,* May 30, 1998)
>
>   The campaign to make Hollywood more responsible . . . should proceed full speed ahead. (*Boston Herald*, April 9, 2000)
>
>   Make no mistake, Hollywood is contributing to a culture that feeds on and breeds violence. . . . When entertainment companies craft the most shocking video games and movies they can, peddle their virulent wares to an impressionable audience with abandon, then shrug off responsibility for our culture of violence, they deserve censure. (*St. Louis Post-Dispatch*, April 12, 2000)

The video game connection took precedence in all these news reports. Some stories mentioned other explanations, such as the shooters' social rejection, feelings of alienation at school, and depression, but these were treated mostly as minor factors compared with video games. Reporters gave these other reasons far less attention than violent video games, and frequently discussed them at the end of the articles.

The news reports typically introduce experts early in the stories who support the video game explanation. David Grossman, a former army lieutenant described as a professor of "killology," has claimed that video games are "murder simulators" and serve as an equivalent to military training. Among the 199 newspaper articles published, 17 of them mentioned or quoted Grossman. Additionally, an attorney who has filed several lawsuits against video game producers wrote an article for the *Denver Post* insisting that the games are to blame. By contrast, only seven articles identified sociologists as experts. Writers routinely presented alternative explanations as rebuttals but rarely explored them in depth.

Reporting on Research

By focusing so heavily on video games, news reports downplay the broader social contexts. While a handful of articles note the roles that guns, poverty, families, and the organization of schools may play in youth violence in general, when reporters mention research to explain the shooters' behavior, the vast majority of studies cited concern media effects, suggesting that video games are a central cause.

Since the early days of radio and movies, investigators have searched for possible effects—typically negative—that different media may have on audiences, especially children. Such research became more intense following the rise in violent crime in the United States between the 1960s and early 1990s, focusing primarily on television. Several hundred studies asked whether exposure to media violence predicts involvement in actual violence.

Although often accepted as true—one scholar has gone so far as to call the findings about the effects of media violence on behavior a "law"—this body of research has been highly controversial. One such study fostered claims that television had led to more than 10,000 murders in the United States and Canada during the 20th century. This and many other media-effects studies rely on correlation analysis, often finding small but sometimes statistically significant links between exposure to media violence and aggressive behavior.

But such studies do not demonstrate that media violence causes aggressive behavior, only that the two phenomena exist together. Excluding a host of other factors (such as the growing unrest during the civil rights and antiwar movements, and the disappearance of jobs in central cities) may make it seem that a direct link exists between the introduction of television and homicides. In all likelihood any connection is incidental.

It is equally likely that more aggressive people seek out violent entertainment. Aggression includes a broad range of emotions and behaviors, and is not always synonymous with violence. Measures of aggression in media-effects research have varied widely, from observing play between children and inanimate objects to counting the number of speeding tickets a person received. Psychologist Jonathan Freedman reviewed every media-violence study published in English and concluded that "the majority of studies produced evidence that is inconsistent or even contradicts" the claim that exposure to media violence causes real violence.

20   Recently, video games have become a focus of research. Reviews of this growing literature have also been mixed. A 2001 meta-analysis in *Psychological Science* concluded that video games "will increase aggressive behavior," while a similar review published that same year in a different journal found that "it is not possible to determine whether video game violence affects aggressive behavior." A 2005 review found evidence that playing video games improves spatial skills and reaction times, but not that the games increase aggression.

The authors of the *Psychological Science* article advocate the strong-effects hypothesis. Two of their studies were widely reported on in 2000, the year after the Columbine High School shootings, with scant critical analysis. But their research was based on college undergraduates, not troubled teens, and it measured aggression in part by subjects' speed in reading "aggressive" words on a computer screen or blasting opponents with sound after playing a violent video game. These measures do not approximate the conditions the school shooters experienced, nor do they offer much insight as to why they, and not the millions of other players, decided to acquire actual weapons and shoot real people.

Occasionally reporters include challenges like this in stories containing media-effects claims, but news coverage usually refers to this body of research as clear, consistent, and conclusive. "The evidence, say those who study violence in culture, is unassailable: Hundreds of studies in recent decades have revealed a direct correlation between exposure to media violence—now including video games—and increased aggression," said the *New York Times* (April 26, 1999). The *Boston Herald* quoted a clinical psychologist who said, "Studies have already shown that watching television shows with aggressive or violent content makes children more aggressive" (July 30, 2000). The psychologist noted that video game research is newer, but predicted that "in a few years, studies will show that video games increase a child's aggression even more than violent TV shows." News reports do not always use academic sources to assess the conclusiveness of media effects research. A *Pittsburgh Post-Gazette* story included a quote by an attorney, who claimed, "Research on this has been well-established" (May 14, 1999).

It is no accident that media-effects research and individual explanations dominate press attempts to explain the behavior of the school shooters. Although many politicians are happy to take up the cause against video games, popular culture itself suggests an apolitical explanation of violence and discourages a broader examination of structural factors. Focusing on extremely rare and perhaps unpredictable outbursts of violence by young people discourages the public from looking closely at more typical forms of violence against young people, which is usually perpetrated by adults.

The biggest problem with media-effects research is that it attempts to decontextualize violence. Poverty, neighborhood instability, unemployment, and even family violence fall by the wayside in most of these studies. Ironically, even mental illness tends to be overlooked in this psychologically oriented research. Young people are seen as passive media consumers, uniquely and uniformly vulnerable to media messages.

Missing Media Studies

News reports of the shootings that focus on video games ignore other research on the meanings that audiences make from media culture. This may be because its qualitative findings are difficult to turn into simple quotations or sound bites. Yet in seeking better understanding of the role of video games in the lives of the shooters and young people more generally, media scholars could have added much to the public debate.

For instance, one study found that British working-class boys boast about how many horror films they have seen as they construct their sense of masculinity by appearing too tough to be scared. Another study examined how younger boys talk about movies and television as a way to manage their anxieties and insecurities regarding their emerging sense of masculinity. Such studies illustrate why violent video games may appeal to many young males.

Media scholars have also examined how and why adults construct concerns about young people and popular culture. One such study concluded that some adults use their condemnation of media as a way to produce cultural distinctions that position them above those who enjoy popular culture. Other researchers have found that people who believe their political knowledge is superior to that of others are more likely to presume that media violence would strongly influence others. They have also found that respondents who enjoy television violence are less likely to believe it has a negative effect.

28   Just as it is too simplistic to assert that video game violence makes players more prone to violence, news coverage alone, however dramatic or repetitive, cannot create consensus among the public that video games cause youth violence. Finger-wagging politicians and other moralizers often alienate as many members of the public as they convert. In an ironic twist, they might even feed the antiauthoritarian appeal that may draw players of all ages to the games.

The lack of consensus does not indicate the absence of a moral panic, but reveals contradictory feelings toward the target group. The intense focus on video games as potential creators of violent killers reflects the hostility that some feel toward popular culture and young people themselves. After adult rampage shootings in the workplace (which happen more often than school shootings), reporters seldom mention whether the shooters played video games. Nor is an entire generation portrayed as potential killers.

Ambivalence about Juvenile Justice

The concern in the late 1990s about video games coincided with a growing ambivalence about the juvenile justice system and young offenders. Fears about juvenile "super-predators," fanned by former Florida Representative Bill McCollom's 1996 warning that we should "brace ourselves" against the coming storm of young killers, made the school shootings appear inevitable. McCollom and other politicians characterized young people as a "new breed," uniquely dangerous and amoral.

These fears were produced partially by the rise in crime during the late 1980s and early 1990s, but also by the so-called echo boom that produced a large generation of teens during the late 1990s. Demographic theories of crime led policymakers to fear that the rise in the number of teen males would bring a parallel rise in crime. In response, virtually every state changed its juvenile justice laws during the decade. They increased penalties, imposed mandatory minimum sentences, blended jurisdiction with criminal courts, and made it easier to transfer juvenile cases to adult criminal courts.

32   So before the first shot was fired in Paducah, politicians warned the public to be on the lookout for killer kids. Rather than being seen as tragic anomalies, these high-profile incidents appeared to support scholarly warnings that all kids posed an increasing threat. Even though juvenile (and adult) crime was in sharp decline by the late nineties, the intense media coverage contributed to the appearance of a new trend.

Blaming video games meant that the shooters were set aside from other violent youth, frequently poor males of color, at whom our get-tough legislation has been targeted. According to the National Center for Juvenile Justice, African-American youth are involved in the juvenile justice system more than twice as often as whites. The video game explanation constructs the white, middle-class shooters as victims of the power of video games, rather than fully culpable criminals. When boys from "good" neighborhoods are violent, they seem to be harbingers of a "new breed" of youth, created by video games rather than by their social circumstances. White, middle-class killers retain their status as children easily influenced by a game, victims of an allegedly dangerous product. African-American boys, apparently, are simply dangerous.

While the news media certainly asked what role the shooters' parents may have played, the press tended to tread lightly on them, particularly the Kinkels of Springfield, Oregon, who were their son's first murder victims. Their middle-class, suburban, or rural environments were given little scrutiny. The white school shooters did more than take the lives of their classmates; their whiteness and middle-class status threatened the idea of the innocence and safety of suburban America.

In an attempt to hold more than just the shooters responsible, the victims' families filed lawsuits against film producers, Internet sites, and video game makers. Around the same time, Congress made it more difficult to sue gun manufacturers for damages. To date, no court has found entertainment producers liable for causing young people to commit acts of violence. In response to a lawsuit following the Paducah shootings, a Kentucky circuit judge ruled that "we are loath to hold that ideas and images can constitute the tools for a criminal act," and that product liability law did not apply because the product did not injure its consumer. The lawsuit was dismissed, as were subsequent suits filed after the other high-profile shootings.

Game Over?

36   Questions about the power of media and the future of the juvenile justice system persist. In March 2005, the U.S. Supreme Court ruled that juvenile executions were unconstitutional. This ruling represents an about-face in the 25-year trend toward toughening penalties for young offenders. While many human rights and children's advocates praised this decision, it was sharply criticized by those who believe that the juvenile justice system is already too lenient. Likewise, critics continue to target video games, as their graphics and plot capabilities grow more complex and at times more disturbing. Meanwhile, youth crime rates continue to decline. If we want to understand why young people, particularly in middle-class or otherwise stable environments, become homicidal, we need to look beyond the games they play. While all forms of media merit critical analysis, so do the supposedly "good" neighborhoods and families that occasionally produce young killers.

PERSONAL RESPONSE

What is your opinion of violent video games? Are they harmless fun, or do you believe that they may have some effect on behavior? What is your experience with playing such games?

QUESTIONS FOR CLASS OR SMALL-GROUP DISCUSSION

1. What do you understand Sternheimer to mean by the term "folk devils"? She suggests that "video games, those who play them, and those who create them have become contemporary folk devils" (paragraph 4). Can you give examples of other such "folk devils?"

2. What criticisms of media-effects research does Sternheimer make? What do you think of her rationale for those criticisms? What do you think of her explanation of factors besides video games that may account for aggressive behavior in teenagers?

3. What point does Sternheimer make about poor males of color who get in trouble with the law versus white middle-class males who kill? Do your own observations confirm or contradict her viewpoint?

4. Analyze the structure of Sternheimer's argument. What is her thesis? Where does she make concessions? What evidence does she supply? How convinced are you by her evidence? Is her argument now outdated, or does it still hold up?

HIP-HOP'S BETRAYAL
OF BLACK WOMEN

JENNIFER McLUNE

Jennifer McLune is a librarian, activist, and writer living in Washington, D.C. This piece appeared in Z Magazine Online. *According to its mission statement,* Z Magazine *is "dedicated to resisting injustice, defending against repression, and creating liberty. It sees the racial, gender, class, and political dimensions of personal life as fundamental to understanding and improving contemporary circumstances; and it aims to assist activist efforts for a better future." You can view* Z *at www.zcommunications.org/zmag.*

Kevin Powell in "Notes of a Hip Hop Head" writes, "Indeed, like rock and roll, hip-hop sometimes makes you think we men don't like women much at all, except to objectify them as trophy pieces or, as contemporary vernacular mandates, as baby mommas, chickenheads, or bitches.

"But just as it was unfair to demonize men of color in the 1960s solely as wild-eyed radicals when what they wanted, amidst their fury, was a little freedom and a little power, today it is wrong to categorically dismiss hip-hop without taking into serious consideration the socioeconomic conditions (and the many record labels that eagerly exploit and benefit from the ignorance of many of these young artists) that have led to the current state of affairs. Or, to paraphrase the late Tupac Shakur, we were given this world, we did not make it."

Powell's "socioeconomic" explanation for the sexism in hip-hop is a way to silence feminist critiques of the culture. It is to make an understanding of the misogynistic objectification of black women in hip-hop so elusive that we can't grasp it long enough to wring the neck of its power over us. His argument completely ignores the fact that women, too, are raised in this environment of poverty and violence, but have yet to produce the same negative and hateful representation of black men that male rappers are capable of making against women.

Powell's understanding also lends itself to elitist assumption that somehow poverty breeds sexism, or at least should excuse it. Yet we all know that wealthy white boys can create the same hateful and violent music as poor black boys. As long as the boys can agree that their common enemy is female and that their power resides in their penis, women must not hesitate to name the war they have declared on us.

Hip-hop owes its success to the ideology of woman-hating. It creates, perpetuates, and reaps the rewards of objectification. Sexism and homophobia saturate hip-hop culture and any deviation from these forms of bigotry is made marginal to its most dominant and lucrative expressions. Few artists dare to embody equality and respect between the sexes through their music. Those who do have to fight to be heard above the dominant chorus of misogyny.

The most well-known artists who represent an underground and conscious force in hip-hop—like Common, The Roots, Talib Kweli, and others—remain inconsistent, apologetic, and even eager to join the mainstream player's club. Even though fans like me support them because of their moments of decency toward women, they often want to remain on the fence by either playing down their consciousness or by offering props to misogynistic rappers. Most so-called conscious artists appear to care more about their own acceptance by mainstream artists than wanting to make positive changes in the culture.

The Roots, for example, have backed Jay-Z on both his *Unplugged* release and Fade to Black tours. They've publicly declared their admiration for him and have signed on to his new "indie" hip-hop imprint Def Jam Left to produce their next album. Yet Jay-Z is one of the most notoriously sexist and materialistic rappers of his generation.

Hip-hop artists like Talib Kweli and Common market themselves as conscious alternatives, yet they remain passive in the face of unrelenting woman-hating bravado from mainstream artists. They are willing to lament in abstract terms the state of hip-hop, but refuse to name names—unless it's to reassure their mainstream brethren that they have nothing but love for their music.

Talib Kweli has been praised for his song "Black Girl Pain," but clearly he's clueless to how painful it is for a black girl to hear his boy Jay-Z rap, "I pimp hard on a trick, look Fuck if your leg broke bitch, hop up on your good foot."

The misogyny in hip-hop is also given a pass because some of its participants are women. But female hip-hop artists remain marginalized within the industry and culture—except when they are trotted out to defend hip-hop against feminist criticism. But the truth is, all kinds of patriarchal institutions, organizations, and movements have women in their ranks in search of power and meaning. The token presence of individual women changes nothing if women as a group are still scapegoated and degraded.

Unlike men, women in hip-hop don't speak in a collective voice in defense of themselves. The pressure on women to be hyper-feminine and hyper-sexual for the pleasure of men, and the constant threat of being called a bitch, a ho—or worse, a dyke—as a result of being strong, honest, and self-possessed, are real within hip-hop culture and the black community at large. Unless women agree to compromise their truth, self-respect, and unity with other women and instead play dutiful daughter to the phallus that represents hip-hop culture, they will be either targeted, slandered, or ignored altogether. As a result, female rappers are often just as male-identified, violent, materialistic, and ignorant as their male peers.

12   Hip-hop artist Eve, who describes herself as "a pit bull in a skirt," makes an appearance in the Sporty Thieves video for "Pigeons," one of the most hateful misogynistic anthems in hip-hop. Her appearance displays her unity not with the women branded "pigeons," but with the men who label them. This is a heartbreaking example of how hip-hop encourages men to act collectively in the interest of male privilege while dividing women into opposing camps of good and bad or worthy and unworthy of respect.

Lip-service protest against sexism in hip-hop culture is a sly form of public relations to ensure that nobody's money, power, or respect is ever really threatened. Real respect and equality might interfere with hip-hop's commercial appeal. We are asked to dialogue about and ultimately celebrate our "progress"—always predicated on a few rappers and moguls getting rich. Angry young black women are expected to be satisfied with a mere mention that some hip-hop music is sexist and that this sexism of a few rappers is actually, as Powell calls it, "the ghetto blues, urban folk art, a cry out for help." My questions then are: "Whose blues? Whose art? Why won't anybody help the women who are raped in endless rotation by the gaze of the hip-hop camera?"

They expect us to deal with hip-hop's pervasive woman-hating simply by alluding to it, essentially excusing and even celebrating its misogyny, its arrogance, its ignorance. What this angry black woman wants to hear from the apologists is that black women are black people too. That any attack on the women in our community is an attack on us all and that we will no longer be duped by genocidal tendencies in black-face. I want to hear these apologists declare that any black man who makes music perpetuating the hatred of women will be named, shunned, and destroyed, financially and socially, like the traitor of our community he is. That until hip-hop does right by black women, everything hip-hop ever does will fail.

If we accept Powell's explanation for why hip-hop is the way it is—which amounts to an argument for why we should continue to consume and celebrate it—then ultimately we are accepting ourselves as victims who know only how to imitate our victimization while absolving the handful of black folk who benefit from its tragic results. I choose to challenge hip-hop by refusing to reward its commercial aspirations with my money and my attention.

16   I'm tired of the ridiculous excuses and justifications for the unjustifiable pillaring of black women and girls in hip-hop. Are black women the guilty parties behind black men's experience of racism and poverty? Are black women acceptable scapegoats when black men suffer oppression? If black women experience double the oppression as both blacks and women in a racist, patriarchal culture, it is our anger at men and white folks that needs to be heard.

The black men who make excuses for the ideology of woman-hating in hip-hop remind me of those who, a generation ago, supported the attacks on black female writers who went public about the reality of patriarchy in our community. The fact that these black female writers did not create incest, domestic violence, rape, and other patriarchal conditions in the black community did not shield them from being skewered by black men who had their feelings hurt by the exposure of their male privilege and domination of black women. Black women's literature and activism that challenges sexism is often attacked by black men (and many male-identified women) who abhor domination when they are on the losing end, but want to protect it when they think it offers them a good deal.

Black women writers and activists were called traitors for refusing to be silent about the misogynistic order of things and yet women-hating rappers are made heroes by the so-called masses. To be sure, hip-hop is not about keeping it real. Hip-hop lies about the ugly reality that black women were condemned for revealing. Hip-hop is a manipulative narrative that sells because it gets men hard. It is a narrative in which, as a Wu Tang Clan video shows, black women are presented as dancing cave "chicks" in bikinis who get clubbed over the head; or where gang rapes are put to a phat beat; or where working class black women are compared to shit-eating birds.

As a black woman who views sexism as just as much the enemy of my people as racism, I can't buy the apologies and excuses for hip-hop. I will not accept the notion that my sisters deserve to be degraded and humiliated because of the frustrations of black men—all while we suppress our own frustrations, angers, and fears in an effort to be sexy and accommodating. Although Kevin Powell blames the negatives in hip-hop on everything but hip-hop culture itself, he ultimately concludes, "What hip-hop has spawned is a way of winning on our own terms, of us making something out of nothing."

20

If the terms for winning are the objectification of black women and girls, I wonder if any females were at the table when the deal went down. Did we agree to be dehumanized, vilified, made invisible? Rather than pretending to explain away the sexism of hip-hop culture, why doesn't Powell just come clean—in the end it doesn't matter how women are treated. Sexism is the winning ticket to mainstream acceptability and Powell, like Russell Simmons and others, knows this. It's obvious that if these are the winning terms for our creativity, black women are ultimately the losers. And that's exactly how these self-proclaimed players, thugs, and hip-hop intellectuals want us—on our backs and pledging allegiance to the hip-hop nation.

If we were to condemn woman-hating as an enemy of our community, hip-hop would be forced to look at itself and change radically and consistently. Then it would no longer be marketable in the way that these hip-hop intellectuals celebrate. As things stand, it's all about the Benjamins on every level of the culture and black women are being thugged and rubbed all the way to the bank.

PERSONAL RESPONSE

Write in response to McLune's statement in paragraph 5 that "[h]ip-hop owes its success to the ideology of woman hating."

QUESTIONS FOR CLASS OR SMALL-GROUP DISCUSSION

1. How well do you think that McLune explains her title? In what ways is hip-hop a betrayal of black women, according to her? Explain in your own words McLune's argument against Kevin Powell's explanation for the "misogynistic objectification of black women in hip-hop" (paragraph 3).

2. McLune writes: "Few artists dare to embody equality and respect between the sexes through their music" (paragraph 5). What do you think of her assessment of those few artists she names who "represent an underground and conscious force in hip-hop" (paragraph 6)? Can you name similar artists who resist using sexist and homophobic lyrics?

3. To what extent do you agree with McLune's comments on female hip-hop artists (paragraphs 10–12)?

4. Discuss your opinion of what McLune calls for apologists of black hip-hop music and the artists themselves to do.

SCIENTISTS AREN'T THE ONLY INNOVATORS: WE REALLY NEED ARTISTS

SARAH LEWIS

Sarah Lewis is the author of The Rise: Creativity, The Gift of Failure, and the Search for Mastery *(2014). She has served on President Obama's Arts Policy Committee and is a Critic at the Yale University School of Art in the MFA program. She has also held curator positions at both the Tate Modern in London and The Museum of Modern Art in New York. This piece was first published at* Salon.com.

"What's your favorite subject in school?" I heard a mother ask her young son and daughter as we were in the elevator riding up in our building.

"Gym," the girl said.

"Art," the boy said.

I smiled and looked down at the elevator floor. Just before I averted my eyes, I had also noticed that my neighbor was most worried by her son's response: "Art." She looked at me, panic-stricken.

Don't look at me, I thought. I know that, to many, pursuing the arts can seem like the height of impracticality. I remember how nervous my parents were when I came home from grade school and declared that I wanted to be a painter. And then, when I told them that after going to Harvard and Oxford, I wanted to be a curator.

4   We may be concerned when a child expresses a love for the arts because we worry that what President Obama has recently said (and as many have before) could be right—skilled mechanics might have a better chance of getting a high-paying job than those with degrees in art history, or those pursuing a career in the arts. Yet what are we most in need of? People who can think creatively and innovate.

In the United States, creativity scores for children from kindergarten to the sixth grade, as measured by Torrance Tests of Creative Thinking, have dropped for the first time since its testing began in 1968. During the same period, IQ scores have increased each decade. In other words, we are smarter, yet less equipped to find novel approaches to problems.

As the arts have been largely eliminated from U.S. public school, a process that began in the 1970s, so has the avenue to one of the arts' irreplaceable gifts: the agency to withstand ambiguity and to discern for yourself whether to pursue a problem or to quit and reassess.

The external binaries of right and wrong don't exist in art as they do in most subjects. In math, the answer to the problem is correct or incorrect. In history, a sequence of events is true or false. In art, only the student can decide what critique to listen to and what to ignore. Art is the arena of activity where we develop the skill most required to innovate—the ability to harness our own agency.

8   Artist and Nobel Prize-winning scientist Richard P. Feynman put it this way as he distinguished between teaching science and art: in physics, Feynman said, "we have so many techniques—so many mathematical methods—that we never stop telling the students how to do things. On the other hand, the

drawing teacher is afraid to tell you anything. If your lines are very heavy, the teacher can't say, 'Your lines are too heavy,' because some artist has figured out a way of making great pictures using heavy lines." In that moment, the art student is learning the validity of their choices, their own direction, and innovative results.

Yet part of the reason for our collective ignorance about the critical importance of the arts is because we believe that the innovation in the lab—something we value, and can monetize and quantify—is worlds apart from the experimentation in the studio, on bandstands, or stages of all kinds. A reminder of how far this idea is from the truth sits right in the Oval Office of the White House—Morse's 1849 telegraph model, on loan from the Smithsonian.

"This is the start of the Internet right here," Mr. Obama told Michael Lewis of *Vanity Fair*, pointing at the model. Indeed. What I suspect Obama might not have also said was this: Morse invented the telegraph after he spent 26 years in pursuit of his main objective: to be a painter. Morse wanted "to revive the splendor of the fifteenth century; to rival the genius of a Raphael, a Michael Angelo [sic], or a Titian; my ambition is to be enlisted in the constellation of genius now rising in this country."

Sometime after 1832, in Washington Square—Morse's lodgings at New York University (then the University of the City of New York) where he was the school's first painting professor—he nailed the wooden backing of the canvas to a table to hold together the telegraph model. The cogs, clock springs and more were all set into a wooden frame—the abandoned canvas stretcher bars for a painting Morse would never complete.

12

The art of making offers us a way to develop a kind of agency required for supple, nimble endurance. It lets us shift our frame, like Morse, who stared at a set of canvas stretcher bars for years and one day saw its potential to be an original communication device, and then persisted for decades to realize its full application for the world.

It is no longer possible to care about innovation and continue to fear fostering creativity in young people. Inventions come from those who can view a familiar set of variables from a radical perspective and see new possibilities. Creative practice is one of the most effective teachers of this reframing.

The list of those who have lived out this understanding is endless: Engineer, inventor and entrepreneur Elon Musk wrote the code for a video game he created at age 12;

statistician Edward Tufte, who pioneered how to clearly present data through elegant visual design, is also a sculptor; Harvard psychologist Ellen Langer, who pioneered the research on the mind-body connection, spends much of her time painting and exhibiting her work. When Steve Jobs dropped out of Reed College, he chose to focus on calligraphy, a field he called "fascinating" and utterly impractical. "But ten years, later when we were designing the first Macintosh computer, it all came back to me," Jobs said. "And we designed it all into the Mac."

So perhaps it should come as no surprise that physiologist Robert Root-Bernstein of Michigan State University has found that a disproportionately high number of Nobel laureates in the sciences had artistic avocations—their hobbies were painting, composition, sculpture and more. Root-Bernstein found, too, that the energy it took to be a success in science did not lead to a decline in reported time spent with artistic avocations. In other words, scientific and artistic avocational skills were complementary. Talent in one supported talent in the other.

16

"The creativity that allowed us . . . to conceive and build and launch the space shuttle," NASA astronaut Mae Jemison said, "springs from the same source as the imagination and analysis it took to carve a Bundu statue, or the ingenuity it took to design, choreograph and stage [Alvin Ailey's] 'Cry.' . . . That's what we have to reconcile in our minds, how these things fit together."

I often regret that I got off of the elevator without saying anything to my panic-stricken neighbor. Within seconds of the exchange, the elevator arrived at my floor. I flashed a smile to the woman, her art-loving son, and daughter as I walked out. I often hope to run into them again. I would ask the mother if I could give her son a paint set.

PERSONAL RESPONSE

What is your view of the creative arts? Do you believe in their "critical importance" (paragraph 11); or do you consider them a waste of time, "the height of impracticality" (paragraph 5)?

QUESTIONS FOR CLASS OR SMALL-GROUP DISCUSSION

1. How do Lewis's examples of scientists who practiced the arts support her central idea?

2. What do you understand Lewis to mean when she refers to "one of the arts' irreplaceable gifts": "the agency to withstand ambiguity and to discern for yourself whether to pursue a problem or to quit and reassess" (paragraph 8)?

3. What connection does Lewis see between science and art? How do they differ?

4. What do you understand Lewis's main point to be. What does she see as the benefit of the arts to society? To what extent do you agree with her?

MindTap Reflect on the theme of this chapter.

PERSPECTIVES ON POPULAR CULTURE AND THE ARTS

Suggested Writing Topics

1. Refute or support this statement in Jennifer McLune's "Hip-Hop's Betrayal of Black Women": "Sexism and homophobia saturate hip-hop culture and any deviation from these forms of bigotry is made marginal to its most dominant and lucrative expressions" (paragraph 5). Use examples from song lyrics to support your position.

2. Do a detailed analysis of a hip-hop, rap, or other song that you are familiar with. What images does it portray? What message, if any, does it send? How do the lyrics work to make the song artistically good?

3. Analyze the lyrics of a song that you believe to be socially responsible or that comments on a current social issue.

4. Using the example of a recent hit movie, analyze the image of American life that you think it projects. What values, whether positive or negative, does the film seem to endorse?

5. Write about a film that has had a profound effect on you, perhaps one that made you aware of a problem you did not know about before or that moved you to act or think differently. Briefly summarize what the film was about and then explain why and how it affected you.

6. Argue for or against extending the First Amendment's guarantee of freedom of speech to include violent or offensive lyrics in hip-hop, rock, or other forms

of music. Consider how far you think First Amendment's protection of free speech should be allowed to go.

7. Argue in support of or against the statement that music or video games influence violent behavior in individuals.

8. Explore the subject of how artists benefit society by answering any of these questions: In what ways do the arts—music, art, drama, literature—contribute to the culture of a people? What is the value of art? What is gained by a culture's interest in and support of the arts? What would be lost without it?

9. Explore the subject of the role that art should play in American education. Consider questions such as this: Should art be taught in schools? If so, should students be required to take it? What grade levels is it most appropriate for?

10. One of the oldest forms of art is personal decoration. The body is still being used as a surface for symbolic expression by some young people, who use such techniques as branding, piercing, and tattooing. Defend or attack these practices by considering their relative artistic or creative merits.

11. Argue your viewpoint on allowing depictions of violence in the creative arts—poetry, drama, short story, novel, dance, or visual arts—in classroom materials. Is the expulsion of students for creating it or the firing of teachers teaching it justifiable in uncertain and dangerous times?

12. Imagine that you are preparing to give a talk to a group of children about the possible dangers of exposure to media violence. Write an essay with that group as your audience and include details, facts, or references to studies that you think would make an impression on them.

Research Topics

1. Research the development of hip-hop or gangsta rap music, taking into consideration Jennifer McLune's "Hip-Hop's Betrayal of Black Women" and other attacks on its lyrics. What conclusions can you draw about the artistic legitimacy of the music?

2. Research the subject of the influence of violent video games on behavior in young people, drawing on Karen Sternheimer's "Do Video Games Kill?" Possible sources include any of Sternheimer's own books on the subject, including her most recent one, *Pop Culture Panics: How Moral Crusaders Construct Meanings of Deviance and Delinquency* (2015).

3. Use an approach similar to that of Karen Sternheimer in "Do Video Games Kill?" to analyze newspaper coverage of recent school shootings, such as the Sandy Hook Elementary school murders in 2012 or the Umpqua Community College shooting in 2015.

4. Research a particular musician, musical group, or entertainer from an earlier decade. Find out the performer's history, the audience he or she appealed to,

what distinguished him or her from others, and what his or her influence seems to have been on popular culture. Formulate your own assessment of the entertainer's significance and make that your thesis or central idea.

5. Research a particular kind of music, such as hip-hop, rap, grunge, alternative, blues, jazz, or salsa, for the purpose of identifying its chief characteristics, the way it differs from and is influenced by other kinds of music, and its artistic merit or social significance. Include opposing viewpoints and argue your own position on its merits or significance.

6. Research the worldwide influence of American popular culture by examining the popular culture of other countries. Limit your research to one, two, or several countries, or focus on certain aspects of American popular culture that have a heavy influence in foreign countries. This is a broad topic, so look for ways to focus your research topic as you do preliminary reading and searching for sources.

7. Examine allegations of racism, sexism, and/or homophobia leveled against a particular video game, song, musician, film, or group, and draw your own conclusions about the fairness, appropriateness, and/or accuracy of those allegations.

8. Research the history of a popular handheld video game, taking into consideration marketing strategy, target audience, responses of users, and/or longevity of the game.

9. Research the latest studies and opinion pieces on the cultural impact of video games, and draw your own conclusions about their importance in shaping culture.

10. Select an issue or a question related to the broad subject of the role of the artist in society to research and then argue your position on that issue. For instance, what is the role of the arts in today's culture? Do we need the arts?

11. In recent years, some people have been highly critical of what they see as obscenity or immorality in contemporary art and want to censor it.. Research the issue of censorship in the arts, and write an opinion paper on the subject. Consider: Does society have a moral obligation to limit what people can say, do, or use in their art, or do First Amendment rights extend to any subject or medium an artist wants to use?

RESPONDING TO VISUALS

Barry Downard/Ikon Images/Getty Images

What mood does this image of hungry wolves circling outside an urban lobby evoke?

1. What is the effect of having the perspective from right behind a close-up of the nearest wolf? What would change if the perspective were from inside the lobby looking out or from some distance away, looking at the entire scene?

2. How might the image be representative of the nature of some kinds of popular culture such as dystopian literature or film?

3. What element of interest is added when we learn (from the caption) that the wolves are hungry and that they are circling an urban lobby?

RESPONDING TO VISUALS

Lisa Pines/Photodisc/Getty Images

In what ways does this image of a young girl playing with her handheld device seem to capture both a traditional and a modern concept of childhood imagination?

1. How does the image combine a traditional concept of "imagination" with a modern one?

2. How would the effect of the image change were the girl photographed with the butterfly wings only? How might the effect of the image change were the girl holding the electronic device but not wearing the wings?

3. Does this image of the girl standing still and focused on her hand-held device rather than an image of her running out of doors with her wings flapping comment in any way on the nature of childhood today?

MEDIA STUDIES

LEARNING OBJECTIVES

Students will demonstrate an ability to do the following:

- ☐ Comment on ways that news media attempt to influence people's attitudes, beliefs, and/or behavior.

- ☐ Explore ways that media technology can be disruptive and have adverse effects on behavior.

- ☐ Assess the positive and negative influences of certain kinds of media, such as advertisements or reality television programs, on self-image.

MindTap   Understand the goals of the chapter and complete a warm-up activity.

CHAPTER OVERVIEW

Because of its pervasiveness in American culture, the media affects people in both obvious and subtle ways. Analysts are interested in how various media such as newspapers, magazines, television, advertising, social media, and artificial intelligence technology influence behavior, habits, thought, and opinions. There are myriad ways that this wide range of media can influence people of all ages. For example, students of media studies may examine the effects of television and film violence on children and impressionable adults; or they may be interested in the effect of advertising on people's self-image, how they perceive others, what they choose to buy at the market, or which fast food restaurant to eat at. Researchers, scholars, and students of media studies might examine how certain television programs influence the behavior of children or, in the case of reality television programs, adult behavior. They might look at the ways in which newspaper, magazine, and television coverage of the news might be partial or slanted. Of special interest in recent years is the way in which social media affects behavior, as it serves as an immediate, real-time way to warn, advise, or even rally people to action. Recent advances in artificial intelligence indicate that it will someday have the ability to "read" your mind and body. Any research on the general topic *media studies* will lead you to dozens of directions that you can go in looking at the ways in which media influence people.

Although the subjects of the readings in Chapter 8 may also be considered *media*, this chapter looks at broader issues relating to *the media* as it considers several kinds of media. Media analysts often serve as watchdogs against threats to freedom of speech and thought. They concern themselves with social issues such as media violence, censorship in the media, biased reporting, discrimination in programming, the ways that advertising manipulates people, and the ways in which the media shape social and political discourse. They analyze the power of the media and the power behind the media.

A look at the goals and purposes of university media studies programs gives an idea of what is involved in *media studies*. Such programs examine the social, cultural, political, ethical, aesthetic, legal, and economic effects of the media and are interested in the variety of contexts in which the media have influence in those areas. They cite in their rationales for their programs the proliferation of media, the interconnectedness of media on a global level, and the pervasiveness of media in our lives. Furthermore, large numbers of groups, agencies, and organizations identify themselves as "media watchers" and many are media activists. You will find both conservatives and liberals, extremists and moderates on such a list.

The first reading in this chapter, written by Clay Shirky, a professor of social media, makes some intriguing comments about student use of electronic devices in the classroom. "Why I Just Asked My Students to Put Their Laptops Away" is an example of the way that media studies people investigate and draw conclusions about the intersection of technology and the personal, that is, the ways in which advances in technology affect individual lives. In this case, Shirky explains a move he made to help ensure the success of students trying to stay focused in his college classroom.

The next reading takes up another area of concern to media analysts, advertising, in particular photoshopping pictures of models. Erin Cunningham raises questions about media tampering with photographs in "Our Photoshopping Disorder: The Truth in Advertising Bill Asks Congress to Regulate Deceptive Images." While wondering if regulating the advertising industry is really a political matter, Cunningham addresses the way in which many advertising images are retouched to achieve a kind of impossible perfection. Of concern is the ways in which these images set up impossible and unrealistic goals for young girls and women, which, in turn, affects their self-esteem and engenders feelings of inadequacy.

Though it is probably hard to believe now, when it was first invented, people thought "the tube" would never replace the radio, especially when its early live-only broadcasts included inevitable comical errors. Once the problems were resolved and television broadcasting became increasingly sophisticated in both technology and programming, television became an established medium. Television programs now number in the thousands, with cable access and computer-controlled satellite dishes bringing a dizzying array of viewing choices into people's homes. Households have two or three (or more) televisions and DVR and DVD players. It is commonplace to download television programs on computers and handheld electronic devices as well. With the seemingly endless demand for television shows from viewers, network producers and local station managers are always looking for programs that will attract viewers and draw sponsors.

While television has been the target of suspicion, attack, and ridicule from the time it was invented, one of the areas of television programming that gets a great deal of negative reviews is reality shows. These programs follow real people over time behaving in unscripted situations, such as surviving on a faraway and exotic island, selecting a potential mate from a group of twenty-five hopefuls, having a new home built for them, or competing to be the top singer or dancer in the nation. The concept is not new: in the 1950s, for instance, *Queen for a Day* was an early variation, where contestants were selected to tell their sad stories and the winner was the one who garnered the loudest audience applause. But the proliferation of such programs is a twenty-first-century phenomenon. The third reading is interested in the way that television reality programs not only invade privacy but may also be responsible for such extreme behavior as suicide. Serena Elavia uses the extended example of Bravo's *The Real Housewives of New Jersey* in her piece, "The Collective Conscience of Reality Television." She looks at the way in which such series as *Real Housewives* are viewer driven rather than producer or network driven, that is, viewers seem to set the boundaries of what is acceptable to broadcast and what isn't. Elavia, like other writer in this chapter, wonders about invasions of privacy, exploitation of individuals, and the encouraging of extreme behavior.

WHY I JUST ASKED MY
STUDENTS TO PUT THEIR
LAPTOPS AWAY

CLAY SHIRKY

Clay Shirky is a professor of media studies at New York University, holding a joint appointment as an arts professor at NYU's graduate Interactive Telecommunications Program in the Tisch School of the Arts, and as an associate professor in the Journalism Department. He is an expert on the effects of the Internet on society. His books include Little Rice: Smartphones, Xiaomi, and the Chinese Dream *(2015),* Here Comes Everybody: The Power of Organizing Without Organizations *(2008), and* Cognitive Surplus: Creativity and Generosity in a Connected Age *(2010). He blogs at shirky.com/weblog/.*

I teach theory and practice of social media at NYU, and am an advocate and activist for the free culture movement, so I'm a pretty unlikely candidate for internet censor, but I have just asked the students in my fall seminar to refrain from using laptops, tablets, and phones in class.

I came late and reluctantly to this decision—I have been teaching classes about the internet since 1998, and I've generally had a *laissez-faire* attitude towards technology use in the classroom. This was partly because the subject of my classes made technology use feel organic, and when device use went well, it was great. Then there was the competitive aspect—it's my job to be more interesting than the possible distractions, so a ban felt like cheating. And finally, there's not wanting to infantilize my students, who are adults, even if young ones—time management is their job, not mine.

Despite these rationales, the practical effects of my decision to allow technology use in class grew worse over time. The level of distraction in my classes seemed to grow, even though it was the same professor and largely the same set of topics, taught to a group of students selected using roughly the same criteria every year. The change seemed to correlate more with the rising ubiquity and utility of the devices themselves, rather than any change in me, the students, or the rest of the classroom encounter.

4   Over the years, I've noticed that when I do have a specific reason to ask everyone to set aside their devices ('Lids down', in the parlance of my department), it's as if someone has let fresh air into the room. The conversation brightens, and more recently, there is a sense of relief from many of the students. Multi-tasking is cognitively exhausting—when we do it by choice, being asked to stop can come as a welcome change.

So this year, I moved from recommending setting aside laptops and phones to requiring it, adding this to the class rules: "Stay focused. (No devices in class, unless the assignment requires it.)" Here's why I finally switched from 'allowed unless by request' to 'banned unless required'.

We've known for some time that multi-tasking is bad for the quality of cognitive work, and is especially punishing of the kind of cognitive work we ask of college students.

This effect takes place over more than one time frame—even when multi-tasking doesn't significantly degrade immediate performance, it can have negative long-term effects on "declarative memory," the kind of focused recall that lets people characterize and use what they learned from earlier studying. (Multi-tasking thus makes the famous "learned it the day before the test, forgot it the day after" effect even more pernicious.)

8   People often start multi-tasking because they believe it will help them get more done. Those gains never materialize; instead, efficiency is degraded. However, it provides emotional gratification as a side-effect. (Multi-tasking moves the pleasure of procrastination *inside* the period of work.) This side-effect is enough to keep people committed to multi-tasking despite worsening the very thing they set out to improve.

On top of this, multi-tasking doesn't even exercise task-switching as a skill. A study from Stanford reports that heavy multi-taskers are *worse* at choosing which task to focus on. ("They are suckers for irrelevancy", as Cliff Nass, one of the researchers put it.) Multi-taskers often think they are like gym rats, bulking up their ability to juggle tasks, when in fact they are like alcoholics, degrading their abilities through over-consumption.

This is all just the research on multi-tasking as a stable mental phenomenon. Laptops, tablets and phones—the devices on which the struggle between focus and distraction is played out daily—are making the problem progressively worse. Any designer of software as a service has an incentive to be as ingratiating as they can be, in order to compete with other such services. "Look what a good job I'm doing! Look how much value I'm delivering!"

This problem is especially acute with social media, because on top of the general incentive for any service to be verbose about its value, social information is immediately and emotionally engaging. Both the form and the content of a Facebook update are almost irresistibly distracting, especially compared with the hard slog of coursework. ("Your former lover tagged a photo you are in" vs. "The Crimean War was the first conflict significantly affected by use of the telegraph." Spot the difference?)

12   Worse, the designers of operating systems have every incentive to be arms dealers to the social media firms. Beeps and pings and pop-ups and icons, contemporary interfaces provide an extraordinary array of attention-getting devices, emphasis on "getting." Humans are incapable of ignoring surprising new information in our visual field, an effect that is strongest when the visual cue is slightly above and beside the area we're focusing on. (Does that sound like the upper-right corner of a screen near you?)

The form and content of a Facebook update may be almost irresistible, but when combined with a visual alert in your immediate peripheral vision, it is—really, actually, biologically—impossible to resist. Our visual and emotional systems are faster and more powerful than our intellect; we are given to automatic responses when either system receives stimulus, much less both. Asking a student to stay focused while she has alerts on is like asking a chess player to concentrate while rapping their knuckles with a ruler at unpredictable intervals.

Jonathan Haidt's metaphor of the elephant and the rider is useful here. In Haidt's telling, the mind is like an elephant (the emotions) with a rider (the intellect) on top. The rider can see and plan ahead, but the elephant is far more powerful. Sometimes the rider and the elephant work together (the ideal in classroom settings), but if they conflict, the elephant usually wins.

After reading Haidt, I've stopped thinking of students as people who simply make choices about whether to pay attention, and started thinking of them as people *trying* to pay attention but having to compete with various influences, the largest of which is their own propensity towards involuntary and emotional reaction. (This is even harder for young people, the elephant so strong, the rider still a novice.)

16

Regarding teaching as a shared struggle changes the nature of the classroom. It's not me demanding that they focus—it's me and them working together to help defend their precious focus against outside distractions. I have a classroom full of riders and elephants, but I'm trying to teach the riders.

And while I do, who is whispering to the elephants? Facebook, Wechat, Twitter, Instagram, Weibo, Snapchat, Tumblr, Pinterest, the list goes on, abetted by the designers of the Mac, iOS, Windows, and Android. In the classroom, it's me against a brilliant and well-funded army (including, sharper than a serpent's tooth, many of my former students.) These designers and engineers have every incentive to capture as much of my students' attention as they possibly can, without regard for any commitment those students may have made to me or to themselves about keeping on task.

It doesn't have to be this way, of course. Even a passing familiarity with the literature on programming, a famously arduous cognitive task, will acquaint you with stories of people falling into code-flow so deep they lose track of time, forgetting to eat or sleep. Computers are not inherent sources of distraction—they can in fact be powerful engines of focus—but latter-day versions have been designed to be, because attention is the substance which makes the whole consumer internet go.

The fact that hardware and software is being professionally designed to distract was the first thing that made me willing to require rather than merely suggest that students not use devices in class. There are some counter-moves in the industry right now—software that takes over your screen to hide distractions, software that prevents you from logging into certain sites or using the internet at all, phones with Do Not Disturb options—but at the moment these are rear-guard actions. The industry has committed itself to an arms race for my students' attention, and if it's me against Facebook and Apple, I lose.

20

The final realization—the one that firmly tipped me over into the "No devices in class" camp—was this: screens generate distraction in a manner akin to second-hand smoke. A paper with the blunt title "Laptop Multitasking Hinders Classroom Learning for Both Users and Nearby Peers" says it all:

> We found that participants who multitasked on a laptop during a lecture scored lower on a test compared to those who did not multitask, and participants who were in direct view of a multitasking peer scored lower on a test compared to those who were not. The results demonstrate that multitasking on a laptop poses a significant

distraction to both users and fellow students and can be detrimental to comprehension of lecture content.

I have known, for years, that the basic research on multi-tasking was adding up, and that for anyone trying to do hard thinking (our *spécialité de la maison*, here at college), device use in class tends to be a net negative. Even with that consensus, however, it was still possible to imagine that the best way to handle the question was to tell the students about the research, and let them make up their own minds.

The "Nearby Peers" effect, though, shreds that rationale. There is no *laissez-faire* attitude to take when the degradation of focus is social. Allowing laptop use in class is like allowing boombox use in class—it lets each person choose whether to degrade the experience of those around them.

Groups also have a rider-and-elephant problem, best described by Wilfred Bion in an oddly written but influential book, *Experiences in Groups*. In it, Bion, who practiced group therapy, observed how his patients would unconsciously coordinate their actions to defeat the purpose of therapy. In discussing the ramifications of this, Bion observed that effective groups often develop elaborate structures, designed to keep their sophisticated goals from being derailed by more primal group activities like gossiping about members and vilifying non-members.

24

The structure of a classroom, and especially a seminar room, exhibits the same tension. All present have an incentive for the class to be as engaging as possible; even though engagement often means waiting to speak while listening to other people wrestle with half-formed thoughts, that's the process by which people get good at managing the clash of ideas. Against that long-term value, however, each member has an incentive to opt out, even if only momentarily. The smallest loss of focus can snowball, the impulse to check WeChat quickly and then put the phone away leading to just one message that needs a reply right now, and then, wait, *what* happened last night??? (To the people who say "Students have always passed notes in class," I reply that old-model notes didn't contain video and couldn't arrive from anywhere in the world at 10 megabits a second.)

I have the good fortune to teach in cities richly provisioned with opportunities for distraction. Were I a 19-year-old planning an ideal day in Shanghai, I would not put "Listen to an old guy talk for an hour" at the top of my list. (Vanity prevents me from guessing where it *would* go.) And yet I can teach the students things they are interested in knowing, and despite all the literature on joyful learning, from Maria Montessori on down, some parts of making your brain do new things are just hard.

Indeed, college contains daily exercises in delayed gratification. "Discuss early modern European print culture" will never beat "Sing karaoke with friends" in a straight fight, but in the long run, having a passable Rhianna impression will be a less useful than understanding how media revolutions unfold.

Anyone distracted in class doesn't just lose out on the content of the discussion, they create a sense of permission that opting out is OK, and, worse, a haze of second-hand distraction for their peers. In an environment like this, students need support for the better angels of their nature (or at least the more intellectual angels), and they need defenses against the powerful short-term incentives to put off complex, frustrating tasks. That support and those defenses don't just happen, and they are not limited to the individual's choices. They are provided by social structure, and that structure is disproportionately provided by the professor, especially during the first weeks of class.

28   This is, for me, the biggest change—not a switch in rules, but a switch in how I see my role. Professors are at least as bad at estimating how interesting we are as the students are at estimating their ability to focus. Against oppositional models of teaching and learning, both negative—Concentrate, or lose out!—and positive—Let me attract your attention!—I'm coming to see student focus as a collaborative process. It's me and them working to create a classroom where the students who want to focus have the best shot at it, in a world increasingly hostile to that goal.

Some of the students will still opt out, of course, which remains their prerogative and rightly so, but if I want to help the ones who do want to pay attention, I've decided it's time to admit that I've brought whiteboard markers to a gun fight, and act accordingly.

PERSONAL RESPONSE

Do you keep your electronic device turned on during classroom? If so, how do you use it—to take notes, to record the lecture, or to look at messages and postings as they occur? If not, are you distracted by others students' use of their devices?

QUESTIONS FOR CLASS OR SMALL-GROUP DISCUSSION

1. What do you understand Shirky to mean when he says that multitasking is "cognitively exhausting" (paragraph 4)? Does your own experience support that statement?

2. What is the point of Shirky's example of the Jonathan Haidt metaphor of the elephant and the rider (paragraph 10)? Explain his comparison of screen-generated distraction to second-hand smoke (paragraph 6).

3. Summarize the evidence that Shirky provides to prove his point about the distracting nature of various social media in the classroom. Do you find the evidence persuasive?

4. Explain whether you are convinced that Shirky made the right decision to ban electronic devices in his classroom.

OUR PHOTOSHOPPING DISORDER

ERIN CUNNINGHAM

Erin Cunningham has served as fashion reporter at The Daily Beast, *has contributed fashion articles to the* New York Times *and the* Washington Post, *and is currently senior fashion editor at* Refinery29. *She holds a bachelor's degree in International Affairs and English from the George Washington University. This article was posted on* The Daily Beast *website.*

Nearly three years ago, Seth Matlins, a former Hollywood marketing executive who spent almost nine years at agency-powerhouse CAA and served as CMO at Live Nation Entertainment, began looking at the world through the eyes of his daughter and the woman she would one day become. He considered the obstacles "that can leap out and get in the way of a little girl trying to grow up happy and trying to becoming a sustainably happy woman," he told *The Daily Beast*. He quit his million-dollar gig to, in conjunction with his wife, Eva, become an empowering resource for girls and young women.

"In August 2011, there was a story that I read about a member of the British parliament [Jo Swinson] who had taken down two Lancôme billboards in London—one had Julia Roberts, the other had Christy Turlington," he said. "And she took them down because she said they provided such a false and unrealistic expectation of what women should and could look like, that it was damaging. I thought to myself, who in the world is looking out for my daughter—for our children—from a legislative perspective here? And I didn't see anyone, because there was no one."

That same month, Matlins published an op-ed on the *Huffington Post* titled "Why Beauty Ads Should Be Legislated." He called for integration from the Federal Trade Commission (FTC) to regulate and eventually prevent deceptive images in advertisements, highlighting the relationship between these unattainable media expectations and a portfolio of public health issues—including "emotional, mental, and physical."

It was also that year—2011—that the American Medical Association said, "We must stop exposing impressionable children and teenagers to advertisements portraying models with body types only attainable with the help of photo editing software," and asked the advertising industry to "develop guidelines . . . that would discourage the altering of photographs in a manner that could promote unrealistic expectations of appropriate body image."

Three years later, the industry has not changed its practice or increased regulation.

Although Matlin's idea dates back to 2011, the official bill, *H.R. 4341: Truth in Advertising Act of 2014*, was introduced to Congress on March 27, 2014. The bipartisan bill aims "to direct the Federal Trade Commission to submit to Congress a report on the use, in advertising and other media for the promotion of commercial products, of images that have been altered to materially change the physical characteristics of the faces and bodies of the individuals depicted." Presented by co-sponsors Representatives Ileana Ros-Lehtinen (R-FL), Lois Capps (D-CA) and Ted Deutch (D-FL), and receiving support from the Eating Disorder Coalition (EDC), 'The Truth in Advertising' bill asks the FTC to produce "a strategy to reduce the use . . . of images that have been altered to materially change the physical characteristics of the faces and bodies of the individuals depicted." It also requests "recommendations for an appropriate, risk-based regulatory framework with respect to such use" following an 18-month period dedicated to researching the links between unrealistic body expectations and mental, emotional, and physical health issues.

"This bill specifically does not require the FTC to take a specific approach to these issues," Capps told *The Daily Beast*. "Instead, it is calling for conversation to begin on what is an altered body image, what effects does it have on the health and well-being of consumers, and if that false advertising is harmful, how to move forward to address it. It also directs the FTC to work with a wide range of stakeholders to not only lead to the most informed product, but to also ensure that the groups who can make a change in this area are engaged in the conversation—and any possible solutions—from the start. While I acknowledge that it is difficult to move legislation in the current Congress, this bipartisan bill is one that has the chance to be a small but meaningful step forward for our youth."

8

Her co-sponsor, Rep. Ros-Lehtinen, agreed that the focus of this bill stems from the harm these advertisements can have on people's health and well-being—especially the young.

"The photoshopped images of children are particularly disturbing," Rep. Ros-Lehtinen told *The Daily Beast* when asked why she got involved with this legislation. "Advertisers are photoshopping children in ads that encourage young women and men to attempt to replicate unrealistic or impossible bodies, leading to serious health problems like eating disorders. Incredibly, one to two of every 100 children in America suffer from an eating disorder. Anorexia is killing more Americans than any other mental illness, and it is time we did something about it."

According to The National Institute on Media and the Family, the medical statistics point to a problem: 53 percent of 13-year-old girls are dissatisfied with their appearance and body image. When they reach age 17, the number jumps to 78 percent. Eating disorders have the highest mortality of all mental illnesses; 30 percent of high school girls and 16 percent of high school boys suffer from disordered eating. But does our government really have the ability to both regulate and improve the current situation without infringing on the rights of advertisers or privatized companies?

"Yes, this is exactly what the FTC was created to do," Matlins explained, when asked if this situation can truly be regulated by the government. "They're the nation's consumer protection agency. Rather than looking at one advertisement and one claim, which is what they do day in and day out, we're asking the FTC to look at an entire class of advertising, because the practice of materially changing people in these ads is not limited to fashion or beauty, or movie studios, record labels, or TV networks. It's across industry, and it's equally deceptive and damaging regardless of what industry it emanates."

12   Yet the main issue with the bill is its omission of the editorial sector, which is protected by the First Amendment. Recent news coverage concerning body image and social media has been particularly focused on photoshop infractions seen in magazine covers and spreads—think Jezebel's campaign for the release of unretouched photos of Lena Dunham's *Vogue* shoot, or young pop star Lorde calling out Canadian glossy *FASHION* magazine for seemingly adjusting her nose in one of the images.

While they have considered adding publishing to the mix, it's difficult to do so without encroaching on First Amendment freedom, or, as Ros-Lehtinen pointed out, "restricting artistic expression." Although advertisements are required to be regulated by the FTC, publications are protected under the idea of "commercial speech."

When asked about the absence of involvement of the publishing industry, Matlins assured me that this bill is not "a silver bullet. It will not solve, nor address, every single problem that affects the way we feel about ourselves, that affects health and happiness. Editorial certainly contributes to it. Other things contribute to it. Our bill is not a First Amendment issue, because we're not going against things that are universally protected."

So what exactly will the bill aim to protect? And more importantly, who will decide what makes an offending image?

16   "What the bill defines as a material change are changes to shape, size, proportion, color, or the enhancement or removal of an individual feature. So, if you change Keira Knightley's bust the way they did on a movie poster, that counts. If you make Melissa McCarthy smaller the way they did in *The Heat*, that counts. That crosses a line to misrepresentation and deception all in the pursuit of selling," Matlin explains. "As a marketer, I know that advertising sells more than the products or services in it."

The tools to get these improvements up and running are already there. While the bill may seem like a ground-breaking move, the foundation of what it is asking for already legally exists under Section Five of the Federal Trade Commission Act, the FTC already has the ability to prohibit "unfair or deceptive acts or practices in or affecting commerce." So it's hard not to wonder, why have they not been doing anything about it? Despite some of its shortfalls in regards to editorial (which is understandable, considering the protections of the Constitution), the bill (and its Congressional support) may be the push the FTC needs to make strides—albeit, small ones— to regulate photoshopping.

"This bill in particular is taking the right steps," Johanna Kandel, president of the EDC, told the *Daily Beast*. "It asks the FTC to take 18 months to do really thorough research and take a look at the implications of these altered images. And then it also asks them what the next steps are. We're not asking them to move mountains. We're just asking them to do the research."

PERSONAL RESPONSE

Have you ever felt compelled to buy something that you have seen advertised because you are convinced that it will change the way you look or feel or perhaps because it might enhance your image or quality of life? Have you ever been made to feel inadequate because of an advertisement?

QUESTIONS FOR CLASS OR SMALL-GROUP DISCUSSION

1. What do you understand the purpose of H. R. 341: *Truth in Advertising Act of 2014* to be? How would it limit or regulate advertisements?

2. Cunningham mentions several times "the harm these advertisements can have on people's health and well-being—especially the young" (paragraph 8). What do you understand that harm to be? How can an advertisement affect health and well-being? How might the young be especially affected?

3. Cunningham asks: "Who will decide what makes an offending image?" (paragraph 15). How would you answer that question? Who decides which images are offensive or harmful and which are not?

4. The First Amendment is mentioned several times in this article. Why would the First Amendment be an issue in relation to the proposed bill? Do you think that is a legitimate concern and that First Amendment rights must always be honored? Are there circumstances in which it might be legitimate to restrict or violate First Amendment rights?

THE COLLECTIVE CONSCIENCE OF REALITY TELEVISION

SERENA ELAVIA

Serena Elavia, a graduate of Trinity College, Hartford, Connecticut, is a reporter/editor for Fox Business Network. Before that, she worked for a year as an Editorial Fellow for The Atlantic *magazine, where this article was published.*

Once famous for flipping dinner tables on *The Real Housewives of New Jersey*, reality star Teresa Giudice and her husband Giuseppe "Joe" were recently sentenced to one and three-and-a-half years in jail, respectively. When Giudice and her husband pleaded guilty to numerous counts of conspiracy to commit wire and mail fraud in March, Bravo's cameras captured every drama-filled moment for the show's sixth season.

Bravo managed to film the sentencing just in time for the season finale, which even showed Teresa's enemies crying. Teresa and Joe may be convicted criminals, but it's difficult to not feel for the couple throughout the season as viewers watch footage of their four young daughters celebrating what may be their last Christmas together as a family for a long time. Or when the eldest daughter looks at her mother and says "I obviously know what's going on. I'm old enough to comprehend and understand what's going on," as tears stream down her face.

Most reality shows in the vein of *Real Housewives* just feature dinner parties gone wrong and screaming matches, which viewers avidly consume. Networks are willing to show almost everything, regardless of the impact on its cast members, until their viewers get upset, lash out on social media, or threaten to stop watching entirely. What viewers will or won't watch matters immensely to networks; in fact, they seem function as the networks' sole "conscience."

4   There is, of course, content that producers will not air, though "that varies from production company to company," a reality-television producer who asked not to be named said in an email. "Personally, I believe a producer, and then in turn the network, will air anything that does not put them at serious risk of lawsuit."

Producers set few boundaries when it comes to airing non-litigious content with potentially damaging consequences for its stars. MTV found itself facing backlash after the series premiere of *Jersey Shore* when trailers for upcoming episodes showed Nicole "Snooki" Polizzi getting punched in the face at a bar by a stranger. The network pulled the footage after receiving complaints from viewers about depicting violence against women. Producers give viewers what they want to see, but at a certain point the audience begins to empathize with the cast members and turns on producers.

Showing Snooki being sucker-punched is extreme, and viewers objected. But if viewers don't care, then the networks essentially have free rein to show what they want. Take the case of *The Real Housewives of Beverly Hills*: Former cast member Taylor Armstrong discussed on-camera her husband Russell's physical abuse toward her and her five-year-old daughter throughout seasons one and two. Then three weeks before the second season premiered and just one month after Taylor filed for divorce, Russell committed suicide. While season two was packed with stories of Taylor's abuse, Bravo suddenly found itself being blamed for Russell's death, as critics said that the network unfairly portrayed him and drove him to suicide. The producers did edit out some scenes, like Taylor buying lingerie to spice up her marriage, but still showed a dinner party she attended with a black eye. One housewife asked her "Is this what it took for you to leave?," to which Taylor responded "Unfortunately." For Bravo, pushing the envelope proved beneficial—the second season of the show has so far had the highest ratings of the show's four-season run.

A year later during season three of the *Beverly Hills* series, another housewife, Brandi Glanville, announced castmate Adrienne Maloof's family secret at a dinner party. Bravo muted out the revelation, but after the episode aired, the tabloids began to investigate the secret, and ultimately the Maloofs admitted that Adrienne had used a surrogate to have her twin boys. After the incident, Maloof told *Us Weekly* that from the beginning of the show, her children would not be a part of the storyline. With a secret like that, Bravo couldn't resist, even if it meant almost going against Adrienne's contract, and found a way to weave it into the season. In an interview with *Life and Style* after the season, Adrienne said the revelation "destroyed her family" and put a strain on her marriage that ended in divorce.

Then there is the humiliation that some reality show participants have to endure. In 2009, on the 13th season of

ABC's *The Bachelor*, Jason Mesnick originally proposed to one contestant on the finale but then six weeks later in a reunion episode, he confessed that his true love was the runner-up and dumped the teary-eyed winner on live television (as if break ups weren't difficult enough already). Mesnick in an interview later said that because of his contract with ABC he couldn't give his fiancé any advance warning before dumping her on the reunion show. Critics said that producers manipulated the show for ratings, but viewers didn't seem to mind, and airing it paid off for ABC. The show is the highest rated episode of all time in the series with about 17 million viewers.

Sometimes networks preempt viewers' reactions. After news surfaced that "Mama June" Shannon of *Here Comes Honey Boo Boo* is dating a man convicted ten years ago of molesting her own daughter, TLC canceled the series effective immediately. In announcing the decision, the network said, "Supporting the health and welfare of these remarkable children is our only priority. TLC is faithfully committed to the children's ongoing comfort and well-being." As a result, TLC hasn't faced any criticism from viewers or accusations of condoning child molestation.

This question of empathy should not be restricted to producers and networks. Because the whims and tastes of viewers drive the content of reality shows, some have argued that viewers should consider their own complicity in what happens to the show's stars. Dr. Bruce Weinstein, who writes an ethics column for Bloomberg, says "if people didn't want to invade people's privacy, nobody would watch these shows."

Even with deaths and families being torn apart, there is an audience for these shows and so networks continue to produce them. People want to indulge in the drama and the hair-pulling as a guilty pleasure, but most people don't enjoy watching others experience tremendous emotional or physical suffering. These shows continue to be defined by a strange conundrum among reality-television fans: They want to see what's "really" happening to other people, as long as it isn't too real. For producers, who don't think in terms of sympathy, it's a delicate balance of exploiting their stars' stories for ratings while trying to determine what viewers will shun. There is no sympathy "code" for producers to follow when choosing what material to air, but it may be wise for them to consider creating one instead of only relying on fan reaction.

PERSONAL RESPONSE

If you watch reality television shows, explain their appeal. If not, explain why they do not appeal to you.

QUESTIONS FOR CLASS OR SMALL-GROUP DISCUSSION

1. Locate Elavia's thesis or central idea. How well do you think that Elavia's examples support her thesis?

2. Elavia writes, "There is, of course, content that producers will not air" (paragraph 4), and she comments that "producers set few boundaries" (paragraph 5). What sort of content is she referring to? Do you think there should be boundaries and if so, what do you think should be off limits in reality television programming? If not, why not?

3. Elavia refers to the "question of empathy" (paragraph 10) and to the lack of a "sympathy 'code'" (paragraph 11), suggesting that producers and networks should consider creating one. Explain what she means by those remarks and whether you agree with her.

4. Comment on this statement by an ethics column writer: "'If people didn't want to invade people's privacy, nobody would watch these shows'" (paragraph 10).

> MindTap   Reflect on the theme of this chapter.

PERSPECTIVES ON MEDIA STUDIES

Suggested Writing Topics

1. Argue in support of or against Clay Shirky's statement that electronic devices are major distractions in the classroom ("Why I Asked My Students to Put Their Laptops Away").

2. Advertisers contend that they do not create problems, but simply reflect the values of society. With Erin Cunningham's "Our Photoshopping Disorder" in mind, explain your position on the subject of how much responsibility advertisers should bear for the images they produce in their advertisements.

3. Survey a selection of magazine or television advertisements and examine them for examples that might support Erin Cunningham's statement in "Our Photoshopping Disorder" about "the harm these advertisements can have on people's health and well-being—especially the young" (paragraph 8). Explain what you find and whether you agree that some advertisements can cause harm.

4. Like advertisers, producers of television shows argue that they do not create problems but simply reflect the values of society. Drawing on Serena Elevia's "The Collective Conscience of Reality Television," explain your position on the subject of how much responsibility television producers and networks should bear for what they televise in their programs.

5. If you are a fan of reality shows on television, choose one that you particularly like and explain why it appeals to you. If you do not like reality shows, pick one that you particularly dislike and avoid watching and explain why you do not like it.

Research Topics

1. With Erin Cunningham's "Our Photoshopping Disorder" as a starting point, research the topic of advertisers' use of photoshopping in their ads. You might consider finding out the progress of H.R. 4341: *Truth in Advertising Act of 2014*, which Cunningham mentions.

2. Research the subject of advertising ethics by locating articles and books representing the opinions of both those who are critical of advertisements and those who defend them. Argue your own position on the subject, supporting it with relevant source materials.

3. Select a particular type of television program, such as reality TV, news program, talk show, children's entertainment, drama, or situation comedy, and research what critics say about such programming. Is there a program that represents the best of the type? The worst of the type?

4. Another approach is to reality television programs is to trace their development. What were the earliest shows? How do they compare with what it broadcast today? Do you see an improvement or a deterioration in their entertainment value?

5. Much has been written about certain images in films or on television, such as the portrayal of women, of minorities, and of class issues. Select a particular image or theme to research for its representation in films or on television. Choose a specific period (films/programs from this year or last year, or films/programs from a previous decade, for instance) and narrow your focus as much as possible. This task will become more manageable once you begin searching for sources and discover the nature of articles, books, and other materials on the general subject.

6. Research the question of whether allegations that the media have a liberal bias are true. Is it simply a perception, or can such bias, if it exists, be documented?

7. In 1961, Newton N. Minnow coined the term *vast wasteland* for what he saw as television's empty content and anti-intellectualism. Argue either that television remains a vast wasteland or that the phrase is does not describe television today. Base your position on research into the views of experts or others who have published opinions on the subject.

RESPONDING TO VISUALS

iStock/Getty Images

What might this image of a human and machine about to touch suggest of the potential of artificial intelligence, especially deep learning?

1. In the context of artificial intelligence, what do the human and machine arms represent?

2. Why are the fingers almost but not quite touching? What significance does the lightburst behind the fingers have?

3. What dimension or layer of possible meaning is suggested by the universe as background and the Earth highlighted, off to the side? Would the meaning change if the two arms were positioned in front of the Earth alone?

RESPONDING TO VISUALS

Alberto Ruggieri/Illustration Works/Motif/Corbis

Why does this figure coming out of a television have a smile on his face and his hand over the child's eyes?

1. What sorts of things is the figure casting behind him? What do they represent?

2. What commentary does the image make on the effects of television advertising on children?

3. What is added by the details of a pacifier in the child's mouth and the remote control in his hand?

CHAPTER 10

EDUCATION

LEARNING OBJECTIVES

Students will demonstrate an ability to do the following:

☐ Determine some of the important issues in education today.

☐ Evaluate their education thus far by identifying both positive and
negative experiences they have had in the process of getting an
education.

☐ Examine arguments for and against going to college.

MindTap*   Understand the goals of the chapter and complete a
warm-up activity.

CHAPTER OVERVIEW

Education is a complex and crucially important subject. Without education, people face obstacles to participating fully in society. Because of its importance, education is also the subject of controversy. People are divided on issues such as what materials and activities are appropriate for the classroom, what methods of delivering material work best, how much homework ought to be required of students, and what skills and knowledge students must demonstrate to go on to subsequent educational levels. Periodically, philosophies of education change, curricula are restructured, classrooms are transformed, and instructors learn new approaches to teaching their subject matter. As a student who has gone through many years of education, beginning in the primary grades, you are uniquely positioned to comment on this subject. You have been immersed in education and are presumably currently enrolled in at least one class, the course for which you are using this textbook. In the essays in this chapter, writers express their opinions on the subject of education, criticize certain aspects of the educational system in America, and praise other aspects. You are likely to find yourself either nodding your head in agreement or shaking your head in disagreement with what they say.

The first essay in this chapter, by *Boston Globe* opinion columnist Diane Ravitch, discusses what she describes as a skill-centered "fad" in K–12 education. In "Critical Thinking? You Need Knowledge," Ravitch explains why she is critical of the "21st-Century Skills" initiative in public schools. As you read her piece, consider how you would define an intelligent person. What skills and knowledge must a truly educated student have?

Next is an excerpt from Mike Rose's book *Why School?* in which he narrates an encounter with a slightly brain-damaged student in a community college basic skills program. As you read about Anthony's achievements, can you think of students you have known who might be similarly challenged and motivated? What does the example of Anthony add to your understanding of the importance of education?

Then, Heather Schilling summarizes the "anti-college" movement, a sentiment that gained widespread attention during the economic slump of the first decade of the twenty-first century when newspapers and magazines began publishing articles arguing that the high cost of a college education was not a good investment. As you read what she says are the arguments for and against going to college, consider your own feelings about it. As a student enrolled in the course for which you are reading this essay, you are likely to have strong feelings about why you chose to go to college and make that investment in your future. You will have an opportunity to discuss in class and/or write about your viewpoint on this subject.

As you read these selections, think about your own education, the courses you have taken, your classroom activities, the teachers who have taught you, and your own reading habits. Where do you agree with the authors, and where do you disagree? Are your experiences similar to or different from what they describe? What is your own philosophy of education? How important do you believe education is to your well-being and sense of self?

CRITICAL THINKING?
YOU NEED KNOWLEDGE

DIANE RAVITCH

Diane Ravitch is a historian of education, an educational policy analyst, and a research professor of education at New York University. She has served as Assistant Secretary of Education and has published numerous articles and books, including The Language Police: How Pressure Groups Restrict What Students Learn *(2003);* The English Reader: What Every Literate Person Needs to Know *(edited with Michael Ravitch) (2006);* Edspeak: The Death and Life of the Great American School System: How Testing and Choice Are Undermining Education *(2010); and* Reign of Error: The Hoax of the Privatization Movement and the Danger to America's Public Schools *(2014). In addition, she has edited fourteen books and published over 500 articles and reviews for both scholarly and popular publications. This article was published in the* Boston Globe.

The latest fad to sweep K–12 education is called "21st-Century Skills." States—including Massachusetts—are adding them to their learning standards, with the expectation that students will master skills such as cooperative learning and critical thinking and therefore be better able to compete for jobs in the global economy. Inevitably, putting a priority on skills pushes other subjects, including history, literature, and the arts, to the margins. But skill-centered, knowledge-free education has never worked.

The same ideas proposed today by the 21st-Century Skills movement were iterated and reiterated by pedagogues across the 20th century. In 1911, the dean of the education school at Stanford called on his fellow educators to abandon their antiquated academic ideals and adapt education to the real life and real needs of students.

In 1916, a federal government report scoffed at academic education as lacking relevance. The report's author said black children should "learn to do by doing," which he considered to be the modern, scientific approach to education.

4

Just a couple of years later, "the project method" took the education world by storm. Instead of a sequential curriculum laid out in advance, the program urged that boys and girls engage in hands-on projects of their own choosing, ideally working cooperatively in a group. It required activity, not docility, and awakened student motivation. It's remarkably similar to the model advocated by 21st-century skills enthusiasts.

The list goes on: students built, measured, and figured things out while solving real-life problems, like how to build a playhouse, pet park, or a puppet theater, as part of the 1920s and 1930s "Activity Movement." From the "Life Adjustment Movement" of the 1950s to "Outcome-Based Education" in the 1980s, one "innovation" after another devalued academic subject matter while making schooling relevant, hands-on, and attuned to the real interests and needs of young people.

To be sure, there has been resistance. In Roslyn, Long Island, in the 1930s, parents were incensed because their children couldn't read but spent an entire day baking nut bread. The Roslyn superintendent assured them that baking was an excellent way to learn mathematics.

None of these initiatives survived. They did have impact, however: They inserted into American education a deeply ingrained suspicion of academic studies and subject matter. For the past century, our schools of education have obsessed over critical-thinking skills, projects, cooperative learning, experiential learning, and so on. But they have paid precious little attention to the disciplinary knowledge that young people need to make sense of the world.

8

For over a century we have numbed the brains of teachers with endless blather about process and abstract thinking skills. We have taught them about graphic organizers and Venn diagrams and accountable talk, data-based decision-making, rubrics, and leveled libraries.

But we have ignored what matters most. We have neglected to teach them that one cannot think critically without quite a lot of knowledge to think about. Thinking critically involves comparing and contrasting and synthesizing what one has learned. And a great deal of knowledge is necessary before one can begin to reflect on its meaning and look for alternative explanations.

Proponents of 21st-Century Skills might wish it was otherwise, but we do not restart the world anew with each generation. We stand on the shoulders of those who have gone before us. What matters most in the use of our brains is our capacity to make generalizations, to see beyond our own immediate experience. The intelligent person, the one who truly is a practitioner of critical thinking, has the capacity to understand the lessons of history, to grasp the inner logic of science and mathematics, and to realize the meaning of philosophical debates by studying them.

Through literature, for example, we have the opportunity to see the world through the eyes of another person, to walk in his shoes, to experience life as it was lived in another century and another culture, to live vicariously beyond the bounds of our own time and family and place.

12   Until we teach both teachers and students to value knowledge and to love learning, we cannot expect them to use their minds well.

PERSONAL RESPONSE QUESTION

Comment on your own high school education. Do you recall any particular approach to learning that teachers had in common? If so, what was it? If not, how would you characterize your teachers' educational philosophy?

QUESTIONS FOR CLASS OR SMALL-GROUP DISCUSSION

1. Summarize in your own words the approaches to teaching that Ravitch complains about.

2. What rhetorical purpose is served by Ravitch's review of twentieth-century educational movements?

3. What is it that Ravitch feels is missing in the current educational movement? Do you agree with her?

4. Explain in your own words Ravitch's definition of an intelligent person. What, if anything, would you add to or change about her definition?

EXCERPT FROM WHY SCHOOL? A STUDENT IN A COMMUNITY COLLEGE BASIC SKILLS PROGRAM

MIKE ROSE

Mike Rose, a professor of Social Research Methodology at UCLA, has a special interest in educational programs for economically impoverished or underprepared students. He has written extensively on language, literacy, and the teaching of writing. Among his eleven books are The Mind at Work: Valuing the Intelligence of the American Worker *(2004);* Lives on the Boundary *(2005);* An Open Language: Selecting Writing on Literacy, Learning, and Opportunity *(2005);* Writer's Block: The Cognitive Dimension *(2009); and* Back to School: Why Everyone Deserves a Second Chance at Education *(2012). Rose posted this excerpt from his book* Why School? *(2009) on his blog.*

Food wrappers and sheets of newspaper were blowing in the wet wind across the empty campus. It was late in the day, getting dark fast, and every once in a while I'd look outside the library—which was pretty empty too—and imagine the drizzly walk to the car, parked far away.

Anthony was sitting by me, and I was helping him read a flyer on the dangers of cocaine. He wanted to give it to his daughter. Anthony was enrolled in a basic skills program, one of several special programs at this urban community college. Anthony was in his late-thirties, had some degree of brain damage from a childhood injury, worked custodial jobs most of his life. He could barely read or write, but was an informed, articulate guy, listening to FM radio current affairs shows while he worked, watching public television at home. He had educated himself through the sources available to him, compensating for the damage done.

The librarian was about to go off shift, so we gathered up our things—Anthony carried a big backpack—and headed past her desk to the exit. The wind pushed back on the door as I pushed forward, and I remember thinking how dreary the place was, dark and cold. At that moment I wanted so much to be home.

Just then a man in a coat and tie came up quickly behind us. "Hey man," he said to Anthony, "you look good. You lose

4

some weight?" Anthony beamed, said that he had dropped a few pounds and that things were going o.k. The guy gave Anthony a cupping slap on the shoulder, then pulled his coat up and walked head down across the campus.

"Who was that?" I asked, ducking with Anthony back inside the entryway to the library. He was one of the deans, Anthony said, but, well, he was once his parole officer, too. He's seen Anthony come a long way. Anthony pulled on the straps of his backpack, settling the weight more evenly across his shoulders. "I like being here," he said in his soft, clear voice. "I know it can't happen by osmosis. But this is where it's at."

I've thought about this moment off and on for twenty years. I couldn't wait to get home, and Anthony was right at home. Fresh from reading something for his daughter, feeling the clasp on his shoulder of both his past and his future, for Anthony a new life was emerging on the threshold of a chilly night on a deserted campus.

These few minutes remind me of how humbling work with human beings can be. How we'll always miss things. How easily we get distracted—my own memories of cold urban landscapes overwhelmed the moment.

8   But I also hold onto this experience with Anthony for it contains so many lessons about development, about resilience and learning, about the power of hope and a second chance. It reminds us too of the importance of staying close to the ground, of finding out what people are thinking, of trying our best—flawed though it will be—to understand the world as they see it . . . and to be ready to revise our understanding. This often means taking another line of sight on what seems familiar, seeing things in a new light.

And if we linger with Anthony a while longer, either in the doorway or back inside at a library table, we might get the chance to reflect on the basic question of what school is for, the purpose of education. What brought Anthony back to the classroom after all those years? To help his economic prospects, certainly. Anthony wanted to trade in his mop and pail for decent pay and a few benefits. But we also get a glimpse as to why else he's here. To be able to better guide his daughter. To be more proficient in reading about the events swirling around him—to add reading along with radio and television to his means of examining the world. To create a new life for himself, nurture this emerging sense of who he can become.

PERSONAL RESPONSE

Write for a few minutes about what you think the purpose of going to school is. Does that purpose change as you move through the educational system, from elementary to secondary to higher education?

QUESTIONS FOR CLASS OR SMALL-GROUP DISCUSSION

1. State in your own words the point or central purpose of this piece.

2. Comment on the rhetorical effectiveness of Rose's use of one extended example to achieve his purpose. Does that strategy work?

3. Rose says that his experience with Anthony contains "so many lessons" (paragraph 8). What do you understand those lessons to be, and how does Anthony illustrate them?

4. In the concluding paragraph, Rose suggests that the experience with Anthony raises "the basic question of what school is for, the purpose of education." Discuss how Rose answers the question of what school is for and whether you agree with him. Would you add other reasons to those that Rose names?

THE ANTI-COLLEGE MOVEMENT: FINDING THE SONG IN THE CLAMOR

HEATHER SCHILLING

Heather Schilling is Associate Professor, Chair, and Director of Teacher Education at Manchester University (North Manchester, Indiana), where she has taught since 2003. Before that she taught high school English for 12 years. She has recently served as president of the Indiana State Reading Association and is especially interested in service learning, progressive education, and the bridge between high school and college.

As the economic recession took hold of the country in the early part of the 21st century, many Americans began to question the value of investing in higher education, which they had once viewed as secure and well worth the expense. Recent headlines in national publications like *Time, The Chronicle of Higher Education, The New York Times Magazine,* and *U.S. News and World Report* screamed the insult "what's the point of a college education?" Editorials entitled "It's the End of College as We Know it (And I Feel Fine)" (Morella) painted dismal pictures of skyrocketing debt for sub-par education and college graduates not employed in the fields of their degrees. Unfortunately, those involved in higher education, especially the private, liberal arts schools, were slow to turn their attention to the mounting dissatisfaction among students, their parents, and the public at large. Instead of doing something about it like emphasizing how a college education contributes to the core of American values and economic prosperity, those in higher education did little or nothing, resting on tradition, on their laurels, and on archaic reasons for getting a college education. The recent release of the annual national report card for institutions of higher education, along with stories of crippling debt incurred by students attending four-year colleges, has been a wake-up call for colleges and universities to emphasize the real merits of a college education. Despite dire warnings in the press and anecdotal stories about college graduates not being able to find jobs that their degrees have qualified them for, the foundational elements of a college education ultimately do underscore its worth: earning a bachelor's degree in the twenty-first century sets a graduate up for unimagined successes as well as intangible rewards.

Pundits point out the apparent adverse side of attaining a college degree, for some recent graduates do find themselves unemployed or underemployed. In fact, the most recent American economic recession that lasted from December 2007 until June 2009 seems to underscore the dangers of investing too much in one's future—at least when that investment is for a college education, especially when the rate of return looks as if it will fail to meet the investor's expectations. Historically, college graduates could expect to see steady economic benefits over their lifetimes in ways proportionately significant when compared with their peers with only high school degrees. Those times, however, have somewhat changed, and, despite the economic recovery of the past few years, the job market has responded slowly. As a result, some college graduates find themselves struggling to find employment or find themselves underemployed. In fact, despite their academic backgrounds, more recent college graduates face unemployment than their counterparts in previous generations (Abel et al. 3). Equally as alarming as unemployment, many recently-graduated millennials find themselves underemployed, taking jobs for which they are overqualified or that do not require a college degree. Data from the U.S. Department of Occupational Information Network (O*NET) indicates that in 2014 nearly one-third of college graduates were temporarily working in jobs that do not require a college degree (Abel et al. 3). The most recent recession deeply hit the millennials, and the current generation of college graduates have so far fared worse than graduates of previous generations ("Rising Costs"), reaching an unemployment peak of 7 percent in 2010 (Abel et al. 2). Landing a good job, especially in the area of one's major, has become increasingly more difficult, and critics are right to point that out.

Coupled with the difficulty of finding a job or being underemployed, the crippling debt accrued by many college graduates adds fuel to the clamor of dissenting voices arguing that a college education is not worth the investment. Over the past two decades, state and federal loan policies have shifted in such a way that the education industry has seen a rather large increase in the number of students borrowing money (Chen and Wiederspan 572). While graduates have always amassed debt to get their degree, the amount of debt assumed by today's college graduates seems proportionally larger than for previous generations of graduates. Today's college co-ed graduates with an average of $30,000 debt, and researchers indicate that of the loans administered in 2013, nearly 23 percent will default on subsidized loans with another 18 percent expected to default on unsubsidized loans (Chen and Wiederspan 575). Graduates who cannot find jobs simply cannot pay their bills. College tuition and the cost of room and board for students living on campus are at an all-time high, thus deepening the criticism of parents and students alike. As consumers, they question whether spending so much money on a college degree will be worth their investment, especially if they have to borrow increasingly more money. What consumers need to keep in mind, however, is the real value of a college education.

4   According to the College Board, providing "postsecondary education to all who are motivated and can benefit is a prerequisite for both a healthy economy and a society that provides meaningful paths to rewarding and independent lives for all individuals," and ultimately, the picture for college graduates is

not as dismal as the media or critics portray. Despite reports in the popular press and despite stories of college students working in jobs which do not require a college degree or struggling to land that first job, the investment in a college education is still worth the cost. The fact is, for a variety of reasons, college graduates often fare better during economic downturns than their peers with only a high school. Thus, while in the period after the most recent American recession, as noted before, the unemployment rate for college graduates in 2010 was 7 percent, their peers with only a high school diploma fared far worse. The trends in unemployment and underemployment have remained relatively steady over the past two decades, so the recent alarm raised by those hearing only part of the story appears to be ill-founded, and the employment outlook seems much brighter than popular media would have one believe.

Furthermore, despite the naysayers' observations that many recent graduates struggle to find employment or find employment outside the field of their degree, younger graduates have always had greater unemployment or been underemployed; so while pundits may use that argument against getting a college degree, the trend is nothing new. In fact, Sandy Baum, co-author of "Student Debt: Who Borrows Most? What Lies Ahead," indicates that most of the college graduates who leave school with loans are doing just fine (qtd. in Barshay). Interestingly, four-year college graduates are not the problem. Instead, just three types of borrowers need attention: students who attend for-profit schools, students who drop out before finishing their college degrees, and graduate students. Graduate students often have unlimited credit lines with the federal government, so statistics such as those for 2012 indicate that of college students who borrowed more than $50,000, sixty-five percent were graduate students (Barshay). Ultimately, it is not the typical four-year college graduate who drives up the debt ceiling, yet this population is often lumped into the equation with graduate students in the argument that the value of a degree is not worth the high debt it takes to achieve it.

More importantly, though, over seventy percent of college graduates indicate that their college degree has benefited them in intangible ways ("Rising Cost"). They report feeling positive about their futures and having a strong sense of well-being. They also feel that their horizons have been expanded far beyond what they might expected had they not gone college. This optimism is linked not only to the knowledge they gained while at college and the practical application of it that led to getting satisfactory jobs after graduation, but also to a strong sense that college provided a place for them to explore interests and meet a wide and disparate range of people. Many of them made friendships that will last a lifetime. When one considers those benefits in combination with a cost analysis of investing in a college degree, it becomes clear that there are many important and compelling arguments for going to college.

One of the most compelling intangible benefits is something that critics of higher education have failed to consider and what colleges need to promote more: the transferrable skills that college students develop when they are deeply engaged in their education. These skills include collaboration, communication, time management, and structured independence, skills that carry into adulthood and manifest themselves in many ways. Students who immerse themselves in their education learn much more than the academic content of their courses. By interacting with their peers in course projects, in class discussions, and in out-of-class social settings, they learn to collaborate and communicate at a much deeper level than their non-degree-seeking counterparts. Businesses want employees who possess collaborative skills and the ability to work through differences. While higher education does not necessarily measure graduates' abilities to collaborate or employ conflict resolution tactics, these transferrable skills are extremely important. Additionally, going to college helps students develop good time management skills as they learn to navigate the expectations of college academics and newfound freedoms of living independently. In the end, it is these transferable skills that separate college graduates from noncollege graduates even further than the financial differences in income, and these immeasurable characteristics enable college graduates to enter the adult world prepared to interact successfully with colleagues and understand the importance of discovering work-life balance.

8

Initially, the clamoring of the critics might seem to make sense, but if people who listen to the discordant sounds would hear instead the voices of the graduates who value everything they learned in college, the real benefits of a degree become clear. While college is not for everyone, those who make the financial investment and then make the commitment to get the most from that investment learn that education is more than just showing up for class or more than looking ahead to a potential salary. College graduates can not only look forward to out-earning those who do not go to college; they can also enjoy those intangible benefits that charts and graphs cannot measure.

Works Cited

Abel, Jason R., et al. "Are Recent College Graduates Finding Good Jobs?" *Current Issues in Economics and Finance*, vol. 20, no. 1, 2014, pp. 2-4. www .newyorkfed.org/medialibrary/media/research /current_issues/ci20-1.pdf.

Chen, Rong, and Mark Wiederspan. "Understanding the Determinants of Debt Burden Among College Graduates." *The Journal of Higher Education*, vol. 85, no. 4 , July/August 2014, pp. 565-98.

College Board. "Trends in College Pricing 2014." *Trends in Higher Education Series*, 2014, /secure-media .collegeboard.org/digitalServices/misc/trends/2014- trends-college-pricing-report-final.pdf.

Barshay, Jill. "Heaviest Debt Burdens Fall on 3 Types of Students." *The Hechinger Report*. 8 June 2015, hechingerreport.org/the-heaviest-college-debt- burdens-fall-on-three-types-of-students/.

Morella, Michael. "It's the End of College as We Know It (And I Feel Fine)." *Knowledge Bank*. U.S. News & World Report, 30 Apr. 2015, 9:00 a.m., www.usnews.com/opinion/knowledge-bank /2015/04/30/kevin-carey-explains-the-end-of- college-and-higher-educations-future.

"The Rising Cost of Not Going to College." *Pew Research Center: Social & Demographic Trends*. 11 Feb. 2014, www.pewsocialtrends.org/2014/02/11 /the-rising-cost-of-not-going-to-college/.

PERSONAL RESPONSE

Write about how you arrived at your decision to attend college despite the cost.

QUESTIONS FOR CLASS AND SMALL-GROUP DISCUSSION

1. Explain what you understand are the chief arguments in the "anti-college movement" against going to college. Did you think about these arguments when you decided whether to attend college?

2. What are the "intangible benefits" that Schilling says students gain from their college careers (paragraph 1)? Why are they "benefits"? Had you realized that there were those benefits before reading this article?

3. Schilling discusses "transferrable skills [that] college students develop when they are deeply engaged in their education" (paragraph 5). Summarize the skills that she is referring to. Do you feel that you have developed any of those skills at college?

4. Explain the metaphor in the title: What is the "song"? What is the "clamor"? How well do you think the metaphor works in the context of this article?

MindTap   Reflect on the theme of this chapter.

PERSPECTIVES ON EDUCATION

Suggested Writing Topics

1. With Diane Ravitch's "Critical Thinking? You Need Knowledge" in mind, define an "intelligent person." You may want to include specific instances of someone you know who exemplifies that term for you.

2. Explain whether you think Diane Ravitch ("Critical Thinking? You Need Knowledge") would consider Anthony of Mike Rose's excerpt from *Why School?* "an intelligent person."

3. With Heather Schilling's "The Anti-College Movement: Finding the Song in the Clamor" in mind, explore your decision to attend college. What possible drawbacks or potential problems did you consider, and how did the benefits of attending college outweigh the drawbacks of not attending? Are you pleased with your decision thus far?

4. Define *education*, using specific examples to illustrate general or abstract statements. You may want to focus specifically on high school education, as you experienced it, or higher education, which you are currently experiencing.

5. Distinguish among the words *education*, *knowledge*, and *wisdom*. How are they similar? How are they different? Would a standardized test measure any of them?

6. Argue the merits of the major that you have chosen or are thinking of choosing. What do you hope to do with your college degree? What career are you aspiring to? How well will do you think your college education will prepare you for that career?

7. Many articles offering advice to young people on how to do well in school stress the importance of cultivating good homework habits and getting an education. Write a personal essay on your study and homework habits, including how you feel about education and what you hope to achieve with it.

8. Write about a teacher who made an impression and had a significant effect on you. What made that teacher so important to you? What were the teacher's personality features and admirable qualities? If a particular incident was especially significant in your relationship, narrate what happened.

9. Some people argue that not everyone deserves to go to college and that admitting average or mediocre students into colleges has debased American higher education. Argue in support of or against that position.

10. Imagine that the number of students admitted to college directly after high school has been limited to the upper 33 percent of all graduating seniors and that you do not meet the requirements for admission to college. Under special circumstances, students who fall below the 33 percent mark may be admitted. In a letter to the admissions officer at the college of your choice, argue that you should be admitted despite your class ranking and give reasons why you would make a good student.

Research Topics

1. Heather Schilling in "The Anti-College Movement" suggests that colleges and universities failed to react quickly to a growing sense during the recession in the first part of the twenty-first century that investing in higher education might be a waste of money. Research the "anti-college movement" and find out what colleges and universities did in response to it.

2. Read one of Mike Rose's books on education and research a subject related to or suggested by that book. Alternatively, select a potentially argumentative subject that Rose writes about, perhaps starting with his blog, one of his books, or articles he has written.

3. Research the tracking systems used in many schools. Find opinions supporting and opposing such systems, consider their advantages and disadvantages, and arrive at your own conclusion based on your reading.

4. Research the conflict of traditional versus revisionist curriculum. Consider interviewing educators as part of your research. Read periodical articles from the last several years on political correctness, defenses for or against the canon, or related topics.

5. Research the "21st-Century Skills movement." Define it, explain its purpose, and assess its usefulness in producing truly educated students.

6. Taking the lists of works cited at the end of Heather Schilling's "The Anti-College Movement: Finding the Song in the Clamor" as a starting point, research the issue of whether the expense of a college education is worth the investment. Consider: Do college graduates do better financially than non-college graduates? Do college graduates have a better quality of life than non-college graduates? What "intangible benefits" do college graduates gain from their college careers?

7. Colleges and universities receiving federal funding are routinely reviewed for how well the institutions educate students. One of the assessment tools to measure learning in institutions of higher education is a standardized test. Research the success or failure of such tests to measure learning and argue your position on the subject. Can a test reveal how much you know?

RESPONDING TO VISUALS

altrendo images/Getty Images

Why do you think this woman, apparently reading a book, is blindfolded?

1. What is the effect of color choice in this image, for instance, the black blindfold and the red book that the woman is reading? Would the effect be different if the colors were reversed or different?

2. Comment on other details that you notice about the image. For instance, what can you say about the woman's expression, even though her eyes are covered? Why is she holding the book so close to her face? What do the positions of her arms and hands suggest about how she is feeling?

3. How effective do you think this image is as a comment on censorship in general and book censorship in particular? How might the meaning change if the image were a close-up of just the woman and the book she is looking at, excluding the stacks of books that she is resting her arms on?

4. Besides its possibly being a comment on censorship, how else might you interpret this image?

RESPONDING TO VISUALS

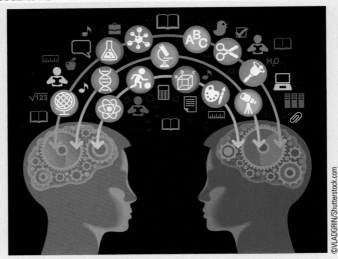

©VLADGRIN/Shutterstock.com

In this representation of the education of children, why do the arrows point both ways?

1. Why do you think the brains are represented as a machine with cogs? Is there significance in the fact that the arrows are pointing to the two largest cogs?

2. What areas of study do the icons on the arrows represent? What are the implications of the mixture of areas of study? What do the icons that are not on the actual arrows represent?

3. What do you think this image says about the nature of education and how children learn? How is knowledge generated in children? Does the process stop at adulthood, or does education continue throughout a lifetime?

POVERTY AND HOMELESSNESS

LEARNING OBJECTIVES

Students will demonstrate an ability to do the following:

- ☐ Articulate approaches that communities use to help people who are living in poverty.

- ☐ Identify potential negative effects on personal well-being or self-esteem of living in poverty or being homeless in children and adults.

- ☐ Debate different approaches to solving the homeless crisis in America.

MindTap®   Understand the goals of the chapter and complete a warm-up activity.

CHAPTER OVERVIEW

Once largely ignored, the issues of poverty, homelessness, and welfare have prompted heated discussion in recent years. At the community level, social workers and staff members at shelters for the homeless and impoverished struggle to meet the needs of desperate people, while at the state and federal levels, legislators argue over whether to cut welfare funding. The number of people living in poverty, especially women and children, has not gone down significantly since before the recession in the first decade of the twenty-first century, with little statistical difference from year to year. Many families whose incomes provide just enough for basic necessities, such as shelter and food, are only a paycheck or two away from living on the streets. Worse, a growing number of the nation's poor actually work full time or at least hold part-time jobs. Compounding the difficulty of these issues are certain attitudes toward or stereotyped beliefs about people on welfare or living on the streets. Charges of laziness and fraud are often leveled at welfare recipients, despite studies that demonstrate that the vast majority of people on welfare want to work and live independent lives.

According to the president of the Children's Defense Fund, as of 2014 over 16 million children lived in poverty in the United States (poverty defined as having an income below the poverty level for a family of four). Of those, 6.8 million children live in extreme poverty, that is, they are living in a family of four with an income less than half the poverty level. By the end of 2015, child poverty had declined slightly from the 2014 level, but although the rates were lower for Hispanic, White, and Asian children, the rate for Black children had increased.

The essays in this chapter examine some of the issues associated with poverty and homelessness. First, Jeff Madrick discusses what he calls "America's child poverty crisis." Although the actual numbers may differ slightly depending on whose figures you are looking at, it is true that somewhere around 20 percent of America's children under age 18 live in poverty. Shockingly, as Madrick points out, "This is a far higher proportion than in any other developed country except Romania." Madrick approaches his subject from the perspective of the cost to society as well as to local, state, and federal governments of all of the problems directly linked to childhood poverty, such as social dysfunction, learning disabilities, health problems, dropping out of school, getting into trouble with the law, and high rates of incarceration. Madrick suggests ways that poverty can be reduced along with solutions to avoid these dire consequences in the first place.

Alana Semuels in "The Resurrection of America's Slums" discusses a related issue, the increasing number of people living in high-poverty areas. According to her, the number of people living in slums has almost doubled since 2000, which, she notes, is "the highest number of Americans living in high-poverty neighborhoods ever recorded." Semuels looks at some of the reasons for this increase and suggests what might be done to alleviate the situation, not only for the sake of those people living in slum areas but also for the sake of the cities themselves.

Next, Greg Kaufmann's "Ignoring Homeless Families" addresses the issue of families who are homeless. Often it is single homeless people who get the most attention and help, but Kaufmann makes a case for trying to end homelessness for both single people and families at the same time. His article not only includes statistics about the number of homeless families as of 2014 but also suggests steps that might be taken to end homelessness, emphasizing especially affordable housing.

As you read these essays, think about your own attitudes toward welfare, homelessness, and poverty. These are tough social problems that just about every society must face, but especially so in countries with large urban areas and great gaps between the rich and the poor. Do the articles in any way reinforce or change your attitudes about these issues? Are you moved by the description of the desperately uncertain lives of the working poor? Do the articles expand your understanding of the issue?

THE COST OF CHILD POVERTY

JEFF MADRICK

Jeff Madrick is a regular contributor to The New York Review of Books *and a former economics columnist for* The New York Times. *He is director of the Bernard L. Schwartz Rediscovering Government Initiative at the Century Foundation, where he is a senior fellow, and he is an editor of* Challenge Magazine. *His books include* The Case for Big Government *(2009);* The Age of Greed *(2011); and* Seven Bad Ideas: How Mainstream Economists Damaged America and the World *(2014). This article was posted on* The New York Review of Books *blog.*

Among the many forces contributing to the recent epidemic of tension between police and mostly black urban communities, from Ferguson to Cleveland to Baltimore, one in particular has been all too little acknowledged: America's child poverty crisis.

There are between 10 and 17 million children under eighteen living in poverty in America today, depending on how you measure it. If we take the measure most often used in international comparisons, up to 20 percent of the young population—one in five children—is poor. This is a far higher proportion than in any other developed country except Romania, according to a 2012 study of thirty-five developed nations by UNICEF. Worse, nearly one in two blacks is born into poverty in the US. And many black men have disappeared into the nation's penal system, often because of harsh prison sentences for minor drug abuses, leaving children to be raised on one income, the mother's.

Meanwhile, years of research have made clear the direct connection between childhood poverty and social dysfunction, ranging from poor health outcomes to higher incarceration rates. Dozens of studies have reported that poor kids are more likely to have learning disabilities, language delays, behavioral problems, and to contract diseases such as asthma and diabetes. They tend not to do as well at school and are more likely to drop out of high school, or even grade school. Women more often have babies in their teenage years. The Children's Defense Fund says the path to prison is often paved in these years. And, most important, neurologists have found virtually incontrovertible evidence that high levels of stress experienced from birth to the age of three can actually damage brain architecture, reducing, for example, the size of the hippocampus.

4   Ignoring these problems is hugely costly to the US government. Harry Holzer of Georgetown University, with co-authors, showed that child poverty cost America $500 billion a year in lost productivity, higher crime rates, and raised health expenditures. Nor is it hard to find government programs that can effectively address these issues. And yet until now, there has been little interest in tackling child poverty on a large scale.

For example, Congress has recently given bipartisan support for a valuable, though limited, home visitation program for poor families—which sends nurses and social workers to poor families to help them raise and nourish their children and which Congress recently extended for another two years. Home visitation is not new and the earlier programs have been closely studied. Infant mortality declines. Children in these families are twice as likely to be screened for developmental delays. At age twelve, the children have better test scores. They get arrested less often before they are sixteen. Mothers are less likely to have a second child in their teens or early twenties. And yet the program, however welcome, is rather small potatoes, having reached only 115,000 families since its inception. It also aims largely at improving the health conditions of poor children, not at reducing the poverty rate.

But there are much more direct ways to alleviate poverty, and some of them have already been shown to have dramatic effect. These include the Earned Income Tax Credit, the

Child Tax Credit, Temporary Assistance for Needy Families (or TANF, the welfare program that replaced the Johnson era welfare program), housing subsidies, food stamps, and others. Indeed, taken together, the programs have reduced child poverty rates by up to 12 percentage points, according to researchers at Columbia University. A new analysis made by the Urban Institute suggests the reduction may be even greater.

These findings may stun readers. But they also carry bad news. The results are based on the new Supplemental Poverty Measure created by the Census Bureau in 2010, according to which the poverty rate was significantly higher in the 2000s than the Official Poverty Measure indicated. (The new measure takes into account government benefits, but also medical expenditures and expenditures required to work, such as the costs of daycare, among other outlays, and also raises estimates of minimal needs for the poor to account for changes in social needs since the adoption of the original poverty line in the 1960s.) Thus, the reduction of up to 12 percentage points according to the Supplemental Poverty Measure still leaves child poverty at about the same inexcusable level reported by the Official Poverty Measure or only a few percentage points less—that is, much too high by any moral standard. Imagine if we didn't have those other programs.

8   There is another, far more sweeping idea that America has until now refused to try, though it has been widely successful in other advanced countries: providing direct cash allowances to poor families for every child they have. Many South American nations provide such allowances for those who meet certain conditions, such as school attendance and doctor visits. Of the thirty-five countries in the UNICEF study, only the US does not have such a policy. Why not?

It's expensive, of course, but so are home visitation and other programs like TANF and the Child Tax Credit; unlike those programs, cash allowances seem to carry a stigma. When I ask economists and policy analysts what they think of the idea, they often say that poor parents will just spend them on themselves. In fact, the experience of the British cash allowance system, instituted in 1999 by the Tony Blair government, shows the opposite. Blair provided generous cash allowances for children among other programs. With support from the allowances and several other Blair programs, the bottom 20 percent of British families received roughly $5000 a year. Columbia University's Jane Waldfogel, who has closely researched the British program, found that the families spent the money on clothes, food, and books for their children—indeed, more so than did higher income parents, who spent the money on items for themselves such as alcohol. A recently published long-term study from Canadian researchers on the effects of a similar Canadian program also found that most parents have spent the allowance constructively on kids.

The British program, which continues today, is, like Social Security in the United States, universal—all children whether rich and poor, receive it. This means it has broader political support. But cash allowances can also be tailored so that they are higher for the poor and lower for the better off. (Cash allowances were reduced for higher income British citizens to meet stringent government budget reductions under the current Prime Minister.) The lack of strings tied to how the money is spent recognizes that the poor can make decisions for themselves, and this can be highly useful. As Clio Chiang points out, a policy associate who works with me on these issues at the Bernard Schwartz "Rediscovering Government Initiative" at the Century Foundation, a poor person in New York City could now buy a discounted monthly Metro Card he or she couldn't previously afford, while a poor parent in Wyoming could fill up the gas tank. Cash allowances reflect a simple idea: treat the poor like people.

But does cash turn poor kids into more productive and well-educated teenagers and adults? It turns out there is substantial evidence for this as well. In one study, the children of poor parents who got a sudden increase in family income due to changes in the Earned Income Tax Credit in the 1990s made substantial educational gains by comparison. A Duke University study of a Cherokee tribe in North Carolina is highly instructive. The tribe opened a casino and distributed $4,000 out of the profits annually to the adults in its community. Compared to families in other Native American communities whose parents didn't receive such allowances, Native American teenagers belonging to the tribe in question had significantly higher school attendance and graduation rates. Indeed, Duncan found that the children of poor families that got an income boost for whatever reason had improved school performance.

12   Based on the relative poverty measure, Waldfogel found that the Blair plan reduced the British child poverty rate by half. The plan cost less than 1 percent of GDP. That would

translate in the US to about $150 billion a year, still a substantial sum, but the British plan was universal and also, as noted, included additional programs, some of which the US already provides. If the US reduced other programs, such as the Child Tax Credit, in order to fund a broad child benefit plan, as financial writer Matt Bruenig has noted, the cost of a cash allowance program that provided $300 to $400 a month per child could be substantially cut. Administering such a program would also be less burdensome than home visitation. Results could be monitored.

For an investment likely to be well less than $100 billion a year, it's plausible that child poverty could be cut in half. And the payoff to the American economy could be large. The reduction in the suffering of innocents may be what would count most. Imagine the effect this might have in poorer neighborhoods of Baltimore or Chicago.

PERSONAL RESPONSE

In paragraph 7, Madrick comments that the child poverty level is still "much too high by any moral standard." To what extent do you agree that child poverty is a moral issue?

QUESTIONS FOR CLASS OR SMALL-GROUP DISCUSSION

1. Before you read this article, were you aware of the statistics on "America's child poverty crisis" (paragraph 1)? What do you make of the statement that the percentage of children living in poverty is "a far higher proportion than in any other developed country except Romania" (paragraph 2). What is the rhetorical effect of such a statement?

2. Why do you think that existing programs for children in poverty that Madrick mentions are not effective enough to eradicate child poverty?

3. Summarize the effects of poverty on children, according to Madrick. From the evidence that he presents, do you agree with Madrick that the problem of child poverty is a crisis?

4. Madrick devotes the entire second half of his article to explaining a program that he believes could cut child poverty "in half" (paragraph 13). State what that program is and whether you think such a program could work in America.

THE RESURRECTION OF
AMERICA'S SLUMS

ALANA SEMUELS

Alana Semuels has a bachelor's degree in history and literature from Harvard and a master's degree from the London School of Economics. While in London, she served as a Boston Globe *correspondent. She has previously been a national correspondent for the* Los Angeles Times *and now writes for* The Atlantic. *This article was first published in* The Atlantic.

Half a century after President Lyndon B. Johnson declared a war on poverty, the number of Americans living in slums is rising at an extraordinary pace. The number of people living in high-poverty areas—defined as census tracts where 40 percent or more of families have income levels below the federal poverty threshold—nearly doubled between 2000 and 2013, to 13.8 million from 7.2 million, according to a new analysis of census data by Paul Jargowsky, a public-policy professor at Rutgers University-Camden and a fellow at The Century Foundation. That's the highest number of Americans living in high-poverty neighborhoods ever recorded.

The development is worrying, especially since the number of people living in high-poverty areas fell 25 percent, to 7.2 million from 9.6 million, between 1990 and 2000. Back then, concentrated poverty was declining in part because the economy was booming. The Earned Income Tax Credit boosted the take-home pay for many poor families. (Studies have shown the EITC also creates a feeling of social inclusion and citizenship among low-income earners.) The unemployment rate fell as low as 3.8 percent, and the first minimum wage increases in a decade made it easier for families to get by. Programs to disassemble housing projects in big cities such as Chicago and Detroit eradicated some of the most concentrated poverty in the country, Jargowsky told me.

As newly middle-class minorities moved to inner suburbs, though, the mostly white residents of those suburbs moved further away, buying up the McMansions that were being built at a rapid pace. This acceleration of white flight was especially problematic in Rust Belt towns that didn't experience the economic boom of the mid-2000s. They were watching manufacturing and jobs move overseas. Cities such as Detroit saw continued white flight as wealthier residents moved to Oakland County and beyond, further and further away from the city's core. They brought their tax dollars with them, leaving the city with little tax base, a struggling economy, and no resources to spend on services.

4   Low-income residents who wanted to follow the wealthy to the suburbs would have had a difficult time. Many wealthy suburbs passed zoning ordinances that prohibited the construction of affordable-housing units or the construction of apartment buildings in general. Some mandated that houses all be detached, or are a minimum size, which essentially makes them too expensive for low-income families. "It's no longer legal to say, 'We don't want African-Americans to live here,' but you can say, 'I'm going to make sure no one who makes less than two times the median income lives here,' "Jargowsky told me.

(Though some affordable-housing developers try to build in the suburbs, many more, especially those in the "poverty-housing industry," advocate for building more developments in high-poverty areas to stimulate economic growth. The Local Initiatives Support Corporation, which has a goal of investing in distressed neighborhoods, for example, has spent $14.7 billion building affordable housing units since 1980.)

Some of the cities where poverty is the most concentrated are in the Midwest and Northeast, where tens of thousands of people have headed to suburbs, and the region itself is shrinking in population. In Syracuse, New York, for example, 65 percent of the black population lived in high-poverty areas in 2013, up from 43 percent of the black population in 2000, Jargowsky found. In Detroit, 58 percent of the black population lived in areas of concentrated poverty in 2013, up from 17 percent in 2000. And in Milwaukee, 43 percent of the Latino population lived in areas of concentrated poverty in 2013, up from 5 percent in 2000.

The number of high-poverty census tracts is also growing in many of these cities. In Detroit, the number of such tracts tripled to 184, from 51 between 2000 and 2013, as concentrated poverty spread to inner suburbs. In Syracuse, the number of high-poverty census tracts grew to 30 from 12.

8   Federal dollars have sometimes been used in ways that increase the concentration of poverty. Most affordable housing is built with low-income housing tax credits, which are distributed by the states. States assign the tax credits through

a process in which they weigh a number of different factors including the location of proposed developments. Many states have favored projects in low-income areas, a practice that was the recent subject of a Supreme Court case known as Inclusive Communities. The Inclusive Communities Project argued, in the case, that the way Texas allocated tax credits was discriminatory, since 93 percent of tax credit units in Dallas are located in census tracts that are more than 50 percent minority, and are predominantly poor. The Supreme Court agreed in June, allowing groups to bring lawsuits about such segregation.

Finally, Housing Choice Vouchers, also known as Section 8, are meant to give poor families better options about where they live, but are instead confining the poor to the few neighborhoods where landlords will accept the voucher.

All of these developments have increased the racial concentration of poverty, especially in mid-sized American cities. "These policies build a durable architecture of segregation that ensures that racial segregation and the concentration of poverty is entrenched for years to come," Jargowsky writes.

Some recent developments, including the Supreme Court decision and a new HUD rule that requires regions to think more carefully about segregation, are positive signs. But Jargowsky says deeper policy prescriptions are needed to reduce these depressing trends in concentrated poverty. First, he says, federal and state governments must ensure that new suburban developments aren't built more quickly than the metropolitan region is growing, so that such developments don't create a population vacuum in cities and inner suburbs. Second, every city and town must ensure that new housing construction reflects the income distribution of the metropolitan area, he said, so that more housing is available to people of all incomes in different parts of town. "If we are serious about breaking down spatial inequality," Jargowsky writes, "We have to overcome our political gridlock and chart a new course toward a more geographically inclusive society."

12   That's important for the future of our cities, but also for our nation, Jargowsky said. His research shows that poor children are more likely to live in high-poverty areas than are poor adults—28 percent of poor black children live in high-poverty areas, for example, compared to 24 percent of poor black adults. Overall, 16.5 percent of poor children live in high-poverty areas, compared to 13.8 percent of poor adults. A child who grows up in a high-poverty area is likely to be poor when

he grows up. Research out this year from Harvard shows that children who moved from poor areas to more affluent areas had higher incomes and better educational achievements than those who stayed in poor areas. Without dramatic changes, today's children who live in high-poverty areas are going to grow up to be poor, too.

PERSONAL RESPONSE

Write in response to Semuels' statement that, as of 2013, the number of people who live in high-poverty areas is "the highest number . . . ever recorded" (paragraph 1). Do you know people who live in slums? What is your experience with high-poverty neighborhoods?

QUESTIONS FOR CLASS OR SMALL-GROUP DISCUSSION

1. What do you understand by the term *white flight* (paragraph 3). In what was does it have a negative effect on a city?

2. Summarize the difficulties that low-income residents face when wanting to move out of high-poverty or slum areas of a city. What problems do you think arise when low-income residents cannot move out of the slum areas they live in?

3. Explain what Semuels means by this statement: "Federal dollars have sometimes been used in ways that increase the concentration of poverty" (paragraph 8).

4. State in your own words some of the developments that, according to Semuels, might help reduce "the racial concentration of poverty" and work toward "a more geographically inclusive society" (paragraphs 8–9).

IGNORING HOMELESS FAMILIES

GREG KAUFMANN

Greg Kaufmann is the former poverty correspondent to The Nation *and a current contributor. He is a senior fellow at the Center of American Progress, editor of TalkPoverty.org, and is an advisor for Barbara Ehrenreich's Economic Hardship Reporting Project. This article was first published on* TheNation.com *blog.*

More than one-third of Americans who use shelters annually are parents and their children. In 2011, that added up to more than 500,000 people. According to Joe Volk, CEO of Community Advocates in Milwaukee, prevalent family homelessness is no accident. "In 2000, we as a nation—and the Department of Housing and Urban Development [HUD]—made the terrible decision to abandon homeless children and their families," said Volk, speaking at a Congressional briefing on *The American Almanac of Family Homelessness*, authored by the Institute for Children, Poverty and Homelessness [ICPH]. "Families for a decade have been ignored."

As the *Almanac* makes clear, federal attention and resources have focused instead on chronically homeless single adults—usually the most visible homeless people in communities across the country, most of whom have severe intellectual or physical disabilities. There was a recognition that it is far less expensive to place these men and women in their own apartments with access to social services—called the "Housing First" model—than to continue paying the long-term costs associated with jail time, and recurring treatment at emergency rooms and hospitals. The federal government's plan was to use the savings gained by reducing homelessness among single adults to fight family homelessness. But that hasn't happened.

Since 2007, there has been a 19 percent decline in chronically homeless single adults. In contrast, family homelessness has *increased* by more than 13 percent over the same period. Matthew Adams, principal policy analyst for ICPH, noted that the number of homeless school-aged children surpassed 1 million for the first time during the 2011-12 school year—a 57 percent increase since 2006-07.

4

"This is basically all a result of focusing our fiscal and human capital solely on single adults," said Adams. Despite a rise in extreme poverty, a decline in affordable housing, a shortage of rental subsidies, high unemployment and a foreclosure crisis, this strategy hasn't changed—with the exception of provisions in the Recovery Act that are now expired.

While the long-term costs of family homelessness are more difficult to quantify than are those costs associated with single adult homelessness, they are nevertheless significant and real (costs to the nation's character aside).

The *Almanac* explores the toll that housing instability, poor nutrition and lack of quality health care takes on homeless children: they experience twice the rate of chronic illnesses; twice the rate of learning disabilities; and three times the rate of emotional or behavioral problems as their peers who have stable housing. Homeless children have less than half the rate of proficiency in math and reading as their housed classmates. It's not surprising that less than one in four homeless children graduates from high school—what's surprising is that that one child manages to graduate at all.

The McKinney-Vento Homeless Education Assistance Improvements Act is supposed to ensure that all homeless students have equal access to education. But despite the dramatic rise in homeless students since 2006, only one in five school districts receives education assistance grants to help them.

8

To the extent that family homelessness is on the federal government's agenda at all—and there is a federal goal to end family homelessness by 2020 (the goal for ending single adult and veteran homelessness is 2015)—there is real concern among many advocates that HUD is attempting to use the "Housing First" approach to help homeless families. Although they agree that it has shown success with single adults, these advocates argue that it simply isn't the right solution for many—or even most—homeless families.

"It's a whole different dynamic for families," said Volk, who operates shelters and permanent housing for both single adults and families. Volk said that an intellectually or physically disabled homeless single adult is usually able to qualify for Supplemental Security Income (SSI), which is $770 per month in Wisconsin. That stable income is sufficient to rent a fully furnished apartment with utilities paid in his state.

In contrast, a single mother must apply for Temporary Assistance for Needy Families (TANF), which in Wisconsin is $653 per month no matter the size of the family. She then must meet a work requirement, arrange for child care, buy furniture and pay for utilities, among other challenges. If her child is sick and she stays home from work, she is sanctioned by the TANF program. She might lose her $653 assistance, consequently fall behind on rent and begin her slide towards homelessness again.

Dona Anderson, director of ICHP, said there is way too much emphasis on getting families out of shelters quickly, rather than making sure they don't return to the shelter again. "What could we do if we could serve families in a dedicated, serious fashion for 12 to 24 months? And really address those education barriers, employment barriers, really get these families stabilized so that once they leave a shelter we don't see them coming back?" said Anderson. "Can we address those deeper-seeded needs rather than just the initial crisis that brought them to the shelter?"

Volk agreed. "We're moving people out of shelters too fast and then we wonder why they don't succeed," he said. "They don't succeed because we didn't give them enough time and enough support before they moved out. We need to rethink how we work with homeless families."

Anderson spoke of a 16-year-old in New York City who was homeless in junior high school. He lived in a shelter "targeted for him" and was able to participate in a high quality after-school program, residential summer camp, and a youth employment program. He's now a successful student who is looking at colleges. In contrast, she met a 4-year-old homeless child in Las Vegas who has no access to a shelter, and is bouncing between motels and hotels with his father, getting by on a fast food diet. He lacks the stable environment "that kids that age especially need in order to develop and grow and be ready for school."

"I tell these stories to illustrate the differences in how children are served, and how they aren't served, when they are experiencing homelessness," said Anderson.

The Almanac includes recommendations for what the 113th Congress can do for homeless families now, including: converting the mortgage interest deduction into a tax credit—as proposed under the Common Sense Housing Investment Act—in order to permanently fund The National Housing Trust Fund (NHTF) and support Section 8 rental assistance. (The NHTF was enacted by Congress in 2008 to increase the supply of affordable housing units, but it has never been funded.) There are now just 3.7 million housing units for every 10 million extremely low-income renters. Another key recommendation is to implement the reforms laid out in the Improving Access to Child Care for Homeless Families Act—pretty fundamental for homeless parents to have access to child care if they are going to find stable housing and jobs.

16   But the first step—the big step—seems to be this: see the problem of family homelessness, admit it and commit to doing something about it. And don't for a second believe that working with a single adult is the same thing as working with a family with so many moving parts.

"We can solve the problem of people living on the street for both singles and families at the same time," said Volk. "It doesn't have to be an either/or, and it can't be—as long as we have children that have to live out on the streets."

PERSONAL RESPONSE

From what you have read here and elsewhere about the homeless, write for a few minutes about your attitude toward them. Would you go out of your way to help a homeless person or family? Would it make a difference to you if it were a single individual versus a family in need?

QUESTIONS FOR CLASS OR SMALL-GROUP DISCUSSION

1. Kauffmann quotes Joe Volk as saying that " 'in 2000, we as a nation . . . made the terrible decision to abandon homeless children and their families. . . . Families for a decade have been ignored' " (paragraph 1). What evidence does he provide to support that statement?

2. Kauffmann writes: "While long-term costs of family homelessness are more difficult to quantify . . . , they are nevertheless significant and real (costs to the nation's character aside)" (paragraph 6). What do you think he means by his parenthetical aside about costs to the nation's character? Do you agree with him?

3. According to this article, what are the effects of housing instability on families, especially on children in homeless families?

4. Why, according to Volk, does the "Housing First" model not work for families when it has seemed to help single adults? That is, why does getting families out of shelters too quickly seem to have a negative effect on families? What issues need to be addressed when working with homeless families, according to Kauffman and those he interviewed for this article? Are you persuaded by his argument that more needs to be done for homeless families?

MindTap   Reflect on the theme of this chapter.

PERSPECTIVES ON POVERTY AND HOMELESSNESS

Suggested Writing Topics

1. Drawing on the readings in this chapter, consider how best to meet the needs of impoverished families or homeless people. From your reading, what do you think are the best ways to solve the problem or reduce the numbers of people living in poverty?

2. Argue in support of or against the statement that society has an obligation to help the poor and homeless.

3. Drawing on the readings in this chapter, write on the subject of the effects of poverty on self-esteem.

4. Drawing on the readings in this chapter, write an essay on the effects of living in poverty on the health and well-being of children.

5. With the readings in this chapter in mind, write your own opinion piece on the subject of poverty and homelessness in America. Select an issue or take a position on one aspect of it.

6. Write a letter to the editor in response to one of the readings in this chapter.

7. If you have ever experienced the effects of poverty, too little income, not enough work, or a need to juggle child care with the demands of a job or school, write an essay describing that experience, how you felt about it, and how you handled it.

8. If you know someone who is homeless or who has lost his or her job because of the economy, write about that person's experiences and the effect it has had on the person and/or his family and friends.

9. Drawing on the readings in this chapter, classify several kinds of poverty by identifying their chief characteristics. How do they differ, and how are they similar?

10. Working in small groups and drawing on the essays in this chapter, create a scenario involving one or more of the following people: a welfare recipient or a homeless person, a welfare caseworker or a staff member at a homeless shelter, a police officer, and either or both a wealthy person and a working-class person with a regular income and a home. Provide a situation, create dialogue, and role-play in an effort to understand the varying perspectives of different people on the issue of welfare or homelessness. Then present your scenario to the rest of your classmates. For an individual writing project, do an analysis of the scenario or fully develop the viewpoint of the person whose role you played.

Research Topics

1. Greg Kaufman in "Ignoring Homeless Families" contends that despite the rising number of families that are homeless, the federal government is not responding to their needs. Research the issue of family homelessness in America. Do your findings support or refute Kaufman's claim?

2. Jeff Madrick contends that child poverty contributes to "the recent epidemic of tension between police and mostly black urban communities" ("The Cost of Child Poverty," paragraph 1). Research for evidence that either supports or refutes that statement.

3. Research the long-effects on children of living in poverty. This is a broad topic, so narrow your focus to one specific area that is affected, such as physical health, success in school, or psychosocial issues such as behavioral and emotional problems.

4. Alana Semuels begins "The Resurrection of America's Slums" with a reference to President Lyndon B. Johnson's "war on poverty." Research the subject of Johnson's war on poverty: What were its goals? What were some of its chief recommendations? How successful was it?

5. Alana Semuels in "The Resurrection of America's Slums" mentions that the Earned Income Tax Credit [EITC] "creates a feeling of social inclusion and citizenship among low-income earners." Research that aspect of the EITC. Begin by learning what it is, how it works, and who is eligible, and then explore ways that it has had benefitted people.

6. Alana Semuels in "The Resurrection of America's Slums" refers to "the acceleration of white flight" and the decline of cities in the Rust Belt. Research the phenomenon of "white flight" and its effects on cities, focusing on one city in particular. For instance, one of the cities that experienced a noticeable economic decline is Detroit, which has now begun to rebuild itself. You might want to focus your research on that city alone, or on a similarly sized city. What led to the decline? What has the city done to rebuild itself?

7. Research the Local Initiatives Support Corporation mentioned in paragraph 5 of Alana Semuels' "The Resurrection of America's Slums." How and when did it originate, what is its purpose, and how effective has it been in reaching its goals?

8. Research your state's policy on welfare, including residency requirements, eligibility for payments, monitoring of recipients, and related issues. Then write a paper outlining your opinion of your state's welfare policy, including any recommendations you would make for changing or improving it, if any.

9. Research the effects of poverty on education: how does it affect school performance, school attendance, or study habits?

10. Research the efforts of an American city to eradicate homelessness or meet the needs of the impoverished. Consider how the city assesses the problem, identifies those in need, and creates programs to meet those needs. Include also any successes or failures in those efforts.

11. From time to time, politicians propose establishing orphanages that would house not only orphaned children but also the children of single parents on welfare or parents deemed unfit to raise their children. Research this subject, and then write a paper in which you argue for or against the establishment of such orphanages. Make sure you consider as many perspectives as possible on this complex issue, including the welfare of the child, the rights of the parent or parents, and society's responsibility to protect children.

12. Research an area of public policy on welfare reform, child welfare, homelessness, public housing, family welfare, food stamps, job training, or any other issue related to any reading in this chapter.

RESPONDING TO VISUALS

Ted Foxx / Alamy Stock Photo

What impression do you get from the sign that the woman is holding?

1. Does this family conform to your image of homeless families? How are they superficially similar to or different from what you expected a homeless family to look like or a homeless family that you know?

2. Contrast the look on the woman's face with the looks on the faces of the rest of her family.

3. What, if anything do the details in the picture tell us about the family itself or what led to the family's homelessness?

RESPONDING TO VISUALS

Con Tanasiuk / Design Pics/Getty Images

What can you tell about the man walking past the homeless person from the way that he is dressed and his facial expression?

1. What does the homeless person's body language say about him? What details surrounding the huddled person tell us, at least at a first impression, about the person's situation?

2. How does the photographer's perspective affect the way viewers see and respond to image? For instance, why do we see the full image of the man, whereas we get a side view of an almost completely covered homeless person?

3. What irony do you see in the contrast between the two men?

GENDER STUDIES

LEARNING OBJECTIVES

Students will demonstrate an ability to do the following:

☐ Identify ways that a culture's definitions of masculinity and femininity
present challenges for men and women.

☐ Define "sex role," and examine issues associated with not conforming
to sex role expectations.

☐ Discuss the effects on children of gender-labeling toys.

MindTap   Understand the goals of the chapter and complete
a warm-up activity.

CHAPTER OVERVIEW

Many people use the word *gender* interchangeably with the word *sex*, but the two have different meanings. Sex is a biological category; a person's sex—whether male or female—is genetically determined. On the other hand, gender refers to the socially constructed set of expectations for behavior based on one's sex. Masculinity and femininity are gender constructs whose definitions vary and change over time and with different cultures or groups within cultures. What is considered appropriate and even desirable behavior for men and women in one culture may be strongly inappropriate in another. Like other cultures, American culture's definitions of masculinity and femininity change with time, shaped by a number of influences, such as parental expectations, peer pressure, and media images. We are born either male or female, and most of us learn to behave in ways consistent with our society's expectations for that sex.

Colleges and universities across the United States (and around the world) have created gender studies programs that examine various aspects of sex and gender. These programs are offered under different names with different emphases: women's studies, men's studies, and lesbian-gay-bisexual-transgender (LGBT) studies, for instance. Courses within these areas of study are typically interdisciplinary in nature, with instructors from traditional disciplines teaching their specialties from the particular perspective of the program. Thus, a political science instructor teaching in a women's studies program would likely offer a feminist perspective on women in politics. An English instructor might look at selected stories and novels for their portrayal of men in a men's studies course or for their portrayal of homosexuality in an LGBT studies program. Gender studies programs may also include courses on sexuality. Whatever the focus of the program, the overarching interest in these courses lies in the ways that one's sex—male or female—or one's gender—masculine or feminine—affects behavior, world view, place in society, role in the home, and other issues associated with being human.

This chapter begins with a review of literature on the debate over what it means to grow up male in America. Thomas Bartlett's "The Puzzle of Boys" looks at a number of recent studies of boys and explains researchers' questions and conclusions about the nature of boyhood. His article gives a general overview of what has become a trend in gender studies toward looking at the difficulties boys face in American culture. This trend marks a shift from decades of studies on girls and women toward more inclusive or balanced efforts to understand both males and females. As you read the essay, consider your feelings about being male or female, recalling especially situations when you were identified on the basis of that characteristic alone.

Next is an article about barriers to men's breaking out of traditional gender roles. While women have made great progress in entering traditionally male fields, the same has not been true for men. Emily Albert Reyes begins by featuring a stay-at-home dad in " 'Men Are Stuck' in Gender Roles, Data Suggest," but she is interested in the larger question of why the "gender revolution has been lopsided." As she mentions various reasons to account for this imbalance, think about whether her explanations are true in your own experience. Do the men and women you know feel that they need to adhere to traditional gender roles, or do they feel free to be and do whatever they want?

Then, Christia Brown in "Target Is Right on Target About the Use of Gender Labels" writes about interviews that she conducted the week that the department store Target announced that it was doing away with gender signage in bedding and toys, that is, doing away with labels that said "girls toys" and "boys toys," for instance. While many people applaud Target's decision, there are also many people who disapprove and even refuse to shop at Target any longer. As a professor, scholar, and author of a book on gender stereotyping, Brown offers evidence to explain why she approves of the move, focusing particularly on the effect that labels have on children. Citing study after study, she builds a case to support her position.

THE PUZZLE OF BOYS

THOMAS BARTLETT

Thomas Bartlett, a senior writer for the Chronicle of Higher Education *since 2001, has covered such subjects as teaching, religion, tenure, plagiarism, diploma mills, and other forms of cheating. He has appeared on national radio and television shows such as National Public Radio's* Talk of the Nation *and ABC News's* Nightline. *Bartlett regularly contributes to the* Chronicle's Off Beat *column, which takes a look at funny or unusual trends in higher education. This piece appeared in the* Chronicle of Higher Education.

My son just turned 3. He loves trains, fire trucks, tools of all kinds, throwing balls, catching balls, spinning until he falls down, chasing cats, tackling dogs, emptying the kitchen drawers of their contents, riding a tricycle, riding a carousel, pretending to be a farmer, pretending to be a cow, dancing, drumming, digging, hiding, seeking, jumping, shouting, and collapsing exhausted into a Thomas the Tank Engine bed wearing Thomas the Tank Engine pajamas after reading a Thomas the Tank Engine book.

That doesn't make him unusual; in fact, in many ways, he couldn't be more typical. Which may be why a relative recently said, "Well, he's definitely all boy." It's a statement that sounds reasonable enough until you think about it. What does "all boy" mean? Masculine? Straight? Something else? Are there partial boys? And is this relative aware of my son's fondness for Hello Kitty and tea sets?

These are the kinds of questions asked by anxious parents and, increasingly, academic researchers. Boyhood studies—virtually unheard of a few years ago—has taken off, with a shelf full of books already published, more on the way, and a new journal devoted to the subject. Much of the focus so far has been on boys falling behind academically, paired with the notion that school is not conducive to the way boys learn. What motivates boys, the argument goes, is different from what motivates girls, and society should adjust accordingly.

4   Not everyone buys the boy talk. Some critics, in particular the American Association of University Women, contend that much of what passes for research about boyhood only reinforces stereotypes and arrives at simplistic conclusions: Boys are competitive! Boys like action! Boys hate books! They argue that this line of thinking miscasts boys as victims and ignores the very real problems faced by girls.

But while this debate is far from settled, the field has expanded to include how marketers target boys, the nature of boys' friendships, and a host of deeper, more philosophical issues, all of which can be boiled down, more or less, to a single question: Just what are boys, anyway?

One of the first so-called boys' books, Michael Gurian's *The Wonder of Boys,* was not immediately embraced by publishers. In fact, it was turned down by 25 houses before finally being purchased by Tarcher/Putnam for a modest sum. This was in the mid-1990s, and everyone was concerned about girls. Girls were drowning in the "sea of Western culture," according to Carol Gilligan. In *Reviving Ophelia,* Mary Pipher bemoaned a "girl-poisoning" culture that emphasized sexiness above all else.

Boys weren't the story. No one wanted to read about them.

8   Or so publishers thought. *The Wonder of Boys* has since sold more than a half-million copies, and Gurian, who has a master's degree in writing and has worked as a family counselor, has become a prominent speaker and consultant on boys' issues. He has written two more books about boys, including *The Purpose of Boys,* published this year, which argues that boys are hard-wired to desire a sense of mission, and that parents and teachers need to understand "boy biology" if they want to help young men succeed.

Drawing on neuroscience research done by others, Gurian argues that boy brains and girl brains are fundamentally dissimilar. In the nature versus nurture debate, Gurian comes down squarely on the side of the former. He catches flak for supposedly over-interpreting neuroscience data to comport with his theories about boys. In *The Trouble with Boys*, a former *Newsweek* reporter, Peg Tyre, takes him to task for arguing that female brains are active even when they're bored, while male brains tend to "shut down" (a conclusion that Ruben Gur, director of the Brain Behavior Laboratory at the University of Pennsylvania, tells Tyre isn't supported by the evidence). Gurian counters that his work has been misrepresented and that the success of his programs backs up his scientific claims.

Close on Gurian's heels was *Real Boys*, by William Pollack. Pollack, an associate clinical professor of psychology at Harvard Medical School and director of the Centers for Men and Young Men, writes that behind their facade of toughness, boys are vulnerable and desperate for emotional connection. Boys, he says, tend to communicate through action. They are more likely to express empathy and affection through an activity, like playing basketball together, than having a heart-to-heart talk. Pollack's view of what makes boys the way they are is less rooted in biology than Gurian's. "What neuroscientists will tell you is that nature and nurture are bonded," says Pollack. "How we nurture from the beginning has an effect." *Real Boys* earned a stamp of approval from Mary Pipher, who writes in the foreword that "our culture is doing a bad job raising boys."

Pollack's book, like Gurian's, was an enormous success. It sold more than 750,000 copies and has been published in 13 countries. Even though it came out a decade ago, Pollack says he still receives e-mail every week from readers. "People were hungry for it," he says.

The following year, *Raising Cain*, by Dan Kindlon, an adjunct lecturer in Harvard's School of Public Health, and Michael Thompson, a psychologist in private practice, was published and was later made into a two-hour PBS documentary. Their book ends with seven recommendations for dealing with boys, including "recognize and accept the high activity level of boys and give them safe boy places to express it." The book is partially about interacting with boys on their own terms, but it also encourages adults to help them develop "emotional literacy" and to counter the "culture of cruelty" among older boys. It goes beyond academic performance, dealing with issues like suicide, bullying, and romance.

Perhaps the most provocative book of the bunch is *The War Against Boys: How Misguided Feminism Is Harming Our Young*

Men, by Christina Hoff Sommers. As the subtitle suggests, Sommers believes that she's found the villain in this story, making the case that it's boys, not girls, who are being shortchanged and that they need significant help if they're going to close the distance academically. But that does not mean, according to Sommers, that they "need to be rescued from their masculinity."

Those books were best sellers and continue to attract readers and spirited debate. While the authors disagree on the details, they share at least two broad conclusions: (1) Boys are not girls, and (2) Boys are in trouble. Why and how they're different from girls, what's behind their trouble, and what if anything to do about it—all that depends on whom you read.

A backlash was inevitable. In 2008 the American Association of University Women issued a report, "Where the Girls Are: The Facts about Gender Equity in Education," arguing not only that the alleged academic disparity between boys and girls had been exaggerated, but also that the entire crisis was a myth. If anything, the report says, boys are doing better than ever: "The past few decades have seen remarkable gains for girls and boys in education, and no evidence indicates a crisis for boys in particular."

So how could the boys-in-trouble crowd have gotten it so wrong? The report has an answer for that: "Many people remain uncomfortable with the educational and professional advances of girls and women, especially when they threaten to outdistance their peers." In other words, it's not genuine concern for boys that's energizing the movement but rather fear of girls surpassing them.

The dispute is, in part, a dispute over data. And like plenty of such squabbles, the outcome hinges on the numbers you decide to use. Boys outperform girls by more than 30 points on the mathematics section of the SAT and a scant four points on the verbal sections (girls best boys by 13 points on the recently added writing section). But many more girls actually take the test. And while it's a fact that boys and girls are both more likely to attend college than they were a generation ago, girls now make up well over half of the student body, and a projection by the Department of Education indicates that the gap will widen considerably over the next decade.

College isn't the only relevant benchmark. Boys are more likely than girls to be diagnosed with attention-deficit disorder, but girls are more likely to be diagnosed with depression. Girls are more likely to report suicide attempts, but boys are more likely to actually kill themselves (according to the Centers for Disease Control and Prevention, 83 percent of suicides between the ages of 10 and 24 are male). Ask a representative of the AAUW about a pitfall that appears to disproportionately affect boys, like attention-deficit disorder, and the representative will counter that the disparity is overplayed or that girls deal with equally troubling issues.

But it's not statistics that have persuaded parents and educators that boys are in desperate straits, according to Sara Mead, a senior research fellow with the New America Foundation, a public-policy institute. Mead wrote a paper in 2006 that argued, much like the later AAUW report, that the boys' crisis was bunk. "What seems to most resonate with teachers and parents is not as much the empirical evidence but this sense of boys being unmoored or purposeless in a vaguely defined way," Mead says in an interview. "That's a really difficult thing to validate more beyond anecdote." She also worries that all this worrying—much of it, she says, from middle-class parents—could have a negative effect on boys, marking them as victims when they're nothing of the sort.

20   Pollack concedes, as Mead and others point out, that poor performance in school is also tied to factors like race and class, but he insists that boys as a group—including white, middle-class boys—are sinking, pointing to studies that suggest they are less likely to do their homework and more likely to drop out of high school. And he has a hunch about why some refuse to acknowledge it: "People look at the adult world and say, 'Men are still in charge.' So they look down at boys and say, 'They are small men, so they must be on the way to success,'" says Pollack. "It's still a man's world. People make the mistake of thinking it's a boy's world."

If the first round of books was focused on the classroom, the second round observes the boy in his natural habitat. The new book *Packaging Boyhood: Saving Our Sons from Superheroes, Slackers, and Other Media Stereotypes* offers an analysis of what boys soak in from TV shows, video games, toys, and other facets of boy-directed pop culture. The news isn't good here, either. According to the book, boys are being taught they have to be tough and cool, athletic and stoic. This starts early with toddler T-shirts emblazoned with "Future All-Star" or "Little Champion." Even once-benign toys like Legos and Nerf have assumed a more hostile profile with Lego Exo-Force Assault Tigers and the Nerf N-Strike Raider Rapid Fire CS-35 Dart

Blaster. "That kind of surprised us," says one of the book's three authors, Lyn Mikel Brown, a professor of education and human development at Colby College. "What happened to Nerf? What happened to Lego?"

Brown also co-wrote *Packaging Girlhood*. In that book, the disease was easier to diagnose, what with the Disney princess phenomenon and sexy clothes being marketed to pre-adolescent girls. Everyone was worried about how girls were being portrayed in the mass media and what that was doing to their self-esteem. The messages about boys, however, were easier to miss, in part because they're so ubiquitous. "We expect a certain amount of teasing, bullying, spoofing about being tough enough, even in animated films for the littlest boys," Brown says.

For *Packaging Boyhood*, the authors interviewed more than 600 boys and found that models of manhood were turning up in some unexpected places, like the Discovery Channel's *Man vs. Wild*, in which the star is dropped into the harsh wilderness and forced to forage. They're concerned that such programs, in order to compete against all the stimuli vying for boys' attentions, have become more aggressively in-your-face, more fearlessly risk-taking, manlier than thou. Says Brown: "What really got us was the pumping up of the volume."

24

Brown thinks boys are more complicated, and less single-minded, than adults give them credit for. So does Ken Corbett, whose new book, *Boyhoods: Rethinking Masculinities*, steers clear of generalizations and doesn't try to elucidate the ideal boyhood (thus the plural "masculinities"). Corbett, an assistant professor of psychology at New York University, wants to remind us not how boys are different from girls but how they're different from one another. His background is in clinical psychoanalysis, feminism, and queer studies—in other words, as he points out in the introduction, "not your father's psychoanalysis."

In a chapter titled "Feminine Boys," he writes of counseling the parents of a boy who liked to wear bracelets and perform a princess dance. The father, especially, wasn't sure how to take this, telling Corbett that he wanted a son, not a daughter.

To show how boys can be difficult to define, Corbett tells the story of Hans, a 5-year-old patient of Sigmund Freud, who had a fear of being castrated by, of all things, a horse. Young Hans also fantasizes about having a "widdler," as the boy puts it, as large as his father's. Freud (typically) reads the kid's issues as primarily sexual, and his desire to be more like his father as Oedipal. Corbett, however, doesn't think Hans's interest in his penis is about sex, but rather about becoming bigger, in developing beyond the half-finished sketch of boyhood. "Wishing to be big is wishing to fill in the drawing," Corbett writes.

Corbett disputes the idea that boys as a group are in peril. They have troubles, sure, but so do other people. Treating boys as problems to be solved, rather than subjects to be studied, is a mistake, he says, and much of the writing on boys "doesn't illuminate the experience of being a boy, but it does illuminate the space between a boy and a parent."

The experience of being a boy is exactly what Miles Groth wants to capture. Groth, a psychology professor at Wagner College, is editor of *Thymos: Journal of Boyhood Studies*, founded in 2007. An article he wrote in the inaugural issue of the journal, "Has Anyone Seen the Boy? The Fate of the Boy in Becoming a Man," is a sort of call to arms for boyhood-studies scholars. For years, Groth says, academics didn't really discuss boys. They might study a certain subset of boys, but boys per se were off the table. "I think there was some hesitancy for scholars to take up the topic, to show that they're paying attention to guys when we should be paying attention to girls," says Groth. "Now I think there's less of that worry. People don't see it as a reactionary movement."

That has opened the door for scholars like Niobe Way. A professor of applied psychology at New York University, Way recently finished a book, scheduled to be published next year by Harvard University Press, on how boys communicate. She's been interviewing teenage boys about their friendships, and what she's found is remarkable. While it's common wisdom that teenage boys either can't express or don't possess strong feelings about their friends, Way has discovered that boys in their early teens can be downright sentimental when discussing their friendships. When asked what they liked about their best friends, boys frequently said: "They won't laugh at me when I talk about serious things." What has emerged from her research is a portrait of emotionally intelligent boys who care about more than sports and cars. Such an observation might not sound revolutionary, but what boys told her and her fellow researchers during lengthy, probing interviews runs counter to the often one-dimensional portrayal of boys in popular culture. "They were resisting norms of masculinity," she says.

Note the past tense. At some point in high school, that expressiveness vanishes, replaced with a more defensive, closed-off posture, perhaps as boys give in to messages about what it means to be a man. Still, her research undermines the stereotype that boys are somehow incapable of discussing their feelings. "And yet," she says, "this notion of this emotionally illiterate, sex-obsessed, sports-playing boy just keeps getting spit out again and again."

Touchy-feely talk about friendships may seem disconnected from boys' academic woes, but Way insists they're pieces of the same puzzle. "If you don't understand the experience of boyhood," she says, "you'll never understand the achievement gaps."

Books cited in this article:

Brown, Lyn Mikel, Sharon Lamb, and Mark Tappan. *Packaging Boyhood: Saving Our Sons from Superheroes, Slackers, and Other Media Stereotypes.* St. Martin's, 2009.

Corbett, Ken. *Boyhoods: Rethinking Masculinities.* Yale UP, 2009.

Gurian, Michael. *The Wonder of Boys: What Parents, Mentors, and Educators Can Do to Shape Boys into Exceptional Men.* Tarcher/Putnam, 1996.

Kindlon, Dan, and Michael Thompson. *Raising Cain: Protecting the Emotional Life of Boys.* Ballantine Books, 1999.

Pollack, William. *Real Boys: Rescuing Our Sons from the Myths of Boyhood.* Henry Holt, 1998.

Sommers, Christina Hoff. *The War Against Boys: How Misguided Feminism Is Harming Our Young Men.* Simon & Schuster, 2000.

Tyre, Peg. *The Trouble with Boys: A Surprising Report Card on Our Sons, Their Problems at School, and What Parents and Educators Must Do.* Crown, 2008.

PERSONAL RESPONSE

Select a passage that offers an opinion on boyhood and respond to it. Consider for example, "Just what are boys, anyway?" (paragraph 5) or "Behind their facade of toughness, boys are vulnerable and desperate for emotional connection" (paragraph 10).

QUESTIONS FOR CLASS OR SMALL-GROUP DISCUSSION

1. What assumptions about the traditional definitions of sex and gender does Bartlett point out?

2. What do you think it means when a child is described as "all boy" or "all girl"? How do you feel about such labels? Do you think it is possible for any society to do away with assigning sex roles?

3. Summarize the chief interests of the recent books on boys that Bartlett covers in his article. What are researchers primarily interested in learning about boys? What conclusions have they drawn?

4. State your understanding of the different approaches among researchers in the area of "boyhood studies." On what points do they seem to agree and disagree? How does Bartlett account for the differences?

"MEN ARE STUCK" IN GENDER ROLES, DATA SUGGEST

EMILY ALPERT REYES

Emily Alpert Reyes covers City Hall for the Los Angeles Times. *She previously reported on the census and demographics, tracking how our lives are changing in Los Angeles, California, and the country. Before joining the* Times, *she worked for the pioneering nonprofit news website voiceofsandiego.org, winning national awards for her reporting on education. This article was first published in the* Los Angeles Times.

Brent Kroeger pores over nasty online comments about stay-at-home dads, wondering if his friends think those things about him. The Rowland Heights father remembers high school classmates laughing when he said he wanted to be a "house husband." He avoids mentioning it on Facebook.

"I don't want other men to look at me like less of a man," Kroeger said.

His fears are tied to a bigger phenomenon: The gender revolution has been lopsided. Even as American society has seen sweeping transformations—expanding roles for women, surging tolerance for homosexuality—popular ideas about masculinity seem to have stagnated.

While women have broken into fields once dominated by men, such as business, medicine and law, men have been slower to pursue nursing, teach preschool, or take jobs as administrative assistants. Census data and surveys show that men remain rare in stereotypically feminine positions.

4   When it comes to gender progress, said Ronald F. Levant, editor of the journal *Psychology of Men and Masculinity*, "men are stuck." The imbalance appears at work and at home: Working mothers have become ordinary, but stay-at-home fathers exist in only 1% of married couples with kids under age 15, according to U.S. Census Bureau data.

In a recent survey, 51% of Americans told the Pew Research Center that children were better off if their mother was at home. Only 8% said the same about fathers. Even seeking time off can be troublesome for men: One University of South Florida study found that college students rated hypothetical employees wanting flexible schedules as less masculine.

Other research points to an enduring stigma for boys whose behavior is seen as feminine. "If girls call themselves tomboys, it's with a sense of pride," said University of Illinois at Chicago sociology professor Barbara Risman. "But boys make fun of other boys if they step just a little outside the rigid masculine stereotype."

Two years ago, for instance, a Global Toy Experts survey found that more than half of mothers wouldn't give a doll to someone else's son, while only 32% said the same about giving cars or trucks to a girl. Several studies have found that bending gender stereotypes in childhood is tied to worse anxiety for men than women in adulthood.

8   In the southern end of Orange County, former friends have stopped talking to Lori Duron and her husband. Slurs and threats arrive by email. Their son calls himself a boy, but has gravitated toward Barbies, Disney princesses and pink since he was a toddler. In a blog and a book she wrote, Duron chronicles worries that would seem trivial if her child were a girl: Whether he would be teased for his rainbowy backpack. Whether a Santa would look askance at him for wanting a doll.

"If a little girl is running around on the baseball team with her mitt, people think, 'That's a strong girl,' " said her husband, Matt Duron, who, like his wife, uses a pen name to shield the boy's identity. "When my 6-year-old is running around in a dress, people think there's something wrong with him."

Beyond childhood, the gender imbalance remains stark when students choose college majors: Between 1971 and 2011, a growing share of degrees in biology, business and other historically male majors went to women, an analysis by University of Maryland, College Park sociologist Philip N. Cohen shows. Yet fields like education and the arts remained heavily female, as few men moved the opposite way. Federal data show that last year less than 2% of preschool and kindergarten teachers were men.

In the last 40 years, "women have said, 'Wait a minute, we are competent and assertive and ambitious,'" claiming a wider range of roles, said Michael Kimmel, executive director of the Center for the Study of Men and Masculinities at Stony Brook University. But "men have not said, 'We're kind, gentle, compassionate and nurturing.'"

As the Durons and other families have discovered, messages of gender norms trickle down early. In Oregon, Griffin Bates was stunned when the little boy she was raising with her lesbian partner at the time came back from a visit with Grandma and Grandpa without his beloved tutu and tiara.

"They were perfectly OK with his mother being gay," Bates said. "But they weren't OK with their grandson playing dress-up in a tutu."

Boys stick with typically masculine toys and games much more consistently than girls adhere to feminine ones, Harvard School of Public Health research associate Andrea L. Roberts found. Biologically male children who defy those norms are referred to doctors much earlier than biologically female ones who disdain "girl things," said Johanna Olson of the Center for Transyouth Health and Development at Children's Hospital Los Angeles. Even the criteria for diagnosing gender dysphoria were historically much broader for effeminate boys than for masculine girls.

Why? "Masculinity is valued more than femininity," University of Utah law professor Clifford Rosky said. "So there's less worry about girls than about boys."

Gender stereotypes do seem to have loosened: The Global Toy Experts survey found that most mothers would let their own sons play with dolls and dress-up sets, even if they shied from buying them for other boys. Parents in some parts of Los Angeles said their boys got barely any flak for choosing pink sneakers or toting dolls to school. And in a recent online survey by advertising agency DDB Worldwide, nearly three quarters of Americans surveyed said stay-at-home dads were just as good at parenting as stay-at-home moms.

But while attitudes may have shifted, Rosky said, "nothing changes until men are willing to act."

Some experts say economic barriers have stopped men from moving further into feminized fields. Jobs held by women tend to pay less, an imbalance rooted in the historical assumption that women were not breadwinners. Women had an economic reason to take many of the jobs monopolized by men, particularly college-educated women trying to climb the economic ladder.

"But if men made the switch, they'd lose money," New York University sociologist Paula England said.

20   Yet it isn't just economics that keeps men from typically female jobs. Men are still rare in nursing, for instance, despite respectable pay. England and other scholars see that dearth as another form of sexism, in which things historically associated with women are devalued.

Men who do enter heavily female fields are often prodded into other ones without even searching, as other people suggest new gigs that better fit the masculine stereotype, said Julie A. Kmec, associate professor of sociology at Washington State University.

While women have "come out" to their families as people who want a life outside the home, men have not "come out" at work as involved fathers, Kimmel said. And that, in turn, holds many working mothers back, Risman argued.

Familiar measures of progress toward gender equality, such as women working in management or men picking up housework, began to plateau in the 1990s. Cohen found that in the first decade of the millennium jobs stayed similarly segregated by gender—the first time since 1960 that gender integration in the workplace had slowed to a virtual halt.

24   "If men don't feel free to go into women's jobs," said Risman, a scholar at the Council on Contemporary Families, "women are not really free."

PERSONAL RESPONSE

How would you answer the Pew Research Center survey questions asking if children were better off if their mothers stay at home with them and if they were better off if their fathers stayed at home (paragraph 5)? Explain your answer.

QUESTIONS FOR CLASS OR SMALL-GROUP DISCUSSION

1. Reyes refers to research that "points to an enduring stigma for boys whose behavior is seen as a feminine" (paragraph 6). What do you think accounts for that stigma? Do you and your friends mock or make fun of males who you perceive as behaving in a "feminine" way?

2. How does Reyes explain such things as, women now frequently go into traditionally male fields but men don't go into women's fields (paragraph 10), and, women now insist that it is fine for them to have typically male traits such as assertiveness and ambition but men do not insist that can be kind and compassionate (paragraph 11)? Do you agree with that explanation?

3. Reyes comments that "gender stereotypes do seem to have loosened" and cites some examples of what she means (paragraph 14). Do your experiences and observations support or refute her comment?

4. Explain what you think this quotation in the last paragraph means and the extent to which you agree with it: "If men don't feel free to go into women's jobs, . . . women are not really free."

TARGET IS RIGHT ON
TARGET ABOUT THE USE
OF GENDER LABELS

CHRISTIA BROWN

Christia Brown is an associate professor of developmental psychology at the University of Kentucky, where she studies the effects of gender stereotypes among children and adolescents. She is author of Parenting Beyond Pink and Blue: How to Raise Your Kids Free of Gender Stereotyping *(2014). She blogs on the* Psychology Today *website in her column "Beyond Pink and Blue," where this article was posted.*

I have been doing a lot of interviews this week after Target announced that they would remove their gender distinctions from toys and bedding. Basically, their decision simply means that toys and bedding will be organized the same way as they currently are, just without the labels "Girls Toys" and "Boys Toys." The doll aisle won't be labeled as just for girls and the pirate bedspread won't be labeled as just for boys. When I read about this, I immediately applauded the decision (especially because I had JUST bought the pirate bedspread for my five year old daughter and was peeved by the signage).

I should have realized that backlash would soon follow, and it quickly did. The criticism boiled down to two main points. To paraphrase, one argument is that this decision will lead to chaos as confused grandmas aimlessly wander the aisles not knowing what to buy for their grandchildren ("My little Maggie likes My Little Pony, but the aisle isn't labeled for girls. I don't know where toys just for girls are."). The second argument is that we are born as boys and girls and Target is trying to make all children transgendered. I was unaware that Target had this much power over our biology; I just thought they had good deals on towels.

The reality, however, is that Target's decision is not coming out of nowhere. They are making a change that grassroots organizations have been championing for years. Let Toys Be Toys, for example, has campaigned for "toy and publishing industries to stop limiting children's interests by promoting some toys and books as only suitable for girls, and others only for boys." Play Unlimited is an organization whose slogan is "Every Toy for Everybody." They push for No Gender December to urge parents to think about gender stereotypes when they buy their holiday presents.

4   The reason these organizations are pushing for stores and marketers to reduce their use of gender labels is because they have been listening to scientists. Science on how gender stereotypes develop in children has shown that Target's decision is good for children. Why? First, toys are important for children.

Play is HOW children learn skills, learn about themselves, and learn about the world. All children need toys that encourage them to be active and develop hand-eye coordination (like balls), toys that help them practice spatial skills and learn basic physics (like construction and technology toys), toys that help them practice empathy and nurturance (like dolls), and toys that foster creativity (like arts and crafts). Unfortunately, these toys are segregated into boys' aisles and girls' aisles, and are explicitly labeled as such.

Many people assume that labeling and sorting by gender doesn't really matter. The argument people have been making against Target's decision is that boys and girls are naturally different, and boys inherently want Legos and action figures and girls inherently want dolls and tea sets. If this is true, then why would adding the label matter?

"Let Toys Be Toys" sums up it up well. They say, "How toys are labelled and displayed affects consumers' buying habits. Many people feel uncomfortable buying a boy a pink toy or a girl a toy labelled as 'for boys'."

8   Other buyers may simply be unaware of the restricted choices they are offered. They may not notice that science kits and construction toys are missing from the "girls" section, or art & crafts and kitchen toys from the "boys". If they're never offered the chance, a child may never find out if they enjoy a certain toy or style of play.

And children are taking in these messages about what girls and boys are 'supposed to like'. They are looking for patterns and social rules – they understand the gender rule 'This is for boys and that is for girls,' in the same way as other sorts of social rules, like 'Don't hit". These rigid boundaries turn children away from their true preferences, and provide a fertile ground for bullying."

This is indeed what children do. In fact, research has shown that the label of the toy – as either girls' toy or boys' toy – is actually more important than the toy itself. In multiple studies that have been replicated often, preschool children have been brought into a research lab and given a toy created by the researchers, one the children have never seen before. Some kids are told it is a toy that boys like to play with, and some are told it is something that girls like to play with. Boys who think they are playing with a boy toy think it is lots of fun. When they are told it is a girl toy, they say it is no fun and don't want it. Girls do the same thing. They love it when it is labeled a girl toy, and dismiss it when it is labeled a boy toy. The toy never changed, just the label. It is not surprising, then, that girls make a beeline for the girls' section of the toy store and boys to the boys' section. It is often less about their interests and more about identifying with the "right" group.

It goes way beyond simply saying the "right" toy is more fun than the "wrong" toy. When children are given new toys and told they are either boy toys or girl toys, children explore the toy for their gender more carefully, spending more time learning about it and figuring it out. They touch it more, inspect it more, and ask more questions about it. Not surprisingly, they also remember more about those toys that were labeled for their group. Remember that this is preschoolers! This is not about boys being born to play with trucks and girls to play with dolls. This is about labeling trucks as boy toys and dolls as girl toys and children knowing which toy they are supposed to play with (and which toy to avoid like the plague). They then, naturally, develop an expertise in their own group's toys. Before age 2, boys and girls like dolls to the same degree. It is only once boys learn about being boys does their interest in dolls plummet.

12   Knowing which is the "right" toy can even influence how good children are at playing with it. Raymond Montemayor, a psychology professor at the Ohio State University, brought six- to eight-year-old children into his lab. He told them about his new throwing game called Mr. Munchie (which was really just a Canadian toy unknown to US Midwestern kids). To score points, children throw as many plastic marbles as they can into a clown's mouth in thirteen seconds. Some of the children were told the game was "for girls, like jacks." Other children were told that the game was "for boys, like basketball." Not only did children like the game better when it belonged to their group, they also performed better when it was for their group. Girls tossed more marbles into the clown when they were told it was a girl game than when they were told it was a boy game. Conversely, boys were more accurate when they thought it was a boy game rather than a girl game.

All of these studies tell us that children, before they start first grade, know they are boys or girls and know all sorts of "rules" about boys and girls. They know which toys boys and girls play with, how boys and girls are supposed to act, and what kinds of jobs boys and girls will grow up to have. More importantly, believing a toy or activity is for boys rather than girls will determine who plays with it, who learns about it, and who is better at it. The label alone is enough to drive kids' behavior.

What we have learned is that labels matter! Not so much for adults, but for children. Labels point out that there are rules about who can play with what. These are rules that children enforce for themselves because boys want to be a good example of a boy and girls want to be a good example of a girl. The problem is that this limits the skills and abilities that children will develop. Every time a boy shies away from the doll aisle (an evitable consequence of labeling it for girls), he misses out on a chance to develop the nurturing and caretaking skills that will be helpful when he becomes a dad. Every time a girl shies away from construction toys (an evitable consequence of labeling it for boys), she misses out on practicing her spatial skills that will later be tested in advanced math classes. Labels drive these choices. If more stores followed the lead of Target, it would be an important step in kids becoming more well-rounded, more successful individuals.

PERSONAL RESPONSE

Target's announcement at its website about removing gender labels in the toy aisles generated over 3,000 comments, many of them praising Target for its decision but also many of them angry and even outraged. If you were to post a comment in response to the announcement, what would you say?

QUESTIONS FOR CLASS OR SMALL-GROUP DISCUSSION

1. What do you think of the chief complaints of those critical of Target's decision? Do you think complaints have merit? Do you agree with them?

2. Summarize your understanding of what scientific research says about why toys are important for children. What do children learn from toys?

3. Explain why Brown and other researchers say that the labels themselves are more important than the actual toys.

4. Do your own observations or personal experiences support the contention that labeling is a problem, as Brown asserts?

MindTap Reflect on the theme of this chapter.

PERSPECTIVES ON GENDER AND SEX ROLES

Suggested Writing Topics

1. Explore the meaning and implication of these common observations about children: "He's all boy" and "She's all girl."

2. Argue in support of or against Emily Alpert Reyes's statement in "'Men are Stuck' in Gender Roles, Data Suggest" that "the gender revolution has been lopsided."

3. Argue in support of or against Christia Brown's assertion that Target made the right choice in removing gender labels in its stores ("Target is Right on Target About the Use of Gender Labels").

4. Drawing on the essays in this chapter, write a reflective essay in which you explore your own concepts of masculinity and femininity (and perhaps androgyny) and the way in which that concept has shaped the way you are today.

5. Write a response to one of the articles in this chapter as if you were going to send it to the editor of the publication where the article was first published.

6. Explore ways in which you would like to see definitions of masculinity and femininity changed. How do you think relationships between the sexes would be affected if those changes were made?

7. Write a personal narrative recounting an experience in which you felt you were being treated unfairly or differently from persons of the other sex. What was the situation, how did you feel, and what did you do about it?

8. Explain the degree to which you consider gender issues to be important. Do you think too much is made of gender? Does it matter whether definitions of masculinity and femininity are rigid?

Research Topics

1. Thomas Bartlett in "The Puzzle of Boys" refers to the "nature versus nurture debate" (paragraph 9). Research some aspect of this debate. As with any research topic, you will need to narrow your focus after doing some preliminary reading on the nature and scope of this issue.

2. Conduct an investigative analysis of any of the following for their depiction of female and male sex roles: fairy tales, children's stories, advertising images, music videos, television programs, or film. Do you find stereotyped assumptions about masculinity and femininity? In what ways do you think the subject of your analysis (the medium you are investigating) reinforces or shapes cultural definitions of masculinity and femininity? Support your findings with research by reading articles and/or books on the subject.

3. Research the history of the contemporary women's movement, the men's movement, or the gay rights movement in America and report on its origins, goals, and influence. You will have to narrow your scope, depending on the time you have for the project and the nature of your purpose.

4. Since June 26, 2015, same-sex marriage has been legal in the United States. Research some aspect of the history of the struggle that culminated in the Supreme Court decision legalizing such marriages. You might focus on a particular city or state or on an organization, looking at strategies used in the fight to legalize same-sex marriage and the resistance of those opposed to it.

5. Conduct research on the subject of sex-role stereotyping and its influence on boys and/or girls. You may want to focus just on girls or just on boys or do a comparative analysis. Consider beginning your research by looking at some of the books mentioned by Thomas Bartlett in "The Puzzle of Boys."

6. Research Title IX of the 1973 Educational Amendments Act and its effect on women's participation in sports before and after it was enacted.

7. Research the areas that women were limited to enrolling in or denied access to in colleges and universities before Title IX of the 1972 Educational Amendments Act and how that changed as a result of the law. You might want to include a comparison of the restrictions on women with those on men.

RESPONDING TO VISUALS

Department of Defense photo by PH2 J. Alan Elliott

How do the Marine and child contrast in this image of a Marine steadying a child playing with a machine gun on top of a High-mobility Multipurpose Wheeled Vehicle (HMMWV) during Marine Appreciation Week?

1. How do the various components of the photograph contribute to its overall impression? For instance, what is the effect of the position of the American flag?

2. What do the looks on the faces of the Marine and child contribute to the overall effect?

3. Can we tell whether the child is a boy or a girl? Would it matter if the child were a girl? Would the effect of the image change if the Marine were a woman?

RESPONDING TO VISUALS

How would you describe the words in this "word cloud"?

1. How do the colors in the background enhance the meaning of the image?

2. Comment on the word *equality* centered in the image.

3. What is the overall effect or "message" of the image?

RACISM AND DISCRIMINATION

LEARNING OBJECTIVES

Students will demonstrate an ability to do the following:

☐ Analyze the damage that racism and discrimination does to people.

☐ Formulate possible explanations for why people discriminate against those who are different from them.

☐ Theorize whether it is possible for a society to eradicate discrimination based on race, color, ethnic background, or nationality.

MindTap˚   Understand the goals of the chapter and complete a warm-up activity.

CHAPTER OVERVIEW

Racial or ethnic heritage is as important to shaping identity as are sex and social class. One's race or ethnicity can also influence quality of life, educational opportunity, and advancement in employment. American society has a long history of struggling to confront and overcome racism and discrimination on the basis of ethnic heritage. Beginning well before the Civil War, American antislavery groups protested the enslavement of African Americans and worked to abolish slavery in all parts of the country. Other groups besides African Americans have experienced harsh treatment and discrimination solely because of their color or ethnic heritage.

These groups include Chinese men brought to America to help construct a cross-country railroad in the nineteenth century, European immigrants who came to America in large numbers near the end of the nineteenth century in search of better lives than they could expect in their homelands, Japanese men who came in the twentieth century to work at hard labor for money to send home, and Latinos/Latinas and Hispanics migrating north to America. As a result of the heightened awareness of the interplay of race, class, and gender, schools at all levels, from elementary through postgraduate, have incorporated course materials on or created whole courses devoted to those important components of individual identity and history. The readings in this chapter focus on racial and ethnic issues in a country that still struggles with inequities and discrimination.

The chapter begins with a report on the controversy created in Virginia when high school students were shown a four-minute animated video on structural discrimination during Black History Month. Although the video had been produced over a decade before and had been shown to thousands of school children over the years, this time a number of white parents complained that it was "racially divisive" and was offensive to whites because it played on "white guilt." Peter Holley, in his *Washington Post* article "Parents Outraged after Students Shown 'White Guilt' Cartoon for Black History Month," explains the position of both those who created and promoted the video and those who felt offended by it. The article raises some interesting points about racial disparity, privileged groups, and race relations in America.

The next reading is an intriguing personal essay by Sarah Valentine. In "When I Was White," she affirms that the racial transition experience is a valid one, having gone through it herself. Raised as white in a white family, it was only in her adulthood that she learned that her biological father was black. This revelation produced a profound dilemma for her: happy to learn the truth about her parentage and therefore some logical explanation for her dark skin, she nonetheless was faced with the questions of what to do with the "white sense of self" that she had lived with for 27 years and how to "become black." The process, she says, changed the way that she had always thought of herself and race—and thoroughly tore her apart.

While the first two articles address the difficulties of understanding truly what it means to be other than what we are, whether the difference is race, color, ethnic background, nationality, class, sex, or any other factor, the next reading addresses the subject of blatant discrimination on the basis of color and physical or mental disability. Marilyn Elias in "The School-to-Prison Pipeline" has in mind an audience of teachers, but what she writes is of interest to students and lay people as well. She explains what the term "school-to-prison pipeline" means, who is most likely to be in that "pipeline," and what teachers and legislators can do to keep children in the classroom instead of incarcerating them. Elias presents data to support her allegation that the number of students pulled out of the classroom for various infractions is disproportionately higher for minority students and students with disabilities than for other groups of students, suggesting a component of discrimination built into the system. Elias ends her piece with a list of suggestions on how school districts can avoid sending so many of their children to correctional institutions.

As with all of the subjects of the readings in Part two, there is much more to a consideration of racism and discrimination than these readings touch upon. Prejudice, discrimination, stereotyping, and similar injustices are found around the world and take many forms. The readings here suggest just a few of the issues associated with race, ethnicity, and national origin and remind us that only by examining our own perspective can we begin to understand each other.

PARENTS OUTRAGED AFTER STUDENTS SHOWN "WHITE GUILT" CARTOON FOR BLACK HISTORY MONTH

PETER HOLLEY

Peter Holley has been a general assignment reporter at The Washington Post *since 2014. Before that, he was an associate editor at* Houstonia *magazine and had worked as a features reporter for* The Houston Chronicle *and a crime reporter for* The San Antonio Express-News. *Holley also spent nearly a year in Lahore, where he was a writer and editor for Pakistan's* Friday Times.

A Virginia school district has banned the use of an educational video about racial inequality after some parents complained that its messaging is racially divisive.

The four-minute, animated video — "Structural Discrimination: The Unequal Opportunity Race" — was shown last week to students at an assembly at Glen Allen High School, in Henrico County, as a part of the school's Black History Month program. The video contextualizes historic racial disparity in the United States using the metaphor of a race track in which runners face different obstacles depending upon their racial background. It has been shown hundreds of thousands of times at schools and workshops across the country since it was created more than a decade ago, according to the African American Policy Forum, which produced it.

"The video is designed for the general public," said Luke Harris, co-founder of the African American Policy Forum and an associate professor of political science at Vassar College. "We produced something you could show in elementary and secondary schools or in college studies courses." He added: "We found that the video has a huge impact on the people that we're showing it to. Most of us know very little about the social history of the United States and its contemporary impact. It was designed as a tool to throw light on American history."

4

But in Glen Allen, about 14 miles north of Richmond, some parents complained, calling it a "white guilt video." Henrico County Public Schools officials initially defended the video, saying it was "one component of a thoughtful discussion in which all viewpoints were encouraged." But after the story began to spread nationally, school officials switched gears, labeling the video "racially divisive" two days later.

"The Henrico School Board and administration consider this to be a matter of grave concern," School Board Chair Micky Ogburn said in a statement released *to The Washington Post*. "We are making every effort to respond to our community. It is our goal to prevent the recurrence of this type of event. School leaders have been instructed not to use the video in our schools. In addition, steps are being taken to prevent the use of racially divisive materials in the future. We do apologize to those who were offended and for the unintended impact on our community."

Ravi K. Perry — an associate professor of political science at Virginia Commonwealth University and President of the National Association for Ethnic Studies — told *The Post* that he worked closely with school officials over several months to plan the presentation, which he also moderated. The video, he said, was just one element of a 30-minute-long, interactive presentation that was shown to two separate groups, each with around 1,000 students. He asked students to fill out a "group membership profile" and write a poem describing their identity. He said the students were "fully engaged" and the response afterwards was overwhelmingly positive.

The objective, Perry said, was to allow students to "engage American history through the lens of African Americans and other marginalized groups" and to understand that "we all have multiple identities." The idea for the presentation came about, he said, after a racist song was played over the loud speakers at a football game in October in which the visiting team was from a predominately black high school. The song, a racist parody of the theme song from Disney's "Duck Tales," included 13 racial epithets in a single minute, according to *Raw Story*.

8

"I feel extremely grateful to the principal and her staff for being courageous enough to provide a comprehensive educational experience on race in America," he said. "That is something that you should be applauded for doing and not something that millions of people across the country should find distasteful." He added: "Had I been presenting at an environment where the state standardized curriculum had fully integrated the experience of African Americans, then perhaps the material selected to present to students would have been different. Because the information that many students nationwide are learning about race in America is limited or wrong, it's important to provide them with historical context."

The scope of the backlash remains unknown, but the statement noted that "school division leaders" received "numerous emails and phone calls objecting to the video." Among the parents who found the video problematic was Don Blake, whose granddaughter attended the Glen Allen High assembly, according to NBC affiliate WWBT. "They are sitting there watching a video that is dividing them up from a racial standpoint," Blake told the station. "It's a white guilt kind of video. I think somebody should be held accountable for this."

Kenny Manning, a student at Glen Allen High, told ABC affiliate WRIC that reaction on campus was mixed. "A lot of people thought it was offensive to white people and made them feel bad about being privileged," Manning said. "Others thought that it was good to get the information out there. There is oppression going on in the world, and that needs to be looked at with a magnifying glass, I guess."

The video begins with four athletes — two of them white, two of them non-white — taking their marks before a race. After the starting gun fires, the two non-white runners are forced to remain in the starting blocks while their white counterparts begin running. The non-white runners are hit with words such as "slavery," "broken treaties," "genocide" and "segregation" as the white runners pass them by. The white runners eventually pick up dollar-symbol-marked batons that grow in size and are eventually passed off to younger white runners who enter the race.

12   It takes more than a minute until the non-white competitors are allowed to begin running. Not long after they do, they are confronted by overwhelming physical obstacles, such as a rainstorm, rocks, a large hole in the track and sharks. Each obstacle, the viewer learns, symbolizes real-life barriers to success, such as discrimination, poor schooling, standardized tests, racial profiling, the school-to-prison pipeline and housing discrimination. The video shows that these obstacles result in shortened lifespans for the non-white runners.

A white male runner then crosses the finish line ahead of everyone else on a rapidly moving conveyor belt. He holds a water bottle labeled "Yale" and the word "privilege" hovers nearby. A white female runner finishes shortly behind him. As the video ends, viewers are left with a written message: "Affirmative action helps level the playing field."

Harris, the African American Policy Forum co-founder, told *The Post* that the video is intended to show that race-conscious programs are not designed to create "favoritism for damaged individuals," but instead are about creating remedies for damaged institutions. The backlash from some white parents in Virginia didn't surprise him, he said. "The anger is a reaction that we expect to get from some Americans, because we live in a society that doesn't have honest discourse about race," Harris said. "Our society is as heterogeneous as any on the planet, but American social history from a multicultural, multiracial perspective is just something that people have not been exposed to. When someone highlights that message, some people go after the messenger."

Henrico Superintendent Pat Kinlaw said in the district's statement that the video presentation at Glen Allen High remains under investigation. "The matter continues to be under review internally after first coming to the attention of school division leadership on the evening of Thursday, Feb. 4," Kinlaw said. "While we as educators do not object to difficult and constructive conversations about American history and racial discourse past and present, we understand why many people feel this video in particular was not the best way to deliver such an important lesson."

16   Perry said it was unfortunate that school officials had chosen not to use anger about the video to engage in a larger dialogue about race within their community and instead chosen to support the views of the loudest voices. "In politics," he told *The Post*, "that's what we call 'pandering.'" It's where you assume, for example, that the only types of folks you should be paying attention to are the ones who call your office. If you only pay attention to the people who call or email you, you are

> immediately shutting off the people who don't have the time or the resources to get in touch and that goes to the heart of what was being talked about in that video."

PERSONAL RESPONSE

How well do you think that your previous schooling has given you "a comprehensive educational experience on race in America" (paragraph 8)?

QUESTIONS FOR CLASS OR SMALL-GROUP DISCUSSION

1. According to Holley, people who objected to the video's being shown at the Glen Allen High School did so because they felt that it is "racially divisive" (paragraphs 1), and the school board eventually agreed with them (paragraphs 4 and 5). Explain your understanding of the reason why some people believed it to be "racially divisive."

2. What do those who defend the video say in defense of it? Where do you position yourself in the controversy?

3. Holley states that "most of us know very little about the social history of the United States and its contemporary impact" (paragraph 3). To what extent do you believe that he is correct? Does his statement apply to you?

4. How accurate do you consider this statement by Ravi K. Perry, who moderated the presentation that included the video: "Because the information that many students nationwide are learning about race in America is limited or wrong, it's important to provide them with historical context" (paragraph 8)?

WHEN I WAS WHITE

SARAH VALENTINE

Sarah Valentine teaches creative writing and comparative literature at Northwestern University. Her research interests include translation theory and practice and Soviet-era Russian African intellectual encounter. Her

books include her translation Into the Snow: Selected
Poems of Gennady Aygi *(2011) and* Witness and
Transformation: The Poetics of Gennady Aygi *(2015).*
She is working on a memoir about discovering her
African American ancestry as an adult and discovering
the identity of her biological father. This article was first
published in the Chronicle of Higher Education.

Rachel Dolezal's recent unmasking as a white woman living
as black sparked a debate about the legitimacy of "transracial"
experience. I cannot speak for Dolezal or anyone else, but
I can state for a fact that racial transition is a valid experience,
because I have gone through it.

While most people would look at [a picture of my two
brothers and me] and see a black girl, two white boys, and a
very surprised cat, they would be wrong. The girl in the photo
is white, just like her brothers. I was raised in a white family
from birth and taught to identify as white. For most of my life,
I didn't know that my biological father was black. Whenever
I asked as a child about my darker skin, my mother corrected
me, saying it was not dark but "olive." When others asked if
I was adopted, my mother ignored them. Eventually everyone,
including me, stopped asking.

When, as an adult, I learned the truth of my paternity,
I began the difficult process of changing my identity from
white to black. The difficulty did not lie in an unwillingness
to give up my whiteness. On the contrary, the revelation of my
paternity was a relief: It confirmed that I was different from my
parents and siblings, something I had felt deeply all my life.

The dilemma I faced was this: If I am mixed race and
black, what do I do with the white sense of self I lived with for
27 years, and how does one become black? Is that even possible?
Now, you may say that the rest of the world already saw me as
black and all I had to do was catch up. True. But "catching up"
meant that I had to blow the lid off the Pandora's box of everything I thought I knew about myself and about race in America.

My first instinct, as an academic, was to approach the
problem intellectually. I read everything I could get my hands
on about the creation of black identity. But that was only a safe
first step down a path that would tear me apart—physically,
emotionally, intellectually, and psychologically.

"Coming out" as black cost me my relationship with my
mother and some of my closest friends. It cleaved my sense

of self in two. As I struggled to come to terms with what the revelation meant for my family (are they my real family?), my integrity (my whole life I had been passing without realizing it!), and my core identity (if I'm not the person I was made to believe I was for the last 27 years, who am I?), I began to experience symptoms of trauma such as exhaustion, weight loss, and constant all-over physical pain. My hair fell out in clumps. I couldn't concentrate. I developed acid reflux and could not tolerate most foods.

"You're making a big deal out of nothing," my mother said when I tried to impress on her the seriousness of what I was going through. "It's only important if you choose to make it important." Needless to say, her dismissive attitude toward race and my existential struggle did not help. For her, I was and always would be the little "white" girl in the photo.

8   We all have a "raced" understanding of ourselves and the world, regardless of the racial group or groups with which we identify. The notion of people changing their racial categorization is conceivable only in societies where race is policed, where it determines your access to or denial of social and economic status. Otherwise, why would it matter?

This is not something I learned growing up. In my family, it was understood, even if it was never directly stated, that only people of color "had" race; whites were just people. Perceived racial neutrality is endemic to whiteness, and so, growing up, I understood race as something that applied exclusively to other people. In my white family and white community, race was a problem for other people, but not for us.

And, despite discredited notions of biological essentialism, it was assumed to be an intrinsic quality. If you were born black, well, too bad for you—you had race, like it was an incurable disease, deep in the bones and blood.

I remember being at a friend's house in first grade with another girl, who happened to be the only (other) black girl in our class. She got a nosebleed and ran to the bathroom to grab a towel, and I stood outside the open bathroom door, out of sight except for part of my face peering around the corner, reflected in the bathroom mirror. I stood transfixed as I wondered what color her blood would be when it came pouring out of her nose. She's black, dark-skinned, different, not like the rest of us, I thought. Surely her blood would be a different color, too. Such an important difference has to be more than skin-deep. Of course, the moment her bright red blood stained the white towel, I lost interest.

12   That was my first real lesson about race: Black people still seemed different—they just weren't as exciting or exotic as I had hoped.

I leave you to judge for yourself the sad irony of this absurd racism coming from a girl who had been so indoctrinated in the delusional psychology of whiteness that she could not see her own dark-skinned face staring back at her from the mirror. It took that girl years of therapy for post-traumatic stress disorder and depression, medication, broken relationships, and painful reckoning to shed that psychology and create a new one that allowed her to see and love her own blackness and to forgive the little white girl who did not know any better.

Did I change my appearance? No. I look pretty much the way I've always looked, just older. But I did change my last name. I needed to make a definitive break with the person I had been, with the person my family had told me I was. I no longer wanted to be complicit in the lie of whiteness; I needed to define my identity on my own terms. That caused a rift between me and the father who raised me, whose last name I had carried since birth. Until then he had been extremely supportive and understanding. Though he hardly spoke of it, I could feel his hurt and disappointment, and it broke my heart. But what could I do? Sarah Valentine is a different person than Sarah D., who had explained her darker skin as owing to her mother's southern Italian and her father's "black Irish" heritage.

It was both exhilarating and panic-inducing to be publicly black for the first time, to be able to answer, when someone asked "What are you?" (and they always asked), that I was a mixed-race African-American. Never mind that I felt like an impostor, that I didn't feel as if I knew "how to be black." Eventually I became comfortable in my own skin.

16   Ten years later, I can look back at that painful period of racial transition and say that I came out of it with a cohesive sense of self that embodies all its contradictions. But there is still much that I am struggling to articulate and understand.

I don't know how others with stories like mine have handled the revelation of their racial identity, nor do I know if Dolezal's is merely a case of passing or something else. But I believe it is time to probe deeper into the nature of racial experience to see if we can entertain the possibility of authentic transracial identity.

PERSONAL RESPONSE

Valentine says that after she learned about her biological father, she read all she could about black identity. If you were telling someone the characteristics of your own racial identity, what details would you include as the most distinctive or definitive?

QUESTIONS FOR CLASS OR SMALL-GROUP DISCUSSION

1. Valentine begins and ends her article with references to Rachel Dolezal, a white woman who identified and lived as black, including serving as president of an NAACP chapter, until her white parents told the press that she had been born white, a revelation that sparked a controversy "about the legitimacy of the 'transracial' experience" (paragraph 1). Valentine was reared by white parents and lived as white until she learned that her biological father was black, and now she asserts that hers is a "valid" transracial experience. What do you understand the term *transracial* to mean? Are both Dolezal and Valentine transracial, or is one's transracial experience valid and the other's not?

2. What do you understand Valentine to mean when she said that her experience tore her apart "physically, emotionally, intellectually, and psychologically" (paragraph 5)? From your perspective, do you see why it was so traumatic for her?

3. What did Valentine's personal experience teach her about race (paragraph 4)? To what extent do you agree with her assessment of race in America?

4. Why did coming to term with her racial identity matter to Valentine? What do you think of Valentine's mother's and father's responses to her struggle? Do you sympathize with either of her parents?

THE SCHOOL-TO-PRISON PIPELINE

MARILYN ELIAS

Marilyn Elias is a Los Angeles journalist and a frequent contributor to publications of the Southern Poverty Law Center. Her work has been honored with awards from the American Psychological Association, the American Academy of Pediatrics, the Council on Contemporary Families, and Mental Health America. This article was first published in the spring 2013 issue of Teaching Tolerance, *a publication of the Southern Poverty Law Center.*

In Meridian, Mississippi, police routinely arrest and transport youths to a juvenile detention center for minor classroom misbehaviors. In Jefferson Parish, Louisiana, according to a U.S. Department of Justice complaint, school officials have given armed police "unfettered authority to stop, frisk, detain, question, search and arrest schoolchildren on and off school grounds." In Birmingham, Alabama, police officers are permanently stationed in nearly every high school.

In fact, hundreds of school districts across the country employ discipline policies that push students out of the classroom and into the criminal justice system at alarming rates—a phenomenon known as the school to-prison pipeline.

Last month, Sen. Richard Durbin, D-Ill., held the first federal hearing on the school to-prison pipeline—an important step toward ending policies that favor incarceration over education and disproportionately push minority students and students with disabilities out of schools and into jails.

In opening the hearing, Durbin told the subcommittee of the Senate Judiciary Committee, "For many young people, our schools are increasingly a gateway to the criminal justice system. This phenomenon is a consequence of a culture of zero tolerance that is widespread in our schools and is depriving many children of their fundamental right to an education."

A wide array of organizations—including the Southern Poverty Law Center, the NAACP and Dignity in Schools—offered testimony during the hearing. They joined representatives from the Departments of Education and Justice to shine a national spotlight on a situation viewed far too often as a local responsibility.

"We have a national problem that deserves federal action," Matthew Cregor, an attorney with the NAACP Legal Defense Fund, explained. "With suspension a top predictor of dropout, we must confront this practice if we are ever to end the 'dropout crisis' or the so-called achievement gap." In the words of Vermont's Sen. Patrick Leahy, "As a nation, we can do better."

What Is the School-to-Prison Pipeline?

Policies that encourage police presence at schools, harsh tactics including physical restraint, and automatic punishments that result in suspensions and out-of-class time are huge contributors to the pipeline, but the problem is more complex than that.

8   The school-to-prison pipeline starts (or is best avoided) in the classroom. When combined with zero-tolerance policies, a teacher's decision to refer students for punishment can mean they are pushed out of the classroom—and much more likely to be introduced into the criminal justice system.

Who's in the Pipeline?

Students from two groups—racial minorities and children with disabilities—are disproportionately represented in the school-to-prison pipeline. African-American students, for instance, are 3.5 times more likely than their white classmates to be suspended or expelled, according to a nationwide study by the U.S. Department of Education Office for Civil Rights. Black children constitute 18 percent of students, but they account for 46 percent of those suspended more than once.

For students with disabilities, the numbers are equally troubling. One report found that while 8.6 percent of public school children have been identified as having disabilities that affect their ability to learn, these students make up 32 percent of youth in juvenile detention centers.

The racial disparities are even starker for students with disabilities. About 1 in 4 black children with disabilities were suspended at least once, versus 1 in 11 white students, according to an analysis of the government report by Daniel J. Losen, director of the Center for Civil Rights Remedies of the Civil Rights Project at UCLA.

12   A landmark study published last year tracked nearly 1 million Texas students for at least six years. The study controlled for more than 80 variables, such as socioeconomic class, to see how they affected the likelihood of school discipline. The study found that African Americans were disproportionately punished compared with otherwise similar white and Latino students. Children with emotional disabilities also were disproportionately suspended and expelled.

In other studies, Losen found racial differences in suspension rates have widened since the early 1970s and that suspension is being used more frequently as a disciplinary tool. But he said his recent study and other research show that removing children from school does not improve their behavior. Instead, it greatly increases the likelihood that they'll drop out and wind up behind bars.

Punishing Policies

The SPLC [Southern Poverty Law Center] advocates for changes to end the school-to-prison pipeline and has filed lawsuits or civil rights complaints against districts with punitive discipline practices that are discriminatory in impact. According to the U.S. Department of Justice, the number of school resource officers rose 38 percent between 1997 and 2007. Jerri Katzerman, SPLC deputy legal director, said this surge in police on campus has helped to criminalize many students and fill the pipeline.

One 2005 study found that children are far more likely to be arrested at school than they were a generation ago. The vast majority of these arrests are for nonviolent offenses. In most cases, the students are simply being disruptive. And a recent U.S. Department of Education study found that more than 70 percent of students arrested in school-related incidents or referred to law enforcement are black or Hispanic. Zero-tolerance policies, which set one-size-fits-all punishments for a variety of behaviors, have fed these trends.

Best Practices

16   Instead of pushing children out, Katzerman said, "Teachers need a lot more support and training for effective discipline, and schools need to use best practices for behavior modification to keep these kids in school where they belong." Keeping at-risk kids in class can be a tough order for educators under pressure to meet accountability measures, but classroom teachers are in a unique position to divert students from the school-to-prison pipeline.

Teachers know their students better than any resource officer or administrator—which puts them in a singularly empowered position to keep students in the classroom. It's not easy, but when teachers take a more responsive and less punitive approach in the classroom, students are more likely to complete their education.

The information in "A Teacher's Guide to Rerouting the Pipeline" [http://www.tolerance.org/magazine/number-43-spring-2013/feature/teachers-guide-rerouting-pipeline] highlights common scenarios that push young people into the school-to-prison pipeline and offers practical advice for how teachers can dismantle the school-to-prison pipeline.

Avoiding the Pipeline

How can school districts divert the school-to-prison pipeline?

1. Increase the use of positive behavior interventions and supports.

2. Compile annual reports on the total number of disciplinary actions that push students out of the classroom based on gender, race and ability.

3. Create agreements with police departments and court systems to limit arrests at school and the use of restraints, such as mace and handcuffs.

4. Provide simple explanations of infractions and prescribed responses in the student code of conduct to ensure fairness.

5. Create appropriate limits on the use of law enforcement in public schools.

6. Train teachers on the use of positive behavior supports for at-risk students.

PERSONAL RESPONSE

Thinking back on your primary and secondary education, how do you now view fellow classmates who were troublemakers, those who disrupted class or disrespected teachers? Did your school have a police presence and, if so, what did you think of having armed protection while you were getting an education? If not, how were school rules enforced?

QUESTIONS FOR CLASS OR SMALL-GROUP DISCUSSION

1. Explain in your own words what the "school-to-prison pipeline" is. Do you think that your school had such a "pipeline"?

2. Elias reports that the first federal hearing on the school-to-prison pipeline had been held in 2013. What do you think the federal government can do to end "policies that favor incarceration over education and disproportionately push minority students and students with disabilities out of schools and into jails" (paragraph 3)? Why do you think such policies were initiated in the first place?

3. Elias writes, "The school-to-prison pipeline starts (or is best avoided) in the classroom" (paragraph 8). What do you think she means by the parenthetical

statement? What do you think teachers can do to avoid putting students on the track to prison?

4. What is your opinion of Elias's list in the final paragraph of ways that school districts can "divert the school-to-prison pipeline"? Select one and comment on how effective you think it would be.

MindTap   Reflect on the theme of this chapter.

PERSPECTIVES ON RACISM AND DISCRIMINATION

Suggested Writing Topics

1. Watch on *You Tube* or another Web site the video discussed in Peter Holley's "Parents Outraged after Students Shown 'White Guilt' Cartoon during Black History Month" and then argue in support of or against the appropriateness of the video for school children. You can locate the video online by searching the title "Structural Discrimination: The Unequal Opportunity Race."

2. Taking into consideration Peter Holley's "Parents Outraged after Students Shown 'White Guilt' Cartoon during Black History Month" and Sarah Valentine's "When I Was White" in mind, explain your own theory on the conditions that prevent blacks and whites in America from understanding one another's perspectives.

3. Write in response to Marilyn Elias's "The School-to-Prison Pipeline." Do you think that your teachers were harsher on racial minorities and students with disabilities than they were on other students when it came to classroom behavior, as Elias suggests? Do you have anecdotal evidence that supports or refutes her argument?

4. With Marilyn Elias's "The School-to-Prison Pipeline" in mind, argue in favor of or against the presence of armed police in schools. Do you think that their presence contributes to creating an environment of discrimination?

5. Write a reflective essay on your own cultural heritage, explaining your family's background and how you feel about that heritage.

6. Explain the importance of race or ethnicity to your own self-identity. Is it as important as your sex, your job, your social class, or your educational level?

7. Explore the role of racial and ethnic diversity in your educational experiences in high school and college. Consider these questions: How diverse are the student populations of schools you have attended? How large a component did multiculturalism play in the curricula of courses you have taken? Have you been satisfied with that aspect of your education?

8. Narrate your first experience with prejudice, discrimination, or bigotry, as either a witness or a victim. Describe in detail the incident and how it made you feel.

9. Narrate a personal experience that changed your views on the issue of racism.

10. Explain the effects of racial prejudice on a person or a group of people familiar to you.

11. With the readings in this chapter in mind, write an essay on some aspect of the subject of racism and discrimination. As you plan your essay, consider the following questions: Where do people get prejudices? What aspects of American culture reinforce and/or perpetuate stereotypes? How can you personally work against stereotyping and prejudice?

Research Topics

1. Research the subject of a public policy like affirmative action, welfare, or bilingual public education as an effective (or ineffective) way to address racial or ethnic inequities in American society.

2. Research the current state of illegal immigration, reasons to account for it, and what you think should be done, if anything, about it.

3. Investigate the controversy caused when Rachel Dolezal revealed that she is white but identifies as black. In particular, what is it about the term *transracial* as applied to her case that has people arguing over its validity? How do Dolezal's circumstances compare with those of Sarah Valentine's? Is the latter's experience valid and Dolezal's not?

4. Research either the black-power movement or the Rev. Martin Luther King's civil rights marches of the 1960s as a tool for advancing the cause of racial equality in America.

5. Research the subject of whether America is a classless society. Do certain factors such as culture, ethnicity, demographics, nativity, citizenship, mother tongue, religion, skin color, or race play a role in an individual's prospects for social mobility?

6. Research the "school-to-prison" phenomenon, drawing on some of the studies mentioned in Marilyn Elias's "The School-to-Prison Pipeline." You might want to find out what the results of the first federal hearing on the subject were (paragraph 3).

7. Select one of the following groups to which the U.S. federal government has made reparations and research reasons why those reparations were made: Japanese Americans interned in American prisons camp during World War II or the Sioux Indians whose lands were confiscated in 1877.

8. Select a topic from any of the suggested writing topics above and expand it to include library research, Internet research, and/or interviews.

RESPONDING TO VISUALS

William B. Plowman/Getty Images News/Getty Images

A friend comforts the Iraqi-born owner of a restaurant after it was burned by apparently racially-motivated arson on September 19, 2001. Without this information about the context in which it was taken, what might this photograph suggest to you?

1. According to the *Time* magazine issue that this image was published in not long after the 9/11 terrorist attacks in New York and Washington, the restaurant owner had received threatening telephone calls for days before the fire. How does that knowledge affect your understanding of this photograph?

2. What does this image convey that a picture of the restaurant ruins alone would not?

3. What emotions does the photograph evoke in you?

RESPONDING TO VISUALS

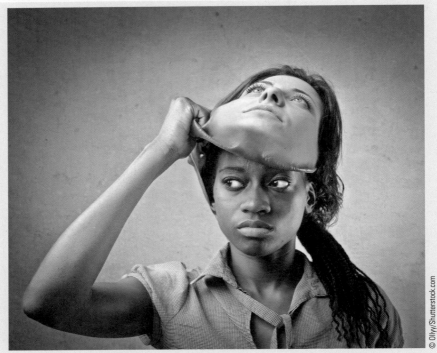

How might this image of an African young woman taking off a mask of a Caucasian be representative of the transracial experience?

1. How do you interpret the look on the young woman's face as she takes off the mask?

2. How does the mask contrast with the young woman's face?

3. What does this photograph suggest to you? That is, what do you think the photographer had in mind with the image?

PSYCHOLOGY AND HUMAN BEHAVIOR

LEARNING OBJECTIVES

Students will demonstrate an ability to do the following:

- ☐ Analyze group dynamics in terms of their influence on individual behavior.

- ☐ Discuss the results of psychological studies on individuals placed in positions of power and submission.

- ☐ Construct scenarios involving authority figures who require blind obedience and hypothesize on their own behavior in such situations.

MindTap˙   Understand the goals of the chapter and complete a warm-up activity.

CHAPTER OVERVIEW

Psychology is the study of the workings of the human mind and human behavior. It attempts to account for how humans act, think, react, and feel in a variety of situations. The field is broad in scope, covering essentially the whole of human action and emotion, so someone looking for a degree or profession in this area will find specialty areas such as clinical psychology, social psychology, counseling, school psychology, criminal psychology, and neuroscience, among others. The articles in this chapter look at several different subjects that psychologists are interested in studying: the behavior of humans when placed in unusual situations, especially those involving power and submission; people's behavior in groups; the effects of punishment on children's behavior; and experiments measuring self-control and delayed gratification.

The chapter begins with Philip Zimbardo's "Revisiting the Stanford Prison Experiment: A Lesson in the Power of Situation," which explains his famous 1971 prison experiment at Stanford University. A classic study of what happens to seemingly psychologically well-adjusted people when they are placed in positions of power and submission, the experiment went in a direction that completely surprised Zimbardo and led to a sudden end six days into a projected two-week project. In this article, he tries to account for what happened in the simulated prison situation; from that, he extrapolates lessons that he suggests have relevance today to law, criminal justice, the penal system, and human behavior. His article concludes with what he sees as the critical message of his experiment for reducing criminal behavior and modifying the behavior of those in charge of prisoners.

Although the Zimbardo article was published in 2007 and the original experiment took place in 1971, the issue of people's behavior in unusual circumstances remains a fascinating subject. Zimbardo's experiment is still talked about and is included in most college psychology textbooks. It is also the subject of a Hollywood film released in 2015 called simply *The Stanford Prison Experiment* and advertised as a thriller. The imminent release provided the impetus for Maria Konnikova's "The Real Lessons of the Stanford Prison Experiment." As the title of her article suggests, Konnikova is interested in what the experiment revealed about human behavior. Many critics have interpreted what happened as evidence of humans' proclivity toward cruelty when placed in positions of power. Konnikova, though, sees a broader application and a slightly different interpretation: "Was the study about our individual fallibility, or about broken institutions? Were its findings about prisons, specifically, or about life in general? What did the Stanford Prison Experiment really show?"

Next, Anne Trafton in "When Good People Do Bad Things" reports on a study by a professor of cognitive neuroscience and her colleagues at MIT to determine factors involved in group dynamics, specifically what happens to individuals when they are part of a group doing things that they would not have considered doing if alone. Researchers studied brain activity to determine "the neural mechanisms behind the group dynamics that produce bad behavior." They looked specifically at the medial prefrontal cortex, which lights up when a person is thinking about him- or herself. The research revealed intriguing results about the way that identifying with groups influences individual behavior.

As the readings in this chapter imply, explaining human behavior definitively is nearly impossible. Psychologists conduct experiments and studies and then draw conclusions as best they can to explain or account for behaviors under certain conditions. Other experts question the research and conclusions and offer counter interpretations. While machines such as the fMRI mentioned in a couple of the essays can scientifically record *what* is happening in the brain, explaining *why* it happens is much more difficult. Behaviors and emotions are not static: they change as people grow and have new experiences, and many of our behaviors are simply inexplicable. For many people, this is what makes psychology exciting, and of course it is a field that has seemingly endless possibilities for exploration.

REVISITING THE STANFORD PRISON EXPERIMENT: A LESSON IN THE POWER OF SITUATION

PHILIP ZIMBARDO

Philip Zimbardo, professor emeritus of psychology at Stanford University, is an internationally recognized scholar, teacher, researcher, and author. Zimbardo's books include The Psychology of Attitude Change and Social Influence *(1991);* Violence Workers: Police Torturers and Murderers Reconstruct Brazilian Atrocities *(2002);* The Lucifer Effect: Understanding How Good People Turn Evil *(2007);* The Time Paradox *(with John Boyd, 2008); and* The Demise of Guys: Why Boys Are Struggling and What We Can Do about It *(with Nikita D. Coulombe, 2012). This article was first published in the* Chronicle of Higher Education.

By the 1970s, psychologists had done a series of studies establishing the social power of groups. They showed, for example, that groups of strangers could persuade people to believe statements that were obviously false. Psychologists had also found that research participants were often willing to obey authority figures even when doing so violated their personal beliefs. The Yale studies by Stanley Milgram in 1963 demonstrated that a majority of ordinary citizens would continually shock an innocent man, even up to near-lethal levels, if commanded to do so by someone acting as an authority. The "authority" figure in this case was merely a high-school biology teacher who wore a lab coat and acted in an official manner. The majority of people shocked their victims over and over again despite increasingly desperate pleas to stop.

In my own work, I wanted to explore the fictional notion from William Golding's *Lord of the Flies* about the power of anonymity to unleash violent behavior. In one experiment from 1969, female students who were made to feel anonymous and given permission for aggression became significantly more hostile than students with their identities intact. Those and a host of other social-psychological studies were showing that human nature was more pliable than previously imagined and more responsive to situational pressures than we cared to acknowledge. In sum, these studies challenged the sacrosanct view that inner determinants of behavior—personality traits, morality, and religious upbringing—directed good people down righteous paths.

Missing from the body of social-science research at the time was the direct confrontation of good versus evil, of good people pitted against the forces inherent in bad situations. It was evident from everyday life that smart people made dumb decisions when they were engaged in mindless groupthink, as in the disastrous Bay of Pigs invasion by the smart guys in President John F. Kennedy's cabinet. It was also clear that smart people surrounding President Richard M. Nixon, like Henry A. Kissinger and Robert S. McNamara, escalated the Vietnam War when they knew, and later admitted, it was not winnable. They were caught up in the mental constraints of cognitive dissonance—the discomfort from holding two conflicting thoughts—and were unable to cut bait even though it was the only rational strategy to save lives and face. Those examples, however, with their different personalities, political agendas, and motives, complicated any simple conceptual attempt to understand what went wrong in these situations.

I decided that what was needed was to create a situation in a controlled experimental setting in which we could array on one side a host of variables, such as role-playing, coercive rules, power differentials, anonymity, group dynamics, and dehumanization. On the other side, we lined up a collection of the "best and brightest" of young college men in collective opposition to the might of a dominant system. Thus in 1971 was born the Stanford prison experiment, more akin to Greek drama than to university psychology study. I wanted to know who wins—good people or an evil situation—when they were brought into direct confrontation.

First we established that all 24 participants were physically and mentally healthy, with no history of crime or violence, so as to be sure that initially they were all "good apples." They were paid $15 a day to participate. Each of the student volunteers was randomly assigned to play the role of prisoner or guard in a setting designed to convey a sense of the psychology of imprisonment (in actuality, a mock prison set up in the basement of the Stanford psychology department). Dramatic realism infused the study. Palo Alto police agreed to "arrest" the prisoners and book them, and once at the prison, they were given identity numbers, stripped naked, and deloused. The prisoners wore large smocks with no underclothes and lived in the prison 24/7 for a planned two weeks; three sets of guards each patrolled eight-hour shifts. Throughout the experiment, I served as the prison "superintendent," assisted by two graduate students.

Initially nothing much happened as the students awkwardly tried out their assigned roles in their new uniforms. However, all that changed suddenly on the morning of the second day following a rebellion, when the prisoners barricaded themselves inside the cells by putting their beds against the door. Suddenly the guards perceived the prisoners as "dangerous"; they had to be dealt with harshly to demonstrate who was boss and who was powerless. At first, guard abuses were retaliation for taunts and disobedience. Over time, the guards became ever more abusive, and some even delighted in sadistically tormenting their prisoners. Though physical punishment was restricted, the guards on each shift were free to make up their own rules, and they invented a variety of psychological tactics to demonstrate their dominance over their powerless charges.

Nakedness was a common punishment, as was placing prisoners' heads in nylon stocking caps (to simulate shaved heads); chaining their legs; repeatedly waking them throughout the night for hour-long counts; and forcing them into humiliating "fun and games" activities. Let's go beyond those generalizations to review some of the actual behaviors that were enacted in the prison simulation. They are a lesson in "creative evil," in how certain social settings can transform intelligent young men into perpetrators of psychological abuse.

Prison Log, Night 5

8   The prisoners, who have not broken down emotionally under the incessant stress the guards have been subjecting them to since their aborted rebellion on Day 2, wearily line up against the wall to recite their ID numbers and to demonstrate that they remember all 17 prisoner rules of engagement. It is the 1 A.M. count, the last one of the night before the morning shift comes on at 2 A.M. No matter how well the prisoners do, one of them gets singled out for punishment. They are yelled at, cursed out, and made to say abusive things to each other. "Tell him he's a prick," yells one guard. And each prisoner says that to the next guy in line. Then the sexual harassment that had started to bubble up the night before resumes as the testosterone flows freely in every direction.

"See that hole in the ground? Now do 25 push-ups [expletive] that hole! You hear me!" One after another, the prisoners obey like automatons as the guard shoves them down. After a brief consultation, our toughest guard (nicknamed "John Wayne" by the prisoners) and his sidekick devise a new sexual game. "OK, now pay attention. You three are going to be female camels. Get over here and bend over, touching your hands to the floor." When they do, their naked butts are exposed because they have no underwear beneath their smocks. John Wayne continues with obvious glee, "Now you two, you're male camels. Stand behind the female camels and hump them."

The guards all giggle at this double-entendre. Although their bodies never touch, the helpless prisoners begin to simulate sodomy by making thrusting motions. They are then dismissed back to their cells to get an hour of sleep before the next shift comes on, and the abuse continues.

By Day 5, five of the student prisoners have to be released early because of extreme stress. (Recall that each of them was physically healthy and psychologically stable less than a week before.) Most of those who remain adopt a zombielike attitude and posture, totally obedient to escalating guard demands.

Terminating the Torment

12   I was forced to terminate the projected two-week-long study after only six days because it was running out of control. Dozens of people had come down to our "little shop of horrors," seen some of the abuse or its effects, and said nothing. A prison chaplain, parents, and friends had visited the prisoners, and psychologists and others on the parole board saw a realistic prison simulation, an experiment in action, but did not challenge me to stop it. The one exception erupted just before the time of the prison-log notation on Night 5.

About halfway through the study, I had invited some psychologists who knew little about the experiment to interview the staff and participants, to get an outsiders' evaluation of how it was going. A former doctoral student of mine, Christina Maslach, a new assistant professor at the University of California at Berkeley, came down late Thursday night to have dinner with me. We had started dating recently and were becoming romantically involved. When she saw the prisoners lined up with bags over their heads, their legs chained, and guards shouting abuses at them while herding them to the toilet, she got upset and refused my suggestion to observe what was happening in this "crucible of human nature." Instead she ran out of the basement, and I followed, berating her for being overly sensitive and not realizing the important lessons taking place here.

"It is terrible what YOU are doing to those boys!" she yelled at me. Christina made evident in that one statement that human beings were suffering, not prisoners, not experimental subjects, not paid volunteers. And further, I was the one who was personally responsible for the horrors she had witnessed (and which she assumed were even worse when no outsider was looking). She also made clear that if this person I had become—the heartless superintendent of the Stanford prison—was the real me, not the caring, generous person she had come to like, she wanted nothing more to do with me.

That powerful jolt of reality snapped me back to my senses. I agreed that we had gone too far, that whatever was to be learned about situational power was already indelibly etched on our videos, data logs, and minds; there was no need to continue. I too had been transformed by my role in that situation to become a person that under any other circumstances I detest—an uncaring, authoritarian boss man. In retrospect,

I believe that the main reason I did not end the study sooner resulted from the conflict created in me by my dual roles as principal investigator, and thus guardian of the research ethics of the experiment, and as the prison superintendent, eager to maintain the stability of my prison at all costs. I now realize that there should have been someone with authority above mine, someone in charge of oversight of the experiment, who surely would have blown the whistle earlier.

By the time Christina intervened, it was the middle of the night, so I had to make plans to terminate the next morning. The released prisoners and guards had to be called back and many logistics handled before I could say, "The Stanford prison experiment is officially closed." When I went back down to the basement, I witnessed the final scene of depravity, the "camel humping" episode. I was so glad that it would be the last such abuse I would see or be responsible for.

Good Apples in Bad Barrels and Bad Barrel Makers

The situational forces in that "bad barrel" had overwhelmed the goodness of most of those infected by their viral power. It is hard to imagine how a seeming game of "cops and robbers" played by college kids, with a few academics (our research team) watching, could have descended into what became a hellhole for many in that basement. How could a mock prison, an experimental simulation, become "a prison run by psychologists, not by the state," in the words of one suffering prisoner? How is it possible for "good personalities" to be so dominated by a "bad situation"? You had to be there to believe that human character could be so swiftly transformed in a matter of days, not only the traits of the students, but of me, a well-seasoned adult. Most of the visitors to our prison also fell under the spell. For example, individual sets of parents observing their son's haggard appearance after a few days of hard labor and long nights of disrupted sleep said they "did not want to make trouble" by taking their kid home or challenging the system. Instead they obeyed our authority and let some of their sons experience full-blown emotional meltdowns later on. We had created a dominating behavioral context whose power insidiously frayed the seemingly impervious values of compassion, fair play, and belief in a just world.

The situation won; humanity lost. Out the window went the moral upbringings of these young men, as well as their middle-class civility. Power ruled, and unrestrained power became an aphrodisiac. Power without surveillance by higher authorities was a poisoned chalice that transformed character in unpredictable directions. I believe that most of us tend to be fascinated with evil not because of its consequences but because evil is a demonstration of power and domination over others.

Current Relevance

Such research is now in an ethical time capsule, since institutional review boards will not allow social scientists to repeat it (although experiments like it have been replicated on several TV shows and in artistic renditions). Nevertheless, the Stanford prison experiment is now more popular than ever in its 36-year history. A Google search of "experiment" reveals it to be fourth among some 132 million hits, and sixth among some 127 million hits on "prison." Some of this recent interest comes from the apparent similarities of the experiment's abuses with the images of depravity in Iraq's Abu Ghraib prison—of nakedness, bagged heads, and sexual humiliation.

20

Among the dozen investigations of the Abu Ghraib abuses, the one chaired by James R. Schlesinger, the former secretary of defense, boldly proclaims that the landmark Stanford study "provides a cautionary tale for all military detention operations." In contrasting the relatively benign environment of the Stanford prison experiment, the report makes evident that "in military detention operations, soldiers work under stressful combat conditions that are far from benign." The implication is that those combat conditions might be expected to generate even more extreme abuses of power than were observed in our mock prison experiment.

However, the Schlesinger report notes that military leaders did not heed that earlier warning in any way. They should have—a psychological perspective is essential to understanding the transformation of human character in response to special situational forces. "The potential for abusive treatment of detainees during the Global War on Terrorism was entirely predictable based on a fundamental understanding of the principles of social psychology coupled with an awareness of numerous known environmental risk factors," the report says. "Findings from the field of social psychology suggest that the conditions of war and the dynamics of detainee operations carry inherent risks for human mistreatment, and therefore must be approached with great caution and careful planning and training." (Unfortunately this vital conclusion is buried in an appendix.)

The Stanford prison experiment is but one of a host of studies in psychology that reveal the extent to which our behavior can be transformed from its usual set point to deviate in unimaginable ways, even to readily accepting a dehumanized conception of others, as "animals," and to accepting spurious rationales for why pain will be good for them.

The implications of this research for law are considerable, as legal scholars are beginning to recognize. The criminal-justice system, for instance, focuses primarily on individual defendants and their "state of mind" and largely ignores situational forces. The Model Penal Code states: "A person is not guilty of an offense unless his liability is based on conduct that includes a voluntary act or the omission to perform an act of which he is physically capable." As my own experiment revealed, and as a great deal of social-psychological research before and since has confirmed, we humans exaggerate the extent to which our actions are voluntary and rationally chosen—or, put differently, we all understate the power of the situation. My claim is not that individuals are incapable of criminal culpability; rather, it is that, like the horrible behavior brought out by my experiment in good, normal young men, the situation and the system creating it also must share in the responsibility for illegal and immoral behavior.

24

If the goals of the criminal system are simply to blame and punish individual perpetrators—to get our pound of flesh—then focusing almost exclusively on the individual defendant makes sense. If, however, the goal is actually to reduce the behavior that we now call "criminal" (and its resultant suffering), and to assign punishments that correspond with culpability, then the criminal-justice system is obligated, much as I was in the Stanford prison experiment, to confront the situation and our role in creating and perpetuating it. It is clear to most reasonable observers that the social experiment of imprisoning society's criminals for long terms is a failure on virtually all levels. By recognizing the situational determinants of behavior, we can move to a more productive public-health model of prevention and intervention, and away from the individualistic medical and religious "sin" model that has never worked since its inception during the Inquisition.

The critical message then is to be sensitive about our vulnerability to subtle but powerful situational forces and, by such awareness, be more able to overcome those forces. Group pressures, authority symbols, dehumanization of others, imposed anonymity, dominant ideologies that enable spurious ends to justify immoral means, lack of surveillance, and other situational forces can work to transform even some of the best of us into Mr. Hyde monsters, without the benefit of Dr. Jekyll's chemical elixir. We must be more aware of how situational variables can influence our behavior. Further, we must also be aware that veiled behind the power of the situation is the greater power of the system, which creates and maintains complicity at the highest military and governmental levels with evil-inducing situations, like those at Abu Ghraib and Guantánamo Bay prisons.

PERSONAL RESPONSE

Although you cannot know for sure unless you were actually in the situation, how do you think you would have treated prisoners had you been a guard in the Stanford prison experiment? How do you think you might have behaved as a prisoner?

QUESTIONS FOR CLASS OR SMALL-GROUP DISCUSSION

1. Are you surprised that the guards behaved so cruelly and that the prisoners were so obedient and "zombielike" (paragraph 11). How would you explain the behavior of each group? What conditions or factors made the participants behave as they did?

2. Assess the conclusions that Zimbardo draws about the prison experiment. Do you see any flaws in his conclusions? What lessons do you think the experiment teaches?

3. To what extent do you agree with Zimbardo's application of the lessons from his prison experiment of 1971 to today's criminal justice system? Besides physically prisons, what other sorts of prisons are there? For instance, in what ways do people turn situations, institutions, even their minds into "prisons" that limit freedoms?

4. Do you think that it made any difference that everybody involved in the experiment was male? Do you think that the experiment would have turned out any differently had everyone been female? What if the prisoners had been female and the guards male, or vice versa?

THE REAL LESSON
OF THE STANFORD
PRISON EXPERIMENT

MARIA KONNIKOVA

Maria Konnikova is a regular contributor to newyorker.com, *writing on psychology and science. Her book* Mastermind: How to Think Like Sherlock Holmes (2013) *was a* Times *bestseller and was nominated for a Mystery Writers of America Agatha Award for Best Nonfiction. Her book* The Confidence Game: Why We Fall For It ... Every Time *was published in 2016. She has also worked as a producer for "Charlie Rose" and has contributed numerous articles and essays to the* Times, theatlantic.com, Scientific American MIND, *and* newrepublic.com, *among other publications. This article was first published at* newyorker.com.

On the morning of August 17, 1971, nine young men in the Palo Alto area received visits from local police officers. While their neighbors looked on, the men were arrested for violating Penal Codes 211 and 459 (armed robbery and burglary), searched, handcuffed, and led into the rear of a waiting police car. The cars took them to a Palo Alto police station, where the men were booked, fingerprinted, moved to a holding cell, and blindfolded. Finally, they were transported to the Stanford County Prison—also known as the Stanford University psychology department.

They were willing participants in the Stanford Prison Experiment, one of the most controversial studies in the history of social psychology. (It's the subject of a new film of the same name—a drama, not a documentary—starring Billy Crudup, of "Almost Famous," as the lead investigator, Philip Zimbardo. It opens July 17th [2015].) The study subjects, middle-class college students, had answered a questionnaire about their family backgrounds, physical- and mental-health histories, and social behavior, and had been deemed "normal"; a coin flip divided them into prisoners and guards. According to the lore that's grown up around the experiment, the guards, with little to no instruction, began humiliating and psychologically abusing the prisoners within twenty-four hours of the study's start.

The prisoners, in turn, became submissive and depersonalized, taking the abuse and saying little in protest. The behavior of all involved was so extreme that the experiment, which was meant to last two weeks, was terminated after six days.

Less than a decade earlier, the Milgram obedience study had shown that ordinary people, if encouraged by an authority figure, were willing to shock their fellow-citizens with what they believed to be painful and potentially lethal levels of electricity. To many, the Stanford experiment underscored those findings, revealing the ease with which regular people, if given too much power, could transform into ruthless oppressors. Today, more than forty-five years later, many look to the study to make sense of events like the behavior of the guards at Abu Ghraib and America's epidemic of police brutality. The Stanford Prison Experiment is cited as evidence of the atavistic impulses that lurk within us all; it's said to show that, with a little nudge, we could all become tyrants.

4 And yet the lessons of the Stanford Prison Experiment aren't so clear-cut. From the beginning, the study has been haunted by ambiguity. Even as it suggests that ordinary people harbor ugly potentialities, it also testifies to the way our circumstances shape our behavior. Was the study about our individual fallibility, or about broken institutions? Were its findings about prisons, specifically, or about life in general? What did the Stanford Prison Experiment really show?

The appeal of the experiment has a lot to do with its apparently simple setup: prisoners, guards, a fake jail, and some ground rules. But, in reality, the Stanford County Prison was a heavily manipulated environment, and the guards and prisoners acted in ways that were largely predetermined by how their roles were presented. To understand the meaning of the experiment, you have to understand that it wasn't a blank slate; from the start, its goal was to evoke the experience of working and living in a brutal jail.

From the first, the guards' priorities were set by Zimbardo. In a presentation to his Stanford colleagues shortly after the study's conclusion, he described the procedures surrounding each prisoner's arrival: each man was stripped and searched, "deloused," and then given a uniform—a numbered gown, which Zimbardo called a "dress," with a heavy bolted chain near the ankle, loose-fitting rubber sandals, and a cap made from a woman's nylon stocking. "Real male prisoners don't wear dresses," Zimbardo explained, "but real male prisoners, we have learned, do feel humiliated, do feel emasculated, and we thought we could produce the same effects very quickly by putting men in a dress without any underclothes." The stocking caps were in lieu of shaving the prisoner's heads. (The guards wore khaki uniforms and were given whistles, nightsticks, and mirrored sunglasses inspired by a prison guard in the movie *Cool Hand Luke*.)

Often, the guards operated without explicit, moment-to-moment instructions. But that didn't mean that they were fully autonomous: Zimbardo himself took part in the experiment, playing the role of the prison superintendent. (The prison's "warden" was also a researcher.) Occasionally, disputes between prisoner and guards got out of hand, violating an explicit injunction against physical force that both prisoners and guards had read prior to enrolling in the study. When the "superintendent" and "warden" overlooked these incidents, the message to the guards was clear: all is well; keep going as you are. The participants knew that an audience was watching, and so a lack of feedback could be read as tacit approval. And the sense of being watched may also have encouraged them to perform. Dave Eshelman, one of the guards, recalled that he "consciously created" his guard persona. "I was in all kinds of drama productions in high school and college. It was something I was very familiar with: to take on another personality before you step out on the stage," Eshelman said. In fact, he continued, "I was kind of running my own experiment in there, by saying, 'How far can I push these things and how much abuse will these people take before they say, 'Knock it off?'"

8   Other, more subtle factors also shaped the experiment. It's often said that the study participants were ordinary guys—and they were, indeed, determined to be "normal" and healthy by a battery of tests. But they were also a self-selected group who responded to a newspaper advertisement seeking volunteers for "a psychological study of prison life." In a 2007 study, the psychologists Thomas Carnahan and Sam McFarland asked whether that wording itself may have stacked the odds. They recreated the original ad, and then ran a separate ad omitting the phrase "prison life." They found that the people who responded to the two ads scored differently on a set of psychological tests. Those who thought that they would be participating in a prison study had significantly higher levels of aggressiveness, authoritarianism, Machiavellianism, narcissism, and social dominance, and they scored lower on measures of empathy and altruism.

Moreover, even within that self-selected sample, behavioral patterns were far from homogeneous. Much of the study's cachet depends on the idea that the students responded en masse, giving up their individual identities to become submissive "prisoners" and tyrannical "guards." But, in fact, the participants responded to the prison environment in all sorts of ways. While some guard shifts were especially cruel, others remained humane. Many of the supposedly passive prisoners rebelled. Richard Yacco, a prisoner, remembered "resisting what one guard was telling me to do and being willing to go into solitary confinement. As prisoners, we developed solidarity—we realized that we could join together and do passive resistance and cause some problems."

What emerges from these details isn't a perfectly lucid photograph but an ambiguous watercolor. While it's true that some guards and prisoners behaved in alarming ways, it's also the case that their environment was designed to encourage—and, in some cases, to require—those behaviors. Zimbardo himself has always been forthcoming about the details and the nature of his prison experiment: he thoroughly explained the setup in his original study and, in an early write-up, in which the experiment was described in broad strokes only, he pointed out that only "about a third of the guards became tyrannical in their arbitrary use of power." (That's about four people in total.) So how did the myth of the Stanford Prison Experiment—"Lord of the Flies" in the psych lab—come to diverge so profoundly from the reality?

In part, Zimbardo's earliest statements about the experiment are to blame. In October, 1971, soon after the study's completion—and before a single methodologically and analytically rigorous result had been published—Zimbardo was asked to testify before Congress about prison reform. His dramatic testimony, even as it clearly explained how the experiment worked, also allowed listeners to overlook how coercive the environment really was. He described the study as "an attempt to understand just what it means psychologically to be a prisoner or a prison guard." But he also emphasized that the students in the study had been "the cream of the crop of this generation," and said that the guards were given no specific instructions, and left free to make "up their own rules for maintaining law, order, and respect." In explaining the results, he said that the "majority" of participants found themselves "no longer able to clearly differentiate between role-playing and self," and that, in the six days the study took to unfold, "the experience of imprisonment undid, although temporarily, a lifetime of learning; human values were suspended, self-concepts were challenged, and the ugliest, most base, pathological side of human nature surfaced." In describing another, related study and its implications for prison life, he said that "the mere act of assigning labels to people, calling some people prisoners and others guards, is sufficient to elicit pathological behavior."

12   Zimbardo released video to NBC, which ran a feature on November 26, 1971. An article ran in the *Times Magazine* in April of 1973. In various ways, these accounts reiterated the claim that relatively small changes in circumstances could turn the best and brightest into monsters or depersonalized serfs. By the time Zimbardo published a formal paper about the study, in a 1973 issue of the *International Journal of Criminology and Penology*, a streamlined and unequivocal version of events had become entrenched in the national consciousness—so much so that a 1975 methodological critique fell largely on deaf ears.

Forty years later, Zimbardo still doesn't shy away from popular attention. He served as a consultant on the new film, which follows his original study in detail, relying on direct transcripts from the experimental recordings and taking few dramatic liberties. In many ways, the film is critical of the study: Crudup plays Zimbardo as an overzealous researcher overstepping his bounds, trying to create a very specific outcome among the students he observes. The filmmakers even underscore the flimsiness of the experimental design, inserting characters who point out that Zimbardo is not a disinterested observer. They highlight a real-life conversation in which another psychologist asks Zimbardo whether he has an "independent variable." In describing the study to his Stanford colleagues shortly after it ended, Zimbardo recalled that conversation: "To my surprise, I got really angry at him," he said. "The security of my men and the stability of my prison was at stake, and I have to contend with this bleeding-heart, liberal, academic, effete dingdong whose only concern was for a ridiculous thing like an independent variable. The next thing he'd be asking me about was rehabilitation programs, the dummy! It wasn't until sometime later that I realized how far into the experiment I was at that point."

In a broad sense, the film reaffirms the opinion of John Mark, one of the guards, who, looking back, has said that

Zimbardo's interpretation of events was too shaped by his expectations to be meaningful: "He wanted to be able to say that college students, people from middle-class backgrounds ... will turn on each other just because they're given a role and given power. Based on my experience, and what I saw and what I felt, I think that was a real stretch."

If the Stanford Prison Experiment had simulated a less brutal environment, would the prisoners and guards have acted differently? In December, 2001, two psychologists, Stephen Reicher and Alexander Haslam, tried to find out. They worked with the documentaries unit of the BBC to partially recreate Zimbardo's setup over the course of an eight-day experiment. Their guards also had uniforms, and were given latitude to dole out rewards and punishments; their prisoners were placed in three-person cells that followed the layout of the Stanford County Jail almost exactly. The main difference was that, in this prison, the preset expectations were gone. The guards were asked to come up with rules prior to the prisoners' arrival, and were told only to make the prison run smoothly. (The BBC Prison Study, as it came to be called, differed from the Stanford experiment in a few other ways, including prisoner dress; for a while, moreover, the prisoners were told that they could become guards through good behavior, although, on the third day, that offer was revoked, and the roles were made permanent.)

16   Within the first few days of the BBC study, it became clear that the guards weren't cohering as a group. "Several guards were wary of assuming and exerting their authority," the researchers wrote. The prisoners, on the other hand, developed a collective identity. In a change from the Stanford study, the psychologists asked each participant to complete a daily survey that measured the degree to which he felt solidarity with his group; it showed that, as the guards grew further apart, the prisoners were growing closer together. On the fourth day, three cellmates decided to test their luck. At lunchtime, one threw his plate down and demanded better food, another asked to smoke, and the third asked for medical attention for a blister on his foot. The guards became disorganized; one even offered the smoker a cigarette. Reicher and Haslam reported that, after the prisoners returned to their cells, they "literally danced with joy." ("That was fucking sweet," one prisoner remarked.) Soon, more prisoners began to challenge the guards. They acted out during roll call, complained about the

food, and talked back. At the end of the sixth day, the three insubordinate cellmates broke out and occupied the guards' quarters. "At this point," the researchers wrote, "the guards' regime was seen by all to be unworkable and at an end."

Taken together, these two studies don't suggest that we all have an innate capacity for tyranny or victimhood. Instead, they suggest that our behavior largely conforms to our preconceived expectations. All else being equal, we act as we think we're expected to act—especially if that expectation comes from above. Suggest, as the Stanford setup did, that we should behave in stereotypical tough-guard fashion, and we strive to fit that role. Tell us, as the BBC experimenters did, that we shouldn't give up hope of social mobility, and we act accordingly.

This understanding might seem to diminish the power of the Stanford Prison Experiment. But, in fact, it sharpens and clarifies the study's meaning. Last weekend brought the tragic news of Kalief Browder's suicide. At sixteen, Browder was arrested, in the Bronx, for allegedly stealing a backpack; after the arrest, he was imprisoned at Rikers for three years without trial. (Ultimately, the case against him was dismissed.) While at Rikers, Browder was the object of violence from both prisoners and guards, some of which was captured on video. It's possible to think that prisons are the way they are because human nature tends toward the pathological. But the Stanford Prison Experiment suggests that extreme behavior flows from extreme institutions. Prisons *aren't* blank slates. Guards do indeed self-select into their jobs, as Zimbardo's students self-selected into a study of prison life. Like Zimbardo's men, they are bombarded with expectations from the first and shaped by preëxisting norms and patterns of behavior. The lesson of Stanford isn't that any random human being is capable of descending into sadism and tyranny. It's that certain institutions and environments demand those behaviors—and, perhaps, can change them.

PERSONAL RESPONSE

Konnikova asserts that the students who participated in the Stanford prison experiment were self-selected in that they had certain characteristics that led them to be interested in a study was specifically about prison life. Discuss whether you would, hypothetically, consider volunteering for a psychological experiment on prison life.

QUESTIONS FOR CLASS AND SMALL-GROUP DISCUSSION

1. State in your own words the factors that Konnikova says influenced or shaped the outcome of the Stanford prison experiment. To what extent, do you agree with the point she makes?

2. Besides the factors shaping outcome, what other points does Konnikova make about the Stanford prison experiment? Do you think her argument is valid?

3. What does Konnikova say is the real lesson of the Stanford prison experiment? How does it differ from Zimbardo's interpretation? Which interpretation do you find more persuasive?

4. What purpose do you think the example of Kalief Browder serves (paragraph 18)? How effective do you find it as a rhetorical strategy?

WHEN GOOD PEOPLE
DO BAD THINGS

ANNE TRAFTON

Anne Trafton writes articles on the life sciences, physical sciences, and biological and chemical engineering for the MIT News *Office. She is also a frequent guest contributor to the* MIT Technology Report. *This article was published in the* MIT News.

When people get together in groups, unusual things can happen—both good and bad. Groups create important social institutions that an individual could not achieve alone, but there can be a darker side to such alliances. Belonging to a group makes people more likely to harm others outside the group.

"Although humans exhibit strong preferences for equity and moral prohibitions against harm in many contexts, people's priorities change when there is an 'us' and a 'them,'" says Rebecca Saxe, an associate professor of cognitive neuroscience at MIT. "A group of people will often engage in actions that are contrary to the private moral standards of each individual in that group, sweeping otherwise decent individuals into 'mobs' that commit looting, vandalism, even physical brutality." Several factors play into this transformation. When people are in a group, they feel more anonymous, and less likely to be caught doing something wrong. They may also feel a diminished sense of personal responsibility for collective actions.

Saxe and colleagues recently studied a third factor that cognitive scientists believe may be involved in this group dynamic: the hypothesis that when people are in groups, they "lose touch" with their own morals and beliefs, and become more likely to do things that they would normally believe are wrong. In a study that recently went online in the journal *NeuroImage*, the researchers measured brain activity in a part of the brain involved in thinking about oneself. They found that in some people, this activity was reduced when the subjects participated in a competition as part of a group, compared with when they competed as individuals. Those people were more likely to harm their competitors than people who did not exhibit this decreased brain activity.

4   [According to the study,] "This process alone does not account for intergroup conflict: Groups also promote anonymity, diminish personal responsibility, and encourage reframing harmful actions as 'necessary for the greater good.' Still, these results suggest that at least in some cases, explicitly reflecting on one's own personal moral standards may help to attenuate the influence of 'mob mentality,'" says Mina Cikara, a former MIT postdoc and lead author of the *NeuroImage* paper.

Group Dynamics

Cikara, who is now an assistant professor at Carnegie Mellon University, started this research project after experiencing the consequences of a "mob mentality": During a visit to Yankee Stadium, her husband was ceaselessly heckled by Yankees fans for wearing a Red Sox cap. "What I decided to do was take the hat from him, thinking I would be a lesser target by virtue of the fact that I was a woman," Cikara says. "I was so wrong. I have never been called names like that in my entire life." The harassment, which continued throughout the trip back to Manhattan, provoked a strong reaction in Cikara, who isn't even a Red Sox fan.

"It was a really amazing experience because what I realized was I had gone from being an individual to being seen as a member of 'Red Sox Nation.' And the way that people responded to me, and the way I felt myself responding back, had changed, by virtue of this visual cue—the baseball hat," she says. "Once you start feeling attacked on behalf of your group, however arbitrary, it changes your psychology."

Cikara, then a third-year graduate student at Princeton University, started to investigate the neural mechanisms behind the group dynamics that produce bad behavior. In the new study, done at MIT, Cikara, Saxe (who is also an associate member of MIT's McGovern Institute for Brain Research), former Harvard University graduate student Anna Jenkins, and former MIT lab manager Nicholas Dufour focused on a part of the brain called the medial prefrontal cortex. When someone is reflecting on himself or herself, this part of the brain lights up in functional magnetic resonance imaging (fMRI) brain scans.

8

A couple of weeks before the study participants came in for the experiment, the researchers surveyed each of them about their social-media habits, as well as their moral beliefs and behavior. This allowed the researchers to create individualized statements for each subject that were true for that person—for example, "I have stolen food from shared refrigerators" or "I always apologize after bumping into someone."

When the subjects arrived at the lab, their brains were scanned as they played a game once on their own and once as part of a team. The purpose of the game was to press a button if they saw a statement related to social media, such as "I have more than 600 Facebook friends."

The subjects also saw their personalized moral statements mixed in with sentences about social media. Brain scans revealed that when subjects were playing for themselves, the medial prefrontal cortex lit up much more when they read moral statements about themselves than statements about others, consistent with previous findings. However, during the team competition, some people showed a much smaller difference in medial prefrontal cortex activation when they saw the moral statements about themselves compared to those about other people.

Those people also turned out to be much more likely to harm members of the competing group during a task performed after the game. Each subject was asked to select photos that would appear with the published study, from a set of four photos apiece of two teammates and two members of the opposing team. The subjects with suppressed medial prefrontal cortex activity chose the least flattering photos of the opposing team members, but not of their own teammates.

12

"This is a nice way of using neuroimaging to try to get insight into something that behaviorally has been really hard to explore," says David Rand, an assistant professor of psychology at Yale University who was not involved in the research. "It's been hard to get a direct handle on the extent to which people within a group are tapping into their own understanding of things versus the group's understanding."

Getting Lost

The researchers also found that after the game, people with reduced medial prefrontal cortex activity had more difficulty remembering the moral statements they had heard during the game. "If you need to encode something with regard to the self and that ability is somehow undermined when you're competing with a group, then you should have poor memory associated with that reduction in medial prefrontal cortex signal, and that's exactly what we see," Cikara says. Cikara hopes to follow up on these findings to investigate what makes some people more likely to become "lost" in a group than others. She is also interested in studying whether people are slower to recognize themselves or pick themselves out of a photo lineup after being absorbed in a group activity.

The research was funded by the Eunice Kennedy Shriver National Institute of Child Health and Human Development, the Air Force Office of Scientific Research, and the Packard Foundation.

PERSONAL RESPONSE

If you have ever done something against your better judgment because of peer pressure, the fact that everyone else was doing it, or any other force that led you to do it, describe the situation. If not, can you imagine yourself ever doing something with a group that you did not want to do?

QUESTIONS FOR CLASS AND SMALL-GROUP DISCUSSION

1. According to Professor Saxe, people often " 'engage in actions that are contrary to the private moral standards of each individual in that group'" (paragraph 2). How does Saxe account for that behavior?

2. Related to question number 1, to what extent do you agree, judging on the basis of your own experience, with this statement: "When people are in groups, they 'lose touch' with their own morals and beliefs, and become more likely to do things that they would normally believe are wrong" (paragraph 3).

3. Comment on Mina Cikara's experience at the Yankee's game when she put on her husband's Red Sox cap (paragraphs 5–6). Have you ever heckled someone in a situation similar to hers? Have you ever been the object of harassment in a similar situation?

4. Summarize Cikara's study of "the neural mechanisms behind the group dynamics that produce bad behavior" (paragraphs 7+). In what contexts, do you think that a "group" could become a "mob"?

MindTap® Reflect on the theme of this chapter.

PERSPECTIVES ON PSYCHOLOGY AND HUMAN BEHAVIOR

Suggested Writing Topics

1. With Philip Zimbardo's "Revisiting the Stanford Prison Experiment: A Lesson in the Power of Situation" and Maria Konnikova's "The Real Lesson of the Stanford Prison Experiment" in mind, write a paper on the subject of "good people pitted against the forces inherent in bad situations" (Zimbardo, paragraph 3).

2. Respond to this statement in Anne Trafton's "When Good People Do Bad Things": "Belonging to a group makes people more likely to harm others outside the group" (paragraph 1).

3. Describe an example of "mindless group-think" (Philip Zimbardo, "Revisiting the Stanford Prison Experiment: A Lesson in the Power of Situation," paragraph 3) that you have either participated in or witnessed, whether with a small group of friends, at an event such as a concert, or in any other situation where large groups or crowds gathered.

4. Argue in support of or against this statement in Philip Zimbardo's "Revisiting the Stanford Prison Experiment: A Lesson in the Power of Situation": "The social experiment of imprisoning society's criminals for long terms is a failure on virtually all levels" (paragraph 24).

Research Topics

1. Research Stanley Milgram's 1961 "obedience to authority" study. What were Milgram's objectives, and what were his conclusions about human behavior? What applications have been made of his study to other situations in which presumably well-meaning people commit atrocities under orders? How are some researchers reinterpreting Milgram's study today?

2. Philip Zimbardo writes in "Revisiting the Stanford Prison Experiment: A Lesson in the Power of Situation" that he "wanted to explore the fictional

notion from William Golding's *Lord of the Flies* about the power of anonymity to unleash violent behavior" (paragraph 2); Maria Konnikova in "The Real Lesson of the Stanford Prison Experiment" calls the Stanford Prison Experiment " 'Lord of the Flies' in the psych lab'" (paragraph 10). Read *Lord of the Flies* and discuss the novel with those statements in mind. Are Zimbardo's and Konnikova's analogy accurate? In what ways is what happens in the novel similar to what happened in the Stanford prison experiment? Research what other writers have to say about the book and argue your own interpretation of its meaning.

3. Find out more about Philip Zimbardo's Stanford prison study. In the original prison study general description (pdf.prisonexp.org/geninfo.pdf), Zimbardo states that two of the problems to be studied are "1) The development of norms which govern behavior in a novel situation. . . . 2) The differential perception of the same situation 'the prison experience' from people who are initially comparable (from the same population) but arbitrarily assigned to play different roles." Read what Zimbardo reported after the study and find out what other psychologists have to say about his experiment.

4. With Philip Zimbardo's "The Stanford Prison Experiment" in mind, research the power of labels (such as "prisoner" and "guard") to influence behavior.

5. Research the results of the BBC Prison Study conducted by Stephen Reicher and Alexander Haslam, mentioned in Maria Konnikova's "The Real Lesson of the Stanford Prison Experiment," and compare their results with those of Zimbardo's Stanford experiment. Try to locate other studies that attempted to replicate Zimbardo's to see if their results were similar to or different from those of the Stanford experiment.

6. Research the influence of groups on individual behavior by searching for studies on "mob mentality" or "herd mentality." When do groups turn into mobs? Why do researchers use the label "herd mentality"?

RESPONDING TO VISUALS

Los Angeles Times/Getty Images

Juvenile offenders at a boot camp wait their turn to use the bathroom before lunch. Why do you think the young men's faces are not visible, except for the partial side view of one of them?

1. What does the young men's body language—their posture, their clasped hands—imply about the expectations at the boot camp for compliant behavior?

2. Describe the look on the face of the only one that we see. What does that look suggest about rules of conduct at boot camp and the willingness of the young man to obey them?

3. What other details of the photograph provide clues about discipline in the camp? Consider how the young men are dressed and the way the beds are made, for instance.

RESPONDING TO VISUALS

How is this image a metaphor for psychology?

1. How might this picture represent mental illness or psychological distress?

2. The silhouette is surrounded by an area that is also part of the puzzle. What does that part of the puzzle suggest about human psychology? How might the missing piece be interpreted?

3. What does the fact that the missing pieces are there, outside of the actual image, suggest about the role of psychology and psychiatry in understanding or healing the mind?

BIOETHICS AND ENVIRONMENTAL STUDIES

LEARNING OBJECTIVES

Students will demonstrate an ability to do the following:

☐ Articulate the ethical issues involved in the sale of human organs.

☐ Debate whether human organ sales should be legalized.

☐ Discuss the subject of individual responsibility for environmental health and species preservation.

☐ Debate ways to address one of today's most pressing environmental issues, such as climate change, air pollution, or water contamination.

CHAPTER OVERVIEW

Bioethics and environmental studies have in common an interest in ensuring a healthy quality of life for people, now and in the future. While these two areas of study are interested in different aspects of human life and the natural environment in which we live, both have at their core the goal of ensuring the health and well-being of humans. There is, in fact, an area of study that specializes in environmental bioethics, which focuses on the interaction among humans, health, and the environment. This chapter has several articles each on the broad areas of bioethics and environmental studies, and you will see as you read the essays how the two separate areas at times become essentially interconnected.

Broadly speaking, bioethics refers to the ethics of biological and health sciences, and its scope encompasses dozens of moral and ethical issues in those areas. Bioethical concerns surround such controversial practices and research as cloning, cryonics, human genetic engineering, research on germline editing, gene therapy, creating artificial life, inserting chip implants into the brains of humans, and genetically modified foods as well as issues concerning organ donation and transplant, life support, population control, medical research, and the like. Of great interest to bioethicists has been the mapping of the human genome and what to do with the knowledge that resulted.

Research into the complex structure of the human body since James D. Watson and Francis Crick discovered in 1953 that deoxyribonucleic acid (DNA) molecules arrange themselves in a double helix has made enormous advances. The discovery of this pattern in DNA, a substance that transmits the genetic characteristics from one generation to the next, led scientists to work on such things as recombinant DNA and gene splicing in the 1970s and eventually to the Human Genome Project, whose goal was to map the entire sequence of human DNA. A genome is the complete set of instructions for making a human being. Each nucleus of the 100 trillion cells that make up the human body contains this set of instructions, which is written in the language of DNA. This major undertaking by scientists around the world promised to provide medical doctors with the tools to predict the development of human diseases. Scientists already are able to identify variations or defects in the genetic makeup of certain cells in human bodies that may result in diseases with genetic origins. Eventually, they will be able to develop tests of an individual's likelihood of developing one of the thousands of inherited diseases such as sickle-cell anemia, cystic fibrosis, or muscular dystrophy, and even heart disease or cancer.

The first two essays in this chapter look at ethical issues raised by the marketing of human organs, specifically kidneys. Miriam Schulman, director of the Ethics Center at Santa Clara University, examines the benefits and drawbacks of legalizing kidney sales. In "Kidneys for Sale: A Reconsideration," she asks, "Should such transactions be legalized? What are the ethical questions we should ask about the sale of kidneys?" She then looks closely at the issues and offers suggestions on how such ethical questions can be addressed. Next, the title of Anthony Gregory's piece, "Why Legalizing Organ Sales Would Help to Save Lives, End Violence," indicates clearly what position he takes on the matter of whether kidney sales should be legalized or not. When reading these essays, pay special attention to the ethical considerations that must be taken into account on the issue of whether kidney sales should be legalized.

Environmental issues such as depletion of the ozone layer, global warming, deforestation, and air and water pollution are just a few of the many causes for concern over the health of animal and vegetable life on Earth. Closely connected to these environmental problems is the rapid rate of increase in the world population. As the number of people grows, pressure increases on natural resources. Will Earth provide enough food for everyone? How can water supplies be kept safe for drinking? How does pollution produced by so many humans affect the quality of the air they breathe? How can people stop the ever-widening hole in the ozone layer that protects us from the harmful rays of the sun? How will future generations sustain the rapidly increasing worldwide population? These are just some of the questions confronting scientists, civic leaders, and ordinary people everywhere.

Although most people recognize that humans must keep their environments safe, not everyone agrees on either the nature of the problems or the severity of their consequences. However, the authors of the next two readings believe very strongly that the environment is in serious jeopardy, and both are fervently devoted to their causes. Bill McKibben makes an impassioned plea for activism in "Global Warning: Get Up! Stand Up!" Pointing out that previously identified environmental problems were fixable with both changes in behavior and legislatively mandated changes, he maintains that Congress has "failed to take on the single greatest challenge human civilization has ever faced." His subtitle, "How to Build a Mass Movement to Halt Climate Change," is a clear indication of the subject of his essay. As you read McKibben's piece, notice his argumentative strategies and ask yourself whether you are persuaded to take action as he so urgently presses his readers to do. Then, Jeff Corwin in "The Sixth Extinction" gives startling facts about the rapid extinction of species. He points out that somewhere on Earth, "every 20 minutes we lose an animal species." With examples of dying species from several areas of the globe, Corwin hopes to persuade readers to "rise to the cause."

KIDNEYS FOR SALE:
A RECONSIDERATION

MIRIAM SCHULMAN

Miriam Schulman is associate director of the Markkula Center for Applied Ethics at Santa Clara University, where she both manages communication and

administrative activities at the Center and edits Issues
in Ethics. *She has published articles on various aspects
of ethics, including ethical choices that college students
face, the ethics of online privacy invasion, the ethics of
business practices, and, as here, the ethics of marketing
kidneys. This article was published on the Markkula
Center Web site.*

In 1988, the Markkula Center for Applied Ethics published
an article, "Kidneys for Sale," which was posted about ten years
later on our Web site. It addressed the ethical issues raised by
the potential for a market in human body parts.

That article has inspired sporadic emails from people asking for advice about how to sell their organs. In recent years, as
the economy has soured, we've noticed an uptick in the number of such messages. Here's a sample:

> I just read your information about how many people need a
> kidney. I would like more information about it and how I could
> sell one of my kidneys to your university because I really need
> money. I want to go to college, but it's really expensive.

These correspondents raise some of the hard questions
that are inspiring a reevaluation of the question: Should
organ donation remain a completely altruistic "gift of life," or
should donors be compensated? The Center's Emerging Issues
Group, which meets weekly to discuss ethical issues in the
news, addressed these questions at a recent session. This article
outlines some of the crucial considerations raised during this
discussion.

A Shortage of Donated Organs

4   First, a few facts about the acute shortage of kidneys. As of
March 6, the waiting list in the United States for all organs
was 113,143, with 91,015 waiting for kidneys. In 2011, there
were a total of 15,417 kidney transplants in the United States,
10,185 from deceased donors and 5,232 from living donors.

"Data such as these underscore just how scarce organs are,"
says Margaret McLean, director of bioethics at the Markkula
Center for Applied Ethics. "About 17 people die every day while
waiting for a suitable organ. Although numerous strategies have
been tried to increase the number of donors—from pink dots
on driver's licenses to PR campaigns to donor reciprocal chains
to organ swapping—we continue to come up short."

That shortage has led to many violations of both US and international laws against kidney sales. For example, this month the Chinese news agency Xinhua reported that a 17-year-old sold his kidney, which is illegal in China, to get enough money for an iPhone. He is now suffering from renal insufficiency. "Only the truly naïve imagine that organs are not currently being sold on the black market," McLean says. The International Business Times estimates that illegal organ sales constitute a $75 million per year industry.

Should such transactions be legalized? What are the ethical questions we should ask about the sale of kidneys?

The Commodification of Human Life

8   Even if legalizing organ sales might inspire more donations, many ethicists reject this approach because they fear where it may lead: to the commodification of human life. Cynthia Cohen from the Kennedy Institute of Ethics at Georgetown writes, "Human beings . . . are of incomparable ethical worth and admit of no equivalent. Each has a value that is beyond the contingencies of supply and demand or of any other relative estimation. They are priceless. Consequently, to sell an integral human body part is to corrupt the very meaning of human dignity."

Despite these concerns, the black market itself has put a value on human organs—about $5,000 according to most reports. Peter Minowitz, professor of political science at SCU, suggests, "The actuality is there's a thriving market for organs, even crossing global boundaries. So even though the sale of organs may, in itself, violate human dignity, that dignity is being violated now on a fairly large scale, especially among the most desperate. Maybe it would be better for them if we legalized the sale and imposed certain standards on it. It's a very complicated series of considerations, mixing moral judgment with what's going on in the real world."

Do No Harm

Undoubtedly, increasing the supply of living donors would be good for organ recipients. According to the Organ Procurement and Transplantation Network, about 90 percent of people who receive a living-donor kidney and 82 percent of those who received a deceased-donor kidney were alive five years after the transplant.

But what happens to the donors? "Usually, in medical ethics, we are looking at harm and good respective to a single patient," says McLean. "Here we are looking at harm and good for two patients where good is going to accrue to one and potential harm to the other."

12 Generally, kidney donation from a living donor is seen as a relatively safe procedure, as the human body functions adequately with only one kidney. The mortality rate for the removal of a kidney (nephrectomy) is between 0.02 and 0.03 percent, major complications affect 1.5 percent of patients, and minor complications affect 8.5 percent. The University of Maryland Transplant Center states:

> The risks of donation are similar to those involved with any major surgery, such as bleeding and infection. Death resulting from kidney donation is extremely rare. Current research indicates that kidney donation does not change life expectancy or increase a person's risks of developing kidney disease or other health problems.

While this picture may accurately reflect the experience of donors in first world countries, those in the developing world report less benign outcomes. Madhav Goyal, Ravindra Mehta, Lawrence Schneiderman, and Ashwini Sehgal studied 305 residents of Chennai, India, who had sold their organs. Participants were asked to rate their health status before and after the operation. Eighty-nine percent of the respondents reported at least some decline in their health. "Fifty percent complained of persistent pain at the nephrectomy site and 33 percent complained of long-term back pain."

McLean points out that society also incurs risks when someone donates a kidney. "Who pays if the donor is harmed or develops renal failure of unrelated etiology 15 years later and needs a transplant?" she asks.

In bioethics, where the first rule is "Do no harm," can the sale of kidneys be judged to conform to this basic principle? Are there better ways to protect donors so that no disproportional harm comes to them?

The Problem of Exploitation and Informed Consent

16 The Indian experience points to another of the key objections that have been raised against the sale of organs: the danger that poor people will be exploited in the transaction. Nicky Santos, S.J., visiting scholar at the Ethics Center and an expert on marketing strategy for impoverished market segments, argues

strongly that desperation "drives the poor to make choices which are not really in their best interests." Such lopsided transactions may exacerbate already existing inequities, where the rich have access to excellent health care and the poor do not.

That was the conclusion of the Bellagio Task Force Report to the International Red Cross on "Transplantation, Bodily Integrity, and the International Traffic in Organs":

> Existing social and political inequities are such that commercialization would put powerless and deprived people at still graver risk. The physical well-being of disadvantaged populations, especially in developing countries, is already placed in jeopardy by a variety of causes, including the hazards of inadequate nutrition, substandard housing, unclean water, and parasitic infection. In these circumstances, adding organ sale to this roster would be to subject an already vulnerable group to yet another threat to its physical health and bodily integrity.

On the other hand, some view this attitude as paternalistic. "You could raise the question," says Michael McFarland, S.J. "Are the rich or those in power in a position to tell the poor they are not capable of making a decision? Doesn't that violate their human dignity? It seems to me that a person in desperate circumstances could be making a perfectly rational decision that the sale of a kidney is in his or her best interests." McFarland, a Center visiting scholar and the former president of College of the Holy Cross, goes on, "You could see the sale of organs as a way for the poor to derive some benefit from donating an organ, which they wouldn't otherwise get. For example, if a poor person was willing to donate a kidney but couldn't afford to take the time off, wouldn't it be reasonable to allow him or her to be compensated for that time?"

More people might be persuaded by this argument if, in fact, kidney sales really did help the poor financially. But in India, donors often did not receive the benefit they expected from the sale of their organs. Ninety-six percent of the people in the study had agreed to the donation to pay off a debt, but six years after the operation, 74 percent of those studied still owed money. Most of the benefit from organ sales goes to middlemen. Havocscope, which monitors black markets, found last May that the average reported amount paid to kidney donors was $5,000, while the average price paid by recipients was $150,000. "The real injustice to the poor is they are getting so little, while those who are involved in these illegal sales are getting all the money," says Rev. Brendan McGuire, vicar general of the Diocese of San Jose. Santos believes that the poor cannot really make free decisions to sell their organs because they are so driven by their dire circumstances. McFarland agrees that the issue of consent is the real sticking point for creating a market for organs. "I think what stops us is the concern about being able to count on a genuine free consent on the part of the donor." But he does not believe any moral absolute makes the sale of kidneys unacceptable. "It comes back to the issue of truly informed consent. Do people understand the risks they are taking on? Are those acceptable risks? Are people capable of making free decisions about whether to take those risks?"

Altruism or Justice

20   Informed consent is, of course, as crucial for organ donation as it would be for organ sale. But donation frames the process as a wholly altruistic act. "For a living donor," says McLean, "it may be a chance to help a family member or friend or even a stranger." For a person signing on to donate organs after death, it may be seen as a way to give back or not to die in vain. And for the family of a deceased donor, it's "a way to have a little bit of someone alive in the world," she continues.

Many people value this altruistic aspect of the current system and do not want to see organ donation reduced to a business transaction. But, McFarland asks, "Is it the wisest and most moral policy to run a social system like kidney donation entirely on altruism?" That may be the ideal, he agrees, but since it has not been very effective at meeting the need for organs, it may be better to "strive for justice and not depend totally on altruism."

The idea of justice encompasses concern about the exploitation of the poor, but it raises even broader concerns about fairness. These might be summed up in another email we received at the Ethics Center:

> So what? Is the sale of one's kidney lawful? Morality or ethics has nothing to do with it when you're down and out. Why doesn't someone ask the same of doctors and hospitals when they sell the transplant operation? Why is it when John Q. Public sees a way into the open markets, that he gets hit with the morality/ethical questions?

Is it fair that everyone involved in organ transplantation—doctors, hospital, nurses, recipient—gets something out of the process except the donor or the donor's family? Also, donors on the black market are rarely paid anything approaching what the kidney is worth. Justice might be better served if donors were paid more. In the Indian study, the average price of an organ in 2001 was $1,410. Nobel Laureate in Economics Gary Becker and his colleague Julio Elias have calculated $45,000 as a fair price. Fairer, still say some ethicists, would be a system that pays the donor a figure closer to the actual cost of maintaining a patient on the waiting list for organs, including the cost of dialysis over many years. Arthur Matas and Mark Schnitzler have calculated that a transplant from a living unrelated donor would save at least $94,579.

24
Alternatively, the donor wouldn't necessarily need to be paid to be compensated. McLean reviews some other proposals to give something back to donors: "One suggestion has been to at least offer to pay funeral expenses for a deceased donor because for many people that's a stumbling block. For live donors—and this could be hugely attractive in the current environment—we might offer to cover their health care for the rest of their lives in exchange for doing this good."

Another cut at fairness has recently been adopted by Israel and is advocated in the United States by the private organization Life Sharers. Top priority on Israel's waiting list goes to candidates who have themselves agreed to be donors. Those who don't sign up as donors get a transplant only if there is an excess of organs.

All proposals to allow the sale of organs raise ethical as well as medical risks. However, as E.A. Friedman and A.L. Friedman argue in Kidney International, Journal of the International Society of Nephrology:

> At least debating the controlled initiation and study of potential regimens that may increase donor kidney supply in the future in a scientifically and ethically responsible manner, is better than doing nothing more productive than complaining about the current system's failure.

PERSONAL RESPONSE

Do you know of anyone who needs or has had an organ transplant? Do you know of anyone who has donated or plans to donate an organ? How do you think you would respond to a friend who says that he or she plans to donate a kidney to a loved one?

QUESTIONS FOR CLASS OR SMALL-GROUP DISCUSSION

1. Schulman asks in paragraph 7 if the sale of kidneys should be legalized. How well does she answer that question?

2. Do you think that the fact that there are numerous black market sales of organs, especially from third-world countries, advance the proposition that kidney sales should be legalized?

3. Schulman sets up a series of questions or issues that need addressing. Summarize the issues, select one that you particularly agree or disagree with, and explain why.

4. Do you think that making organ sales legal and regulating compensations for donors are workable solutions to the problem? What about legalizing other currently illegal trafficking such as prostitution, drugs, or other behaviors that support underground criminal activities? Would making them legal solve the problems?

WHY LEGALIZING ORGAN SALES WOULD HELP TO SAVE LIVES, END VIOLENCE

ANTHONY GREGORY

Anthony Gregory is a research fellow and student programs director at the Independent Institute and is the author of The Power of Habeas Corpus in America: From the King's Prerogative to the War on Terror *(2013). He has written hundreds of articles for a wide range of magazines and newspapers. This article was first published in* The Atlantic.

Last month, New Yorker Levy Izhak Rosenbaum pled guilty in federal court to the crime of facilitating illegal kidney transplants. It has been deemed the first proven case of black market organ trafficking in the United States. His lawyers argue that his lawbreaking was benevolent: "The transplants were successful and the donors and recipients are now leading full and healthy lives."

Indeed, why are organ sales illegal? Donors of blood, semen, and eggs, and volunteers for medical trials, are often compensated. Why not apply the same principle to organs?

The very idea of legalization might sound gruesome to most people, but it shouldn't, especially since research shows it would save lives. In the United States, where the 1984 National Organ Transplantation Act prohibits compensation for organ donating, there are only about 20,000 kidneys every year for the approximately 80,000 patients on the waiting list. In 2008, nearly 5,000 died waiting.

4   Many protest that an organ market will lead to unfair advantages for the rich, but this is a characteristic of the current trade.

A global perspective shows how big the problem is. "Millions of people suffer from kidney disease, but in 2007 there were just 64,606 kidney-transplant operations in the entire world," according to George Mason University professor and Independent Institute research director Alexander Tabarrok, writing in the *Wall Street Journal*.

Almost every other country has prohibitions like America's. In Iran, however, selling one's kidney for profit is legal. There are no patients anguishing on the waiting list. The Iranians have solved their kidney shortage by legalizing sales.

Many will protest that an organ market will lead to exploitation and unfair advantages for the rich and powerful. But these are the characteristics of the current illicit organ trade. Moreover, as with drug prohibition today and alcohol prohibition in the 1920s, pushing a market underground is the way to make it rife with violence and criminality.

8   In Japan, for the right price, you can buy livers and kidneys harvested from executed Chinese prisoners. Three years ago in India, police broke up an organ ring that had taken as many as 500 kidneys from poor laborers. The World Health Organization estimates that the black market accounts for 20 percent of kidney transplants worldwide. Everywhere from Latin America to the former Soviet Republics, from the Philippines to South Africa, a huge network has emerged typified by threats, coercion, intimidation, extortion, and shoddy surgeries.

Although not every black market transaction is exploitative—demonstrating that organ sales, in and of themselves, are not the problem—the most unsavory parts of the trade can be attributed to the fact that it is illegal. Witnessing the horror stories, many are calling on governments to crack down even more severely. Unfortunately, prohibition drives up black-market profits, turns the market over to organized crime, and isolates those harmed in the trade from the normal routes of recourse.

Several years ago, transplant surgeon Nadley Hakim at St. Mary's Hospital in London pointed out that "this trade is going on anyway, why not have a controlled trade where if someone wants to donate a kidney for a particular price, that would be acceptable? If it is done safely, the donor will not suffer."

Bringing the market into the open is the best way to ensure the trade's appropriate activity. Since the stakes would be very high, market forces and social pressure would ensure that people are not intimidated or defrauded. In the United States, attitudes are not so casual as to allow gross degeneracy. Enabling a process by which consenting people engage in open transactions would mitigate the exploitation of innocent citizens and underhanded dealing by those seeking to skirt the law.

12   The most fundamental case for legalizing organ sales—an appeal to civil liberty—has proven highly controversial. Liberals like to say, "my body, my choice," and conservatives claim to favor free markets, but true self-ownership would include the right to sell one's body parts, and genuine free enterprise would imply a market in human organs. In any event, studies show that this has become a matter of life and death.

Perhaps the key to progress is more widespread exposure to the facts. In 2008, six experts took on this issue in an Oxford-style debate hosted by National Public Radio. By the end, those in the audience who favored allowing the market climbed from 44 to 60 percent.

Yet, the organ trade continues to operate in the shadows and questionable activities occur in the medical establishment under the color of law. Even today, doctors sometimes legally harvest organ tissue from dead patients without consent. Meanwhile, thousands are perishing and even more are suffering while we wait for the system to change.

The truly decent route would be to allow people to withhold or give their organs freely, especially upon death, even if in exchange for money. Thousands of lives would be saved. Once again, humanitarianism is best served by the respect for civil liberty, and yet we are deprived both, with horribly unfortunate consequences, just to maintain the pretense of state-enforced propriety.

PERSONAL RESPONSE

Would you be willing to donate an organ to a close friend or relative? Write for a few minutes explaining your answer.

QUESTIONS FOR CLASS OR SMALL-GROUP DISCUSSION

1. What explanation does Gregory give for why legalizing organ sales would help save lives and end violence? Are you convinced?

2. In paragraph 4, Gregory writes that people protest that "an organ market will lead to unfair advantages for the rich." Do you agree with what he says in response to that argument?

3. Gregory says that "the most fundamental case for legalizing organ sales [is] an appeal to civil liberty" (paragraph 12). What does he mean by that? To what extent, do you agree with him?

4. Assess this article as an argument. What are its strengths and weaknesses? Do you find it logical, with valid evidence and/or convincing proof? If you have read Miriam Schulman's "Kidneys for Sale: A Reconsideration," how do the two arguments compare?

GLOBAL WARNING:
GET UP! STAND UP!

BILL McKIBBEN

Bill McKibben, author, educator, and environmentalist, is a contributing editor of OnEarth. His books include The End of Nature, *the first book for a general audience on global warming (1989);* The Age of Missing Information *(1992);* Hope, Human and Wild: True Stories of Living Lightly on Earth *(1995);* Maybe One: The Case for Smaller Families *(1998);* Long Distance: Testing the Limits of Body and Spirit in a Year of Living Strenuously *(2000);* Enough: Staying Human in an Engineering Age *(2003);* Deep Economy: The Wealth of Communities and the Durable Future *(2007);* EAARTH *[sic]:* Making a Life on a Tough New Planet *(2008);* The Global Warming Reader *(2012); and* Oil and Honey: The Education of an Unlikely Activist (2013). OnEarth, *the quarterly journal of the Natural Resources Defense Council, explores politics, nature, wildlife, culture, science, health, the challenges that confront our planet, and the solutions that promise to heal and protect it.*

Here's a short list of the important legislation our federal government has enacted to combat global warming in the years since 1988, when a NASA climatologist, James Hansen, first told Congress that climate change was real:

1.

2.

3.

And what do you know? That bipartisan effort at doing nothing has been highly successful: Our emissions of carbon dioxide have steadily increased over that two-decade span.

Meanwhile, how have the lone superpower's efforts at leading international action to deal with climate change gone? Not too well. We refused to ratify the Kyoto treaty, while the rest of the developed world finally did so. And while we've pressured China over world-shaking issues like DVD piracy, we've happily sold them the parts to help grow their coal-fired electric utility network to a size that matches ours.

4   In other words, Washington has utterly and completely failed to take on the single greatest challenge human civilization has ever faced.

What's more, Washington, at least so far, couldn't care less about the failure. A flurry of legislation has been introduced in the last couple of months, but scarcely a member of Congress felt compelled to answer in the last election for failing to deal with climate change. A simple "I'm concerned" was more than enough.

Not only that, but scientists revealed last December that a piece of ice the size of 11,000 football fields had broken off an Arctic ice shelf.

So, and here I use a technical term that comes from long study of the intricate science, we're screwed. Unless.

8   If we're going to change any of those nasty facts, we need a movement. A real, broad-based public movement demanding transformation of the way we power our world. A movement as strong, passionate, and willing to sacrifice as the civil rights movement that ended segregation more than a generation ago. This essay is about the possible rise of such a movement— about the role that you might play in making it happen.

It's not the fault of our environmental organizations that such a movement doesn't yet exist. It's the fault of the molecular structure of carbon dioxide.

Modern environmentalism arose in the early 1960s in the wake of *Silent Spring*. That's the moment advocates of "conservation"—the idea that we should protect some areas as refuges amid a benign modernity—began to realize that modernity itself might be a problem, that the bright miracles of our economic life came with shadows. First DDT, but before long phosphates in detergent and sulfur in the smoke stream of coal plants and chlorofluoro-carbons (CFCs) in our air conditioners. And carbon monoxide, carbon with one oxygen atom, the stuff that was helping turn the air above our cities brown.

All were alike in one crucial way: You could take care of the problems they caused with fairly easy technical fixes. Different pesticides that didn't thin eggshells; scrubbers on smokestacks. DuPont ended up making more money on the stuff that replaced CFCs, which had been tearing a hole in the ozone layer. None of these battles was easy: The Natural Resources Defense Council (NRDC) and Greenpeace and Environmental Defense and the Sierra Club and the Union of Concerned Scientists and a thousand Friends of the You-Name-It had to fight like hell to make sure that the fixes got made. But that was the war we armed for: We had the lawyers and the scientists and the regulatory experts and the lobbyists and the fund-raisers. We didn't always win, but the batting average was pretty high: You can swim in more rivers, breathe in more cities. It was a carbon monoxide movement, and the catalytic converter, which washed that chemical from your exhaust, was its emblem. You could drive your car; you just needed the right gear on your tailpipe.

12   But carbon dioxide—carbon with two oxygen atoms—screwed everything up. Carbon dioxide in itself isn't exactly a pollutant. It doesn't hurt you when you breathe it; in fact, for a very long time engineers described a motor as "clean-burning" if it gave off only CO_2 and water vapor. The problem that emerged into public view in the late 1980s was that its molecular structure trapped heat near the planet that would otherwise radiate back out to space. And, worse, there wasn't a technofix this time—CO_2 was an inevitable by-product of burning fossil fuels. That is to say, the only way to deal with global warming is to move quickly away from fossil fuels.

When you understand that, you understand why Congress has yet to act, and why even big and talented environmental organizations have been largely stymied. Fossil fuel is not like DDT or phosphates or CFCs. It's the absolute center of modern life. An alien scientist arriving on our planet might well conclude that Western human beings are devices for burning coal and gas and oil, since that is what we do from dawn to dusk, and then on into the brightly lit night. When societies get richer, they start reducing other pollutants—even in China some cities have begun to see reductions in sulfur and nitrogen as people demand better pollution controls. But as the Harvard economist Benjamin Friedman conceded in a landmark book in 2005, *The Moral Consequences of Economic Growth*, carbon dioxide is the only pollutant that economic growth doesn't reduce. It is economic growth. It's no accident that the last three centuries, a time of great prosperity, have also been the centuries of coal and oil and gas.

Which means that this is a war that environmentalism as currently constituted simply can't win. Our lobbyists can sit down with congressional staffers and convince them of the need for, say, lower arsenic levels in water supplies; they have enough support to win those kinds of votes. We've managed, brilliantly, to save the Arctic National Wildlife Refuge from drilling. But we lack (by a long shot) the firepower to force, say, a carbon tax that might actually cut fossil fuel use. We've been outgunned by the car companies and the auto unions when it comes to gasoline mileage. We can save the Arctic refuge from oil drilling, but we can't save it from thawing into a northern swamp no caribou would ever wander through. In essence, we have a problem opposite to that of the American military: Well armed for small battles with insurgent polluters, we suddenly find ourselves needing to fight World War II.

What we have now is the superstructure of a movement. We have brilliant scientists, we have superb economists, we have some of the most battle-hardened lawyers and lobbyists you could hope for. The only thing the climate movement lacks is the movement part.

16   Consider this: last Labor Day weekend, a few of us led a five-day, 50-mile march across our home state of Vermont to demand that our candidates for federal office take stronger stands on climate legislation. We started at Robert Frost's summer writing cabin high in the Green Mountains, happy with the symbolism of choosing a road less taken. As we wandered byways and main roads, we were happy too with the reception we got—crowds waiting to greet us at churches and senior centers and farms, motorists waving and honking even from the largest SUVs. By the time we reached Burlington, the state capital, we had a thousand marchers. (It was more

than enough to convince all our candidates, even the conservative Republicans, to endorse strong carbon reductions; they all
signed a pledge backing 80 percent cuts in carbon emissions by
2050.) But here's the not-so-happy thing: The newspapers said
that a rally of 1,000 people was the largest that had yet taken
place in this nation against global warming. That's pathetic.

But not hopeless. Because that movement is starting to
gather, less inside the main environmental organizations than
on their fringes.

The student movement, for instance, has come out of
nowhere in the last three years. All of a sudden there are hundreds of high schools and college campuses where kids are
working for real change in how their dorms and classrooms
are heated and lit. And emboldened by their success on campus, they're increasingly involved in state and national and
international efforts. Whenever I'm feeling disheartened about
how slowly change is coming, I stop by a meeting of the Sunday
Night Group at Middlebury College, the campus where I work.
A hundred or more students show up for the weekly meetings,
and they get right down to business—some on making sure
that every light bulb in town is a compact fluorescent, some
on making sure that every legislator in the state is a climate
convert. On the national level, the group Energy Action has
joined 16 student organizations into an effective force. The
group's Campus Climate Challenge will soon involve a thousand schools, and its leaders are planning a summer of marches
and a platoon of youth to bird-dog presidential candidates.

Or look at the churches and synagogues. Ten years ago
there was no religious environmental movement to speak of.
Now, "creation care" is an emerging watchword across the
spectrum, from Unitarians to evangelicals among the Chris-
tian traditions and in Jewish, Buddhist, and Muslim communities as well. And the rhetoric is increasingly matched by
action: Groups such as Interfaith Power and Light are organizing congregations to cut energy use, and groups such as
Religious Witness for the Earth are organizing people of faith
for marches of their own.

20   There's even one very sweet by-product of the roadblock
in Washington: In cities and states across the union, big environmental groups and local citizen activists have focused their
energy on mayors and governors and learned a good deal in
the process. Including this: It's possible to win. If California's
Republican governor can decide it's in his interest to embrace
strong climate legislation, you know people have done good

groundwork. They've worked in public as well as behind the scenes. Activists from the Maryland-based Chesapeake Climate Action Network were arrested last fall for blocking the doors to federal offices to demand more accurate federal science.

The moment is ripe. Hurricane Katrina blew open the door of public opinion, and Al Gore walked valiantly through it with his movie. There are, finally, lots and lots of people who want to know how they can make a difference. Not 51 percent of the people, but we don't need 51 percent. We can do just fine with 15 percent. As long as they're active. As long as they're a movement.

Which brings me, finally, to the point. It's time to unleash as much passion and energy as we can. It's movement time.

What we need is nothing less than a societal transformation. Not a new gizmo, not a few new laws, but a commitment to wean America from fossil fuels in our lifetime and to lead the rest of the world, especially India and China, in the same direction. The shorthand we're using in our April stepitup07.org campaign is the same as it was in our Vermont march: 80 percent cuts by 2050. What we need is big change, starting right now.

24   And that's a message Congress needs to hear. Though the November elections opened new possibilities, they also raised new perils. Instead of James Inhofe, who thought global warming was a hoax, the relevant Senate committee now answers to Barbara Boxer, who understands that it's very real. But the very chance of a deal raises the specter of a bad deal—some small-potatoes around-the-edges kind of action that substitutes the faux realism of Washington politics for the actual physics-and-chemistry realism of our predicament. For instance, when John McCain introduced legislation five years ago that asked for small and more or less voluntary cuts, it was a step forward, and I saluted him on the cover of this magazine. But the current draft of his bill is fairly weak. Even the strongest bills, introduced by Henry Waxman and Bernie Sanders, barely meet the test for what the science demands. And chances are, unless we really do our job on the ground, the measures they're proposing will barely be discussed.

NASA's James Hansen—our premier climatologist—has made it clear we have 10 years to reverse the flow of carbon into the atmosphere. Actually, he made it clear in the fall of 2005, so we have eight and a half years before we cross certain thresholds (Arctic melt, for instance) that commit us to an endless cycle of self-reinforcing feedback loops and, in Hansen's words, a "totally different planet."

That requires transformation, not tinkering. It's not like carbon monoxide or DDT—it's like the women's movement or the civil rights movement, which changed the basic taken-for-granted architecture of our nation. Except it's harder, because this time we don't need the system to accommodate more people; we need the system to change in profound ways.

The only chance is for those of us who see the risk and the opportunity to act—as quickly and as powerfully as ever we can.

PERSONAL RESPONSE

How committed are you to the kind of activism that McKibben calls for?

QUESTIONS FOR CLASS OR SMALL-GROUP DISCUSSION

1. Describe the tone in the opening paragraphs. What is the effect of that tone? Where does the tone change?

2. In paragraph 4, McKibben writes that Washington, DC, has failed "to take on the single greatest challenge human civilization has ever faced." What is that challenge? Do you agree that it is the greatest challenge humans have faced? If not, what other challenge(s) are greater?

3. The subtitle of this essay is "How to Build a Mass Movement to Halt Climate Change." Summarize in your own words the actions that McKibben recommends for building a mass movement to halt climate change. Do you agree with him that such a movement will work?

4. How persuasive do you find this article? Are you moved to act?

THE SIXTH EXTINCTION

JEFF CORWIN

Jeff Corwin, biologist, Emmy Award-winning producer, and television host of Animal Planet *is the author of* Living on the Edge: Amazing Relationships in the

*Natural World (2004) and 100 Heartbeats: The
Race to Save the World's Most Endangered Animal
Species (2009), a book about his experiences tracking
the sixth extinction. A companion documentary to the
book aired on MSNBC in 2009. He has also published a
number of pamphlets in his Explorer Series on topics like
the world of wild cats and the world of sharks.*

There is a holocaust happening. Right now. And it's not confined to one nation or even one region. It is a global crisis.

Species are going extinct en masse.

Every 20 minutes we lose an animal species. If this rate continues, by century's end, 50% of all living species will be gone. It is a phenomenon known as the sixth extinction. The fifth extinction took place 65 million years ago when a meteor smashed into the Earth, killing off the dinosaurs and many other species and opening the door for the rise of mammals. Currently, the sixth extinction is on track to dwarf the fifth.

4   What—or more correctly—who is to blame this time? As Pogo said, "We have met the enemy, and he is us."

The causes of this mass die-off are many: overpopulation, loss of habitat, global warming, species exploitation (the black market for rare animal parts is the third-largest illegal trade in the world, outranked only by weapons and drugs). The list goes on, but it all points to us.

Over the last 15 years, in the course of producing television documentaries and writing about wildlife, I have traveled the globe, and I have witnessed the grim carnage firsthand. I've observed the same story playing out in different locales.

In South Africa, off the coast of Cape Horn, lives one of the most feared predators of all—the great white shark. Yet this awesome creature is powerless before the mindless killing spree that is decimating its species at the jaw-dropping rate of 100 million sharks a year. Many are captured so that their dorsal fins can be chopped off (for shark fin soup). Then, still alive, they are dropped back into the sea, where they die a slow and painful death.

8   Further east, in Indonesia, I witnessed the mass destruction of rain forests to make way for palm oil plantations. Indonesia is now the world's leading producer of palm oil—a product used in many packaged foods and cosmetic goods—and the victims are the Sumatran elephant and orangutan. These beautiful creatures are on the brink of extinction as

their habitats go up in smoke, further warming our planet in the process.

One day while swimming off the coast of Indonesia, I came across a river of refuse and raw sewage stretching for miles. These streams and islands of refuse now populate all our oceans; in the middle of the Pacific, there is an island of garbage the size of Texas. This floating pollution serves to choke off and kill sea turtles—driving them closer to extinction. At the same time, the coral reefs where sea turtles get their food supply are dying due to rising sea temperatures from global warming. To top it off, sea turtles are hunted and killed for their meat—considered a delicacy in many Asian countries. It is an ugly but altogether effective one-two-three punch for this unique species.

It's important to understand that this is not just a race to save a handful of charismatic species—animals to which we attach human-inspired values or characteristics. Who wouldn't want to save the sea otter, polar bear, giant panda or gorilla? These striking mammals tug at our heartstrings and often our charitable purse strings. But our actions need to be just as swift and determined when it comes to the valley elderberry longhorn beetle or the distinctly uncuddly, pebbly-skinned Puerto Rican crested toad or the black-footed ferret, whose fate is inextricably intertwined with that of the prairie dog. The reality is that each species, no matter how big, small, friendly or vicious, plays an important and essential role in its ecosystem. And we're in a race to preserve as much of the animal kingdom as possible.

Meanwhile, around the planet there are massive die-offs of amphibians, the canaries in our global coal mine. When frogs and other amphibians, which have existed for hundreds of millions of years, start to vanish, it is a sign that our natural world is in a state of peril. Bat and bee populations are also being decimated. Without bees, there will be no pollination, and without pollination, the predator that is decimating these other species—humankind—will also be headed toward its own extinction. Yes, there is a certain irony there.

This was all brought home to me in an intimate way after a recent trip to Panama. My young daughter, Maya, asked if she could accompany me on my next trip there so that she could see one of her favorite animals—the Panamanian golden frog—up close and personal in the jungle. Sadly, I had to tell her no. This small, beautiful frog—the national symbol of Panama—no longer exists in the wild. Only a few live in captivity.

Is there hope? Yes. Because in every place I visited to witness the sixth extinction unfold, I met brave and selfless conservationists, biologists and wildlife scientists working hard to save species.

In Panama, biologist Edgardo Griffith has set up an amphibian rescue center to protect and quarantine rare frogs (including the Panamanian golden frog) before they are all wiped out by the deadly fungus *Chytrid*, which is rapidly killing off frogs on a global scale. In Africa, zoologist Iain Douglas Hamilton is one of many seeking to stop the illegal trade in elephant ivory and rhino horn. In Namibia, zoologist Laurie Marker is making strides to save the cheetah before it goes the way of the saber tooth tiger (or India's Bengal tiger, which is also on the precipice of extinction). In Indonesia, Ian Singleton is raising orphaned orangutans, training them to return to the remaining rain forest—giving them a second chance at living in the wild. In South Africa, Alison Kock is leading a crusade to educate the world about the wholesale destruction of sharks.

Here in the United States, Chris Lucash of the U.S. Fish and Wildlife Service is working to reintroduce the red wolf, now found only in captivity, to the woods of North Carolina. They are just a few of the many who are trying to reverse the species holocaust that threatens the future of our natural world.

16   These committed scientists bring great generosity and devotion to their respective efforts to stop the sixth extinction. But if we don't all rise to the cause and join them in action, they cannot succeed. The hour is near, but it's not too late.

PERSONAL RESPONSE

Write for a few minutes about a detail in this essay that impressed you in some way.

QUESTIONS FOR CLASS OR SMALL-GROUP DISCUSSION

1. Explain what Corwin means by his title, "The Sixth Extinction."

2. Where does Corwin use examples effectively? What do you understand Corwin to mean by the metaphor of canaries in a coal mine (paragraph 11)?

3. What argumentative strategies does Corwin use to persuade his reader to action? Are you persuaded?

4. In his concluding paragraph, Corwin urges readers to "rise to the cause and join [scientists] in action." How do you think readers can practically join scientists around the globe? What else might individuals do to help stop species extinction?

MindTap® Reflect on the theme of this chapter.

PERSPECTIVES ON BIOETHICS AND ENVIRONMENTAL STUDIES

Suggested Writing Topics

1. Compare the views of Miriam Schulman ("Kidneys for Sale: A Reconsideration") and Anthony Gregory ("Why Legalizing Organs Would Help to Save Lives, End Violence"). Explain where you agree with them, where you disagree, and/or whether you have real concerns about what the writers say.

2. Explore one of the ethical, social, or legal problems associated with the selling of human organs. State and defend your own position on the subject.

3. If you are committed to the kind of activism that Bill McKibben urges in "Global Warning: Get Up! Stand Up!" explain the nature of your activism and analyze its effectiveness for you personally.

4. Jeff Corwin in "The Sixth Extinction" urges us all "to rise to the cause and join [scientists] in action." Explain what you can do personally to respond to Corwin's call for action.

5. Explain your position on the subject of individual responsibility for environmental health and/or reducing your carbon footprint.

6. Write an essay that offers possible solutions to one of the major environmental issues confronting people today.

7. Propose practical conservation steps that students on your campus or the campus as a whole can take. If your campus is already "green," explain what it does and what you think it accomplishes.

8. Argue the extent to which you think that pressure from lobbyists should influence the thinking of legislators considering measures that would tighten regulations on environmental issues.

9. Although the writers in this chapter address a wide range of bioethical and environmental issues, these selections do not provide exhaustive coverage. Select an environmental issue that is not addressed in these essays, explain the problem in detail, and if possible, offer solutions.

Research Topics

1. Research the National Organ Transplant Act of 1984—what it restricts and allows, what its impact has been on organ transplants, and whether you think it should remain in effect as it is, be amended or revised, or be repealed.

Consider the opinions of Miriam Schulman in "Kidneys for Sale: A Reconsideration" and Anthony Gregory in "Why Legalizing Organs Would Help to Save Lives, End Violence" in your research.

2. Research the current state of the controversy over stem cell research, perhaps looking at what both your own state's and federal laws prohibit or allow, and then state your own position on the subject, giving its current ethical and legal status.

3. Besides the issues discussed in the readings in this chapter, there are numerous other medical issues that raise moral and ethical questions. Research one of the following, explore differing viewpoints on the controversy, and arrive at your own conclusion: increasing incentives for organ donation, access to expensive treatments for self-induced health problems, embryo research, mandatory testing for HIV diseases, compulsory genetic screening for certain risk groups or during premarital examinations, the status of genetic disease and genetic therapy, cryonics, human genetic engineering, gene therapy, artificial life, or genetically modified foods.

4. One of the results of identifying the entire genetic makeup of humans is that some pharmaceutical companies now hold patents on genes and therefore can charge high prices for drugs to treat certain diseases. Some people argue that gene patents prevent further research, whereas others argue that such patents work the way they are supposed to, thus benefitting patients. Research the subject of gene patents and draw your own conclusion about the benefits and drawbacks of patenting genes.

5. Research the question: Should scientists create human life? Consider pros and cons and arrive at your own conclusion.

6. Select an issue in the area of neurotechnology, such as cell therapy in the brain; using neuroscience to enhance military personnel's performance or weaken that of the enemy; transcranial magnetic stimulation to treat depression; implantable brain chips; deep brain stimulators to treat debilitating neurological symptoms, such as those associated with Parkinson's disease; brain computer interfaces; or forensic neuroscience. Research the controversy over the issue and arrive at your own conclusion.

7. Research some aspect of the history and/or practice of eugenics, such as the program of Nazi Germany under Hitler or U.S. programs for forced sterilization for mentally ill patients.

8. Research the progress of Greenpeace's "Detox My Fashion" campaign.

9. Find out more about the sixth extinction and focus on one specific aspect of it to research.

10. Conduct research on the impact of socioeconomic inequities on environmental issues and argue your position on the subject.

RESPONDING TO VISUALS

In this depiction of a man attempting to block the flow of toxic waste, what do the smokestacks in the shape of guns represent?

1. Comment on the perspective from which we see this image, with the man very close to the front and the factory extending far into the distance.

2. What does the man in the river represent? Why is he masked?

3. How effective do you find this image as a statement on environmentalism?

RESPONDING TO VISUALS

Alberto Ruggieri/Illustration Works/Getty Images

Why are the two bodies in this image overlapping?

1. Comment on the composition of the image and its use of color.

2. Can we tell what organ is being transplanted? Does it matter?

3. What would you guess is the artist's opinion of organ transplants?

MARKETING, THE AMERICAN CONSUMER, AND THE WORKPLACE

LEARNING OBJECTIVES

Students will demonstrate an ability to do the following:

☐ Determine ways that commercialism has invaded everyday lives.

☐ Debate whether commercialism has a negative effect on the quality of American life.

☐ Discuss tactics that employers use to hire qualified workers.

☐ Explore ways to succeed in a job search.

MindTap   Understand the goals of the chapter and complete
a warm-up activity.

CHAPTER OVERVIEW

With their reputation for conspicuous consumption and materialism, Americans are both the envy of people in other nations and the objects of their criticism. America has long been regarded as the "land of plenty," with a plethora of products to buy and a standard of living that allows most citizens to buy them. Yet such plenitude can lead to overconsumption, creating a need to buy for the sake of buying that can become a kind of obsession. Some people seek psychological counseling for this compulsion, whereas others seek financial counseling to manage the debts they have built up as a result of their need to buy things.

Indeed, shopping is so central to the lives of Americans that malls have become more than places to find virtually any product people want and need; they have become social centers, where people gather to meet friends, eat, hang out, exercise, and be entertained. Some regard this penchant for spending money and acquiring goods as a symptom of some inner emptiness, with malls, shopping strips, and discount stores replacing the spiritual centers that once held primary importance in people's lives. Others, especially manufacturers of products and the people who sell them, regard consumerism as a hearty indicator of the nation's economic health.

Smartphones and other handheld devices have made shopping from anywhere a breeze, as electronic technology has essentially transformed the way that people shop. Social media has become a gold mine for advertisers, as merchants track consumers' browsing and purchasing online and then populate websites with ads targeted specifically for them. Now it is not only "Black Friday," the day after Thanksgiving when Christmas shopping kicks off with a zest as shoppers flock to stores with prices deeply discounted for that day, and "Cyber Monday," when retailers offer deep discounts on online purchases, but many other days when vendors offer flash sales or deep discounts to lure buyers to purchase their products. The Internet may well have replaced shopping malls and the traditional store fronts of Main Street.

In the first selection in this chapter, Gary Ruskin and Juliet Schor discuss the negative effects of the pervasive spread of commercialism throughout far too many aspects of American life. "Every Nook and Cranny: The Dangerous Spread of Commercialized Culture" cites numerous examples of the commercialization of government and culture and argues that the effects are almost all negative. Noting that advertising has only recently "been recognized as having political and social merit," Ruskin and Schor complain that it now invades "nearly every nook and cranny of life." You may find yourself nodding in agreement as they mention many ways in which advertising has invaded everyday life. Whether you agree with them that such pervasiveness is dangerous is something you will have to decide for yourself.

In order to earn money to purchase food, clothing, and other items, most people must work, and the workplace, too, can have enormous influence on people's lives.

Most Americans work outside of the home, either full-time or part-time, spending significant portions of their lives on the job. The physical atmosphere of the workplace, the friendliness of coworkers, wages and benefits, and the attitudes of supervisors or bosses all play pivotal roles not only in the way workers perform but also in the way they feel about themselves. Tension, anxiety, and stress in the workplace can lower production for the company and produce actual illnesses in workers, whereas a pleasant atmosphere, good benefits, and relatively low stress can boost production and make employees look forward to going to work. Research has demonstrated that the quality of life in the workplace has a direct effect on the quality of work employees do and on their general well-being.

Related to the subject of the workplace is the subject of the job market, which the next two readings discuss, one from the perspective of companies looking for workers, and the other from the perspective of a job seeker looking for work. Peter Cappelli in "Why Companies Aren't Getting the Employees They Need" looks at the job market from the perspective of the employer. A number of large companies complain that there are not enough qualified, skilled workers to fill vacant positions. Cappelli notes that these companies blame schools and the government, but he argues that the fault is theirs, explains why they are at fault, and offers some practical solutions to the problem. In contrast, Peter Weinberg in "Escape from the Job Jungle" describes his months-long search for work. Using humor to explain his search methods and their lack of success, he represents the age group of newly graduated twenty- to twenty-four-year-olds who begin the job search with great optimism, only to discover that it takes hard work and persistence to find the right job for their qualifications.

If, like most college students, you have had a job or are currently working, think about your own experiences as a worker. Do you feel a sense of community in your workplace? Is your work fun? Tedious? Challenging? How would you characterize the relationship between management and employees where you work (or have worked)? Is what you earn adequate enough to meet your financial needs? Do you have benefits with your job? These questions all relate to the quality of your work experience, and how you answer them reveals a great deal about your workplace.

EVERY NOOK AND CRANNY: THE DANGEROUS SPREAD OF COMMERCIALIZED CULTURE

GARY RUSKIN AND JULIET SCHOR

Gary Ruskin is executive director of Commercial Alert, a nonprofit organization whose mission, according to its website, is "to keep the commercial culture within its proper sphere, and to prevent it from exploiting children and subverting the higher values of family, community, environmental integrity and democracy." Ruskin is an expert on the effects of advertising on children and the over-commercialization in many areas of American life. He has published widely and is a frequent guest on television news programs. Juliet Schor is a professor of sociology at Boston College and the author of The Overworked American: The Unexpected Decline of Leisure *(1991);* The Overspent American: Upscaling, Downshifting and the New Consumer *(1998);* Born to Buy: The Commercialized Child and the New Consumer Culture *(2004); and* True Wealth *(2011). She serves on the board of directors of Commercial Alert. This article was first published in* Multinational Monitor, *a publication that tracks activity in the corporate world, especially in third-world countries.*

In December, many people in Washington, D.C., paused to absorb the meaning in the lighting of the National Christmas Tree, at the White House Ellipse. At that event, President George W. Bush reflected that the "love and gifts" of Christmas were "signs and symbols of even a greater love and gift that came on a holy night."

But these signs weren't the only ones on display. Perhaps it was not surprising that the illumination was sponsored by MCI, which, as MCI WorldCom, committed one of the largest corporate frauds in history. Such public displays of commercialism have become commonplace in the United States.

The rise of commercialism is an artifact of the growth of corporate power. It began as part of a political and ideological response by corporations to wage pressures, rising social expenditures, and the successes of the environmental and consumer movements in the late 1960s and early 1970s. Corporations fostered the anti-tax movement and support for corporate welfare, which helped create funding crises in state and local governments and schools, and made them more willing to carry commercial advertising. They promoted "free market" ideology, privatization and consumerism, while denigrating the public sphere. In the late 1970s, Mobil Oil began its decades-long advertising on the *New York Times* op-ed page, one example of a larger corporate effort to reverse a precipitous decline in public approval of corporations. They also became adept at manipulating the campaign finance system, and weaknesses in the federal bribery statute, to procure influence in governments at all levels.

4   Perhaps most importantly, the commercialization of government and culture and the growing importance of material acquisition and consumer lifestyles were hastened by the co-optation of potentially countervailing institutions, such as churches (papal visits have been sponsored by Pepsi, Federal Express, and Mercedes-Benz), governments, schools, universities, and nongovernmental organizations.

While advertising has long been an element in the circus of U.S. life, not until recently has it been recognized as having political or social merit. For nearly two centuries, advertising (lawyers call it commercial speech) was not protected by the U.S. Constitution. The U.S. Supreme Court ruled in 1942 that states could regulate commercial speech at will. But in 1976, the Court granted constitutional protection to commercial speech. Corporations have used this new right of speech to proliferate advertising into nearly every nook and cranny of life.

Entering the Schoolhouse

During most of the twentieth century, there was little advertising in schools. That changed in 1989, when Chris Whittle's Channel One enticed schools to accept advertising, by offering to loan TV sets to classrooms. Each school day, Channel One features at least two minutes of ads, and 10 minutes of news, fluff, banter, and quizzes. The program is shown to about 8 million children in 12,000 schools.

Soda, candy and fast food companies soon learned Channel One's lesson of using financial incentives to gain access to schoolchildren. By 2000, 94 percent of high schools allowed the sale of soda, and 72 percent allowed sale of chocolate candy. Energy, candy, personal care products, even automobile manufacturers have entered the classroom with "sponsored educational materials"—that is, ads in the guise of free "curricula."

8   Until recently, corporate incursion in schools has mainly gone under the radar. However, the rise of childhood obesity has engendered stiff political opposition to junk food marketing, and in the last three years, coalitions of progressives, conservatives and public health groups have made headway. The State of California has banned the sale of soda in elementary,

middle and junior high schools. In Maine, soda and candy suppliers have removed their products from vending machines in all schools. Arkansas banned candy and soda vending machines in elementary schools. Los Angeles, Chicago and New York have city-wide bans on the sale of soda in schools. Channel One was expelled from the Nashville public schools in the 2002–2003 school year, and will be removed from Seattle in early 2005. Thanks to activist pressure, a company called ZapMe! which placed computers in thousands of schools to advertise and extract data from students, was removed from all schools across the country.

Ad Creep and Spam Culture

Advertisers have long relied on 30-second TV spots to deliver messages to mass audiences. During the 1990s, the impact of these ads began to drop off, in part because viewers simply clicked to different programs during ads. In response, many advertisers began to place ads elsewhere, leading to "ad creep"—the spread of ads throughout social space and cultural institutions. Whole new marketing sub-specialties developed, such as "place-based" advertising, which coerces captive viewers to watch video ads. Examples include ads before movies, ads on buses and trains in cities (Chicago, Milwaukee and Orlando), and CNN's Airport channel. Video ads are also now common on ATMs, gas pumps, in convenience stores and doctors' offices.

Another form of ad creep is "product placement," in which advertisers pay to have their product included in movies, TV shows, museum exhibits, or other forms of media and culture. Product placement is thought to be more effective than the traditional 30-second ad because it sneaks by the viewer's critical faculties. Product placement has recently occurred in novels, and children's books. Some U.S. TV programs (*American Idol, The Restaurant, The Apprentice*) and movies (*Minority Report, Cellular*) are so full of product placement that they resemble infomercials. By contrast, many European nations, such as Austria, Germany, Norway and the United Kingdom, ban or sharply restrict product placement on television.

Commercial use of the Internet was forbidden as recently as the early 1990s, and the first spam wasn't sent until 1994. But the marketing industry quickly penetrated this sphere as well, and now 70 percent of all e-mail is spam, according to the spam filter firm Postini Inc. Pop-ups, pop-unders and ad-ware have become major annoyances for Internet users. Telemarketing became so unpopular that the corporate-friendly Federal Trade Commission established a National Do Not Call Registry, which has brought relief from telemarketing calls to 64 million households.

12   Even major cultural institutions have been harnessed by the advertising industry. During 2001–2002, the Smithsonian Institution, perhaps the most important U.S. cultural institution, established the General Motors Hall of Transportation and the Lockheed Martin Imax Theater. Following public opposition and Congressional action, the commercialization of the Smithsonian has largely been halted. In 2000, the Library of Congress hosted a giant celebration for Coca-Cola, essentially converting the nation's most important library into a prop to sell soda pop.

Targeting Kids

For a time, institutions of childhood were relatively uncommercialized, as adults subscribed to the notion of childhood innocence, and the need to keep children from the "profane" commercial world. But what was once a trickle of advertising to children has become a flood. Corporations spend about $15 billion marketing to children in the United States each year, and by the mid-1990s, the average child was exposed to 40,000 TV ads annually.

Children have few legal protections from corporate marketers in the United States. This contrasts strongly to the European Union, which has enacted restrictions. Norway and Sweden have banned television advertising to children under 12 years of age; in Italy, advertising during TV cartoons is illegal, and toy advertising is illegal in Greece between 7 AM and 11 PM. Advertising before and after children's programs is banned in Austria.

Government Brought to You by . . .

As fiscal crises have descended upon local governments, they have turned to advertisers as a revenue source. This trend began inauspiciously in Buffalo, New York, in 1995 when Pratt & Lambert, a local paint company, purchased the right to call itself the city's official paint. The next year the company was bought by Sherwin-Williams, which closed the local factory and eliminated its 200 jobs.

16

In 1997, Ocean City, Maryland, signed an exclusive marketing deal to make Coca-Cola the city's official drink, and other cities have followed with similar deals with Coke or Pepsi. Even mighty New York City has succumbed, signing a $166 million exclusive marketing deal with Snapple, after which some critics dubbed it the "Big Snapple."

At the United Nations, UNICEF made a stir in 2002 when it announced that it would "team up" with McDonald's, the world's largest fast food company, to promote "McDonald's World Children's Day" in celebration of the anniversary of the United Nations adoption of the Convention on the Rights of the Child. Public health and children's advocates across the globe protested, prompting UNICEF to decline participation in later years.

Another victory for the anti-commercialism forces, perhaps the most significant, came in 2004, when the World Health Organization's Framework Convention on Tobacco Control became legally binding. The treaty commits nations to prohibit tobacco advertising to the extent their constitutions allow it.

Impacts

Because the phenomenon of commercialism has become so ubiquitous, it is not surprising that its effects are as well. Perhaps most alarming has been the epidemic of marketing-related diseases afflicting people in the United States, and especially children, such as obesity, type 2 diabetes and smoking-related illnesses. Each day, about 2,000 U.S. children begin to smoke, and about one-third of them will die from tobacco-related illnesses. Children are inundated with advertising for high calorie junk food and fast food, and, predictably, 15 percent of U.S. children aged 6 to 19 are now overweight.

Excessive commercialism is also creating a more materialistic populace. In 2003, the annual UCLA survey of incoming college freshmen found that the number of students who said it was a very important or essential life goal to "develop a meaningful philosophy of life" fell to an all-time low of 39 percent, while succeeding financially has increased to a 13-year high, at 74 percent. High involvement in consumer culture has been shown (by Schor) to be a significant cause of depression, anxiety, low self-esteem and psychosomatic complaints in children, findings which parallel similar studies of materialism among teens and adults. Other impacts are more intangible. A 2004 poll by Yankelovich Partners, found that 61 percent of the U.S. public "feel that the amount of marketing and advertising is out of control," and 65 percent "feel constantly bombarded with too much advertising and marketing." Is advertising diminishing our sense of general well-being? Perhaps.

20   The purpose of most commercial advertising is to increase demand for a product. As John Kenneth Galbraith noted 40 years ago, the macro effect of advertising is to artificially boost the demand for private goods, thereby reducing the "demand" or support for unadvertised, public goods. The predictable result has been the backlash to taxes, and reduced provision of public goods and services.

This imbalance also affects the natural environment. The additional consumption created by the estimated $265 billion that the advertising industry will spend in 2004 will also yield more pollution, natural resource destruction, carbon dioxide emissions and global warming.

Finally, advertising has also contributed to a narrowing of the public discourse, as advertising-driven media grow ever more timid. Sometimes it seems as if we live in an echo chamber, a place where corporations speak and everyone else listens.

Governments at all levels have failed to address these impacts. That may be because the most insidious effect of commercialism is to undermine government integrity. As governments adopt commercial values, and are integrated into corporate marketing, they develop conflicts of interest that make them less likely to take stands against commercialism.

Disgust among Yourselves

24   As corporations consolidate their control over governments and culture, we don't expect an outright reversal of commercialization in the near future.

That's true despite considerable public sentiment for more limits and regulations on advertising and marketing. However, as commercialism grows more intrusive, public distaste for it will likely increase, as will political support for restricting it. In the long run, we believe this hopeful trend will gather strength.

In the not-too-distant future, the significance of the lighting of the National Christmas Tree may no longer be overshadowed by public relations efforts to create goodwill for corporate wrongdoers.

PERSONAL RESPONSE

Ruskin and Schor ask in paragraph 20: "Is advertising diminishing our sense of general well-being?" Look at the examples they give in that and the previous paragraph and then answer the question by examining whether your own general well-being has been affected by advertising.

QUESTIONS FOR CLASS OR SMALL-GROUP DISCUSSION

1. Ruskin and Schor mention ways in which commercialism has entered the schoolroom (paragraphs 6–8). Were any of the examples they cite part of your own school experience? Can you give other examples of the invasion of commercialism into schools?

2. What other examples of "ad creep" (paragraph 9) can you give besides the ones that Ruskin and Schor mention? Discuss whether you believe that such advertising should be banned or restricted in the United States, as it is in other countries.

3. Summarize the effects cited by Ruskin and Schor of the "ubiquitous" nature of commercialization (paragraph 19). Do you think that they provide enough evidence to support their contention?

4. Are you convinced by Ruskin and Schor's argument that the spread of commercialism is "dangerous"? Explain your answer.

WHY COMPANIES AREN'T GETTING THE EMPLOYEES THEY NEED

PETER CAPPELLI

Peter Cappelli is the George W. Taylor professor of management at the University of Pennsylvania's Wharton School and director of Wharton's Center for Human Resources. He is also a research associate at the National Bureau of Economic Research, served as a senior advisor to the Kingdom of Bahrain for Employment Policy from 2003 to 2005, and is a distinguished scholar of the Ministry of Manpower for Singapore. His books include Talent Management: Managing Talent in an Age of Uncertainty *(2008);* Managing the Older Worker *(with Bill Novelli) (2010); and* Why Good People Can't Get Jobs *(2012).*

Everybody's heard the complaints about recruiting lately. Even with unemployment hovering around 9%, companies are grousing that they can't find skilled workers, and filling a job can take months of hunting. Employers are quick to lay blame. Schools aren't giving kids the right kind of training. The government isn't letting in enough high-skill immigrants. The list goes on and on. But I believe that the real culprits are the employers themselves.

With an abundance of workers to choose from, employers are demanding more of job candidates than ever before. They want prospective workers to be able to fill a role right away, without any training or ramp-up time.

Bad for Companies, Bad for Economy

In other words, to get a job, you have to have that job already. It's a Catch-22 situation for workers—and it's hurting companies and the economy.

To get America's job engine revving again, companies need to stop pinning so much of the blame on our nation's education system. They need to drop the idea of finding perfect candidates and look for people who could do the job with a bit of training and practice. There are plenty of ways to get workers up to speed without investing too much time and money, such as putting new employees on extended probationary periods and relying more on internal hires, who know the ropes better than outsiders would. It's a fundamental change from business as usual. But the way we're doing things now just isn't working.

The Big Myths

The perceptions about a lack of skilled workers are pervasive. The staffing company ManpowerGroup, for instance, reports that 52% of U.S. employers surveyed say they have difficulty filling positions because of talent shortages. But the problem is an illusion. Some of the complaints about skill shortages boil down to the fact that employers can't get candidates to accept jobs at the wages offered. That's an affordability problem, not a skill shortage. A real shortage means not being able to find appropriate candidates at market-clearing wages. We wouldn't say there is a shortage of diamonds when they are incredibly expensive; we can buy all we want at the prevailing prices.

The real problem, then, is more appropriately an inflexibility problem. Finding candidates to fit jobs is not like finding pistons to fit engines, where the requirements are precise and can't be varied. Jobs can be organized in many different ways so that candidates who have very different credentials can do them successfully. Only about 10% of the people in IT jobs during the Silicon Valley tech boom of the 1990s, for example, had IT-related degrees. While it might be great to have a Ph.D. graduate read your electrical meter, almost anyone with a little training could do the job pretty well.

A Training Shortage

And make no mistake: There are plenty of people out there who could step into jobs with just a bit of training—even recent graduates who don't have much job experience. Despite employers' complaints about the education system, college students are pursuing more vocationally oriented course work than ever before, with degrees in highly specialized fields like pharmaceutical marketing and retail logistics.

8   Unfortunately, American companies don't seem to do training anymore. Data are hard to come by, but we know that apprenticeship programs have largely disappeared, along with management-training programs. And the amount of training that the average new hire gets in the first year or so could be measured in hours and counted on the fingers of one hand. Much of that includes what vendors do when they bring in new equipment: "Here's how to work this copier." The shortage of opportunities to learn on the job helps explain the phenomenon of people queueing up for unpaid internships, in some cases even paying to get access to a situation where they can work free to get access to valuable on-the-job experience.

Companies in other countries do things differently. In Europe, for instance, training is often mandated, and apprenticeships and other programs that help provide work experience are part of the infrastructure. The result: European countries aren't having skill-shortage complaints at the same level as in the U.S., and the nations that have the most established apprenticeship programs—the Scandinavian nations, Germany and Switzerland—have low unemployment.

Employers here at home rightly point to a significant constraint that they face in training workers: They train them and make the investment, but then someone else offers them more money and hires them away.

The Way Forward

That is a real problem. What's the answer? We aren't going to get European-style apprenticeships in the U.S. They require too much cooperation among employers and bigger investments in infrastructure than any government entity is willing to provide. We're also not going to go back to the lifetime-employment models that made years-long training programs possible.

But I'm also convinced that some of the problem we're up against is simply a failure of imagination. Here are three ways in which employees can get the skills they need without the employer having to invest in a lot of upfront training.

Work with Education Providers: If job candidates don't have the skills you need, make them go to school before you hire them.

Community colleges in many states, especially North Carolina, have proved to be good partners with employers by tailoring very applied course work to the specific needs of the employer. Candidates qualify to be hired once they complete the courses—which they pay for themselves, at least in part. For instance, a manufacturer might require that prospective job candidates first pass a course on quality control or using certain machine tools.

Going back to school isn't just for new hires, either; it also works for internal candidates. In this setup, the employer pays the tuition costs through tuition reimbursement. But the employees make the bigger investment by spending their own time, almost always off work, learning the material.

Bring Back Aspects of Apprenticeship: In this arrangement, apprentices are paid less while they are mastering their craft—so employers aren't paying for training and a big salary at the same time. Accounting firms, law firms and professional-services firms have long operated this way, and have made lots of money off their young associates.

Of course, a full apprenticeship model—with testing and credentials associated with different stages of experience—wouldn't work in all industries. But a simpler setup would: Companies could give their new workers a longer probationary period—with lower pay—until they get up to speed on the requirements of the job.

Promote from Within: Employees have useful knowledge that no outsider could have and should make great candidates for filling jobs higher up. In recent years, however, an incredible two-thirds of all vacancies, even in large companies, have been filled by hiring from the outside, according to data from Taleo Corp., a talent-management company. That figure has dropped somewhat lately because of market conditions. But a generation ago, the number was close to 10%, as internal promotions and transfers were used to fill virtually all positions.

These days, many companies simply don't believe their own workers have the necessary skills to take on new roles. But, once again, many workers could step into those jobs with a bit of training. And there's one on-the-job education strategy that doesn't cost companies a dime: Organize work so that employees are given projects that help them learn new skills. For example, a marketing manager may not know how to compute the return on marketing programs but might learn that skill while working on a team project with colleagues from the finance department.

20   Pursuing options like these vastly expands the supply of talent that employers can tap, making it both cheaper and easier to fill jobs. Of course, it's also much better for society. It helps build the supply of human capital in the economy, as well as opening the pathway for more people to get jobs. It's an important instance where company self-interest and societal interest just happen to coincide.

PERSONAL RESPONSE

If you were ever turned down for a job because you did not have the skills to perform it, describe that experience. If that has not been your experience and you have been hired for a job, describe that experience.

QUESTIONS FOR CLASS OR SMALL-GROUP DISCUSSION

1. According to Cappelli, who do companies blame for their not being able to recruit qualified people? Who does Cappelli blame?

2. How does Cappelli answer the question posed by his title?

3. State in your own words what the "big myths" are, as explained in the section with that subheading, and then state what the reality is, according to Cappelli.

4. Summarize the recommendations that Cappelli makes to help companies get the people they need for skilled jobs. What do you think of his recommendations? Do you think they are practical?

ESCAPE FROM THE JOB JUNGLE

PETER WEINBERG

Peter Weinberg is a Ph.D. graduate fellow in neurobiology at Columbia University. This piece was posted on the Huffington Post website.

At first, I was sure I'd find a job. I graduated Phi Beta Kappa from a well-branded college, I did hard time in the internship trenches for four consecutive summers, and according to Indeed.com, there were hundreds of job openings in New York City. All I had to do was pick one with the words "assistant" "junior" or "associate" in the title, upload my resume, and go back to watching *Curb Your Enthusiasm*. A few days later, employers would swamp my inbox, promising me big stacks of money and a swivel chair of my very own. That's how the Internet works: you click what you want and you get it.

I applied to 53 jobs in July, according to the tally marks I carved into my parents' dining room table while playing the harmonica. But the big sack I bought to hold all my salary never filled up, and I began to suspect something just wasn't right.

I googled "economy," and found all sorts of disconcerting information.

Especially this one: the unemployment rate among recent college graduates was 9.6%. Also, according to a recent study from the Buzz Kill Institute, the longer it took me to find a job, the more scarred I'd be for the rest of my life. Then I stumbled upon an article by Thomas Friedman, who insisted that nowadays, people have to invent their own jobs. So I invented NemAssist.com. It's like Match.com, but instead of finding true love, you find an archenemy. It's a speed hating service that helps you find loathe at first sight.

It was a brilliant invention, but none of my friends in finance wanted to invest, and NemAssist never started up (thanks for nothing, Tom). Back at square one, I decided to write up a list of Four Strategies for Finding Work. I crossed out "Online Applications" and "Entrepreneurship" and moved on to Strategy 3: "Loco-Motion."

Loco-Motion is when doing something completely insane moves you forward in life. You hear the success stories all the time: "I hired a plane to skywrite my resume above the beach in South Hampton. Two days later I started at Morgan

Stanley." So I called the Drug Policy Alliance and asked for the e-mail address of the director. Then I sent him a long rambling e-mail about my history thesis on Reagan's war on drugs. The next day, I had my first interview.

I didn't get the job, but I started to believe in the power of Loco-Motion. So I tried it again, except this time I called Google and asked to speak to Larry Page. The sound of the phone hanging up is still ringing in my ears.

8

I wrote "50/50 odds" next to Loco-Motion, and moved on to Strategy 4: Networking. For the whole month of September, I spun an intricate networking web, like some kind of exotic Jewish spider. I talked to 28 strangers. Friends of friends of friends. They worked at HBO and ABC, Time Inc. and the Daily Beast, BBDO and Dentsu, Penguin and Simon & Shuster, and more. Assistants steered me through cubicle labyrinths and deposited me on plush couches in big offices. No one had any jobs to offer, but everyone had advice, which I jotted down diligently in a legal pad. On the way out, I'd look around at all the lucky workers, entranced, like a little boy at an aquarium, his face flush against the glass.

I liked networking, but it didn't seem to work. By September, it still hadn't landed me one single interview. I did pick up two part time gigs as a writing tutor and a manager for a small theater company, both procured through Strategy 1, which actually had 2/55 odds in the end.

On September 8th, a switch flipped on inside me. My mood plummeted from "cautious optimism" to "nihilistic despair." On that day, for 20 of my 23 years, I'd been sitting in a classroom. Now I was sitting in a La-Z-Boy in a bathrobe. What really pushed me over the edge that day was an article in *The Atlantic*, which claimed that I belonged to a "Lost Generation." At first I assumed this referred to young adults who were severely disappointed by the season finale of *Lost*. It didn't, but that was the idea that stuck with me. Maybe life is just like *Lost*: you invest so much time and energy throughout so many seasons, and it all adds up to nothing.

And then, a fly landed in my networking web. I hurried over to inspect the body—it was a full-time freelancing gig at an ad agency. Could I come in for an interview on Thursday? I checked my schedule. Thursday was free (and so was every day after Thursday).

12

As I sat and waited in an awfully swank lobby, I started flipping through that legal pad I'd spent my summer filling up. As the snippets of wisdom fluttered by, I realized how well networking had prepared me for an interview. Four ad execs had poured their brains out to me. I had prepared answers for any possible question, even those horrible HR-type ones like "what is your greatest weakness?" ("You mean besides being a perfectionist? Kryptonite.") That's the thing about networking—it's the only job-getting strategy that actually makes you more employable.

Flash forward to December 9th, and I'm in a swivel chair, spinning round and round in the sickly white light of an office. After three months of freelancing, my boss, Jack, had just offered me a job.

Lucky. Unbelievably lucky. That's how I felt as I swiveled. Also, a little dizzy. Also, a little guilty.

I started thinking about all the other 20- to 24-year-olds out there, still stuck in the search, bleeding out in the job jungle, their ankles shackled by debt with miles and miles to go till the next interview. Can they all network their way out of there? Will Indeed.com throw them a vine? Can they find a part-time path to prosperity? Will Lady Luck bail them out?

16   I'd hate to play the odds on that one.

PERSONAL RESPONSE

Write about any failure or success you have had in trying to find work. If you have never applied for a job, write about the experience of someone you know.

QUESTIONS FOR CLASS OR SMALL-GROUP DISCUSSION

1. Why do you think that Weinberg describes his job search as a "jungle" (title)?

2. What misconceptions about how easy it would be to get a job after graduation does Weinberg dispel?

3. Despite his humor, does Weinberg make any serious recommendations on how to get a job? What do you think of his advice?

4. Is Weinberg pessimistic or optimistic about job prospects for young people? He specifically mentions the 20–24 age group because that is the group he fits into. Do you think his observations about searching for a job apply to any age group?

MindTap   Reflect on the theme of this chapter.

PERSPECTIVES ON MARKETING, THE AMERICAN CONSUMER, AND THE WORKPLACE

Suggested Writing Topics

1. Argue against or in support of the contention of Gary Ruskin and Juliet Schor in "Every Nook and Cranny" that commercialism is "dangerous" to the public.

2. Argue for or against the proposition that the United States should "ban or sharply restrict product placement on television" (Gary Ruskin and Juliet Schor, "Every Nook and Cranny," paragraph 10).

3. Classify consumers' shopping and buying habits on the basis of what generation they belong to, using millennials, generation X members, and baby boomers as your three groups.

4. Respond to an accusation that is often leveled against Americans that they are addicted to buying and accumulating material goods. Is that a fair analysis of American consumerism?

5. Write an essay analyzing the positive and negative effects of America's emphasis on consumerism on one particular group of people, such as young people, the elderly, working-class people, the wealthy, or those living in poverty.

6. Imagine that you are marketing a product that has traditionally been sold to one particular segment of the market, such as white, middle-class males. Now, you want to increase your sales by targeting other groups. Select a particular group and create a sales campaign aimed at that group.

7. Explain what you think shopping malls, discount stores, and overstocked supermarkets suggest about Americans' values. For instance, what impression do you think that foreign visitors get of America when they see the sizes of and selections in those marketplaces?

8. Argue whether you agree with the suggestions that Peter Cappelli makes in "Why Companies Aren't Getting the Employees They Need" for how companies can get the recruits they want.

9. Write about your own experience searching for a job, as Peter Weinberg does in "Escape from the Job Jungle."

10. Explain what you value most in a job and why. Is it having fun, making lots of money, meeting challenges, or some other aspect of it?

11. Describe what you see as the ideal job or ideal working conditions.

12. Describe your work experiences and the extent to which self-satisfaction or self-motivation contributes to your performance.

Research Topics

1. Although Gary Ruskin and Juliet Schor's "Every Nook and Cranny" was published in 2005, it makes many points that are likely still true and relevant today. Research one of the subjects that they mention, such as their assertion in paragraph 4 that "the commercialization of government and culture and the growing importance of material acquisition and consumer lifestyles was hastened by the co-optation of potentially countervailing institutions, such as churches . . . , governments, schools, universities, and nongovernmental organizations." Consider whether what they assert in their article still holds true.

2. Research the subject of whether America has become a market society.

3. Research the marketing strategies of a major business. Assess what you see as its successes and/or failures in promoting its products.

4. Select a particular product (such as automobiles, cosmetics, clothing, or beer) or a particular target population (such as children, overweight women, millennials, or the elderly) and research the market strategies used by major companies for that particular product or group.

5. Research the recent advertising campaign of a major corporation whose product poses a threat to the environment or to human health and well-being.

6. Research the subject of American consumerism and arrive at your own conclusion about its effects on Americans and American values. This is a broad subject, so look for ways to narrow your focus as quickly as you can.

7. Research the impact of suburban malls on city-center or small mom-and-pop neighborhood businesses.

8. Research the impact that the Internet has had on suburban malls and neighborhood businesses.

9. Starting with Peter Cappelli's "Why Companies Aren't Getting the Employees They Need," research the subject of which jobs are the hardest for companies to fill and why they are hard to fill.

10. Research the European regulations outlawing wage and benefit discrimination against part-time workers and argue whether you think the United States ought to have such a goal and, if so, whether it could realistically attain it.

RESPONDING TO VISUALS

JOHN MACDOUGALL/AFP/GettyImages

Does it matter that this picture of a woman walking by an advertisement was taken on a street in Berlin, or could it have been taken anywhere?

1. The original caption for the image tells us that this is a "fashion ad," but what product is being advertised? How can you tell?

2. What details of the advertisement do you find persuasive? Would you be inclined to consider buying the product because of this advertisement?

3. Comment on the composition of this photograph: what is the effect of the woman walking past the ad being dominated by the woman jumping in the advertisement? How do the two figures contrast?

RESPONDING TO VISUALS

Tetra Images/Getty Images

What do the most obvious components of this picture of a bar code in the form of an American flag represent?

1. What does the word *SALE* add to the impact of the image?

2. What comment on American commercialism does this image make or imply?

3. Do you think the comment being made about America is a fair representation of American values?

GLOSSARY

abstract. A summary of the essential points of a text. It is usually quite short, no more than a paragraph.

ad hominem **arguments.** Attacking the character of the arguer rather than the argument itself.

analogy. A comparison of two things to show their similarity.

analysis. Dividing a subject into its separate parts for individual study.

appeal. A rhetorical strategy used in argumentation to be persuasive; a persuasive technique that goes beyond fact or logic to engage audience's sympathy, sense of higher power or authority, or reasoning. Classic persuasion relies on a combination of *ethical, logical*, and *emotional appeals* to sway an audience.

argument/persuasion. An argument is an attempt to prove the validity of a position by offering supporting proof. Persuasion takes argument one step further by convincing an audience to adopt a viewpoint or take action.

Aristotelian logic. Formal, classic argumentation that typically follows one of two common lines of reasoning, *deductive* and *inductive* reasoning.

attributive tag. A short identifying phrase or clause that identifies ("attributes") the source of a quotation or paraphrase: *Mugabane explains . . . ; According to Sissela Bok, . . . ; Singer, a Princeton University professor who publishes widely on bioethics issues, recommends . . . .*

audience. The readers of a piece of writing, the individual or group for whom a writer writes.

backing. According to the Toulmin model of reasoning, the support or evidence for a warrant.

begging the question (circular reasoning). Making a claim that simply rephrases another claim in other words.

blog. A personal website that the owner uses for whatever purpose he or she likes, such as a daily record of thoughts or experiences or links to other sites. The term derives from the phrase "web log."

body of an essay. The paragraphs between the introduction and conclusion of an essay that develop, support, explain, or illustrate the thesis or central idea of a paper.

book review. A report that summarizes only the main ideas of a book and provides critical commentary on it. Usually in a book review, you will also be asked to give your personal response to the book, including both your opinion of the ideas it presents and an evaluation of its worth or credibility.

brainstorming. Writing for a short, set period of time everything related to a general subject in order to generate a workable topic for a paper.

cause–effect analysis. An expository mode explaining why something happened or showing what happened as a result of something—or perhaps both.

citation. A reference that provides supporting illustrations or examples for your own ideas; the authority or source of that information is identified.

claim. In the Toulmin model of reasoning, the proposition, a debatable or controversial assertion, drawn from the data or grounds, based on the *warrant* (the underlying assumption). The point your paper is making, your thesis or arguable position statement.

classification/division. The process of sorting information and ideas into categories or groups (classification); the act of breaking information, ideas, or concepts into parts in order to better understand them (division).

comparison/contrast. Showing a strong similarity or a strong dissimilarity between two things. Comparing or contrasting usually promotes one of two purposes: to show each of two subjects distinctly by considering both side by side, or to evaluate or judge two things.

concession. Agreement with an opponent on certain points or acknowledging that an opposing argument cannot be refuted.

conclusion. In an essay, the final paragraph(s) that bring the paper to a satisfying close.

conditions of rebuttal. Weaknesses in the opposing argument that provide ways to counter the argument, usually by showing flaws in logic or weakness of supporting evidence.

connotation. The emotional associations of a word, as distinct from *denotation*, the literal meaning. Connotative meaning applies to images and things as well.

context. The circumstances, setting, or surrounding of a word, an image, or an event.

critique. An evaluation of a work's logic, rhetorical soundness, and overall effectiveness.

data or grounds. In the Toulmin model of reasoning, the evidences that support a claim. They constitute proof and demonstrate that the claim is true.

debate. A discussion involving opposing points in an argument. In formal debate, opposing teams defend and attack a specific proposition.

deductive reasoning. In argumentation, the movement from a general principle or shared premise to a conclusion about a specific instance.

definition. The process of making clear a precise meaning or significance. In definition, a writer conveys the essential characteristics of something by distinguishing it from all other things in its class.

description. A conveyance through words of the essential nature of a person, place, or thing by appealing to the senses, that is, by evoking through words certain sights, smells, sounds, or tactile sensations. The purpose of description may be objective—to convey information without bias; or it may be subjective—to express feelings, impressions, or attitudes about a person, place, or thing.

diction. A writer's word choice and level of usage, which varies in informal and formal language; slang, regional, nonstandard, and colloquial language; and jargon.

dropped quotation. A quotation that appears without an introduction, as if it had just been dropped into a paper.

editing. Re-examining written work for errors in grammar, mechanics, and punctuation.

either/or reasoning. Admitting only two sides to an issue and asserting that the writer's is the only possible correct one.

ellipsis points. Consisting of three spaced periods, used in quoting source material to indicate that words have been omitted.

emotional appeal. A rhetorical strategy that attempts to move an audience on an affective or emotional level with startling, disturbing, or touching examples.

ethical appeal. A rhetorical strategy that calls upon authority or the credibility of sources to persuade.

evaluation. A judgment about worth, quality, or credibility.

exemplification. Showing by example; using specific details or instances to illustrate, support, or make specific.

expository writing. Writing with the goal of informing or presenting an objective explanation on a subject. Types of expository writing include cause–effect analysis, classification–division, comparison or contrast, and definition.

expressive writing. Emphasizes the writer's feelings and subjective view of the world.

fallacies or common flaws. Components of argument that are false or misleading, thus making the reasoning illogical and the argument essentially invalid.

false analogy. Falsely claiming that, because something resembles something else in one way, it resembles it in all ways.

forum. An open discussion or exchange of ideas among many people.

freewriting. The act of writing down every idea that occurs to you about your topic without stopping to examine what you are writing.

grammar. Refers to sentence construction, especially avoiding fragments and run-ons; subject–verb and pronoun–antecedent agreement; correct use of case for nouns and pronouns; and using adjectives and adverbs correctly.

hasty or faulty generalization. The drawing of a broad conclusion on the basis of very little evidence.

hypothesis. A tentative explanation to account for some phenomenon or set of facts. It is in essence a theory or an assumption that can be tested by further investigation and is assumed to be true for the purpose of argument or investigation.

illustration. An explanation or clarification, usually using example or comparison.

inductive reasoning. In argumentation, the movement from a number of specific instances to a general principle.

introduction. The opening words, sentences, or paragraphs that begin a piece of writing.

invention. Generating ideas for writing.

journal. A personal record of experiences, thoughts, or responses to something, usually kept separate from other writings, as in a diary or notebook.

listserv. An e-mail-based discussion group of a specific topic.

loaded words (emotionally charged language). Language guaranteed to appeal to audiences on an emotional rather than an intellectual level. A loaded word has highly charged emotional overtones or connotations that evoke a strong response, either positive or negative, that goes beyond the denotation or specific definition given in a dictionary. Often the meaning or emotional association of the words varies from person to person or group to group.

logical appeal. A rhetorical strategy that applies sound reasoning in order to persuade.

mechanics. In writing, refers to spelling words correctly, including correct hyphenation; correct use of italics; and use of capital letters, numbers, and abbreviations.

narration. The re-creation of an experience for a specific purpose, such as to illustrate a point, report information, entertain, or persuade. A narrative may be a brief anecdote, a story, or a case history.

non sequitur. Drawing inferences or conclusions that do not follow logically from available evidence.

oversimplification. Offering a solution or an explanation that is too simple for the problem or issue being argued.

paraphrase. A restatement of a passage in your own words. A paraphrase is somewhat shorter than the original but retains its essential meaning.

persuasive writing. Seeks to convince readers of the validity of an author's position on an issue and sometimes even to move them to action.

point of view. The perspective from which a piece is written: first person (I, we), second person (you), or third person (he/she/it/one, they).

position paper. A detailed report that explains, justifies, or recommends a particular course of action.

post hoc, ergo propter hoc **reasoning.** Assuming that something happened simply because it followed something else without evidence of a causal relationship.

précis. A concise summary of the highlights of a written text.

premise. An assumption or a proposition on which an argument is based or from which a conclusion is drawn.

prewriting. The first stage of the writing process, when writers determine their purpose, identify their audience, discover their subject, narrow their focus, and plan their writing strategy.

proposition. A statement of a position on a subject, a course of action, or a topic for discussion or debate.

punctuation. Refers to the use of commas, colons, semicolons, apostrophes, and quotation marks.

qualifiers. Words or phrases that, when added to a word or phrase, modify its meaning by limiting (she is partially correct) or enhancing (he is completely correct) it. In argumentation, such words allow the writer to make concessions to the opposition.

reading critically. The process of making a careful, thoughtful, and thorough consideration of a piece of writing by looking at its different parts.

rebuttal. Response addressed to opposing arguments, such as demonstrating a flaw in logic or reasoning or exposing faulty or weak supporting evidence.

red herring. Diverting the audience's attention from the main issue at hand to an irrelevant issue.

revision. Re-examination of written work. *Global revision* examines the whole essay or entire paragraphs and addresses the issues of purpose, audience, organization, and content as well as style and clarity. *Sentence revision* looks at individual sentences for clarifying or refining.

rhetoric. The art or study of using written or spoken language effectively.

rhetorical analysis. The process of making a careful, thoughtful, and thorough consideration of a piece of writing by looking at its different parts.

rhetorical fallacy. A flaw or error in reasoning that renders an argument invalid or weakens it considerably.

rhetorical mode. A strategy used to organize and develop ideas in a writing assignment. Broadly, there are four traditional modes: exposition, argumentation, narration, and description.

Rogerian argument. Based on the work of the American psychologist Carl R. Rogers, an approach to argumentation that adopts the stance of listening to opposing arguments with an open mind, making concessions, and attempting to find a common ground.

slanted word. A word whose connotation (suggestive meaning as opposed to actual meaning) is used to advance an argument for its emotional association.

social networking sites. Online service or platform whose function is to provide a forum for messages, pictures, weblinks, and other means of establishing connections among people.

stereotyping. A form of generalization or oversimplification in which an entire group is narrowly labeled or perceived on the basis of a few in the group.

strategy. A plan of action to achieve a specific goal; the way that an assignment is organized and developed.

subject. A general or broad area of interest.

summary. A concise presentation of the main points or highlights of a text.

syllogism. Traditional form of deductive reasoning that has two premises and a conclusion.

syntax. The arrangement of words or phrases to create sentences.

synthesis. Combining the ideas of two or more authors and integrating those ideas into your own discussion.

thesis statement. A statement of the specific purpose of a paper. A thesis is essentially a one-sentence summary of what you will argue, explain, illustrate, define, describe, or otherwise develop in the rest of the paper. It usually comes very early in a paper.

tone. A writer's attitude toward subject and audience, conveyed through word choice and diction.

topic. A specific, focused, and clearly defined area of interest. A topic is a narrow aspect of a subject.

topic sentence. Sentence stating the focus or central idea of a paragraph.

Toulmin model of reasoning. A model of informal argumentation, or practical reasoning, described by Stephen Toulmin, a twentieth-century philosopher, mathematician, and physicist.

transition. A linking of ideas, thoughts, or points; making the connection between clauses, sentences, and/or paragraphs clear.

transitional words. Words that show the connection between ideas, clauses, sentences, and paragraphs.

warrant. According to the Toulmin model of reasoning, the underlying assumptions or inferences that are taken for granted and that connect the claim to the data.

workshop. Similar in intent to a forum, a workshop is characterized by exchanges of information, ideas, and opinions, usually among a small group of people. Both workshops and forums involve interaction and exchange of ideas more than panel discussions, which typically allot more time to panel members than to audience participants.

CREDITS

THOMAS BARTLETT, "The Puzzle of Boys." Reprinted by permission from The Chronicle of Higher Education, The Chronicle Review. 22 Nov. 2009.

CHRISTIA BROWN, "Target is Right on Target about the Use of Gender Labels," Psychology Today, 14 Aug. 2015.

PETER CAPPELLI, "Why Companies Aren't Getting the Employees They Need," Wall Street Journal, 24 Oct. 2011.

JEFF CORWIN, "The Sixth Extinction," The Los Angeles Times, 30 Nov. 2009. Reprinted with permission of the author.

ERIN CUNNINGHAM, "Our Photoshopping Disorder: The Truth in Advertising Bill Asks Congress to Regulate Deceptive Images," The Daily Beast, 22 Apr. 2014.

SERENA ELAVIA, "The Collective Conscience of Reality Television," 29 Oct. 2014, © 2015 The Atlantic Media Co., as first published in The Atlantic Magazine. All rights reserved. Distributed by Tribune Content Agency, LLC.

MARILYN ELIAS, "The School-to-Prison Pipeline." Reprinted with permission of Teaching Tolerance, a project of the Southern Poverty Law Center. www.tolerance.org.

ANTHONY GREGORY, "Why Legalizing Organ Sales would Help to Save Lives, End Violence." Reprinted by The Atlantic, 9 Nov. 2011, by permission of the author.

ABIGAIL HALL, "The Gender Wage Gap—A Myth that Just Won't Die," from Independent Institute, retrieved from http://blog.independent.org. Reprinted by permission of Abigail Hall.

PETER HOLLEY, "Parents outraged after students shown 'white guilt' cartoon for Black History Month," Washington Post, 11 Feb. 2016.

GREG KAUFMANN, "Ignoring Homeless Families," The Nation, 19 Apr. 2013.

MARIA KONNIKOV, "The Real Lesson of the Stanford Prison Experiment," Copyright © 2015 Conde Nast. From The New Yorker, 12 June 2015. All rights reserved. Reprinted by permission.

SARAH LEWIS, "Scientists aren't the only Innovators! We Really Need Artists," This article first appeared in Salon.com, at http://www.Salon.com. An online version remains in the Salon archives. Reprinted with permission.

JEFF MADRICK, "The Cost of Child Poverty," The New York Review of Books Daily. Copyright © 2015 by Jeff Madrick. Reprinted by permission.

INDEX

388